Program Construction

Program Construction

Calculating Implementations from Specifications

Roland Backhouse
The University of Nottingham, UK

WILEY

Library of Congress Cataloging-in-Publication Data

(to follow)

British Library Cataloguing in Publication Data

A catalogue record for this book is available from the British Library

0 470 84882 0

Typeset in 10/12.5pt Lucida Bright by T&T Productions Ltd, London.
Printed and bound in Great Britain by Biddles Ltd, Guildford and Kings Lynn.
This book is printed on acid-free paper responsibly manufactured from sustainable
forestry in which at least two trees are planted for each one used for paper production.

Contents

Preface

Programming is a highly skilled activity, and good programmers are few and far between. In few other professions is the 90–10 rule (90% of the effort goes into the last 10% of the work) so vitally important. Many programmers are able to write programs that 'work' in most circumstances; few programmers know the basic principles of program specification, let alone how to construct programs that guarantee to meet their specifications in *all* circumstances.

It is no wonder. Many texts have been written that explain how to *encode* computational processes in some specific programming language (C, Java, Visual Basic, or whatever), but few tackle the much harder problem of presenting the problem-solving skills that are needed to formulate programming problems precisely and concisely, and to convert those formulations into elegant implementations.

This book is about programming *per se*. It is about the most elementary principles of program construction—problem decomposition, invariant properties, and guarantees of progress. It is intended to appeal to both novice programmers, who wish to start on the right track, and to experienced programmers who wish to properly master their craft.

Although the subject matter of the book is 'elementary', in the sense of foundational, it is not 'easy'. Programming is challenging, and it is wrong to skirt the issues or to wrap it up in a way that makes it seem otherwise. I have lectured on this material for many years, mostly to undergraduates on computing science degrees, and, occasionally, to professional programmers. Inevitably, it is the experienced programmers who appreciate its value the most. Novice programmers have the additional hurdle of learning how to write code—too often in a highly complex programming language. For them, the problem is the programming language, whereas, of course, the programming language should not be a problem, but part of the solution.

In order to present the real challenges of programming without obfuscation, the book uses a very simple programming language, with just four programming constructs—assignment, sequential composition, conditionals and loops. I have omitted variable declarations, so that the focus of the book remains clear. Experts will recognize the language as the Guarded Command Language, a simple, elegant language designed by Dijkstra specifically for this purpose.

The book is a major revision of my earlier book *Program Construction and Verification*, published in 1986. Some sections remain the same, but there is much that is different. The main difference is reflected in the omission of 'verification' in the title. The primary goal of the book is to show how programs are *constructed* to meet their specifications, by means of simple, mathematical calculations. The emphasis on construction is crucial; the fact that the calculations can be formally *verified* is also important, but much less so. Unfortunately, however, the emphasis in many related texts is the reverse; the fundamental principles of program construction are introduced as a mechanism for performing a *post hoc* validation of the program's correctness, and their integral role in the activity of developing programs is neglected. Even worse, *automatic* verification is often given as the primary justification for their use. I have no doubt that this misplaced emphasis on verification rather than construction has, for long, stood in the way of the acceptance and active use of the principles by practising programmers. Quite rightly, professional programmers will strive to ensure that their programs are correct *by construction*; it is this endeavour that this text aims to support.

Another aspect of the text that has undergone major revision is the discussion of logical reasoning. I now realize just how inadequate my own education in logic has been. The traditional style of reasoning in mathematics is to verify a conjecture by means of a sequence of true statements, each statement being a self-evident truth or *implied* by earlier ones. Calculational logic, as presented in this book, places *equality* of propositions at the forefront. Mathematical theorems are derived (not verified) by a process of algebraic calculation, just as in school algebra and in differential and integral calculus.

The basis for calculational logic was formulated by Dijkstra and Scholten, in their 1990 book *Predicate Calculus and Program Calculus*. In my view, their work has initiated a major revolution in the art of effective reasoning. As yet, however, it is largely unknown in mathematical circles. Hopefully, this book will help to foster the widespread acceptance and application of their ideas.

Intended Readership

The book has been written primarily for self-study. Many exercises have been supplied, with complete solutions, interspersed throughout the text. Only by making a serious attempt at the exercises can the material be properly mastered. My hope is that readers will do the exercises as they read, rather than postponing them until the chapter has been completed. Many of the exercises are quite challenging; the solutions are there to be consulted, so that the reader can build up confidence and experience in an effective, calculational style of reasoning.

I anticipate that all readers will have an elementary, operational understanding of at least one programming language. (By this, I mean that they will know about the store ('memory') of a computer, and how an assignment statement updates the store. They will also know how conditional statements, sequences of statements, and loops are executed.) Most benefit will be gained by studying the book simultaneously with, or shortly after, learning how to code in a conventional (preferably simple!) programming language. In this way, it is possible to appreciate just how easy it is to get things wrong, and to gain the satisfaction of being confident that you are right.

The assumed mathematical knowledge is minimal. Only simple properties of arithmetic (including inequalities between integers and reals) are required. However, my experience of where students have difficulty (apart from the intrinsic difficulty of the subject matter) is primarily in the mathematical skill of algebraic manipulation. Allowing sufficient time in the curriculum for the students to develop this skill, rather than trying to cram it into an already overfull syllabus, is the best remedy.

Lots more examples and exercises could have been included in the book. I have deliberately refrained from doing so in order to keep the book relatively short. My plan is to publish additional supporting material from time to time, access to which can be gained via the URL http://www.wiley.com/go/backhouse.

Acknowledgments

It is a pleasure to record my gratitude to some of the people who have helped in the realization of this book, however indirect their help may have been.

First and foremost, I am indebted to my own teachers, without whom my own work would not have been possible. It will soon become very evident to the reader of the 'Bibliographic Remarks' who has influenced me the most. I am particularly indebted to the late Edsger W. Dijkstra, whose writings have been a major inspiration for many years. I have also learnt much from David Gries's books; David also reviewed an early draft of this book, in exceptionally comprehensive and helpful detail, for which I am very grateful. Thanks, too, to Tony Hoare, for his support and encouragement; I am also grateful to him and the Queen's University of Belfast for kind permission to reproduce a major part of his inaugural lecture.

I learnt a very great deal during the 13 years that I spent in the Netherlands, about mathematical method, about teamwork, and about academic and scientific values. Many thanks go to Henk Doornbos, Paul Hoogendijk, Ed Voermans and Jaap van der Woude, whose loyalty and enthusiasm are unforgettable. Thanks, also, to Doaitse Swierstra for his support and friendship in difficult times. Special thanks must go to Netty van Gasteren, who tragically died only recently, from whom I learnt more than I really appreciated at the time.

A number of people have helped directly by reading drafts of the text, pointing out errors and making suggestions for improvements. Robert L. Baber and Tony Seda both gave me extensive and very thoughtful reviews of an earlier draft. I hope that I have done justice to their criticisms. Diethard Michaelis has also sent me many invaluable comments and corrections.

The book was prepared using Mathʃpad, a system that aims to integrate the process of doing mathematics and writing about it. Its use, in combination with the TEX and LATEX systems, has been of immeasurable benefit to me. I am grateful to Eindhoven University of Technology and the Dutch government for their generous support of the development and implementation of Mathʃpad. I am greatly indebted to Richard Verhoeven, who not only implemented the system, working many long hours in doing so, but who also has always been, and continues to be, extremely helpful, willing and generous, giving of his time far beyond the call of duty.

Thanks are also due to the staff of John Wiley & Sons, Ltd, for their friendly and professional help in producing this book. Thanks also to Sam Clark, of T&T Productions Ltd, for the cheerful and competent way he has assisted in trying to make sure that everything is exactly right.

As always, my biggest thanks go to my wife, Hilary.

Roland Backhouse
January 2003

1

A Science of Computing

The hallmark of a science is the avoidance of error.

J. Robert Oppenheimer

The electronic, digital computer is a marvel of modern technology. Within a lifetime, it has developed from nothing to a tool whose use is so widespread that we are often unaware that it is there. The first computers, built in the 1940s, were monstrous. As recently as the 1960s and 1970s, it was common for new employees in a company to be shown 'the computer'—housed in a special-purpose, air-conditioned room, to which admission was restricted to a select few. Nowadays, computers are used in many household appliances, they are also used in cars, trains and aircraft, and we even carry them around with us—laptops, palm-tops, what would we do without them?

The developments in computer *hardware* have been truly phenomenal. But developments in computer *software* have not kept pace. The programming languages that are in use today have changed little from the programming languages that were developed in the 1950s, and programming remains a highly skilled activity. It is the nature of the task that is the problem. The hardware designer must build a dumb machine, whose sole purpose is to slavishly execute the instructions given to it by the programmer; the programmer has to design general-purpose systems and programs, at a level of detail at which they can be faithfully executed, without error, by even the dumbest of machines.

1.1   Debugging

There is a story about the current state of computer software that is widely reported on the Internet. The chief executive of a multi-billion dollar software company compared the computer industry with the car industry.

> 'If the automobile industry had kept up with technology like the computer industry has,'

he is reported to have said,

> 'we would all be driving $25 cars that get 1000 to the gallon'.

> 'That may be true,'

was the swift response of the president of one automobile company,

> 'but who would want to drive a car that crashes twice a day?'

This story is, most likely, just a joke[1]. But, like all good jokes, it succeeds because it reflects profoundly on modern-day reality.

At the time of writing (December 2002), it is still the case that computer software is liable to spontaneously 'crash', due to simple programming errors (or 'bugs' as they are called in the software industry). In contrast, the car industry is often held up as an exemplar of excellence in standards of safety and reliability.

Memories are short. Cars may be (relatively) safe and reliable today but, in the 1950s, as highlighted by Ralph Nader in his acclaimed book *Unsafe At Any Speed*, cars were knowingly made and sold that were liable to spontaneous crashes, and car manufacturers were guilty of deliberately undermining efforts to invest in improved standards. ('Safety and sales strategies do not mix' was the argument used at the time.)

The computer industry of today is very much like the car industry of the 1950s. Computers are still relatively new, and the novelty factor has not worn off, so that guarantees of reliability and fitness-for-purpose are, for many, a low priority. Few programmers are trained in scientific methods of constructing programs and, consequently, they waste substantial amounts of effort 'debugging' their programs, rarely with complete success. ('Debugging' is the process of repeatedly testing, followed by patching, the program, in an attempt to remove discovered errors.)

The need for alternative, mathematically rigorous, program construction techniques was recognized in the late 1960s when the large computer manufacturers first began to realize that the costs of producing computer software were

---

[1]At least, I think it is. It may be true, but it is difficult to verify the authenticity of material on the Internet. For this reason, names have been omitted in this account.

outstripping by far the costs of producing computer hardware. They spoke of a 'software crisis'. The problems of producing reliable computer software were aired at two conferences on Software Engineering, held in 1968 and 1969 and sponsored by the NATO Science Committee. Typical of the sort of facts laid bare at these conferences was the following statement by Hopkins of the IBM Corporation.

> We face a fantastic problem in big systems. For instance, in OS/360[2] we have about 1000 errors per release.

Tellingly, he added:

> Programmers call their errors 'bugs' to preserve their sanity; that number of 'mistakes' would not be psychologically acceptable.

The process of debugging has several drawbacks: it is useless as a methodology for constructing programs, it can never be used to establish the correctness of a correct program, and it cannot be relied upon to establish the incorrectness of an incorrect program.

Let us look in detail at these drawbacks. Here are two examples, each illustrating a different aspect.

1.2   Testing a Correct Program

One well-known method of computing n^2, for some positive integer n, without performing a multiplication is to sum the first n odd numbers. This is based on the property that

$$n^2 = 1+3+5+\ldots+(2n-1) \ .$$

Not so well known is that a similar method can be used to compute n^3, n^4, n^5, etc., without performing a multiplication. To see how this is done let us re-express the computation of n^2 as follows.

First, write down all the positive integers up to (and including) $2n-1$. For $n=6$, this means the numbers 1 through 11.

$$1 \quad 2 \quad 3 \quad 4 \quad 5 \quad 6 \quad 7 \quad 8 \quad 9 \quad 10 \quad 11$$

Cross out every second number:

$$1 \quad\quad 3 \quad\quad 5 \quad\quad 7 \quad\quad 9 \quad\quad 11$$

Finally, add these together to form a running total:

$$1 \quad\quad 4 \quad\quad 9 \quad\quad 16 \quad\quad 25 \quad\quad 36$$

To compute n^3, begin as before by writing down all the positive numbers, but this time up to $3n-2$. For $n=6$, this means the numbers 1 through 16.

---

[2] At that time, OS/360 was a widely used operating system for IBM computers.

1	2	3	4	5	6	7	8	9	10	11	12	13	14	15	16

Cross out every third number:

1	2		4	5		7	8		10	11		13	14		16

Add these together to form a running total:

1	3		7	12		19	27		37	48		61	75		91

Cross out every second number:

1			7			19			37			61			91

Finally, form a running total:

1			8			27			64			125			216

The general algorithm for computing n^m is to write down all the positive numbers up to $mn - m + 1$. Then we iterate $m-1$ times the process of crossing out numbers followed by forming a running total. On the kth iteration every $(m-k+1)$th number is crossed out. (In this way, the set of numbers crossed out changes from every mth number on the first iteration to every second number on the last iteration.)

Now, we can test this algorithm in two ways. We can extend one of the existing tables to the right; for example, the table for n^2 can be extended to calculate 7^2 and 8^2:

1	2	3	4	5	6	7	8	9	10	11	12	13	14	15
1		3		5		7		9		11		13		15
1		4		9		16		25		36		49		64

Alternatively, we can add new tables to the ones we already have; for example, the table for 3^4:

1	2	3	4	5	6	7	8	9
1	2	3		5	6	7		9
1	3	6		11	17	24		33
1	3			11	17			33
1	4			15	32			65
1				15				65
1				16				81

We can continue this testing as much as we like (indeed, for ever and a day). Each time we add more entries and verify the correct result, our confidence in the algorithm grows. But, this process will never make us totally confident. Can we be sure that it will correctly compute 21^5 or 6^{12}? On the evidence presented so far would you be willing to gamble on its correctness?

Edsger W. Dijkstra, an eminent computer scientist, has summarized the flaw in testing in a now-famous quotation.

> Program testing can be used to show the presence of bugs, but never to show their absence.

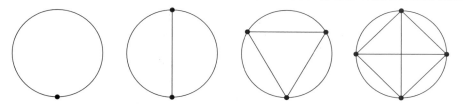

Figure 1.1   Cutting the cake.

Exercise 1.1 (Cutting the cake). This exercise demonstrates the fallacy of using 'poor man's induction', i.e. extrapolating from a few cases to a more general claim.

Suppose n points are marked on the circumference of a circular cake and then the cake is cut along the chords joining them. The points are chosen in such a way that all intersection points of pairs of chords are distinct. The question is: in how many portions does this cut the cake?

Figure 1.1 shows the case when n is 1, 2, 3 or 4.

Suppose $n = 5$. Determine the number of portions. On the basis of these five cases make a conjecture about the number of portions for arbitrary n. Now, suppose $n = 0$. Does this support or refute the conjecture? Next, suppose $n = 6$. Determine the number of portions. What do you discover?   □

1.3   Testing an Incorrect Program

Testing cannot be used to establish the absence of errors in a program. Nor can testing be relied upon to show the presence of errors.

I once had a very graphic illustration of this when I had to mark a programming assignment. The problem the students had been set was to write a program that would compare two strings for equality. One student's solution was to assign the value true or false to a boolean $equal$ as follows[3]:

$$equal := (string1.length = string2.length);$$

if $equal$

then for $i := 1$ **to** $string1.length$

   do $equal := (string1.character[i] = string2.character[i])$

The problem with this code is that it returns the value true whenever the two strings have equal length and their last characters are identical. For example, the two strings 'cat' and 'mat' would be declared equal because they both have length three and end in 't'.

The student was quite taken aback when I demonstrated the error. Indeed, upon further questioning, it emerged that the program had been tested quite system-

---

[3]The program is coded in Pascal. The characters of a string s are assumed to be stored in the array $s.character$, indexed from 1 to $s.length$.

atically. First, it had been tested on several pairs of identical strings, and then on several pairs of strings of unequal length. Both these tests had produced satisfactory results. The final test had been to input several pairs of equal length but unequal strings, such as 'cat' and 'dog', or 'house' and 'river'.

This final test is interesting because it is possible to use simple probability theory to make a rough estimate of the chances of discovering the programming error. The details are not relevant here. Suffice it to say that, assuming pairs of words of equal length are generated with equal letter frequencies (that is, each letter in the alphabet is chosen with a probability of $1/26$), there is only a one in three chance of discovering the error after ten tests; increasing the number of tests to 20 would still only yield a one in two chance, and one would need to perform over 50 tests to achieve a 90% chance of discovering the error. Finally, and most importantly, there is no certainty that one would ever discover the error, no matter how many tests have been performed.

So, you see that program testing is never-ending. We can never be sure that all avenues have been tried; we can never be sure that there is not one more error lurking unseen, just waiting for the most crucial opportunity to show itself.

(Needless to say, I observed the error by reading the code, not by testing. The student was blameless. The error was the responsibility of the student's teacher for having failed to teach proper design principles and suggesting that testing was adequate.)

1.4   Correct by Construction

That debugging is not fail-safe is a drawback, but not its main limitation. The main problem with debugging is that it is useless as the basis for program *design*, of which fact even a small acquaintance with programming will convince you. An alternative to debugging is the development of a *science* of programming. Such a science should provide the techniques to enable the verification of a program against its specification. But it should do more than that; it should provide a discipline for the *construction* of programs that guarantees their correctness.

Of course, the science guarantees correctness only if it is used correctly, and people will continue to make mistakes. So testing is still wise, and debugging will occasionally be necessary. But now, rather than chance, it is our own skill in applying the science on which we rely. The aim of this book is to impart that skill and to enable you to take a pride in your programming ability.

Bibliographic Remarks

The Internet is awash with accounts of bugs and other programming errors that have made headline news over the years. For a particularly tragic case, search on the word 'Therac' for details of a software error that resulted in at least three deaths by an overdose of radiation in 1986. Searching on 'Risks' (short for 'Forum on Risks to the Public in Computers and Related Systems') yields details of many other examples.

The summary of the state of the car industry in the 1950s (see Section 1.1) is based on *Unsafe At Any Speed* by Nader (1965). The reports on the two NATO Science Committee-sponsored conferences (Naur and Randell, 1969; Buxton and Randell, 1970) are available on the Internet.

A very large part of the text has been directly influenced by the work of Edsger W. Dijkstra. The quotation attributed to Dijkstra in Section 1.2 appears in Buxton and Randell (1970), which is also the source of Hopkins's remarks.

I first saw the algorithm for computing the powers of n, discussed in Section 1.2, in Polya (1954); it was originally discovered by Mössner (1951) and verified by Perron (1951).

The case $n = 0$ in the cutting-the-cake problem (Exercise 1.1) was pointed out to me by Diethard Michaelis. A formula giving the number of portions is quite complicated. See Dijkstra (1990) for a derivation of the correct formula.

2

A Searching Problem and Its Solution

Examples are better than precepts; let me get down to examples—I much prefer examples to general talk.

G. Polya

This chapter is about the systematic development of a search algorithm and its proof of correctness. The algorithm is presented in English rather than in a mathematical language so that you can begin to understand the process of algorithm design without being distracted by perhaps unfamiliar notation. A disadvantage is that the description is imprecise and relies on your good will in understanding what is meant.

2.1 Problem Statement

The problem we consider is this. Suppose you are presented with a deck of cards, as shown in Figure 2.1. On each card is printed the name of a student together with personal details (date of birth, address, examination record, etc.). The cards are all in alphabetical order (according to surname). Suppose you are also presented with one additional card on which is printed the name of a student X. The task is to describe a procedure for splitting the deck of cards into two parts in such

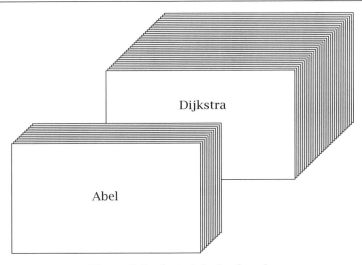

Figure 2.1   Sorted deck of cards.

a way that (a) *all* of the cards in the first part precede X in alphabetical order, and (b) *none* of the cards in the second part precedes X in alphabetical order. Otherwise, the original deck should be left intact.

We call this a searching problem because we are effectively looking for the position in the deck at which to insert the new card.

When presented with a problem like this, the first step is to ensure that you have a clear understanding of the problem. For programming purposes, the demands on clarity and unambiguity of the problem specification are much higher than if the task is to be carried out manually by a colleague, when one can rely on common sense and intelligence. We discuss program specification in detail later, but for the purposes of this exposition we rely on goodwill in making sense of some of the actions to be described.

One point needing clarification is that the process of splitting the original deck may result in one of the parts being empty. For example, if the deck contains the student surnames

> Einstein
> Newton
> Russell

and the name X is Galileo, the deck should be split into the two parts consisting of, first, the card belonging to Einstein and, second, the two cards belonging to Newton and Russell. However, if the name is Turing, the first part consists of all three cards in the original deck and the second part is empty.

The mathematical abstraction of regarding no cards as being nonetheless a deck of cards is a useful one with the very practical effect of reducing the number of cases one has to consider from three (X is at the beginning, X is in the middle, and

X is at the end) to one. As a bonus, the original problem statement now applies to an empty deck of cards, in which case the process of splitting the deck would result in two parts, each of which is also empty.

2.2 Problem Solution

Here is an efficient algorithm to solve the problem. We maintain at all times three decks of cards. The first of these, which we call the *left deck*, contains cards that are all known to precede X in alphabetical order; the third deck, which we call the *right deck*, contains cards that are all known to not precede X in alphabetical order; finally, the second deck, which we call the *middle deck*, contains cards that may or may not precede X in alphabetical order. All three decks are alphabetically ordered and are such that recombining the left, middle and right decks, in that order, returns the deck to its original form.

Initially, the left and right decks are both empty. The task is complete when the middle deck is empty. We make progress to this state by repeatedly removing cards from the middle deck and adding them to either the left or right deck.

In more detail, the procedure to be used is the following. Arrange space on a table for the three decks of cards. Initially, the entire deck is placed face up in the space reserved for the middle deck. The left and right decks are empty. Subsequently, the following process is repeated until the middle deck is empty.

Pick up the middle deck and split it in two. This splitting may take place in an arbitrary fashion except that the deck containing the cards that are later in alphabetical order should be non-empty. Call the two decks the *lower* and *upper* decks, where the lower deck contains the cards that are earlier in alphabetical order and the upper deck contains the cards that are later in alphabetical order. Then, depending on the student name revealed at the start of the upper deck, do one of two things.

(R1) If the name precedes X in alphabetical order, place the entire lower deck and the first card of the upper deck face down on the left deck and return the remainder of the upper deck to the middle deck.

(R2) If the name does not precede X in alphabetical order, place the entire upper deck face up on the right deck and return the lower deck to the middle deck.

When the middle deck is empty, the goal of splitting the deck in two will have been achieved.

This completes the description of the algorithm. Let us now see what would constitute a proof of correctness.

2.3   Proof of Correctness

The first thing to be completely clear about is that 'correctness' as used in this text is a relative notion. The word 'correct' sounds absolute—and that may be the way you use it in everyday conversation—but it is being used here as a technical term. When we refer to a program being 'correct', we mean relative to some given *specification*. Generally, the specification of a programming problem consists of a *precondition*, describing the properties of the input data, and a *postcondition*, describing the desired effect of the computation. In our searching problem, the precondition comprises a description of the given deck of cards and the information it contains together with the important requirement that the names on the cards be alphabetically ordered. The postcondition states that the given deck of cards is to be split into two and details the properties required of the two parts. In terms of the solution we have presented, these properties are:

(P1) every card in the left deck precedes X in alphabetical order;

(P2) none of the cards in the right deck precedes X in alphabetical order;

(P3) the original deck can be retrieved by recombining the left and right decks in that order.

The proof of correctness hinges on two aspects of the repeated process, the so-called *bound function* and the *invariant*.

In general, the *bound function* is an integer function of the data being manipulated. It measures, in some sense, the 'size' of the problem remaining to be solved. We use it to prove that the repeated process will always terminate, i.e. that the program will not 'get into a loop' and repeat the same sequence of actions indefinitely.

The *invariant* is a property of the data being manipulated that holds irrespective of the number of repetitions that have been executed. We use the invariant to establish so-called 'conditional correctness', meaning that the program meets its specification under the assumption of (or 'conditional' on) a proof of termination.

(a) Proof of Termination.   For the bound function, we take the number of cards in the middle deck. To use it to prove that the process of repeatedly executing (R1) or (R2) will always terminate, we make two observations.

(T1) There is a lower bound (zero) on the number of cards in the middle deck. In this case, the lower bound is dictated by the physical characteristics of a deck of cards. In general, we look to the condition for terminating the repeated process to provide such a bound.

(T2) Every time the repeated part of the search process is executed, the number of cards in the middle deck decreases by at least one. This is because we have been careful to ensure that the inspected card is always removed from the middle deck and added to either the left or right deck.

Together, these two observations make it obvious that the number of times the repeated part of the algorithm is executed is at most equal to the number of cards in the original deck.

It is worth noting in passing that this proof of termination does not depend on how the middle deck is split at each iteration. It is allowed, for example, to always split it so that the lower deck is empty. This is correct but inefficient. A more efficient strategy is to always split the middle deck into two (as near as possible) equal parts, since this means that its size is (approximately) halved at each repetition. We return to the issue of efficiency in Chapter 4 but, for the moment, correctness is our only concern.

(b) Conditional Correctness.   The second part of the proof of correctness is given the name *conditional correctness*[1]. A proof of conditional correctness assumes that the execution of a program terminates and concentrates on establishing that its specification is met.

The properties we use to establish the conditional correctness of our searching algorithm have already been stated. They are:

(I1) every card in the left deck precedes X in alphabetical order;

(I2) none of the cards in the right deck precedes X in alphabetical order;

(I3) the original deck may be retrieved by recombining the left, middle and right decks, in that order.

Note that these properties hold no matter how often the splitting process has been executed, and so we refer to them as *invariants*.

Note, also, that properties (I1)–(I3) *generalize* the properties (P1)–(P3) above. Indeed, (I1) and (P1) are identical, as are (I2) and (P2). Properties (I3) and (P3) are, however, different; they are the same only when the middle deck is empty. It is in this sense that (I3) generalizes (P3). The invention of invariants is a crucial process in program construction. Typically, as this example illustrates, invariants are generalizations of the required postcondition.

We use the principle of mathematical induction to prove that these three properties really are invariant. Generally, the principle of mathematical induction is used to prove that some property $P.n$ is true for all natural numbers n. (The natural numbers are the whole numbers beginning at 0, thus 0, 1, 2, 3 and so on. The notation '$P.n$' indicates that P is a function of n.) In this case, n refers to the number of times the middle deck has been split and property P is property (I1) *and* property (I2) *and* property (I3). In other words, what we wish to prove is that, for any natural number n, each of properties (I1), (I2) and (I3) hold after n iterations of the repeated process.

---

[1] Many texts use the term 'partial correctness' instead. The statement that a program is 'partially' correct can be misleading, since it suggests that there is something wrong with the program. 'Conditional' correctness is the term introduced and favoured by C. A. R. Hoare, the computing scientist to whom the techniques on which this text is based are widely attributed.

The first step is to show that they all hold after 0 iterations—i.e. initially. This is true of (I1) as initially the left deck is empty. Similarly, (I2) is true initially. Property (I3) is also true because the combination of the left, middle and right decks is just the middle deck, which is identical to the original deck.

The next step is to make the induction hypothesis that all three properties hold just before execution of the repeated part. Then we examine in turn the two cases considered within the splitting process and show that, in each case, properties (I1)–(I3) remain true after its execution. Let us examine just one of these cases to see how the argument goes.

We are assuming that the original deck has been split into three decks—the left, middle and right decks—and that all the cards in the left deck and none of the cards in the right deck precede X in alphabetical order. Let us suppose that cutting the deck reveals a name that precedes X in alphabetical order. Then, as the original deck was sorted, the name on every card in the lower part of the middle deck must also precede X. Thus, removing the lower deck and the revealed card from the middle deck and appending them to the left deck preserves property (I1). The right deck is not affected, so (I2) remains true. Finally, we leave the deck intact, in the sense of (I3), by adding the removed cards to the end of the left deck.

A similar argument applies in the case that cutting the deck reveals a name that does not precede X in alphabetical order.

The final step in our use of mathematical induction is to argue that, as properties (I1)–(I3) hold initially, they must, by the above argument, also hold after one iteration of the repeated part and, therefore, after two and three, and so on. We conclude that (I1)–(I3) are invariants, i.e. their truth is independent of the number of times the repeated part has been executed.

There is one more step remaining before our proof is complete. This is to show that the postcondition of the algorithm is a logical consequence of the condition for termination and the invariant property. This is clearly true because, on termination, the middle deck is empty, which is equivalent to saying that the original deck has been split into two. More formally, when the middle deck is empty, invariant (Ii) is equivalent to postcondition (Pi), where i is 1, 2 or 3.

2.4   What, Why and How

The objective of this chapter has been to summarize the main elements of program construction, using a concrete example as illustration. A brief summary is that there are three essential ingredients: the '*what*', the '*why*' and the '*how*'.

The 'what' is the program's specification. A specification acts as a contract between the client, who commissions the software, and the programmer, who implements the software; it says *what* the program should compute.

The 'how' is the implementation itself. It consists of a number of instructions that are executed by a computer. The implementation thus prescribes *how* to meet the specification.

The 'why' is the justification that the implementation does indeed meet its specification. It documents the program by explaining the function of the instructions in the implementation; it says *why* the program is as it is.

A *precise* specification is essential to the construction of reliable programs; without one, there is simply no basis for verifying that the client's requirements have been met. Also, because it is to be executed by an unforgiving machine, the implementation needs to be precise and unambiguous. Finally, the justification that the program meets its specification needs to be precise, in order to have complete confidence in the correctness of the implementation.

In this chapter, we have foregone precision for the sake of illustration. This lack of precision means that we cannot truly claim to have developed a correct implementation of the given specification. The problem lies in the use of an imprecise language (English) to discuss the program; at times you have been expected to interpret the statements generously. (For example, the way in which the lower and upper decks, or the left and right decks, are combined into one was never precisely stated, although it is crucial to keeping the original deck intact.) In later chapters, we rectify the problem. We introduce a simple language for program specification, and a separate language for program implementations. We also relate the two, precisely and concisely.

2.5 Exercises

Exercise 2.1 (Find). The development of the mathematics of program construction was pioneered by, most prominently, Edsger W. Dijkstra and C. A. R. Hoare (now Sir Tony Hoare). In his inaugural lecture at The Queen's University of Belfast in February 1971, Hoare presented the design of an algorithm which he enacted with a deck of cards. In this question, you are asked to study Hoare's description of the algorithm and then analyse the correctness argument he gave.

This is Hoare's description of the algorithm[2]. Study it carefully and then answer the questions which follow.

... So in order to explain my understanding of computer science, it is essential to describe the nature of the activity of computer programming. To do this I have chosen an example of one of the first programs which I designed and wrote some ten years ago for the solution of a simple but nontrivial practical problem. It is a problem that can arise in the collection and tabulation of statistics, for example, the discovery of the median and other quantiles of a set of statistical observations. Suppose we have a large number of observations, say a hundred

---

[2]Reproduced with the permission of the author and by courtesy of the Queen's University of Belfast.

thousand—perhaps the heights of school entrants, or the distances of stars, or marks in some examination. It is required to single out those 20 thousand observations with smallest value; perhaps the 20 thousand nearest stars, or the 20 thousand shortest schoolchildren, or the 20 thousand students with lowest marks.

The first guide in the discovery of a method for computer solution of a problem is to see how the problem could be solved by hand by a human being. In order not to be overwhelmed by the sheer numbers involved, we will scale down the problem to only one hundred observations, of which the twenty with lowest values are to be selected. Imagine for convenience that the values of the observations are recorded on a hundred cards; these cards must be separated into two heaps, the left-hand heap containing the twenty lowest cards, and the right-hand heap containing the rest. We can now regard the problem as one of designing, as it were, the rules for a game of patience, whose outcome is the one we desire, and which has the delightful property that it always comes out.

Perhaps the first idea which occurs to us is to sort the cards into ascending order; for then the selection of the required twenty cards is trivial. All that is needed is to deal the first twenty cards off the top of the pack. So all we have to do is to find some efficient method of sorting the pack. But further consideration shows that it would be a waste of time to sort the *whole* pack, when all we require is to single out twenty of them, the twenty cards with smallest value. So we turn attention again to this problem.

Our second proposed method is to look through the whole pack for the smallest card, and remove it; then look for the smallest again in the reduced pack; and to repeat the process until twenty cards have been singled out. Before accepting this solution, we ask ourselves how efficient the method is. In order to find the lowest card in a pack it is in principle necessary to look at every card in the pack, i.e. a hundred cards; to find the second lowest card requires ninety-nine inspections, and so on. Thus assuming optimistically that each inspection takes a second, the total time taken will be about half an hour—a rather daunting prospect. Going back to the original computer program of 100 thousand observations, and assuming our computer can examine about a hundred thousand observations in one second, it would take about five hours to select the least 20 000 observations. So it is worth while to seek an alternative more efficient solution.

As our third idea, it may occur to us that if we happened to know the value of the observation which was the twenty-first smallest one, we could use this as a sort of *borderline* value in the process of splitting the pack into two heaps. For example, supposing we think that 367 is the twentieth smallest value. All we need to do is to go through the pack, putting all the cards lower than the borderline value on a left-hand heap, and all cards higher than it on a right-hand heap, and so on. At the end, we expect that the left-hand heap will contain exactly the required twenty values. This process requires only one scan of the entire pack, and will take just over one and a half minutes in our small manual example. Returning to the computer problem, it could carry out the whole process on a hundred thousand observations in one second—very much better than the five hours required if the previous method had been used. But it seems that this gain in speed can be achieved only if we have prior knowledge of the correct borderline value, and this knowledge we do not have.

But now suppose we make a *guess* of the correct borderline value, and carry out the partitioning process as before. I suggest that we choose the borderline as the value of an actual card in the pack, since this will ensure that we never choose a ridiculously high or low value. Now if our guess, say 367, was too high, the left-hand heap ends up too large, containing more than twenty cards; and the right-hand heap is too small, containing less than eighty cards. Similarly, if our guess was too low, the left-hand heap is too small and the right-hand heap is too large. Thus we always know afterwards whether the first guess was too high or too low, and perhaps we can use this knowledge to make a better guess next time.

As before, it is a good idea to select as next guess an actual card of the pack, which is known to be better than the previously guessed wrong borderline. This can be done very easily by selecting a card from the appropriate heap, for example, the left-hand heap if the original guess was too high; for it is known that all cards in this heap are smaller that the previous (too high) borderline. So we can repeat the process with this new borderline.

But now consider the right-hand heap which was too small. This heap contains only cards which *should* be there, in the sense that they are already in the same heap as they will be in when the correct borderline is found. There is no point in scanning the cards of this heap again. This suggests that in any subsequent scan we can put these cards aside, say at the top of the card table. The importance of this suggestion arises from the fact that subsequent scans will be shorter than earlier ones, so eventually we will get down to a single card, which must then be the right borderline.

So having put to the top the right-hand heap which was too small, we move the other heap to the middle, select a new borderline, say 196,

and proceed with the split. At the end of the second split, we will have
a borderline value and three heaps:

1. A top right heap, with cards higher than the first borderline 367.

2. A bottom right heap, with cards lying between the two borderlines
   196 and 367.

3. A bottom left heap, with cards lower than the second smaller borderline 196.

It may happen now that it is the left of the two bottom heaps which
is too small; it will therefore contain only cards which properly belong
to the left heap; and as before, we can put it on the card table, and
omit it from future examination. Then we place the borderline value on
that heap. Next we move the remaining bottom heap up to the middle
and repeat the process, selecting again an arbitrary trial borderline
(say 229), and splitting the middle heap into a bottom left heap and a
bottom right heap. Then we have a picture as shown in Figure 2.2.

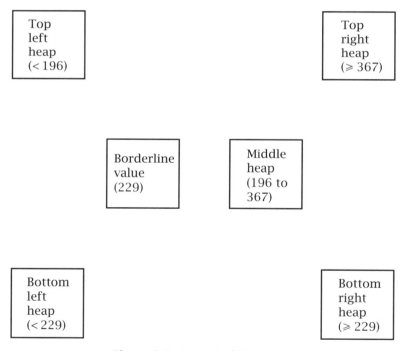

Figure 2.2   Layout of the game.

Obviously we don't want to continue to proliferate more and more
heaps, and we must seek every opportunity to amalgamate them, for
example, by putting the bottom right heap on top of the top right heap.

(1) Put all 100 cards on the middle heap.

(2) Repeat the following until the middle heap is empty:

  (2.1) Take a card from the middle heap as borderline.

  (2.2) Repeat the following until the middle heap is empty:
  If the top card of the middle heap is less than the borderline, put it on the bottom left heap; otherwise on the bottom right heap.

  (2.3) If the combined size of top left and bottom left heaps is less than 21, amalgamate them; and if it is still less than 20 put the borderline card on as well.

  (2.4) If the combined size of top right and bottom right heaps is less than 81, amalgamate them; and if it is still less than 80 put the borderline card on as well.

  (2.5) Move the remaining bottom heap (if any) to the middle heap.

(3) The required 20 observations will now be found on the top left heap.

Figure 2.3 Rules of the game.

This operation is permissible whenever the resulting combined heap is not too large. Similarly the left-hand heaps can be amalgamated if this would not make the top left heap too large. It is evident that one at least of these amalgamations is always possible; and if they are both possible, the whole problem is solved. But if one of them cannot be amalgamated, we must continue the process of splitting on this remaining heap, and so continue until the problem is solved.

It seems now that we have a grasp of a solution to our original problem; and to verify this, it is worthwhile to write the rules of the game rather more precisely, as is done in Figure 2.3.

Now answer the following questions.

(a) Does the algorithm make any assumption about the given pack of cards? What is the weakest assumption for the algorithm to function correctly?

(b) What can you say about the size of the individual heaps? (For example, what can you say about the size of the top-right heap?)

(c) What relationships exist between the values in the different heaps? (For example, which heap contains the smallest values?)

(d) Suppose all cards in the pack have the same value. Describe what happens. Suppose the pack is sorted in ascending order and suppose the borderline card is chosen to be the 20th in the pack. Is it the case that step (2) will be repeated exactly once? If not, give a necessary and sufficient condition for this to be the case.

(e) Why is it important that the borderline is a card in the middle heap? Show by example what may go wrong if the chosen borderline value is not the value of one of the cards. (Hint: think about why the algorithm is guaranteed to terminate.)

(f) Generalize your answers to (a)–(c) for the case that the problem is to find the *M* lowest values in a pack of *N* cards, where *M* and *N* are input parameters to the algorithm. Modify the algorithm accordingly. Check that your algorithm works for the extreme cases when *M* and/or *N* is zero, and when *M* equals the number of cards in the pack.   □

The exercises below are aimed at getting you to think in terms of invariant properties. The invariant properties are very simple—even 'obvious' once pointed out. Finding them can be difficult, however, because thinking in terms of invariants is a skill that is rarely taught properly, if at all. The solutions are provided at the back of the book, but try not to give up too early!

Exercise 2.2 (The Domino Problem). A chess board has had its top-right and bottom-left squares removed so that there are 62 squares remaining. (See Figure 2.4.)

Figure 2.4   Mutilated chess board.

An unlimited supply of dominoes has been provided; each domino will cover exactly two squares of the chessboard. Is it possible to cover all 62 squares of the chessboard with the dominoes without any domino overlapping another domino or sticking out beyond the edges of the board?   □

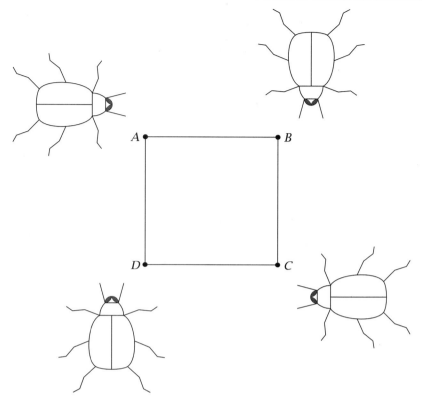

Figure 2.5 The amorous beetles.

Exercise 2.3 (The Amorous Beetles). Four beetles—A, B, C and D—occupy the corners of a square (Figure 2.5). A and C are male, B and D are female. Simultaneously A crawls towards B, B towards C, C towards D, and D towards A. If all four beetles crawl at the same rate, they will describe four congruent logarithmic spirals which meet at the centre of the square.

How far does each beetle travel before they meet? The problem can be solved without calculus. □

2.6 Summary

The purpose of this chapter has been to introduce, informally, the concepts underlying program construction. The *specification* of a program by means of a *precondition* and *postcondition* has been illustrated. The design of a repetitive process (a 'loop') using an *invariant* property to precisely describe the function of the iteration, and the use of a bound function as a measure of progress towards the termination condition have been introduced. Finally, the relation between invariants and mathematical induction has been explained.

All these topics will be amplified and made rigorous in later chapters.

Bibliographic Remarks

The algorithm discussed in this chapter is a variant on the well-known binary search method. We return to it again in Chapter 4. The idea of using a deck of cards to illustrate the algorithm was suggested to me by Stuart Anderson. Hoare's inaugural 1971 lecture (see Exercise 2.1) is published in Hoare and Jones (1989, pp. 89–101). See Section 14.2 for a formal specification of Hoare's problem, and how an implementation is calculated from the specification.

The problem of the amorous beetles (Exercise 2.3) is from Gardner (1959). The origin of the domino problem (Exercise 2.2) is unknown to me.

3

Calculational Proof

In earlier chapters, we have argued that proof is necessary to guarantee that programs meet their specifications. What is meant by a 'proof' is, however, not as clear cut as one might at first imagine. In this chapter, we discuss different sorts of proofs. We advocate 'calculational proofs' in which reasoning is goal directed and justified by simple axiomatic laws that can be checked syntactically rather than semantically. We introduce a notation for presenting calculations and give several examples.

3.1 The Nature of Proof

The word 'proof' can be understood in several ways. An *informal proof*, the sort most commonly encountered in mathematical texts, consists of a mixture of natural language (for example, English) and mathematical calculations. The English text outlines the main steps in the proof, and the mathematical calculations fill in some of the details. Figure 3.1, a proof of Pythagoras's theorem, is a typical example. It uses English to describe the construction of a square from four copies of a right-angled triangle, combined with an outline of an algebraic calculation using properties of arithmetic.

Informal proofs place a large burden on the reader. The reader is expected to have a good understanding of the problem domain, and the meaning of the natural language statements, as well as the language of mathematics. Because of their reliance on meaning, we say that they are *semantic* proofs. Figure 3.2 is an example of a proof where the burden of understanding of the English language

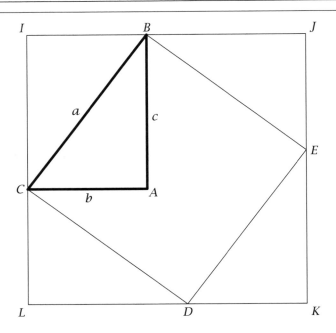

Let ABC be a triangle with $\widehat{BAC} = 90^0$. Let the lengths of sides BC, AC, AB be, respectively, a, b and c. We wish to prove that $a^2 = b^2 + c^2$. Construct a square $IJKL$, of side $b+c$, and a square $BCDE$, of side a, as shown in the figure. Clearly,

$$area(IJKL) \ = \ (b+c)^2 \ .$$

But,

$$area(IJKL) \ = \ area(BCDE) + 4 \times area(ABC) = a^2 + 2bc \ .$$

That is,

$$(b+c)^2 \ = \ a^2 + 2bc \ .$$

Whence,

$$b^2 + c^2 = a^2 \ .$$

Figure 3.1 Proof of Pythagoras's theorem.

statements is particularly great. The theorem proved is deep and interesting—if a map is placed on the ground anywhere in the area covered by the map, then there will be a point on the map that is directly above the point on the ground that it

Suppose a map of London is placed on the ground in the middle of Trafalgar Square. (Readers unfamiliar with London should note that Trafalgar Square is in Central London.) Then, there is a point on the map that is directly above the point on the ground that it represents.

> *Proof.* The map (of London) is directly above a part of London. Thus the (entire) map is directly above a part of the area which it represents. Now, the (smaller) area of the map representing Central London is also above a part of the area which it represents. Within the area representing Central London, Trafalgar Square is marked, and this (yet smaller) part of the map is directly above a part of the area which it represents. Continuing in this way, we can find smaller and smaller areas of the map each of which is directly above a part of the area which it represents. In the limit we reduce the area on the map to a single point which is directly above a part of the area it represents. That is, a point has been found that is directly above the point on the ground that it represents.

Figure 3.2 A semantic proof.

represents—but it is quite difficult to understand even the statement of the theorem, and yet more difficult to understand the proof. Without a good understanding of the semantics of the proof, the reader cannot check its validity. Many would feel uneasy about the validity of the proof and would demand a more detailed justification for some of the steps. The difficulty is compounded, of course, for those for whom English is not the mother tongue. What is meant, for example, by 'the area represented' by a section of the map, and the meaning of 'in the limit'. In comparison, the language of mathematics is much simpler; moreover, unlike natural language, it is universal!

At the other end of the scale, a *formal proof* is conducted entirely in the language of mathematics. A *formal proof* is a sequence of steps, each of which is a well-established fact or which follows from earlier statements by a process so simple that it is deemed to be self-evident. Figure 3.3 is an example of a formal proof. It is a proof of the fact that $\sqrt{2} + \sqrt{7}$ is greater than $\sqrt{3} + \sqrt{5}$. The first three lines of the proof state well-known facts. Each subsequent line combines one or more previous lines in order to derive some new fact; next to each of these lines is a hint explaining how the line is derived.

Checking each line of Figure 3.3 is straightforward. The lines where the hint mentions 'arithmetic' involve squaring and other simple arithmetic calculations. For example, to check line 7 it is necessary to check that $(1 + 2\sqrt{14})^2$ is $57 + 4\sqrt{14}$ and that $(2\sqrt{15})^2$ is $57+3$. The remaining lines are checked by confirming that the line is an instance of either line 0 or line 1. That is, one has to check that

$$
\begin{array}{lll}
0. & \text{if } a > 0 \text{ and } b > c > 0 \text{ then } a+b > a+c > 0 & \\
1. & \text{if } a > b > 0 \text{ then } \sqrt{a} > \sqrt{b} > 0 & \\
2. & 224 > 9 > 0 & \\
3. & \sqrt{224} > \sqrt{9} > 0 & (1 \text{ and } 2) \\
4. & 4\sqrt{14} > 3 > 0 & (3 \text{ and arithmetic}) \\
5. & 57 + 4\sqrt{14} > 57+3 > 0 & (0 \text{ and } 4) \\
6. & \sqrt{57 + 4\sqrt{14}} > \sqrt{57+3} > 0 & (1 \text{ and } 5) \\
7. & 1 + 2\sqrt{14} > 2\sqrt{15} > 0 & (6 \text{ and arithmetic}) \\
8. & 8 + 1 + 2\sqrt{14} > 8 + 2\sqrt{15} > 0 & (0 \text{ and } 7) \\
9. & \sqrt{8 + 1 + 2\sqrt{14}} > \sqrt{8 + 2\sqrt{15}} > 0 & (1 \text{ and } 8) \\
10. & \sqrt{2} + \sqrt{7} > \sqrt{3} + \sqrt{5} > 0 & (9 \text{ and arithmetic}) \\
\end{array}
$$

Figure 3.3   A formal proof of $\sqrt{2} + \sqrt{7} > \sqrt{3} + \sqrt{5}$.

the line is obtained by a valid substitution of numbers for the variables a, b and c.

Most proofs of theorems in mathematics go through a 'social process' to check their validity. This process involves the proof being checked by a number of experts in the field; eventually the proof is accepted or shown to be flawed. For example, Andrew Wiles's first announced 'proof' of Fermat's Last Theorem was discovered to be flawed. His second proof has been accepted by the mathematical community even though it is said that no one but he understands the proof in its entirety. In the course of time, understanding of Wiles's proof should grow, leading to simpler, shorter proofs, or, possibly, the discovery of another flaw in the proof. This social process is inappropriate for proving properties of programs. The delay is too long and there are too many of them to be proved. Fortunately, properties of programs are often rather shallow; proof is still necessary, because the devil lies in the detail.

Exercise 3.1. The proof in Figure 3.1 assumes a lot of knowledge about geometric figures. Can you fill in some of the details?   □

3.2   Construction versus Verification

Informal proofs are often favoured because they are claimed to be easier to understand and they appeal to 'intuition'. In reality, informal proofs have their own characteristic types of complexity, namely the complexity of hidden details, assumed knowledge and the imprecision of natural language. Also, intuition (meaning understanding without conscious reasoning) is a fickle ally which should never be relied upon.

On the other hand, formal proofs can be difficult to understand, particularly when done badly. The proof in Figure 3.3 is a good example of how *not* to present a formal proof. Unfortunately, it is typical of how many formal proofs are presented.

The problem with the proof in Figure 3.3 is that it is oriented to *verification* rather than *construction*. Each step in the proof is relatively easy to check, but it is very difficult to see how the proof was constructed. The goal is to determine which of $\sqrt{2} + \sqrt{7}$ or $\sqrt{3} + \sqrt{5}$ is the largest, but the proof begins in line 2 with the numbers 224 and 9—completely out of the blue! Because of this, the proof is very difficult to reproduce, even though the individual steps are easy to understand, and it is yet more difficult to apply the underlying method to a problem of a similar form. The proof offers no guidance on how to determine, for example, the ordering relation between $\sqrt{3} + \sqrt{11}$ and $\sqrt{5} + \sqrt{7}$. In fact, the proof was not constructed in the way it is presented but rather by *inverting* a *construction* of the ordering relation.

In this text we employ a calculational proof style. 'Calculational' means that the proofs are syntactic rather than semantic. In other words, our proofs are like a game with meaningless symbols conducted according to a set of predetermined rules. It also means that our calculations are directed towards determining what is true rather than verifying some conjectured truth.

To illustrate calculational proof let us consider the problem just mentioned of determining a relation between $\sqrt{3} + \sqrt{11}$ and $\sqrt{5} + \sqrt{7}$. We denote the relation by X. So, X is one of '<', '=' or '>'.

This is the first step in every calculation—introduce a variable to denote the *unknown*, the value to be calculated. Undoubtedly, it is a step very familiar to the reader in other circumstances. (Examples that the reader may have encountered elsewhere include calculating the distance d travelled by a falling body in a given time, and calculating the temperature T of a gas contained within a given volume at a given pressure.) What may well be unfamiliar is that the unknown in this case is a relation (rather than a distance, a time, a temperature, a voltage, or some other measurable quantity). If it is unfamiliar, don't let it worry you!

The next step is to identify properties of the unknown that will help to identify it. The problem statement involves two arithmetic operators, addition and taking square roots. So it is properties of these two operators with respect to the three ordering relations that we seek.

The crucial property of addition is that it is *invertible* with respect to all three relations. To explain what we mean by 'invertible', we first have to explain equality between 'booleans'. Suppose a, b and c are arbitrary numbers. Then, clearly, $a+b \; X \; a+c$ will be true or false, whichever of the three relations X is. For example, $1+2 < 1+3$ is true, and $1+2 = 1+3$ is false. Also, $b \, X \, c$ will be true or false. We say that $a+b \; X \; a+c$ and $b \, X \, c$ are *booleans*: their values are either true or false.

Invertibility of addition is the property that these booleans are always equal. That is, $a+b \; X \; a+c$ is true exactly when $b \, X \, c$ is true. Vice versa, $a+b \; X \; a+c$ is false exactly when $b \, X \, c$ is false. Mathematically, for all numbers a, b and c,

$$(a+b \ X \ a+c) \ = \ (b \, X \, c) \ . \tag{3.2}$$

In words, the truth value of $a+b \ X \ a+c$ is equal to the truth value of $b \, X \, c$. Spelling the three instances of the property out in detail, we have

$$(a+b < a+c) \ = \ (b < c) \ ,$$
$$(a+b = a+c) \ = \ (b = c) \ ,$$
$$(a+b > a+c) \ = \ (b > c) \ .$$

Note that the parentheses are necessary here in order to avoid confusion: it is common to write so-called *continued* orderings and/or equalities, these being read *conjunctionally*. For instance, the *continued equality*

$$a+b \ = \ a+c \ = \ b \ = \ c$$

means $a+b = a+c$ *and* $a+c = b$ *and* $b = c$ (i.e. the *conjunction* of three equalities). This is quite different from

$$(a+b = a+c) \ = \ (b = c)$$

which means that the boolean $a+b = a+c$ is equal to the boolean $b = c$.

Later, we introduce another symbol for equality between booleans (symbol '$\equiv$') partly to avoid confusion with continued equalities, but also for more significant reasons.

Squaring of *positive* numbers is also 'invertible' with respect to the three ordering relations. This means that, whatever X is among the three relations, we have, for all numbers a, b and c, that the boolean $a^2 \, X \, b^2$ is equal to the boolean $a \, X \, b$. That is, for all positive numbers a and b,

$$(a^2 \, X \, b^2) \ = \ (a \, X \, b) \ . \tag{3.3}$$

For example,

$$(a^2 > b^2) \ = \ (a > b) \ .$$

The two properties (3.2) and (3.3) are all we need to know to calculate the relationship X between $\sqrt{3} + \sqrt{11}$ and $\sqrt{5} + \sqrt{7}$. Here is how it goes. It is a sequence of equalities, just like a calculation in algebra, in which the equality between the first and last terms is the result of the calculation. To help you understand the calculation, a *hint* has been added at each step, indicating the property that is being applied. (The parentheses needed to disambiguate in-line formulae are no longer needed because the layout of the calculations makes clear what is intended.)

$$\sqrt{3} + \sqrt{11} \ X \ \sqrt{5} + \sqrt{7}$$

$$= \qquad \{ \qquad \text{squaring is invertible with respect to } X \colon (3.3) \quad \}$$

$$(\sqrt{3} + \sqrt{11})^2 \ X \ (\sqrt{5} + \sqrt{7})^2$$

=   {   arithmetic   }

$$14 + 2\sqrt{33} \ X \ 12 + 2\sqrt{35}$$

=   {   addition is invertible with respect to X: (3.2)   }

$$2 + 2\sqrt{33} \ X \ 2\sqrt{35}$$

=   {   squaring is invertible with respect to X: (3.3)   }

$$(2 + 2\sqrt{33})^2 \ X \ (2\sqrt{35})^2$$

=   {   arithmetic   }

$$136 + 8\sqrt{33} \ X \ 140$$

=   {   addition is invertible with respect to X: (3.2)   }

$$8\sqrt{33} \ X \ 4$$

=   {   squaring is invertible with respect to X: (3.3)

           and arithmetic   }

$$2112 \ X \ 16 \ .$$

Summarizing, we have established that

$$(\sqrt{3} + \sqrt{11} \ X \ \sqrt{5} + \sqrt{7}) \ = \ (2112 \ X \ 16) \ .$$

So, the boolean $\sqrt{3} + \sqrt{11} < \sqrt{5} + \sqrt{7}$ is false, since $2112 < 16$ is false; for the same reason, $\sqrt{3} + \sqrt{11} = \sqrt{5} + \sqrt{7}$ is false. But, $\sqrt{3} + \sqrt{11} > \sqrt{5} + \sqrt{7}$ is true, since $2112 > 16$. In this way, we have *calculated* that $\sqrt{3} + \sqrt{11}$ is greater than $\sqrt{5} + \sqrt{7}$.

    Note that we could now repeat the calculation with X replaced everywhere by '>', adding the additional final step $(2112 > 16) = $ true, as outlined below:

$$\sqrt{3} + \sqrt{11} > \sqrt{5} + \sqrt{7}$$

=   {   squaring is invertible with respect to X: (3.3)   }

$$(\sqrt{3} + \sqrt{11})^2 > (\sqrt{5} + \sqrt{7})^2$$

=   {   …   }

    …

=   {   …   }

$$2112 > 16$$

=   {   arithmetic   }

true .

This would be a *verification* that $\sqrt{3} + \sqrt{11}$ is greater than $\sqrt{5} + \sqrt{7}$ because we start with the answer and verify its validity. A verification is undesirable because it hides the process of discovery. Worse still would be to turn the calculation upside down:

true

$=$ {   arithmetic   }

2112 > 16

$=$ {   ...   }

...

$=$ {   ...   }

$(\sqrt{3}+\sqrt{11})^2 > (\sqrt{5}+\sqrt{7})^2$

$=$ {   squaring is invertible with respect to X: (3.3)   }

$\sqrt{3}+\sqrt{11} > \sqrt{5}+\sqrt{7}$.

Now the process of discovery has been completely obliterated; a straightforward calculation has been turned into a piece of magic!

Exercise 3.4. The arithmetic in the calculation could have been made simpler if $2 + 2\sqrt{33}\ X\ 2\sqrt{35}$ had been simplified to $1 + \sqrt{33}\ X\ \sqrt{35}$. State the rule that allows this simplification to be made. (Take care with positive and negative numbers.)   □

Exercise 3.5. Determine the ordering relation between $\sqrt{3}+\sqrt{13}$ and $\sqrt{5}+\sqrt{11}$. Try to copy the style of calculation used above.   □

Exercise 3.6. Below is an algorithm to determine the ordering relation between $\sqrt{a}+\sqrt{b}$ and $\sqrt{c}+\sqrt{d}$ for given natural numbers a, b, c and d. What is wrong with the algorithm? Construct a counterexample to demonstrate the error. (Hint: examine each step to see whether it makes a valid use of a property of squaring or addition. Also, note that counterexamples do not need to be complicated!) Identify a suitable invariant property to be maintained by the algorithm in order to avoid the error; using the invariant, modify the algorithm so that it is correct.

We refer to $\sqrt{a}+\sqrt{b}$ and $\sqrt{c}+\sqrt{d}$ as the *left* and *right sides* of the relation, respectively.

Step 1. Square the left side and simplify it to the form $u + \sqrt{v}$. (For example, $(\sqrt{3}+\sqrt{13})^2$ is simplified to $16 + 2\sqrt{39}$.) Similarly, square and simplify the right side to the form $x + \sqrt{y}$.

Step 2. Subtract u from both sides and simplify. The left side is now in the form $\sqrt{v}$ and the right side is in the form $z + \sqrt{y}$.

Step 3. Square both sides again. Simplify the right side to the form $p + \sqrt{q}$. The left side is simplified to v.

Step 4. Subtract p from both sides and square again.

The relation between the original left and right sides is the same as the relation between the left and right sides obtained by carrying out steps 1-4. □

3.3 Formatting Calculations

The message of Section 3.2 is that reducing problem solving to calculation can be very effective, but, the use of a verificational, as opposed to constructive, style of reasoning can make simple calculations opaque and complex. In this text, we will develop a style of calculation that aims to elucidate the process of constructing solutions to non-trivial mathematical and programming problems.

Throughout, we use a uniform format for presenting calculations. We summarize the format in this section, but discuss it again when we begin to use it in earnest. The reader may therefore wish to omit this section on a first reading, returning to it when the need arises.

3.3.1 Basic Structure

Our calculations have a number of *steps* (usually more than one). A mandatory element is that each step is accompanied by a *hint* providing a justification for the validity of the step. For example, a two-step calculation might have the following shape.

$$R$$
$$= \qquad \{ \quad p \ \}$$
$$S$$
$$= \qquad \{ \quad q \ \}$$
$$T \ .$$

In this calculation, R, S and T are expressions, and p and q are hints why $R = S$ and $S = T$, respectively. The *conclusion* of the calculation is that $R = T$.

Here is a concrete example, where we use the laws of arithmetic to simplify an arithmetic expression. The goal of the calculation is to simplify the expression $(n+1)^2 - n^2$ by eliminating the squaring operator.

$$(n+1)^2 - n^2$$
$$= \qquad \{ \quad x^2 - y^2 \ = \ (x-y) \times (x+y),$$
$$\qquad \text{with } x, y \ := \ n+1, n \ \}$$
$$((n+1) - n) \times ((n+1) + n)$$
$$= \qquad \{ \qquad \text{addition is symmetric and associative} \ \}$$
$$((n-n) + 1) \times ((n+n) + 1)$$

$$= \qquad \{ \qquad n-n=0, \; n+n=2\times n \quad \}$$

$$(0+1)\times(2\times n + 1)$$

$$= \qquad \{ \qquad \text{arithmetic} \quad \}$$

$$2\times n + 1 \; .$$

The calculation is parametrized by the variable n which, by convention, denotes an arbitrary (natural) number. The conclusion of the calculation is the equality between the first and last lines:

$$(n+1)^2 - n^2 \;=\; 2\times n + 1$$

for all (natural) numbers n.

3.3.2 Hints

The *hints* in a calculation serve a number of purposes. The simple device of bracketing allows them to be of any size whatsoever. As a consequence, we may not only give detailed information about the formal justification for an individual step but also, whenever necessary, explain where we are going and why. We can also include a subcalculation in the hint, should we choose to do so.

In the above calculation, the hints get progressively simpler so let us begin with the last one.

The final hint, 'arithmetic', says almost nothing; it simply says that some property of arithmetic is being used. Here, the general laws actually being used are that $0+x=x$, and $1\times x=x$, irrespective of the value of x. These are very basic laws, which we expect the reader to be completely familiar with, and the presence of a hint is deemed to be superfluous. In more complicated cases, a hint like 'arithmetic' can be very useful. If, for example, an expression involves both arithmetic and boolean operators, such a hint focuses attention on the arithmetic operators rather than the boolean operators.

In contrast, the first hint is quite complicated. It states a property of arithmetic that holds for all values of the variables x and y. The accompanying text 'with $x,y \;:=\; n+1 \,, n$' indicates that the property is being used in the case that x has the value $n+1$ and y has the value n. Formally, the equality between the first and second expressions in the calculation

$$(n+1)^2 - n^2 \;=\; ((n+1)-n)\times((n+1)+n)$$

is the *instance* of the law

$$x^2 - y^2 \;=\; (x-y)\times(x+y)$$

obtained by *instantiating* x to $n+1$ and y to n.

Note that $n+1$ is parenthesized in order to make it clear how the instance is obtained. Sometimes, as in this case, parentheses are unnecessary when forming an instance of a law. In many cases, however, precedence conventions dictate the insertion of parentheses. For example, instantiating x to $n+1$ in the law $0 \times x = 0$, we get $0 \times (n+1) = 0$. Had we not parenthesized '$n+1$' in the left side, we would have got $0 \times n+1 = 0$. According to the convention that multiplication has precedence over addition, this is read as $(0 \times n) + 1 = 0$, which is blatantly untrue!

Instances of properties are most often indicated by a *simultaneous* assignment[1] where, as in this case, more than one variable is instantiated simultaneously. Although simultaneous assignments are rarely allowed in conventional programming languages their use should not cause any difficulty.

The second hint is less detailed than the first, but more detailed than the last. Formally, the step uses three properties of arithmetic: two explicitly mentioned in the hint, and one not mentioned at all. The two that are mentioned are that $x+y = y+x$, for all x and y (addition is 'symmetric'), and $(x+y)+z = x+(y+z)$, for all x, y and z (addition is 'associative'). The third property is that $x-y = x+(-y)$. The step is thus quite large. One should beware of large steps—this is where errors can occur, and the steps need to be checked carefully.

The third hint uses what is called *substitution of equals for equals*. The hint states that $n - n$ and 0 are equal, and the step replaces one by the other. The hint also states that $n+n$ and $2 \times n$ are equal, again justifying the step of replacing one by the other.

A difficulty that you may encounter, when carrying out calculations in this style for the first time, is that you can 'see' that a step is valid but cannot give a formal justification. The temptation to write 'arithmetic' or a similar hint becomes very great. The problem is that it is usual to first develop substantial skills in arithmetic before beginning to explore the basic laws (the 'axioms') on which those skills are based. Also, reduction of calculation steps to primitive axioms, each accompanied by the appropriate hint, can lead to a huge expansion in their lengths.

Documenting a calculation requires experience in order to achieve the right grain of detail. The omission of detail is, however, a common cause of error. So, it is better to include more detail than less, unless you are very confident of a step's accuracy.

A case in point is the use of arithmetic. Because the axioms of arithmetic are not the topic of this text, the grain of detail will vary, depending on the circumstances. Often, we will abbreviate a calculation to just one or two steps, giving the very briefest of explanations and leaving the reader to fill in the details:

$$(n+1)^2 - n^2$$

$$= \qquad \{ \qquad \text{arithmetic} \quad \}$$

$$2 \times n + 1 \ .$$

---

[1] Sometimes referred to as a 'multiple' assignment.

On the other hand, calculations that involve the topics introduced in this text—calculational logic and program construction—will be presented in much greater detail. Our policy is that, when a topic is first introduced, we use very small steps, each making use of just one formal rule. Later, as experience is gained, we combine small steps into one larger step.

Exercise 3.7. We commonly use the notation $E[x_0, x_1, \ldots, x_n := e_0, e_1, \ldots, e_n]$ to denote the simultaneous substitution of expressions $e_0, e_1, \ldots, e_n$ for the variables $x_0, x_1, \ldots, x_n$ in expression E. In the process, it is important to respect precedence conventions, adding parentheses around the expressions $e_0, e_1, \ldots, e_n$ when necessary.

Perform the following substitutions. Be careful with parenthesization and remove unnecessary parentheses. (A raised infix dot denotes multiplication. Multiplication has precedence over addition. Exponentiation is denoted by a superscript. Exponentiation has precedence over multiplication.)

(a) $x[x := x+2]$.

(b) $(y \cdot x)[x := x+y]$.

(c) $(x+y)[x := x+y]$.

(d) $(x+1)[y := x]$.

(e) $x[x, y := 0, x+2]$.

(f) $(x + y \cdot x)[x, y := x-y, x+y]$.

(g) $(x+y)[x, y := x \cdot y, x \cdot y]$.

(h) $(x + x \cdot y^z)[x, y, z := x+2, x \cdot y, 2]$.   □

3.3.3 Relations between Steps

A calculation with a number of steps, in which each step relates one expression to the next by equality, establishes that all the expressions are equal. However, it is usually the equality between the first and last expressions that is important to us. As mentioned earlier, the conclusion of the above four-step calculation is the equality between the first and last lines, that is,

$$(n+1)^2 - n^2 \;=\; 2 \times n + 1 \;.$$

Formally, equality is a *transitive* relation. That is, if $R = S$ and $S = T$, it is also the case that $R = T$.

Two other relations that are transitive are the less-than relation, denoted by '$<$', and the at-most relation, denoted by '$\leq$'[2]. Sometimes, our calculations use these

---

[2]It is strongly recommended that you pronounce the symbol '$\leq$' as 'at most' rather than the more cumbersome 'less than or equal to'. Similarly, we recommend that you pronounce '$\geq$' as 'at least' rather than 'greater than or equal to'.

relations in successive steps. Here, for example, is a calculation that constructs a rough estimate of the difference between 256 and 367:

$$367 - 256$$

$$< \qquad \{ \qquad 367 < 400 \quad \}$$

$$400 - 256$$

$$< \qquad \{ \qquad 200 < 256 \quad \}$$

$$400 - 200$$

$$= \qquad \{ \qquad \text{arithmetic} \quad \}$$

$$200 \ .$$

The conclusion of this calculation is that $367 - 256 < 200$. It illustrates the so-called *conjunctional* use of the less-than operator. In general, $R < S < T$ means $R < S \ and \ S < T$. Transitivity of less-than means that a consequence of $R < S < T$ is that $R < T$.

Different relations may be combined in the same proof, but then there should be a logical justification for doing so. For instance, one step of a proof may assert, say, $R < S$, whereas the next asserts $S \leqslant T$. The inference is then that $R < T$. All such steps can be combined with equality steps, as in the last line above. However, it would be nonsense to combine '<' with '>' or '$\geqslant$' in one calculation since then no inference can be made of the relation between the first and last expressions.

The type of the expressions is arbitrary. They may denote real values, integer values, sets, relations, etc. In each case, the familiar equality symbol, '=', is used to denote equality of values. In particular, if R, S and T denote boolean values, we still use the equality symbol to denote equality. For example, a step in a proof might be

$$E \leqslant F$$

$$= \qquad \{ \qquad E \text{ and } F \text{ denote integer values.}$$

$$\text{Property of integer arithmetic} \quad \}$$

$$E < F+1$$

Here we are using the fact that the statement $E \leqslant F$ *is the same as* the statement $E < F+1$ whenever E and F denote integer values. In other words, the value of $E \leqslant F$ (which is either true or false) *is equal to* the value of $E < F+1$. In in-line expressions, we often use the symbol '$\equiv$' to denote equality of boolean values. One reason for this is to avoid ambiguity. For example, we write

$$E \leqslant F \ \equiv \ E < F+1$$

in order to avoid confusion with

$$E \leqslant F = E < F+1$$

which means $E \leqslant F$ *and* $F = E$ *and* $E < F+1$. (So equality here means equality of integer values rather than equality of boolean values.) There is another reason for having two notations for equality of boolean values. This second reason, which is much more important than the first, is discussed in Chapter 5.

Generally, in such calculations, the connecting relations will have lower precedence than the operators in the expressions they connect, this convention superseding any other precedence conventions. You should have no problem with this convention since it is clearly what is suggested by the layout.

3.3.4 'If' and 'Only If'

Steps relating boolean values will sometimes be related by 'if' or 'only if'. The 'if' relation is denoted by '$\Leftarrow$' and the 'only if' relation by '$\Rightarrow$'. We introduce these relations formally in Section 7.3. For the moment we use them informally (although in a formally correct way).

Here is an example of a calculation involving an 'if' step. (Read the second step as $10{\times}20 \leqslant 11{\times}23$ *if* both $10{\times}20 \leqslant 11{\times}20$ and $11{\times}20 \leqslant 11{\times}23$.) It establishes that $200 \leqslant 11{\times}23$ is true.

$$
\begin{array}{cl}
& 200 \leqslant 11{\times}23 \\[4pt]
= & \{ \quad 200 = 10{\times}20 \quad \} \\[4pt]
& 10{\times}20 \leqslant 11{\times}23 \\[4pt]
\Leftarrow & \{ \quad \text{'}\leqslant\text{' is a transitive relation} \quad \} \\[4pt]
& 10{\times}20 \leqslant 11{\times}20 \leqslant 11{\times}23 \\[4pt]
= & \{ \quad \text{multiplication is invertible with respect to '}\leqslant\text{'} \\
& \qquad \text{(applied twice), and } 10 \leqslant 11 \text{ and } 20 \leqslant 23 \quad \} \\[4pt]
& \textit{true} \ .
\end{array}
$$

An 'if' step is a *strengthening* step. In this example, the inequality $10{\times}20 \leqslant 11{\times}23$ is replaced by the stronger statement $10{\times}20 \leqslant 11{\times}20 \leqslant 11{\times}23$. Because they are strengthening steps, 'if' steps in calculations are much less welcome than equality steps; it may be the case that the strengthening is too coarse. In the following example, the pattern of the above calculation is used, but the strengthening leads to a property that cannot be established. As a consequence, the calculation stalls.

$$
\begin{array}{cl}
& 243 \leqslant 11{\times}23 \\[4pt]
= & \{ \quad 243 = 9{\times}27 \quad \} \\[4pt]
& 9{\times}27 \leqslant 11{\times}23 \\[4pt]
\Leftarrow & \{ \quad \text{'}\leqslant\text{' is a transitive relation} \quad \} \\[4pt]
& 9{\times}27 \leqslant 11{\times}27 \leqslant 11{\times}23 \ .
\end{array}
$$

(Note that the calculation is correct even though $11 \times 27 \leqslant 11 \times 23$ is false. As we see later, '$243 \leqslant 11 \times 23$ if false' is a valid, although meaningless, conclusion.)

'Only if' steps are the converse of 'if' steps; an 'only if' step is a *weakening* step. An important use of 'only if' steps is in determining circumstances in which a boolean expression is false. An example is the following. (x mod 3 is the remainder after dividing x by 3.)

$$23 \times 11 = 243$$

$\Rightarrow$ { Leibniz (substitution of equals for equals) }

$$(23 \times 11) \text{ mod } 3 \ = \ 243 \text{ mod } 3$$

$=$ { $(23 \times 11) \text{ mod } 3 \ = \ 1$

  $243 \text{ mod } 3 \ = \ 0$

  (details of calculation omitted) }

$$1 = 0$$

$=$ { arithmetic }

false .

The first step should be read as '$23 \times 11 = 243$ *only if* $(23 \times 11) \text{ mod } 3 = 243 \text{ mod } 3$'. The hint 'Leibniz (substitution of equals for equals)' refers to the fact that application of a function to equal values results in equal values[3]. In this case, the function that is being applied is the 'mod 3' function, which computes the remainder after dividing a given number by 3. The omitted details in the second step involve the use of properties of remainder computation which make it easy to evaluate $(23 \times 11) \text{ mod } 3$ and $243 \text{ mod } 3$. (See Chapter 15.) The conclusion is that $23 \times 11 = 243$ only if false, i.e. $23 \times 11 \neq 243$.

Section 3.4 gives a non-trivial example of the use of 'only if'.

3.4 A Classic Example

This section is more advanced and intended for readers who already have some training in the conventional style of presenting proofs in mathematics. It is intended as a demonstration of the effectiveness of calculational proof. Other readers may return to it at a later stage in their reading.

The problem we consider is to prove that $\sqrt{2}$ is irrational, i.e. $\sqrt{2}$ cannot be expressed in the form $\frac{m}{n}$ for natural numbers m and n.

The standard textbook proof begins by assuming that $\sqrt{2}$ is equal to $\frac{m}{n}$ and then establishes a contradiction. This is, of course, the only way to proceed. The

---

[3]Baron Gottfried Wilhelm von Leibniz, 1646–1716, a famous German mathematician, was the first to formulate the rule. In his honour, we frequently abbreviate the hint to 'Leibniz'; 'substitution of equals for equals' is longer, but decidedly more self-explanatory.

next step in the standard textbook proof is, however, a very big one. The claim is made that, without loss of generality, it may be assumed that m and n have no common factors. This is a major step, most often taken without proof, if only because it is not entirely clear what 'without loss of generality' means.

Here is the calculational proof. The strategy is the same: we assume that $\sqrt{2}$ is equal to $\frac{m}{n}$ and then deduce false, but the assumption that m and n have no common factors is not needed.

$$\sqrt{2} = \frac{m}{n}$$

= { Use arithmetic to eliminate the square root operator. }

$$2{\times}n^2 = m^2$$

⇒ { This and the next are the crucial steps. We use the fact that if two values are equal then the result of applying any function to them yields equal values. (This is called 'substitution of equals for equals' or 'Leibniz's rule'.) For the validity of this step, the identity of the function is not needed. We call it exp. }

$$\mathsf{exp}.(2{\times}n^2) = \mathsf{exp}.(m^2)$$

= { Now we choose the function exp.

Let exp.k be the number of times that 2 divides k.

For example, exp.$48 = 4$ and exp.$49 = 0$.

The function exp has two important properties:

exp.$2 = 1$ and

exp.$(k{\times}l) = \mathsf{exp}.k + \mathsf{exp}.l$.

We apply these properties to simplify the left and right sides. }

$$1 + 2 \times \mathsf{exp}.n = 2 \times \mathsf{exp}.m$$

= { The left side is an odd number, the right side is an even number. Odd numbers and even numbers are different. }

false .

Exercise 3.8. Examine the above proof carefully to see how it can be generalized. Specifically, consider replacing the number 2 by k. Derive a condition on k that guarantees that $\sqrt{k}$ is irrational.   □

3.5 Summary

In this chapter, we have discussed the difference between formal, syntactic proofs and semantic proofs. Syntactic proofs involve a game with symbols in which each step of a proof involves the application of a well-defined rule. They are precise and each step can be easily verified. Presented badly, however, it can be difficult to understand how the proof was constructed, making it difficult to apply the proof method to examples of a similar form. Semantic proofs employ natural language to convey the essential details of a logical argument and rely heavily on the reader's understanding of the terms used and ability to fill in the missing detail. For this reason, semantic proofs are difficult to check thoroughly and usually undergo a 'social process' whereby, in the course of time, they become accepted or rejected by a community of mathematicians.

This text is about the formal, syntactic calculation of programs and their properties. This ensures the highest possible level of confidence in their correctness and reduces to a minimum the social process of checking their validity (although we can never guarantee 100% correctness and an independent check is still indispensable). We avoid the shortcomings of syntactic proof by making our calculations goal directed and adding copious hints in order to make clear the strategy being used. We call such proofs *calculational* because they are about calculating solutions to (mathematical and programming) problems in the style of ordinary arithmetic.

Bibliographic Remarks

The proof format is due to W. H. J. Feijen and was first used in Dijkstra and Feijen (1984); nowadays it is used very widely. I learnt the proof of the irrationality of $\sqrt{2}$ given here from Hoogerwoord (2001).

4

Implementation Issues

In Chapter 2, we showed how to design a card-searching algorithm in a way that guaranteed the algorithm's correctness. This chapter is about the issues that arise when we implement the algorithm in a conventional programming language. The main issues are about how to represent a deck of cards in a computer program. Another issue is how to implement the choice of a particular card in the deck. This leads us on to a discussion of the mathematical properties of integer division.

4.1 Binary Search

This section is about implementing the card-searching algorithm discussed in Section 2.2. We use Java as the implementation language in the first instance in order to illustrate the problems that arise when using a 'real' programming language. In Chapter 9 and beyond, we use an idealized programming language that allows us to focus on program design rather than the intricacies of one particular programming language.

A word of caution is needed in advance. Java uses the symbol '=' for the assignment operator and the symbol '==' for the equality operator. So, in Java, 'x==0' has the same meaning as 'x = 0' in mathematics, but 'x=0' means something quite different. The difference between the two is evident from that fact that $x = 0$—conventional equality—has the same meaning as $0 = x$, whereas x=0—in Java—does not have the same meaning as 0=x. (In fact, the latter is not even a valid statement.) Mathematical equality is symmetric, whereas assignment is not.

In words, the Java assignment x=0 means that the value referenced by the variable x becomes 0. More briefly, it is read as 'x gets 0' or 'x becomes 0'. This misuse of the equality symbol is a frequent cause of error in Java programs. In order to avoid confusion, we use the teletype font when the Java assignment is intended. We also emphasize the fact that assignment is not symmetric by putting a space immediately after, but not before, the assignment operator in Java programs. On the other hand, we place the equality operator symmetrically between its two operands. Thus, we write 'x= 0' to mean the assignment of the value 0 to the variable x, and 'x == 0' (or 'x = 0', using a non-teletype font) for equality between x and 0.

The search algorithm in Section 2.2 manipulates an actual deck of cards. In a computer program, we have to *represent* the physical operations on the decks of cards in terms of operations that are primitive to the programming language. That is, we have to decide how to represent each of the decks of cards, how to represent splitting a deck into two and how to represent the transfer of cards between decks. Also, we have to decide on a specific implementation of the choice of a card in the middle deck of cards.

The simplest and most convenient way to represent a deck of cards in a language like Java is an *array*. An array is a sequence of numbered values. Below is such a sequence. In this case, numbering begins at zero and the values are all names of animals.

0	1	2	3	4	5
cat	cow	dog	fox	fox	hen

The values *stored* in an array are called the *elements* of the array. In our example, the elements are 'cat', 'cow', 'dog', etc. The number assigned to each element is called its *index*. Note that the values in an array may occur more than once (as, for example, 'fox') but the elements are distinct, because each has a unique index. The above array has six elements, but only five values are stored in the array. (The above array is also alphabetically ordered, but, in general, array values need not be ordered.)

In Java and similar languages, array elements can be quite complex objects. In a real-life situation, an array element might represent, for example, all the information about a book in a library: its title, author and publisher, date of purchase, location, etc. For simplicity, in our implementation of the searching algorithm of Section 2.2, we assume that the information on each card in the given deck of cards is an integer, and the given card X is an integer value. The representation we choose for the whole deck of cards is thus an array of integers.

In a Java program, the text

```
int[] card
```

declares an array ('[]') of integers ('int') with the name card, implicitly indexed from zero onwards. The *length* of the array is its number of elements; its value is denoted in Java by `card.length`. The declaration means that elsewhere in the program (more precisely, within the 'scope' of the declaration) the individual elements of the array can be accessed by `card[0]`, `card[1]`, etc. For brevity, we use N to denote the length of the array of cards. It is important to note that N may be zero, in which case the array represents an empty deck of cards.

We use the notation $m..n$ to denote a *range* of integers, the set of all integers at least m and at most n. For example, 2..5 denotes the set of integers {2,3,4,5}. When m is greater than n, $m..n$ denotes the empty set. For example, 1..0 is the empty set; there are no integers in the range 1..0. (The notation was introduced in the language Pascal. It is not a standard notation in Java, so we use it to specify Java programs, but not in the programs themselves.)

An attempt to access an array element `card[k]`, where k is an integer outside the range 0..N−1 and N is the length of the array, will result in a so-called 'array bound exception'. Note that if the length of an array is zero, any attempt to access an array element will result in such an error when the program is executed.

A *segment* of an array is identified by a range of integers; it is the sequence of array elements indexed by the integers in the range. If an array represents a deck of cards, a segment represents a contiguous subdeck of the deck. In this way, the computation of a single integer, j say, represents splitting a deck into two: the deck represented by the segment indexed by integers up to, but not including, j, and the deck represented by the segment indexed by integers from j onwards.

Given that we propose to represent the deck of cards by an array indexed from 0 up to, but not including, N, splitting the deck into two can be represented by computing an index in the range 0..N. The index j represents splitting the original deck into a lower and upper deck, namely the subdecks represented by the segments 0..j−1 and j..N−1, respectively. Note that j equal to zero represents the situation in which the lower deck is empty, whilst j equal to N represents the situation in which the upper deck is empty. (Check your understanding by saying what is meant by j and N both being equal to zero.)

A summary of the foregoing is that our searching algorithm is represented in Java by a function `split` that returns an integer when given two parameters: an (ordered) integer array `card` and an integer X. The declaration of such a function in Java is as follows[1]:

```
public static int split(int[] card, int X); .
```

More precisely, the input array is ordered and the function returns an integer index in the range 0..N, where N equals `card.length`; if the returned index is j, all cards in the segment 0..j−1 should be less than X, and all cards in the segment j..N−1 should be at least X.

---

[1]The keywords 'public static' in this declaration are not relevant to this discussion and can safely be ignored by readers unfamiliar with Java. The declaration of the function can, in fact, be made more precise and more general by relaxing the assumption that the array values are integers. The details are not relevant to our discussion.

4.1.1 Implementation

In the implementation of the algorithm, we need to represent the left, right and middle decks. However, since the 'left' deck is always an initial segment of the deck of cards, the range of integer values representing the left deck always begins with 0. We can therefore represent the left deck by a single integer l. To be precise, the left deck will be represented by the segment $0..l-1$ of the array card, where index l is in the range $0..N$. (Recall that N is the length of the array card.) The use of upper bound '$l-1$' means that l equal to 0 represents the situation that the left deck is empty.

Similarly, the right deck is always a final segment of the deck of cards. It can therefore be represented by a single integer r. To be precise, the right deck will be represented by the segment $r..N-1$ of the array card, where index r is in the range $0..N$. Note that r equal to N represents the situation that the right deck is empty.

This leaves the representation of the middle deck. But, this is easy, as the middle deck is what is left over after removing the left and right decks. No new variables need to be introduced to represent the middle deck; it is represented by the array segment $l..r-1$. In particular, l equal to r represents the situation that the middle deck is empty.

To guarantee that the left, middle and right decks represented by the indices l and r are all disjoint, we require l and r to satisfy the invariant property

$$0 \leqslant l \leqslant r \leqslant N .$$

An empty left deck is represented by $l = 0$ and an empty right deck is represented by $r = N$.

The middle deck is empty when $l = r$; choosing a card in the middle deck occurs when it is known that $l < r$. The choice is represented by choosing an (integer) index k in the range $l..r-1$. For correctness, any choice in this range will do; for efficiency, a good idea is to try to reduce the size of the middle deck by a half at each iteration. This is achieved by choosing k in the middle of the range, using the assignment:

```
k= (l+r-1)/2 .
```

We postpone checking that this does return a value in the right range until later.

The final pieces of the implementation represent adding the cards in the lower deck to the left deck and adding cards in the upper deck to the right deck. These are implemented by the assignments

```
l= k+1
```

and

```
r= k ,
```

respectively. The complete implementation is shown in Figure 4.1.

```
/* card is an array of integers sorted in ascending order
 * (repetitions are allowed), and X is an integer
 *
 * returns an index l in the range 0..N, such that
 * all cards in segment 0..l-1 are less than X, and
 * all cards in segment l..N-1 are at least X,
 * where N is card.length
 */
public static int split(int[] card, int X) {
  int N= card.length;
  int l= 0; int r= N;
  /* Invariant: all cards in segment 0..l-1 are less than X
   *            all cards in segment r..N-1 are at least X
   *            0 <= l <= r <= N
   * Bound function: r-l
   */
  while (l < r)
    {int k= (l+r-1)/2;
     if (card[k] < X) l= k+1;
     else r= k;
    }
  /* All cards in segment 0..l-1 are less than X
   * All cards in segment l..N-1 are at least X
   */
  return l;
}
```

Figure 4.1   Implementation of search program in Java.

Exercise 4.1. Add code to the program in Figure 4.1 that assigns the value true to the variable found if there is an index i such that card[i] == X.   □

4.2   Verifying Correctness—A Taster

The step from manipulating decks of cards to a Java program is quite large and raises the question of whether we can be really sure that the Java implementation correctly meets its specification.

Later, we will be discussing formal techniques for verifying that the construction of a program has been carried out correctly. This section is a taster of what is to come.

One particular aspect of the Java program in Figure 4.1 that gives rise to some doubt is the assignment to k:

```
int k= (l+r-1)/2 .
```

The right side of this assignment is an *integer division* and not an exact division[2]. Can we be really sure that the assignment will set k to a value that is in the correct range; does it depend on how the exact division is rounded to an integer value? In order to be absolutely sure we need to understand properly the effect of an integer division.

In order to avoid any confusion that may be caused by the overloading of the division operator, it is useful to switch from the monospaced ASCII notation of Java to a good old-fashioned mathematical notation. (Mathematical notation has been developed over many centuries to enhance readability—fortunately becoming well-established long before the development of the teletype technology that has tyrannized programming language notation during the last half century.) We will use $m \div n$ to denote the integer value obtained by dividing integer m by integer n. This is different from $\frac{m}{n}$ and m/n, which both denote the real value obtained by dividing m by n. We also use ':=' to denote the assignment operator, avoiding the confusion (and errors) that occur when the Java '=' symbol is mistaken for equality. In this notation the assignment is

$$k \ := \ (l+r-1) \div 2 \ .$$

The assignment to k is executed when $0 \leqslant l < r \leqslant N$. The requirement is that the value assigned to k is at least l and less than r—otherwise we cannot guarantee termination of the program. So what we have to verify is that

$$l \leqslant (l+r-1) \div 2 < r \ \ \Leftarrow \ \ 0 \leqslant l < r \leqslant N \ .$$

(Note: read the symbol '⇐' as 'if'.)

In order to do this, we need to have a precise definition of integer division. The official documentation on Java gives such a definition but that definition is complicated by the inclusion of all sorts of special cases (such as that one of the arguments is a so-called 'NaN'—'Not a Number'). For our purposes it is reasonable to assume the following properties of the integer division $m \div n$.

- Dividing a multiple of n by n is *exact*. That is,

$$(m \times n) \div n \ = \ m \ .$$

- Integer division by (positive number) n is *monotonic* with respect to the at-most relation. That is, for integers i and j,

$$i \div n \leqslant j \div n \ \ \Leftarrow \ \ i \leqslant j \ .$$

In addition, we may require the following property.

---

[2]In programming language jargon, we say that the division operator '/' is *overloaded*. The computation that is executed depends on the type of the arguments. When both its arguments are integers, the result is an integer; if both arguments are floating point values, the result is a floating point value.

- Integer division rounds *towards* 0. In particular,

$$m \div n \leqslant m/n \quad \Leftarrow \quad 0 \leqslant m \wedge 0 \leqslant n \ .$$

(We will not need to consider the case when either of m or n is negative.)

The first two of these properties are properties that one can reasonably expect to hold of any implementation of integer division, independently of how one chooses to round the real division. The third property is a design choice. Other choices are to round away from zero, or round up, or round down, and other programming languages may choose differently. For this reason, we are careful to avoid using the property in our calculations wherever possible. See Exercise 4.4 for further evidence of why the exploitation of this property should be avoided.

Now, recall that what we have to prove is

$$l \leqslant (l+r-1) \div 2 < r \quad \Leftarrow \quad 0 \leqslant l < r \leqslant N \ .$$

This is the same as showing that

$$l \leqslant (l+r-1) \div 2 \quad \Leftarrow \quad 0 \leqslant l < r \leqslant N$$

and

$$(l+r-1) \div 2 < r \quad \Leftarrow \quad 0 \leqslant l < r \leqslant N \ .$$

The proof of the first of these properties proceeds as follows. First, we begin with the property $l \leqslant (l+r-1) \div 2$ and calculate a simpler formula that guarantees its truth (simpler in the sense of not involving integer division).

$$l \leqslant (l+r-1) \div 2$$

=   { $l = (2 \times l) \div 2$

(division by 2 is introduced here in order to

eliminate it at the next step)   }

$$(2 \times l) \div 2 \leqslant (l+r-1) \div 2$$

⟸   {   division by 2 is monotonic   }

$$2 \times l \leqslant l+r-1$$

=   {   addition is monotonic   }

$$l \leqslant r-1$$

=   { l and r are integers   }

$$l < r \ .$$

We have thus shown that

$$l \leqslant (l+r-1) \div 2 \quad \Leftarrow \quad l < r \ .$$

But

$$l < r \quad \Leftarrow \quad 0 \leqslant l < r \leqslant N \ .$$

So it follows that

$$l \leqslant (l+r-1) \div 2 \quad \Leftarrow \quad 0 \leqslant l < r \leqslant N \ ,$$

as required.

The calculational proof style used above was introduced in Section 3.3. Since this is the first significant application, let us briefly recall the main elements of the format. The calculation has four steps beginning with

$$l \leqslant (l+r-1) \div 2$$

and ending with

$$l < r \ .$$

Each step asserts either an equality between two properties or that the upper property is true if ('$\Leftarrow$') the lower property is true. A reason or *hint* why a step is valid is stated between braces. For example, the hint in the first step is that l and $(2 \times l) \div 2$ are equal so that $l \leqslant (l+r-1) \div 2$ is the same as $(2 \times l) \div 2 \leqslant (l+r-1) \div 2$. The second and third hints state the property being used. The final hint states that the step is valid because l and r are integers. (It would not be valid if l and r were real values.)

The fact that the four step calculation allows us to conclude that

$$l \leqslant (l+r-1) \div 2 \quad \Leftarrow \quad l < r \ ,$$

i.e. that the first line follows from the last line, is a consequence of simple properties of equality. The second step asserts that

$$(2 \times l) \div 2 \leqslant (l+r-1) \div 2 \quad \Leftarrow \quad 2 \times l \leqslant l+r-1 \ ,$$

but the first step asserts that the left side of this proposition is equal to $l \leqslant (l+r-1) \div 2$, and the third and fourth steps assert that the right side is equal to $l < r$. So the conclusion is obtained from the second step by 'substitution of equals for equals'—the replacement of subexpressions by equal subexpressions.

Note that we use plain old '=' for equality of booleans (and not, for example, '$\Leftrightarrow$'). To avoid ambiguities, we often use the symbol '$\equiv$' for equality of booleans in in-line formulae. For example, the final step in the above proof uses the property

$$l \leqslant r-1 \equiv l < r \ .$$

(Read this as: 'the boolean $l \leqslant r-1$ is equal to the boolean $l < r$'.) Here, we need to distinguish between equality of booleans and equality of integers. It would be confusing to write

$$l \leqslant r-1 \ = \ l < r$$

even if lots of white space were used to separate the two booleans.

Note that, last but not least, the calculation simplifies '$l \leqslant (l+r-1) \div 2$' to '$l < r$'. It is always good practice to prove properties in a goal-oriented way, working from complicated statements to simpler statements. In this case, the goal was to prove

$$l \leqslant (l+r-1) \div 2 \ \Leftarrow \ 0 \leqslant l < r \leqslant N \ .$$

The strategy is to take the left side of this statement, since this is the more complicated side, and simplify it. In the process, we learn that the properties $0 \leqslant l$ and $r \leqslant N$ are not relevant.

Exercise 4.2. Prove

$$(l+r-1) \div 2 < r \ \ \Leftarrow \ \ l < r$$

in the same way. Prove it also using that $m \div 2 \leqslant m/2 \ \Leftarrow \ 0 \leqslant m$. (That is, integer division by 2 rounds down for positive m.) ☐

Exercise 4.3.

(a) Integer division by positive number n is monotonic with respect to the at-most relation. Is it monotonic with respect to the less-than relation? That is, prove or disprove that, for all integers i and j, and all positive integers n,

$$i \div n < j \div n \ \Leftarrow \ i < j \ .$$

(b) Is it the case that the 'if' in the monotonicity of integer division by n can be replaced by an equality? That is, prove or disprove that, for all integers i and j, and all positive integers n,

$$(i \div n \leqslant j \div n) \ = \ (i \leqslant j) \ .$$

(c) Compare your answers to (a) and (b) with the following properties of addition. Why is there a difference?

$$(i+n < j+n) \ = \ (i < j) \ ,$$
$$(i+n \leqslant j+n) \ = \ (i \leqslant j) \ .$$

(d) Suppose n is negative. Which of the following do you expect to be true?

$$i \div n \leqslant j \div n \ \Leftarrow \ i \leqslant j \ ,$$
$$i \div n \leqslant j \div n \ \Leftarrow \ j \leqslant i \ .$$

☐

Exercise 4.4. The searching algorithm shown in Figure 4.1 is correct so long as k is assigned a value satisfying $l \leqslant k < r$. Determine which of the following assignments meet this requirement. In the cases that the requirement is not met give an example showing how the program would not function correctly.

$$k := l \ ,$$
$$k := r \ ,$$
$$k := (l+r) \div 2 \ .$$

Suppose that integer division is defined to round *away* from zero rather than *towards* zero. That is, suppose

$$m/n \leqslant m \div n \quad \Leftarrow \quad 0 \leqslant m \wedge 0 \leqslant n \ .$$

If this is the case, would the following assignments to k be correct?

$$k := (l+r-1) \div 2 \ ,$$
$$k := (l+r) \div 2 \ .$$

Draw a conclusion about the safest assignment to k in the case in which it is not known whether integer division is implemented by rounding up or down.   □

Exercise 4.5. Rather than cutting the middle deck into two roughly equal decks, one might try to estimate where in the middle deck the value X can be found. For example, if the deck of cards contains the numbers from 0 to M in steps of roughly $\frac{M}{N}$, the value X might be found roughly at position $X \times \frac{M}{N}$. As more and more of the deck has been eliminated from the search, the array values at positions l and $r-1$ can be used to interpolate an estimate of the position of X in the array.

   A suggested implementation of this idea is to use the following assignment to k:

$$k \ := \ l + \frac{X - card[l]}{card[r-1] - card[l]} \times (r-l) \ .$$

What is wrong with this idea? (Assume that real arithmetic is used to evaluate the right side and then the value is converted to an integer by rounding. The answer does not depend on how rounding is done.)   □

Exercise 4.6. The implementation of binary search below is taken from a textbook on developing Java software.

   The class `Comparator`, which is used in the implementation, provides a method `relation` which compares its two arguments. Assume that array `v` is sorted in ascending order (possibly with duplicate entries) and `c.relation(x,y)` implements the test $x < y$.

   The notation `b ? e1 : e2` denotes a conditional expression. If boolean `b` evaluates to `true`, the value of the expression is given by `e1`, otherwise it is given by `e2`.

   (a) Suppose array `v` has length 2 and elements 10 and 20. Suppose also that the object `o` being searched for has the value 30. Trace the execution sequence of the method and identify a run-time error in the program.

(b) Write a critique of the implementation focusing on its correctness, the roles
   of the variables `hi` and `lo`, and its robustness in extreme circumstances.

```
/**
 *  The statically accessible sort operation
 *
 *  @param v the sorted array of <code>Object</code>s to be
 *  searched.
 *
 *  @param o the object to be searched for.
 *
 *  @param c the <code>Comparator</code> used to compare the
 *  <code>Object</code> during the search process.  Must either be
 *  "less than" or "greater than" and the same comparator that
 *  defines the order on the array.
 *
 *  @return index of the item or -1 if it is not there.
 */
public static int execute(final Object[] v,
                          final Object o,
                          final Comparator c)
{
    int hi = v.length ;
    int lo = 0 ;
    while (true)
    {
        int centre = (hi + lo) / 2 ;
        if (centre == lo)
        {
            //
            //  Only two items left to test so it is either centre
            //  or centre+1 or it is not in.  This is an exit
            //  point of the infinite loop.
            //
            return ( v[centre].equals(o)
                        ? centre
                        : ( v[centre+1].equals(o)
                          ? centre+1
                          : -1)) ;
        }
        if (c.relation(v[centre], o))
        {
            lo = centre ;
        }
        else if (c.relation(o, v[centre]))
        {
            hi = centre ;
        }
        else
        {
            return centre ;
        }
    }
}
```

□

4.3 Summary

In this chapter, we have shown how the card-searching algorithm of Chapter 2 is implemented in Java. A possible source of error—non-termination due to the approximate nature of integer division—was identified and we showed how to verify that the implementation is indeed correct. This involved identifying the mathematical properties of integer division rather than relying on a description of how integer division is implemented. The exercises explore the freedom we have in the implementation; in particular, they demonstrate instances where the implementation goes wrong.

Bibliographic Remarks

Binary search is notorious for catching out programmers (Knuth, 1973, p. 407); although the 'idea' is very simple, many programmers have failed to implement it correctly. Unfortunately, many textbooks continue to present its implementation without any justification. Fortunately, nowadays, most published implementations are correct. The program in Exercise 4.6 (from Winder and Roberts (1998, pp. 592, 593)) demonstrates how easy it is to get it wrong and, thereby, the importance of a scientific approach to program construction.

5

Calculational
Logic: Part 1

In a proof, whether formal or informal, we may distinguish two types of reasoning. There is reasoning that involves properties of the data and is therefore problem dependent, and there is reasoning that is independent of the problem domain. The latter form of reasoning we call *logical reasoning*. For example, if the goal is to prove that

$$l \leqslant (l+r-1) \div 2 < r \;\; \Leftarrow \;\; 0 \leqslant l < r \leqslant N \;,$$

logical reasoning justifies splitting the proof into two parts, a proof that

$$l \leqslant (l+r-1) \div 2 \;\; \Leftarrow \;\; 0 \leqslant l < r$$

and a proof that

$$(l+r-1) \div 2 < r \;\; \Leftarrow \;\; 0 \leqslant l < r \;.$$

This step is quite independent of the fact that the property we are required to prove is a property of integer division. However, to prove these two parts we need to exploit the properties of arithmetic and integer division. The first step is thus domain independent, whereas subsequent steps are domain dependent. Logic is the glue that binds together the properties of the data.

The computer programmer is a voracious consumer of logic, and an excellent understanding of logical reasoning is vital to building reliable software. In this chapter, we begin a study of logic. The focus of the chapter is *equality* of boolean values. It is appropriate to begin with a study of equality because it is the most fundamental operator in any calculus. In addition, we study the negation operator. In Chapter 6, we apply what we have learnt here to reasoning about the conversion between real and integer numbers.

Section 5.1 is a brief introduction to what logic is about. We assume that most readers will have had an elementary introduction already. Section 5.2 onwards contains the meat of the chapter. We observe that equality of boolean values is transitive, symmetric *and associative*. The associativity of boolean equality is a property that is very important and it is vital that it is reflected in the notation used. So, an underlying theme of this chapter is choice of notation and how it helps in calculational proofs.

5.1   Logical Connectives

Mathematics is the art of effective reasoning. Progress in mathematics is encoded and communicated via its own language—a universal language that is understood and accepted throughout the world. Indeed, communication via the language of mathematics is typically easier than communication via a natural language. This is because mathematical language is clear and concise.

Logic is a part of mathematics. It is the glue that binds together other mathematical statements. Traditionally, logic has been conducted in natural language. Mathematical statements are interspersed with phrases or sentences like—'a necessary condition is. . .', 'therefore. . .', 'because', 'if and only if', 'every number can be factorized into a product of prime numbers', etc. But, from the time of Leibniz (1646–1716), who dreamt of reducing all mathematics to calculation, efforts have been made to formalize logic. George Boole's aim in his book *Laws of Thought* was specifically to

> 'investigate the fundamental laws. . . by which reasoning is performed,
> . . . give expression to them in the language of a Calculus, and upon this
> foundation. . . establish the Science of Logic.'

The basis of logic is very simple. It consists of the two so-called *boolean* values true and false. *Propositions* are statements that are either true or false. Examples of propositions are $0 = 0$ (a true proposition), the word 'logic' begins with the letter 'c' (a false proposition), and the number $\sqrt{2}^{\sqrt{2}}$ is rational (which is either true or false, but I don't know which). *Atomic* propositions are ones that cannot be broken down into simpler propositions.

Logic is not at all concerned with the truth or otherwise of atomic propositions; that is the concern of the problem domain being discussed. Logic is concerned with whether the combination of atomic propositions leads to a valid or 'logical' conclusion. Compare, for example,

> If a book is a recommended text, a copy will be held in the library. The
> book *Logic is Glue* is a recommended text. Therefore, a copy of *Logic
> is Glue* will be held in the library.

with

> The knowledge in universities grows and grows. Each new student brings a little in and the graduates do not take any away.

The first is a logical argument. It has two *premises*, the statements

> If a book is a recommended text, a copy will be held in the library.

and

> The book *Logic is Glue* is a recommended text.

and one *conclusion*:

> A copy of *Logic is Glue* will be held in the library.

And, clearly, the conclusion is indeed a consequence of the first two statements. Note, however, that logic does not enable us to tell whether or not the premise that all recommended texts are held in the library is true, nor whether or not the premise that the book *Logic is Glue* is a recommended text is true. Logic is about the properties of the logical *connectives* and not about the truth or otherwise of the atomic propositions.

The second argument has the same structure, the two premises

> Each new student brings a little [knowledge] in.

and

> The graduates do not take any [knowledge] away.

and one conclusion

> The knowledge in universities grows and grows.

The argument is illogical, *not* because we may dispute the validity of the premises, but because the conclusion is just not a logical consequence of the premises.

The logical connectives are functions from booleans to booleans. Since their domain and range are finite sets we can give them a precise mathematical meaning by simply enumerating all possible combinations of input and output value. This is done in a *truth table*.

There are four truth tables with one propositional variable. That is, there are exactly four functions that map a single boolean value into a boolean value.

p	true	p	$\neg p$	false
true	true	true	false	false
false	true	false	true	false

The first column is the 'constant true' function, the second is the identity function, the third is negation, and the last column is the 'constant false' function.

This means that any expression in one propositional variable p can always be simplified to either true, p, $\neg p$ or false.

There are 16 binary functions from booleans to booleans. Eight correspond to the most frequently used ones: six binary operators and the constant true and false functions.

p	q	true	$p = q$ $p \equiv q$	$p \neq q$ $p \not\equiv q$	$p \wedge q$	$p \vee q$	$p \Leftarrow q$	$p \Rightarrow q$	false
true	true	true	true	false	true	true	true	true	false
true	false	true	false	true	false	true	true	false	false
false	true	true	false	true	false	true	false	true	false
false	false	true	true	false	false	false	true	true	false

Of all these logical operators, the most important is equality. So, it is with this operator that we begin.

5.2 Boolean Equality

The history of mathematics shows that it is often the most fundamental concepts that have taken the longest to be recognized and properly incorporated into the body of mathematical knowledge. The number zero, indispensable to the conventional positional notation for numbers, is the classic example—the Greek mathematicians did not even recognize one as a number, let alone zero. Equality is another example. It was not until 1557 that the '=' symbol was introduced by Robert Recorde in his book *The Whetstone of Witte* 'containying...the rule of Equation...'. Before then, equal values were written side by side. In historical terms, equality is a relatively modern concept.

Recorde's symbol for equality is used universally to denote the fact that two values are the same. It is used, for example, for equality of numbers (integers, reals, complex numbers, etc.), for equality of sets, for equality of functions, and so on. Curiously, however, it is rarely used in logic texts for equality of propositions.

Equality—on any domain of values—has a number of characteristic properties. First, it is *reflexive*. That is $x = x$ whatever the value (or type) of x. Second, it is *symmetric*. That is, $x = y$ is the same as $y = x$. Third, it is *transitive*. That is, if $x = y$ and $y = z$, then $x = z$. Finally, if $x = y$ and f is any function, then $f.x = f.y$ (where the infix dot denotes function application). This last rule is called *substitution of equals for equals* or *Leibniz's rule*.

Equality is a binary relation. When studying relations, reflexivity, symmetry and transitivity are properties that we look out for. Equality is, however, also a function. It is a function with range the boolean values true and false. When we study functions, the sort of properties we look out for are associativity and symmetry. For example, addition and multiplication are both associative: for all x, y and z,

$$x + (y + z) = (x + y) + z$$

and

$$x \times (y \times z) = (x \times y) \times z \ .$$

They are also both symmetric: for all x and y,

$$x + y = y + x$$

and

$$x \times y = y \times x \ .$$

Symmetry of the equality function is just the same as symmetry of the equality relation. But what about associativity of equality? Is equality an associative operator?

The answer is that, in all but one case, the question does not make sense. Associativity of a binary function only makes sense if the domains of its two arguments and the range of its result are all the same. The expression $(p = q) = r$ just does not make sense when p, q and r are numbers, or characters, or sequences, etc. The one exception is equality of boolean values. When p, q and r are booleans, $p = q$ is also a boolean; so it makes sense to compare $p = q$ with r for equality. That is, $(p = q) = r$ is a meaningful boolean value. Similarly, so too is $p = (q = r)$. It also makes sense to compare these two values for equality. In other words, it makes sense to ask whether equality of boolean values is associative—and, perhaps surprisingly, *it is*. That is, for all booleans p, q and r,

$$\textbf{[Associativity]} \quad ((p = q) = r) = (p = (q = r)) \ . \tag{5.1}$$

Please complete the following exercise before continuing. It will help you understand the discussion that follows better.

Exercise 5.2. Check that equality of boolean values is associative by constructing the truth tables for $(p = q) = r$ and $p = (q = r)$, where p, q and r are boolean values. Identify a general rule, based on how many of p, q and r are true, that predicts when the two expressions are true. □

Associative functions are usually denoted by infix operators[1]. The benefit is immense. If a binary operator $\oplus$ is associative (that is, $(x \oplus y) \oplus z = x \oplus (y \oplus z)$ for all x, y and z), then we can write $x \oplus y \oplus z$ without fear of ambiguity. The expression becomes more compact because of the omission of parentheses. But the

---

[1] An *infix operator* is a symbol used to denote a function of two arguments that is written between the two arguments. The symbols '+' and '×' are both infix operators, denoting addition and multiplication, respectively.

omission of parentheses is not that important. The real benefit comes in calculations. A major advantage is that the notation is unbiased; a calculation in which an expression of the form $x \oplus y \oplus z$ occurs may begin by simplifying $x \oplus y$ or it may begin by simplifying $y \oplus z$, no preliminary manipulation being required to get the expression in the right form. Also, what frequently happens is that (for example) $x \oplus y$ is replaced by, say, $u \oplus v$ so that the subterm becomes $u \oplus v \oplus z$. This simplification is then immediately followed by the simplification of $v \oplus z$ to some term w, say. Thus in *two* steps the term $x \oplus y \oplus z$ has been replaced by $u \oplus w$, whereas, formally, the calculation has *three* steps, the invisible middle step being application of the associativity of the operator. Indeed, a good notation guides calculations by making the most important steps (almost) invisible. If the operator is also symmetric (that is, $x \oplus y = y \oplus x$ for all x and y), the gain is even bigger because then, if the operator is used to combine several subexpressions, we can choose to simplify any pair of subexpressions.

Infix notation is also often used for binary relations. We write, for example, $0 \leqslant m \leqslant n$. Here, the operators are being used *conjunctionally*: the meaning is $0 \leqslant m$ *and* $m \leqslant n$. In this way, the formula is more compact (since m is not written twice). More importantly, we are guided to the inference that $0 \leqslant n$. The algebraic property that is being hidden here is the transitivity of the at-most relation. If the relation between m and n is $m < n$ rather than $m \leqslant n$ and we write $0 \leqslant m < n$, we may infer that $0 < n$. Here, the inference is more complex since there are two relations involved. But it is an inference that is so fundamental that the notation is designed to facilitate its recognition.

In the case of equality of boolean values, we have a dilemma. Do we understand equality as a relation and read a continued expression of the form

$$x = y = z$$

as asserting the equality of all of x, y and z? Or do we read it 'associatively' as

$$(x = y) = z \ ,$$

or, equally, as

$$x = (y = z) \ ,$$

in just the same way as we would read $x + y + z$? The two readings are unfortunately not the same (for example, true = false = false is false according to the first reading but true according to the second and third readings). As we shall see, there are advantages in both readings and it is a major drawback to have to choose one in favour of the other.

It would be very confusing and, indeed, dangerous to read $x = y = z$ in any other way than $x = y$ and $y = z$; otherwise, the meaning of a sequence of expressions separated by equality symbols would depend on the type of the expressions. Also, the conjunctional reading (for other types) is so universally accepted—for good reasons—that it would be quite unacceptable to try to impose a different convention.

The solution to this dilemma is to use two different symbols to denote equality of boolean values—the symbol '=' when the transitivity of the equality relation is to be emphasized and the symbol '≡' when its associativity is to be exploited. Accordingly, we will write both $p = q$ and $p \equiv q$. (As the reader will have observed, we have been doing this for some time now. It is only now, however, that we have been able to provide a full explanation.) When p and q are expressions denoting boolean values, these both mean the same. But a continued expression

$$p \equiv q \equiv r \ ,$$

comprising more than two boolean expressions connected by the '≡' symbol, is to be evaluated *associatively*—i.e. as $(p \equiv q) \equiv r$ or $p \equiv (q \equiv r)$, whichever is the most convenient—whereas a continued expression

$$p = q = r$$

is to be evaluated *conjunctionally*—i.e as $p = q$ *and* $q = r$. More generally, a continued *equality* of the form

$$p_1 = p_2 = \ldots = p_n$$

means that all of $p_1, p_2, \ldots, p_n$ are equal, whilst a continued *equivalence* of the form

$$p_1 \equiv p_2 \equiv \ldots \equiv p_n$$

has the meaning given by fully parenthesizing the expression (in any way whatsoever, since the outcome is not affected) and then evaluating the expression as indicated by the chosen parenthesization. Note that when n is 2 we may use either symbol. That is, $p \equiv q$ and $p = q$ have the same meaning.

Moreover, we recommend that the '≡' symbol is pronounced as 'equivales'; being an unfamiliar word, its use will help to avoid misunderstanding.

5.3 Examples of the Associativity of Equivalence

This section contains a number of examples illustrating the effectiveness of the associativity of equivalence.

Even and Odd Numbers. The first example is particularly beautiful. It is the following property of the predicate **even** on numbers. (A number is even exactly when it is divisible by two.)

$$m+n \text{ is even} \ \equiv \ m \text{ is even} \ \equiv \ n \text{ is even} \ .$$

It will help if we refer to whether or not a number is even or odd as the *parity* of the number. Then, if we parenthesize the statement as

$$m+n \text{ is even} \ \equiv \ (m \text{ is even} \ \equiv \ n \text{ is even}) \ ,$$

it states that the number $m+n$ is even exactly when the parities of m and n are both the same. Parenthesizing it as

$$(m+n \text{ is even} \ \equiv \ m \text{ is even}) \ \equiv \ n \text{ is even} \ ,$$

it states that the operation of adding a number n to a number m does not change the parity of m exactly when n is even.

Another way of reading the statement is to use the fact that, in general, the equivalence $p \equiv q \equiv r$ is true exactly when an odd number of p, q and r is true (see Exercise 5.2). So the property captures four different cases:

$$
\begin{array}{lllll}
& ((m+n \text{ is even}) & \text{and } (m \text{ is even}) & \text{and} & (n \text{ is even})) \\
\text{or} & ((m+n \text{ is odd}) & \text{and } (m \text{ is odd}) & \text{and} & (n \text{ is even})) \\
\text{or} & ((m+n \text{ is odd}) & \text{and } (m \text{ is even}) & \text{and} & (n \text{ is odd})) \\
\text{or} & ((m+n \text{ is even}) & \text{and } (m \text{ is odd}) & \text{and} & (n \text{ is odd})) \ .
\end{array}
$$

The beauty of this example lies in the avoidance of case analysis. There are four distinct combinations of the two booleans 'm is even' and 'n is even'. Using the associativity of equivalence the value of '$m+n$ is even' is expressed in one simple formula, without any repetition of the component expressions, rather than as a list of different cases. Avoidance of case analysis is vital to effective reasoning.

Exercise 5.3. The *sign* of a number says whether or not the number is positive. For non-zero numbers x and y, the product $x \times y$ is positive if the signs of x and y are equal. If the signs of x and y are different, the product $x \times y$ is negative.

Assuming that x and y are non-zero, this rule is expressed as

$$x \times y \text{ is positive} \ \equiv \ x \text{ is positive} \ \equiv \ y \text{ is positive} \ .$$

Interpret the two different ways of parenthesizing the equivalences and enumerate the different properties of the sign of a number that this one equivalence captures. □

Full Adder. A *full adder* is a component of a circuit to add two binary numerals. An addition unit comprises a chain of full adders, the number of full adders being equal to the bit length of the numerals to be added. Each full adder has three inputs and two outputs. The three inputs are two bits to be added and a carrier bit, the carrier bit being 'carried over' from previous additions in the chain. Let us suppose the bits to be added are a and b and the carrier bit is c. Let A, B and C be the propositions $a=1$, $b=1$ and $c=1$. The output is a bit d, which is the least significant bit of $a+b+c$, and a new carrier bit, the most significant bit of $a+b+c$. Let us suppose that D is the proposition $d=1$. It is easy to see that $d=1$ exactly when an odd number of a, b and c is 1 (i.e. when all are 1 or when just one is 1 and the other two are 0). Now the proposition $p \equiv q \equiv r$ is true exactly when an odd number of p, q and r is true. So we have

$$D = (A \equiv B \equiv C) \ .$$

Now, using the associativity of boolean equality, we get

$$(D \equiv A) = (B \equiv C) \ .$$

In words, the least significant bit of $a+b+c$ is equal to a when the other two bits b and c are equal; if the bits b and c are different, then the bits d and a are different.

5.4 Continued Equivalences

The associativity of equivalence is exploited in almost all laws of the propositional calculus. A first example is the law

$$[\textbf{Constant true}] \quad \textsf{true} \equiv p \equiv p \ . \tag{5.4}$$

There are two ways to parenthesize this formula. Reading it as $\textsf{true} \equiv (p \equiv p)$, which we write in the form

$$\textsf{true} = (p \equiv p)$$

for greater emphasis, the law states that equivalence is a reflexive relation. According to the other parenthesization,

$$(\textsf{true} \equiv p) = p \ ,$$

the law states that $\textsf{true}$ is a unit[2] of the equivalence operator.

The law (5.4), in conjunction with the symmetry of equivalence, provides an easy way of simplifying continued equivalences in which one or more terms is repeated. Suppose, for example, we want to simplify

$$p \equiv p \equiv q \equiv p \equiv r \equiv q \ .$$

Symmetry of equivalence allows us to rearrange all the terms so that repeated occurrences of 'p' and 'q' are grouped together. Thus we get

$$p \equiv p \equiv p \equiv q \equiv q \equiv r \ .$$

Now we can use (5.4) to replace occurrences of '$p \equiv p$' and '$q \equiv q$' by 'true' obtaining

$$\textsf{true} \equiv p \equiv \textsf{true} \equiv r \ .$$

---

[2]A *unit* of a symmetric binary operator $\otimes$ is a value $1_\otimes$ such that, for all x of the appropriate type, $x \otimes 1_\otimes = x$. A *zero* of a binary operator $\otimes$ is a value $0_\otimes$ such that $x \otimes 0_\otimes = 0_\otimes$.

Finally, we use (5.4) again to replace 'true $\equiv x$' by 'x'. The result is that the original formula is simplified to

$$p \equiv r \ .$$

In general, the rule is that an expression of the form

$$p_1 \equiv p_2 \equiv \ldots \equiv p_n$$

is simplified by replacing any term that is repeated an odd number of times by a single occurrence of the term, and any term that is repeated an even number of times by removing all occurrences of the term (replacing the original expression by true if all terms are repeated an even number of times). Applying this process, the expression

$$p \equiv p \equiv q \equiv p \equiv r \equiv q \equiv q \equiv r \equiv p$$

is simplified to

$$q \ ,$$

because both p and r occur an even number of times, whilst q occurs an odd number of times.

Compare this process with the simplification of an arithmetic expression involving continued addition. The expression

$$p + p + q + p + r + q + q + r + p$$

is simplified to

$$4p + 3q + 2r \ .$$

This is made possible because addition is associative and symmetric. So, although some details of the simplification process are different, in essence the process is identical.

Exercise 5.5. Simplify the following.

(a) $p \equiv p \equiv p \equiv p \equiv p$.

(b) $p \equiv \text{true} \equiv q \equiv p$.

(c) $q \equiv p \equiv q \equiv p \equiv q \equiv p$.

(d) $\text{false} \equiv \text{false} \equiv \text{false}$.

(e) $p = p = p$.

(f) $(\text{false} \equiv \text{false}) = \text{false} = \text{false}$.

(g) $(p = p) = p = p$.   □

5.5 The Island of Knights and Knaves

The island of knights and knaves is a fictional island that is often used to test students' ability to reason logically. The island has two types of inhabitants: 'knights', who always tell the truth; and 'knaves', who always lie. Logic puzzles involve deducing facts about the island from statements made by its inhabitants without knowing whether or not the statements are made by a knight or a knave. We will use this, and similar sorts of logic puzzle, from time to time to provide practice in effective, calculational reasoning.

Suppose A is the proposition 'person A is a knight' and suppose A makes a statement S. Then A is true is the same as S is true. That is,

$$A \equiv S \ .$$

This is the basic rule that is used in solving logic puzzles about the island. For example, if A says 'I am a knight', we can infer $A \equiv A$. Since this is always true, we get no information from the statement. A moment's thought confirms that this is what one would expect. Both knights and knaves would claim that they are knights. A more informative statement is, for example, if A says 'I am the same type as B'. For then we infer $A \equiv (A \equiv B)$, which by associativity of equivalence and the rule (5.4) simplifies to B. So, from this statement, we can infer that B is a knight, but nothing about A.

If native A is asked a yes/no question Q, then the response to the question is $A \equiv Q$. That is, the response will be 'yes' if A is a knight and the answer is really yes, or A is a knave and the answer is really no. Otherwise the response will be 'no'. For example, asked the question 'are you a knight' all natives will answer 'yes', as $A \equiv A$. Asked the question 'is B a knight?' A will respond 'yes' if they are both the same type, otherwise 'no'. That is, A's response is 'yes' or 'no' depending on the truth or falsity of $A \equiv B$.

Because these rules are equivalences, we expect the algebraic properties of equivalence to play a central role in the solution of logic puzzles formulated about the island. In this section, we consider two examples: one very simple, the other more complicated. Then it is your turn.

Example 5.6. In this first example, it is rumoured that there is gold buried on the island. You ask one of the natives, A, whether there is gold on the island. He makes the following response: 'There is gold on this island equivales[3] I am a knight.' The problem is as follows.

(a) Can it be determined whether A is a knight or a knave?

(b) Can it be determined whether there is gold on the island?

You may wish to try the example yourself before consulting the solution. □

---

[3]The knights and knaves had had a proper training in calculational logic, otherwise they would not always be able to give the right response!

Solution. Let G denote the proposition 'There is gold on the island'. A's statement is $A \equiv G$. So what we are given is

$$A \equiv A \equiv G \ .$$

This, by (5.4), is equivalent to G. So we deduce that there is gold on the island, but it is not possible to tell whether A is a knight or a knave. □

Example 5.7. A tourist comes to a fork in the road, where one branch leads to a restaurant and one does not. A native of the island is standing at the fork. Formulate a single yes/no question that the tourist can ask such that the answer will be yes if the left fork leads to the restaurant, and otherwise the answer will be no.

Again, you may wish to try the example yourself before consulting the solution. □

Solution. Let Q be the question. Let A be 'the native is a knight'. Let L be the proposition 'the left fork leads to the restaurant'. We require that L equivales the response to the question is yes. But the response to the question Q is yes equivales $Q \equiv A$. So we require that $L \equiv (Q \equiv A)$. Equivalently, using the symmetry and associativity of equivalence, $Q \equiv (L \equiv A)$. The question is thus: is the statement that the left fork leads to the restaurant equivalent to your being a knight?

Note that this analysis is valid independently of what L denotes. It might be that the tourist wants to determine whether there is gold on the island, or whether there are any knaves on the island, or whatever. In general, if it is required to determine whether some proposition P is true or false, the question to be posed is $P \equiv A$. In the case of more complex propositions P, however, the question may be simplified. □

Here are some exercises to try yourself. More will be given later.

Exercise 5.8. Suppose you come across two of the inhabitants. You ask both of them whether the other one is a knight. Will you get the same answer in each case? □

Exercise 5.9. There are three natives A, B and C. Suppose A says 'B and C are the same type.' What can be inferred about the number of knights? □

Exercise 5.10. Suppose C says 'A and B are as like as two peas in a pod'. What question should you pose to A to determine whether or not C is telling the truth? □

Exercise 5.11. What single question allows you to determine whether A is a knight? Justify your question using the construction given above. □

Exercise 5.12. What question should you ask A to determine whether B is a knight? Justify your question using the construction given above. □

Exercise 5.13. What question should you ask A to determine whether A and B are the same type? Justify your question using the construction given above. □

Exercise 5.14. You would like to determine whether an odd number of A, B and C is a knight. You may ask one yes/no question to any one of them. What is the question you should ask? □

5.6 Negation

We now consider the negation operator. Negation is a unary operator (meaning that it is a function with exactly one argument) mapping a boolean to a boolean and is denoted by the symbol '¬', written as a prefix to its argument. If p is a boolean expression, '¬p' is pronounced '*not p*'. The law governing ¬p is

$$\textbf{[Negation]} \quad \neg p \equiv p \equiv \mathsf{false} \ . \tag{5.15}$$

Reading this as

$$\neg p = (p \equiv \mathsf{false}) \ ,$$

it functions as a definition of negation. Reading it the other way,

$$(\neg p \equiv p) = \mathsf{false} \ ,$$

it provides a way of simplifying propositional expressions. In addition, the symmetry of equivalence means that we can rearrange the terms in a continued equivalence in any order we like. So, we also get the property:

$$p = (\neg p \equiv \mathsf{false}) \ .$$

The law (5.15), in conjunction with the symmetry and associativity of equivalence, provides a way of simplifying continued equivalences in which one or more terms are repeated and/or negated. Suppose, for example, we want to simplify

$$\neg p \equiv p \equiv q \equiv \neg p \equiv r \equiv \neg q \ .$$

We begin by rearranging all the terms so that repeated occurrences of 'p' and 'q' are grouped together. Thus we get

$$\neg p \equiv \neg p \equiv p \equiv q \equiv \neg q \equiv r \ .$$

Now we can use (5.4) and (5.15) to reduce the number of occurrences of 'p' and 'q' to at most one (possibly negated). In this particular example we obtain

$$\mathsf{true} \equiv p \equiv \mathsf{false} \equiv r \ .$$

Finally, we use (5.4) and (5.15) again. The result is that the original formula is simplified to

$$\neg p \equiv r \ .$$

Just as before, this process can be compared with the simplification of an arithmetic expression involving continued addition, where now negative terms may also appear. The expression

$$p + (-p) + q + (-p) + r + q + (-q) + r + p$$

is simplified to

$$q + 2r$$

by counting all the occurrences of p, q and r, an occurrence of $-p$ cancelling out an occurrence of p. Again the details are different but the process is essentially identical.

The two laws (5.4) and (5.15) are all that is needed to define the way that negation interacts with equivalence; using these two laws we can derive several other laws. A simple example of how these two laws are combined is a proof that $\neg\mathsf{false} = \mathsf{true}$:

$$\neg\mathsf{false}$$

$=\qquad\{\qquad \text{law } \neg p \equiv p \equiv \mathsf{false} \text{ with } p := \mathsf{false} \quad\}$

$$\mathsf{false} \equiv \mathsf{false}$$

$=\qquad\{\qquad \text{law } \mathsf{true} \equiv p \equiv p \text{ with } p := \mathsf{false} \quad\}$

$$\mathsf{true} \ .$$

Let us now see how associativity of equivalence is used in a simple calculation. We investigate the expression $\neg(p \equiv q)$ to see whether it is possible to distribute negation through equivalence:

$$\neg(p \equiv q)$$

$=\qquad\{\qquad \text{the law } \neg p \equiv p \equiv \mathsf{false} \text{ with } p := (p \equiv q) \quad\}$

$$p \equiv q \equiv \mathsf{false}$$

$=\qquad\{\qquad \text{the law } \neg p \equiv p \equiv \mathsf{false} \text{ with } p := q \quad\}$

$$p \equiv \neg q \ .$$

We have thus proved

[Inequivalence] $\neg(p \equiv q) \equiv p \equiv \neg q$.   (5.16)

Note how associativity of equivalence has been used silently in this calculation. Note also how associativity of equivalence in the summary of the calculation gives us two properties for the price of one. The first is the one proved directly:

$$\neg(p \equiv q) = (p \equiv \neg q) \ ,$$

the second comes free with associativity:

$$(\neg(p \equiv q) \equiv p) = \neg q \ .$$

The proposition $\neg(p \equiv q)$ is usually written $p \not\equiv q$. The operator is called *inequivalence* (or *exclusive-or*, abbreviated *xor*). As a final worked example, we show that inequivalence associates with equivalence:

$$(p \not\equiv q) \equiv r$$

$=$ {   expanding the definition of $p \not\equiv q$ }

$$\neg(p \equiv q) \equiv r$$

$=$ { $\neg(p \equiv q) \equiv p \equiv \neg q$ }

$$p \equiv \neg q \equiv r$$

$=$ {   using symmetry of equivalence, the law (5.16)

                 is applied in the form $\neg(p \equiv q) \equiv \neg q \equiv p$

                 with $p,q := q,r$ }

$$p \equiv \neg(q \equiv r)$$

$=$ {   definition of $q \not\equiv r$ }

$$p \equiv (q \not\equiv r) \ .$$

Exercise 5.17. Simplify the following. (Note that in each case it does not matter in which order you evaluate the subexpressions. Also, rearranging the variables and/or constants does not make any difference.)

(a) false $\not\equiv$ false $\not\equiv$ false .

(b) true $\not\equiv$ true $\not\equiv$ true $\not\equiv$ true .

(c) false $\not\equiv$ true $\not\equiv$ false $\not\equiv$ true .

(d) $p \equiv p \equiv \neg p \equiv p \equiv \neg p$.

(e) $p \not\equiv q \equiv q \equiv p$.

(f) $p \not\equiv q \equiv r \equiv p$.

(g) $p \equiv p \not\equiv \neg p \not\equiv p \equiv \neg p$.

(h) $p \equiv p \not\equiv \neg p \not\equiv p \equiv \neg p \not\equiv \neg p$.   □

Exercise 5.18. Using only equivalences and/or inequivalences, formalize the following statements.

(a) None or both of p and q is true.

(b) Exactly one of p and q is true.

(c) Zero, two, or four of p, q, r and s is true.

(d) One or three of p, q, r and s is true.   □

Exercise 5.19. Prove that $\neg$true $=$ false.   □

Exercise 5.20 (Double Negation). Prove the rule of double negation

$$\neg\neg p = p \ .$$

$\square$

Exercise 5.21. The proof that inequivalence and equivalence associate with each other is summarized in the law

$$p \not\equiv q \equiv r \equiv p \equiv q \not\equiv r \ ,$$

any parenthesization being allowed. In addition, any rearrangement of the variables is allowed because both equivalence and inequivalence are symmetric.

Use these observations to list as many individual properties of equivalence and inequivalence as you can. In particular, deduce that inequivalence is associative.

$\square$

Exercise 5.22 (Encryption). The fact that inequivalence is associative, that is

$$(p \not\equiv (q \not\equiv r)) \equiv ((p \not\equiv q) \not\equiv r) \ ,$$

is used to encrypt data. To encrypt a single bit b of data, a key a is chosen and the encrypted form of b that is transmitted is $a \not\equiv b$. The receiver decrypts the received bit, c, using the same operation[4]. That is, the receiver uses the same key a to compute $a \not\equiv c$. Show that, if bit b is encrypted and then decrypted in this way, the result is b independently of the key a.

$\square$

Exercise 5.23. Let us return to the island of knights and knaves. In this question, there are two natives, A and B. Now, A says, 'B is a knight is the same as I am a knave'. What can you determine about A and B?

$\square$

Exercise 5.24. On the island of knights and knaves, you encounter two natives, A and B. What question should you ask A to determine whether A and B are different types?

$\square$

5.7 Summary

In this chapter, we have explored the basic properties of equivalence (the equality of boolean values), negation and inequivalence. Equivalence is highly unusual in that it is reflexive, symmetric, transitive *and* associative. Inequivalence is symmetric and also associative. We have shown how these properties are exploited in a variety of situations and we have begun the introduction of an axiomatization of the logical connectives.

See the appendix for a list of properties that have been established.

---

[4]This operation is usually called 'exclusive-or' in texts on data encryption; it is not commonly known that exclusive-or and inequivalence are the same. Inequivalence can be replaced by equivalence in the encryption and decryption process. But, very few scientists and engineers are aware of the algebraic properties of equivalence, and this possibility is never exploited!

Bibliographic Remarks

The fact that equality of boolean values is associative has been known since at least the 1920s, having been mentioned by Alfred Tarski in his PhD thesis, where its discovery is attributed to J. Lukasiewicz. (See the paper 'On the primitive term of logistic' (Tarski, 1956); Tarski is a famous logician.) Nevertheless, its usefulness was never recognized until brought to the fore by E.W. Dijkstra in his work on program semantics and mathematical method (see, for example, Dijkstra and Scholten 1990). Even now, however, it appears to be unknown to most mathematicians and logicians (and many computing scientists).

The origin of the logic puzzles is Raymond Smullyan's book *What is the Name of this Book* (Smullyan, 1978). This is a very entertaining book which leads on from simple logic puzzles to a discussion of the logical paradoxes and Gödel's undecidability theorem. But Smullyan's proofs invariably involve detailed case analyses. The exploitation of the associativity of equivalence in the solution of such puzzles is due to Wiltink (1987). The textbook by Gries and Schneider (1993) is highly recommended for further reading. The slogan 'logic is the glue' is theirs. The example of a full adder is also theirs.

6

Number Conversion

In Chapter 4, we discussed the properties of integer division. In this chapter, we discuss the related issue of converting real numbers to integers. We introduce a method for defining such operations, called a *Galois connection*. The use of a Galois connection to define a function is particularly elegant, as we hope to demonstrate in this and later chapters.

6.1 The Floor Function

Casting is the name given in languages like C and Java for the operation of converting a value of one type to another. Casts often occur automatically, but the programmer should still be aware of when they occur because they can cause errors if not used properly.

The cast from real numbers to integers occurs when evaluating an integer division. The real value of the division is first computed and then the value is converted to an integer, for example by rounding towards zero. The cast from integers to reals may seem unnecessary—one might argue that an integer is a real value anyway—but it is required in languages like Java, and indeed sometimes needs to be made explicit. This is because the division operator '/' is overloaded in Java. The text 1/2 (for example) means an integer division and evaluates to zero. So, if the real value is intended, one has to write, say, 1.0/2.0. Adding decimal points does not help, however, when the values being divided are expressions. So if, for example, m and n have been declared to be integers, we have to write something like (real)m/(real)n to force the compiler to compute the real value of m/n.

(We say 'something like' here because we do not want to go into all the intricacies of a specific language. In fact there is no 'real' type in Java; there are two integer types and two floating point types.)

Most languages specify how conversion from reals to integers is done. Java, for example, specifies that it is to be done by rounding towards zero. But there are circumstances when a programmer wishes the cast to be evaluated differently. For example, when completing a tax return, the tax payer is allowed to round in a direction in their own favour. Thus, interest received would be rounded down whilst interest paid would be rounded up. The values entered may also be computed, for example by dividing interest between two partners according to a pre-negotiated ratio. The programmer of a tax-calculator must therefore fully understand the properties of the casting operators. This is the topic of this chapter.

In mathematics, there is no specific notation for casting an integer value to a real value. Mathematicians call it an 'embedding' and usually rely on a notational convention, like using m and n to denote integers and x and y to denote reals, in order to make clear what is intended. When specific reference to the embedding is needed, it is usual to introduce some local ad hoc notation. There is, however, a well-established mathematical notation for converting reals to integers. Mathematicians have identified two such functions, the *floor* function and the *ceiling* function. For real value x, the floor of x is an integer and is denoted $\lfloor x \rfloor$. Also, for real value x, the ceiling of x is an integer and is denoted $\lceil x \rceil$. To begin with we consider only the floor function; we return to the ceiling function later.

The *floor* function from reals to integers is defined as follows: for all real x we take $\lfloor x \rfloor$ (read 'floor x') to be the greatest integer that is at most x. Formally, this is captured by a simple equivalence.

Definition 6.1 (Floor Function). For all real x, $\lfloor x \rfloor$ is an integer such that, for all integers n,

$$n \leqslant \lfloor x \rfloor \equiv n \leqslant x \ .$$

□

In the definition of the floor function we use the mathematical convention of *not denoting* the conversion from integers to reals. It is implicit in the inequality $n \leqslant x$, which seems to compare an integer with a real. In fact, what is meant is the comparison of the real value corresponding to n with the real value x. On the right side of the equivalence the at-most relation ('$\leqslant$') is between reals, whereas on the left side it is between integers.

Making explicit both conversions, temporarily adopting a Java-like notation, is illuminating. Doing so the definition becomes that, for all real x, (floor)x is an integer such that for all integers n,

$$n \ \leqslant \ (\text{floor})x \ \equiv \ (\text{real})n \ \leqslant \ x \ .$$

So, the floor of x is defined by connecting it to the conversion from integers to reals in a simple equivalence. The definition of the floor function is an instance of what is called a *Galois connection*. In general, a Galois connection relates (or connects) two functions by a simple equivalence of the same shape as that above; Galois connections are used to define a complicated function (like the floor function) by mapping its properties into the properties of a simpler function (like the embedding of integers into the reals). This said, it is useful to adopt the mathematical convention of omitting explicit mention of the embedding function and this is what we do from now on.

6.2   Properties of Floor

The first time that one encounters a definition like Definition 6.1, it can be difficult to see how it is used. But, it is not as difficult as it may seem.

The first thing we can do is to try to identify some special cases that simplify the definition. Two possibilities present themselves immediately; both exploit the fact that the at-most relation is reflexive. The equation

$$n \leqslant \lfloor x \rfloor \equiv n \leqslant x$$

is true for all integers n and reals x. Also, $\lfloor x \rfloor$ is by definition an integer. So we can instantiate n to $\lfloor x \rfloor$. We get

$$\lfloor x \rfloor \leqslant \lfloor x \rfloor \equiv \lfloor x \rfloor \leqslant x \ .$$

The left side that is obtained—$\lfloor x \rfloor \leqslant \lfloor x \rfloor$—is true, and so the right side is also true. That is,

$$\lfloor x \rfloor \leqslant x \ .$$

This tells us that the floor function rounds down. It returns an integer that is at most the given real value. (Note that this is not the same as rounding towards zero. For negative numbers, rounding down rounds away from zero. So the Java real-to-integer conversion coincides with the floor function only for positive values.)

The second possibility is to instantiate x to n. This is allowed because every integer is a real. Strictly, however, we are instantiating x to the real value obtained by converting n. We get

$$n \leqslant \lfloor n \rfloor \equiv n \leqslant n \ .$$

In this case, it is the right side of the equivalence that is true. So we can simplify to

$$n \leqslant \lfloor n \rfloor \ .$$

Earlier, we determined that $\lfloor x \rfloor \leqslant x$ for all real values x. Instantiating x to n, we get

$$\lfloor n \rfloor \leqslant n \ .$$

Combining the two inequalities, we have derived that, for all integers n,

$$\lfloor n \rfloor = n \ . \tag{6.2}$$

(Formally, the property of the at-most relation we use is that it is *antisymmetric*. That is, for all numbers m and n, $m = n$ exactly when both $m \leqslant n$ and $n \leqslant m$.)

Note that it is *not* permissible to instantiate n with some real value x. The defining equation is true for all *integers* n, but a real value is not an integer.

A good understanding of the equivalence operator suggests something else we can do with the defining equation: in general, we have

$$p \equiv q \equiv \neg p \equiv \neg q \ .$$

This is the rule of *contraposition*. So the contrapositive of the definition of the floor function is, for all integers n and real x,

$$\neg(n \leqslant \lfloor x \rfloor) \ \equiv \ \neg(n \leqslant x) \ .$$

But $\neg(n \leqslant m) \equiv m < n$. So

$$\lfloor x \rfloor < n \ \equiv \ x < n \ .$$

Equally, using that for integers m and n, $m < n \ \equiv \ m+1 \leqslant n$,

$$\lfloor x \rfloor + 1 \leqslant n \ \equiv \ x < n \ .$$

Now we can exploit reflexivity of the at-most relation again. Instantiating n with $\lfloor x \rfloor + 1$ and simplifying we deduce:

$$x < \lfloor x \rfloor + 1 \ .$$

Recalling that $\lfloor x \rfloor \leqslant x$, we have established

$$\lfloor x \rfloor \ \leqslant \ x \ < \ \lfloor x \rfloor + 1 \ .$$

In words, $\lfloor x \rfloor$ is such that $\lfloor x \rfloor$ is at most x and x is less than $\lfloor x \rfloor + 1$. Because $\lfloor x \rfloor$ is an integer, this defines it *uniquely*. We can express the unicity by a simple equivalence: for all integers m and all reals x,

$$m = \lfloor x \rfloor \ \equiv \ m \leqslant x < m+1 \ . \tag{6.3}$$

Recalling the discussion of integer division, we now ask whether the floor function is monotonic. That is, we want to show that

$$\lfloor x \rfloor \leqslant \lfloor y \rfloor \ \Leftarrow \ x \leqslant y \ .$$

Here we calculate:

$$\lfloor x \rfloor \leqslant \lfloor y \rfloor$$

$$= \qquad \{ \qquad \text{Definition 6.1, } x,n := y,\lfloor x \rfloor \ \}$$

$$\lfloor x \rfloor \leqslant y$$

$$\Leftarrow \qquad \{ \qquad \text{transitivity of } \leqslant \ \}$$

$$\lfloor x \rfloor \leqslant x \leqslant y$$

$$= \qquad \{ \qquad \lfloor x \rfloor \leqslant x \ \}$$

$$x \leqslant y \ .$$

Thus, the floor function is, indeed, monotonic.

6.3 Indirect Equality

Let us now demonstrate how to derive more complicated properties of the floor function. In the process we introduce an important technique for reasoning with Galois connections called the rule of *indirect equality*.

The following property illustrates the technique:

$$\left\lfloor \sqrt{\lfloor x \rfloor} \right\rfloor = \lfloor \sqrt{x} \rfloor \qquad\qquad (6.4)$$

for all x, $0 \leqslant x$.

Suppose we want to establish this property. It is an *equality* between two floor values; yet the definition of the floor function, Definition 6.1, seems to suggest that we should prove it by proving the two inequalities

$$\left\lfloor \sqrt{\lfloor x \rfloor} \right\rfloor \leqslant \lfloor \sqrt{x} \rfloor$$

and

$$\left\lfloor \sqrt{\lfloor x \rfloor} \right\rfloor \geqslant \lfloor \sqrt{x} \rfloor \ .$$

This strategy turns out to be rather difficult to carry out. A better strategy is this: the form of the left side of Definition 6.1 is an inequality between an arbitrary integer and a floor value. So let us begin with the expression

$$n \leqslant \left\lfloor \sqrt{\lfloor x \rfloor} \right\rfloor \ ,$$

where n is arbitrary, and see what we can discover. This is how the calculation goes.

$$n \leqslant \left\lfloor \sqrt{\lfloor x \rfloor} \right\rfloor$$

$$= \qquad \{ \qquad n \text{ is an integer, Definition 6.1} \ \}$$

$$n \leqslant \sqrt{\lfloor x \rfloor}$$

$$= \qquad \{ \qquad \text{arithmetic} \ \}$$

$$n^2 \leqslant \lfloor x \rfloor \ \vee \ n < 0$$

$$= \qquad \{ \qquad n^2 \text{ is an integer, Definition 6.1} \quad \}$$

$$n^2 \leqslant x \ \vee \ n < 0$$

$$= \qquad \{ \qquad \text{arithmetic, assuming that } 0 \leqslant n \quad \}$$

$$n \leqslant \sqrt{x}$$

$$= \qquad \{ \qquad n \text{ is an integer, Definition 6.1} \quad \}$$

$$n \leqslant \lfloor \sqrt{x} \rfloor \quad .$$

So we have proved that, for all integers n, where $0 \leqslant n$,

$$n \leqslant \left\lfloor \sqrt{\lfloor x \rfloor} \right\rfloor \ \equiv \ n \leqslant \lfloor \sqrt{x} \rfloor \quad .$$

Since n is an arbitrary integer, and $\left\lfloor \sqrt{\lfloor x \rfloor} \right\rfloor$ is an integer, by definition, we can now instantiate n to $\left\lfloor \sqrt{\lfloor x \rfloor} \right\rfloor$. We can also instantiate n to $\lfloor \sqrt{x} \rfloor$, for the same reason. In the former case, we get

$$\left\lfloor \sqrt{\lfloor x \rfloor} \right\rfloor \leqslant \left\lfloor \sqrt{\lfloor x \rfloor} \right\rfloor \ \equiv \ \left\lfloor \sqrt{\lfloor x \rfloor} \right\rfloor \leqslant \lfloor \sqrt{x} \rfloor \quad .$$

That is,

$$\left\lfloor \sqrt{\lfloor x \rfloor} \right\rfloor \leqslant \lfloor \sqrt{x} \rfloor \quad .$$

Similarly, in the latter case, we get

$$\lfloor \sqrt{x} \rfloor \leqslant \left\lfloor \sqrt{\lfloor x \rfloor} \right\rfloor \quad .$$

Property (6.4) now follows from the antisymmetry of the at-most relation.

Note that the decision on how to prove the theorem, i.e. the introduction of the integer n, is entirely inspired by the shape of Definition 6.1. The only way we can calculate something about the floor function is to use its specification. That specification allows one to rewrite the floor function only when it is in some special shape. In this case: it is on the *greater* side of the at-most relation and on the *smaller* side there is an (arbitrary) integer. That the specification of the floor function is indeed a good basis for calculating properties of the function is due to the rule of 'indirect equality'.

Rule of indirect equality.

Two numbers l and m are equal if it is the case that, for all numbers n of the same type as l and m,

$$n \leqslant l \equiv n \leqslant m \quad .$$

The qualification on n in the rule means that (for example) if l and m are reals, the property $n \leqslant l \equiv n \leqslant m$ must be true of all real numbers, n; if, however, l and m are known to be, say, natural numbers, the property must be true of all natural numbers, n, and, if l and m are, say, even integers, the property must be true of all even integers, n.

Exercise 6.5. Prove the rule of indirect equality making clear how the properties of equivalence and the at-most ordering are used. Where does the requirement that all of l, m and n have the same type enter into the proof? ☐

Exercise 6.6. Using the same calculational style exemplified above, prove the following properties of the floor function:

(a) $\lfloor x+m \rfloor = \lfloor x \rfloor + m$;

(b) $\lfloor x/m \rfloor = \lfloor \lfloor x \rfloor / m \rfloor$ (assuming m is a positive integer). ☐

Exercise 6.7. What is wrong with the following 'proof'?
We have, for integers m and n, where n is strictly positive, and all real x,

$$m \leqslant \lfloor n \times x \rfloor$$

$$= \qquad \{ \qquad \text{definition of floor} \quad \}$$

$$m \leqslant n \times x$$

$$= \qquad \{ \qquad \text{arithmetic} \quad \}$$

$$m/n \leqslant x$$

$$= \qquad \{ \qquad \text{definition of floor} \quad \}$$

$$m/n \leqslant \lfloor x \rfloor$$

$$= \qquad \{ \qquad \text{arithmetic} \quad \}$$

$$m \leqslant n \times \lfloor x \rfloor \ .$$

Thus, by indirect equality, $n \times \lfloor x \rfloor = \lfloor n \times x \rfloor$ for all positive n. (Hint: check every step carefully to see that all requirements have been met.)

Give examples of n and x for which $n \times \lfloor x \rfloor \neq \lfloor n \times x \rfloor$. (Hint: find values m, n and x that demonstrate the error in the above proof.) ☐

6.4 Rounding Off

To round off this chapter, we show how the programmer can take control of rounding in integer division.

Recall the discussion at the beginning of the chapter where we said that in a tax calculation it is sometimes necessary to round down and sometimes to round up. We want to show how to implement rounding up integer divisions supposing that our programming language always rounds down.

In order to express the problem we need the *ceiling* function. The definition is a dual of the definition of the floor function.

Definition 6.8. For all real x, $\lceil x \rceil$ is an integer such that, for all integers n,

$$\lceil x \rceil \leqslant n \equiv x \leqslant n \ .$$

$\square$

We leave it as an exercise to the reader to derive properties of the ceiling function dual to the properties of the floor function derived in Section 6.2.

Rounding down, an integer division of positive numbers m and n is expressed by

$$\left\lfloor \frac{m}{n} \right\rfloor \ ,$$

where $\frac{m}{n}$ is the real division of m and n. Dually, rounding up is expressed by

$$\left\lceil \frac{m}{n} \right\rceil \ .$$

Implementing rounding up given an implementation of rounding down amounts to finding suitable values p and q so that

$$\left\lfloor \frac{p}{q} \right\rfloor = \left\lceil \frac{m}{n} \right\rceil \ .$$

The values p and q should be expressed as arithmetic functions of m and n (that is, functions involving addition and multiplication, but not involving the floor or ceiling functions).

We can *calculate* suitable expressions for p and q using the rule of indirect equality. Specifically, for arbitrary integer k, we aim to eliminate the ceiling function from the inequality

$$k \leqslant \left\lceil \frac{m}{n} \right\rceil$$

obtaining an inequality of the form

$$k \leqslant e \ ,$$

where e is an arithmetic expression in m and n. We may then conclude that

$$\lfloor e \rfloor = \left\lceil \frac{m}{n} \right\rceil \ .$$

The first step in the calculation is perhaps the most difficult. This is because the definition of the ceiling function, Definition 6.4, provides a rule for dealing with inequalities where a ceiling value is on the lower side of an at-most relation but not when it is on the higher side (which is the case we are interested in).

However, recalling our discussion of the floor function, the solution is to consider
the contrapositive of the defining equation. Specifically we have, by negating both
sides of Definition 6.4,

$$n < \lceil x \rceil \equiv n < x \ .$$
(6.9)

We can now proceed with the derivation:

$$k \leqslant \left\lceil \frac{m}{n} \right\rceil$$

$=$ $\{$ integer arithmetic $\}$

$$k-1 < \left\lceil \frac{m}{n} \right\rceil$$

$=$ $\{$ contrapositive of definition of ceiling (rule (6.9)) $\}$

$$k-1 < \frac{m}{n}$$

$=$ $\{$ arithmetic, assuming $0 < n$ $\}$

$$n \times (k-1) < m$$

$=$ $\{$ integer inequalities $\}$

$$n \times (k-1) + 1 \leqslant m$$

$=$ $\{$ arithmetic, assuming $0 < n$ $\}$

$$k \leqslant \frac{m+n-1}{n}$$

$=$ $\{$ definition of floor function: (6.1) $\}$

$$k \leqslant \left\lfloor \frac{m+n-1}{n} \right\rfloor \ .$$

Here k is arbitrary. So, by indirect equality, we get, for all m and n, where $0 < n$,

$$\left\lceil \frac{m}{n} \right\rceil = \left\lfloor \frac{m+n-1}{n} \right\rfloor \ .$$
(6.10)

In Java, therefore, if it is required to round up the result of dividing integer m by
strictly positive integer n, one should compute (m+n-1)/n. (If n is negative, then,
of course, both m and n should be negated before applying the formula.)

Exercise 6.11. Note how the assumption $0 < n$ emerged naturally during the
above calculation; multiplication by n is only monotonic with respect to the less-
than relation when n is strictly positive. Show that the assumption is necessary
by using (6.10) to evaluate

$$\left\lceil \frac{-1}{-1} \right\rceil \ .$$

What do you get? $\square$

Exercise 6.12. What is wrong with the following derivation?

$$\left\lceil \frac{m}{n} \right\rceil \leqslant k$$

$$= \qquad \{ \qquad \text{definition of ceiling} \quad \}$$

$$\frac{m}{n} \leqslant k$$

$$= \qquad \{ \qquad \text{inequalities} \quad \}$$

$$\frac{m}{n} < k+1$$

$$= \qquad \{ \qquad \text{contrapositive of definition of floor} \quad \}$$

$$\left\lfloor \frac{m}{n} \right\rfloor < k+1$$

$$= \qquad \{ \qquad \text{inequalities} \quad \}$$

$$\left\lfloor \frac{m}{n} \right\rfloor \leqslant k \ .$$

Thus, by indirect equality,

$$\left\lfloor \frac{m}{n} \right\rfloor = \left\lceil \frac{m}{n} \right\rceil \ .$$

□

Exercise 6.13. Construct a function f such that $f.(-x) = -\lfloor x \rfloor$.   □

Exercise 6.14. Integer division can be defined independently of real division. A possible definition is: for integers m and n (where $n \neq 0$), $m \div n$ is the largest integer k such that $k \times n \leqslant m$.

Rephrase this definition in the form of an equivalence connecting division to multiplication. Use your definition to establish

$$m \div n = \left\lfloor \frac{m}{n} \right\rfloor \ .$$

Suppose the definition is: for integers m and n (where $n \neq 0$), $m \div n$ is the smallest integer k such that $k \times n \geqslant m$. What is the equivalence in this case?

(The definition in Java amounts to a case analysis on whether the sign of m is equal to the sign of n. If so, the first definition above is taken, if not, the second.)

□

6.5 Summary

In this chapter, we have seen how the conversion of real numbers to integer numbers is given a mathematical definition by connecting it to the opposite conversion, from integer numbers to real numbers. Specifically, we have studied the floor and ceiling functions and their mathematical properties. The concluding example showed how to construct a definition of rounding up an integer division in terms of rounding down.

Bibliographic Remarks

A good source for further discussion of the floor and ceiling functions is the book *Concrete Mathematics* (Graham, Knuth and Patashnik, 1989).

7

Calculational
Logic: Part 2

This chapter continues the axiomatization of the propositional connectives begun in Chapter 5. The axioms for disjunction (the logical 'or' of two statements) are added to the axioms for equivalence and negation, and then it is shown how to define the remaining logical connectives (conjunction, i.e. logical 'and', 'if' and 'only if') in terms of these three primitives. Additional laws are derived in examples and exercises.

7.1 Disjunction

The *disjunction* $p \lor q$ is the (inclusive) 'or' of p and q. Stating that $p \lor q$ is true means that one or more of p and q is true.

Disjunction has three obvious properties, namely *idempotence*, *symmetry* and *associativity*. *Idempotence* of disjunction is the rule:

$$\textbf{[Idempotence]} \quad p \lor p \equiv p \ . \tag{7.1}$$

Note that, for convenience, we assume that the operator '$\lor$' takes precedence over the operator '$\equiv$'. Fully parenthesized, (7.1) reads $(p \lor p) \equiv p$ and *not* $p \lor (p \equiv p)$. As an aid to reading, we try to indicate precedence by suitably spacing the subexpressions, adding more space around the operators with lower precedence, but sometimes the formulae become too large to be able to do this well.

The *symmetry* and *associativity* of disjunction are expressed as follows:

$$\textbf{[Symmetry]} \quad p \lor q \equiv q \lor p \ . \tag{7.2}$$

$$\textbf{[Associativity]} \quad p \lor (q \lor r) \equiv (p \lor q) \lor r \ . \tag{7.3}$$

The associativity of disjunction allows us to omit parentheses in continued disjunctions, as in, for example,

$$p \vee q \vee p \vee r \vee q \vee q \ .$$

The symmetry of disjunction means that the terms in such a continued disjunction can be rearranged at will, and the idempotence of disjunction means that multiple occurrences of the same term can be reduced to one. So the above expression would be simplified as follows:

$$p \vee q \vee p \vee r \vee q \vee q$$

$=$ {   rearranging terms—allowed because

                   disjunction is symmetric and associative   }

$$p \vee p \vee r \vee q \vee q \vee q$$

$=$ {   idempotence of disjunction (applied three times)   }

$$p \vee r \vee q \ .$$

Exercise 7.4. What is the difference between the simplification rule just given for continued disjunctions and the simplification rule for continued equivalences?

$\square$

The fourth law governing disjunction is not so obvious. Disjunction distributes through equivalence:

[Distributivity] $p \vee (q \equiv r) \ \equiv \ p \vee q \ \equiv \ p \vee r \ .$ (7.5)

The fifth and final law is called the rule of the *excluded middle*; it states that, for each proposition p, either p or its negation is true. These are the only two possibilities and a third 'middle' possibility is excluded:

[Excluded Middle] $p \vee \neg p \ .$ (7.6)

Using this basis, we can derive many other laws. Here is how to show that false is a unit of disjunction:

$$p \vee \mathsf{false}$$

$=$ {   definition of false (5.15)   }

$$p \vee (\neg p \equiv p)$$

$=$ {   disjunction distributes over equivalence (7.5)   }

$$p \vee \neg p \ \equiv \ p \vee p$$

$=$ {   excluded middle (7.6) and

                   idempotence of disjunction   }

$$\mathsf{true} \equiv p$$

$$= \qquad \{ \qquad \text{unit of equivalence (5.4)} \quad \}$$

$$p \ .$$

Exercise 7.7. Prove that $p \lor \text{true} \equiv \text{true}$. (In words, true is a *zero* of disjunction.)

$\square$

Exercise 7.8. Construct a truth table for (7.5) and verify that it is always true. $\square$

7.2 Conjunction

In this section, we define conjunction (logical 'and') in terms of disjunction and equivalence. We show how to use the definition to derive the basic properties of conjunction.

The definition of conjunction uses the so-called *golden rule*:

$$[\text{Golden Rule}] \quad p \land q \ \equiv \ p \ \equiv \ q \ \equiv \ p \lor q \ . \tag{7.9}$$

The convention is that the conjunction operator ('$\land$', read 'and') has the same precedence as disjunction ('$\lor$'), which is higher than the precedence of equivalence.

Giving conjunction and disjunction the same precedence means that an expression like $p \land q \lor r$ is ambiguous. It is not clear whether it means $(p \land q) \lor r$ or $p \land (q \lor r)$. You should, therefore, always parenthesize, so that the meaning is clear. (Giving conjunction precedence over disjunction, as is often done, is bad practice, because it obscures symmetries in their algebraic properties.)

The golden rule can be seen as a definition of conjunction in terms of equivalence and disjunction if we read it as

$$(p \land q) \ = \ (p \ \equiv \ q \ \equiv \ p \lor q) \ .$$

But, it can also be read in other ways. For example, the golden rule asserts the equality

$$(p \land q \ \equiv \ p) \ = \ (q \ \equiv \ p \lor q) \ .$$

This reading will be used later when we define logical implication. It can also be read as a definition of disjunction in terms of conjunction:

$$(p \land q \ \equiv \ p \ \equiv \ q) \ = \ (p \lor q) \ .$$

This reading is sometimes useful when, in a calculation, it is expedient to replace disjunctions by conjunctions.

The golden rule is so named because it can be used in so many different ways. Its beauty comes from exploiting the associativity and symmetry of equivalence. Here is how it is used to prove some basic properties of conjunction.

It is easy to see that conjunction is symmetric:

$$p \wedge q$$

$=$ {   golden rule   }

$$p \equiv q \equiv p \vee q$$

$=$ {   equivalence and disjunction are symmetric   }

$$q \equiv p \equiv q \vee p$$

$=$ {   golden rule, $p,q := q,p$ }

$$q \wedge p \quad .$$

Exercise 7.10. Prove that $p \wedge p \equiv p$. (Begin with $p \wedge p$ and simplify.)   □

So-called *absorption* of conjunctions by disjunctions is derived as follows:

$$p \vee (p \wedge q)$$

$=$ {   golden rule   }

$$p \vee (p \equiv q \equiv p \vee q)$$

$=$ {   disjunction distributes over equivalence   }

$$p \vee p \equiv p \vee q \equiv p \vee (p \vee q)$$

$=$ {   idempotence and associativity of disjunction   }

$$p \equiv p \vee q \equiv p \vee q$$

$=$ {   unit/reflexivity law of equivalence   }

$$p \quad .$$

Thus,

[Absorption] $p \vee (p \wedge q) \;\equiv\; p \quad .$ (7.11)

Exercise 7.12. Prove that $p \wedge (p \vee q) \equiv p$.   □

Now we prove that conjunction is associative. First, we observe a lemma:

$$p \wedge (q \wedge r)$$

$=$ {   golden rule: $p,q := p, q \wedge r$ }

$$p \equiv q \wedge r \equiv p \vee (q \wedge r)$$

$=$ {   golden rule: $p,q := q,r$ }

$$p \equiv q \equiv r \equiv q \vee r \equiv p \vee (q \equiv r \equiv q \vee r)$$

$=$ {   distributivity of disjunction over equivalence   }

$$p \equiv q \equiv r \equiv q \vee r \equiv p \vee q \equiv p \vee r \equiv p \vee q \vee r \quad .$$

Note that the formula in the last line is completely symmetric in p, q and r. That is, because of the symmetry of equivalence and disjunction, any permutation of the three variables leaves the formula unchanged. To complete our task we use the lemma twice, once with a different permutation of the variables:

$$p \wedge (q \wedge r)$$

=   {   above   }

$$p \equiv q \equiv r \equiv q \vee r \equiv p \vee q \equiv p \vee r \equiv p \vee q \vee r$$

=   {   equivalence is symmetric, disjunction is symmetric   }

$$r \equiv p \equiv q \equiv p \vee q \equiv r \vee p \equiv r \vee q \equiv r \vee p \vee q$$

=   {   above, $p,q,r := r,p,q$ }

$$r \wedge (p \wedge q)$$

=   {   conjunction is symmetric   }

$$(p \wedge q) \wedge r \ .$$

From now on, we often omit parentheses in continued conjunctions, silently exploiting the associativity property.

Exercise 7.13. Prove that disjunction distributes over conjunction. That is, prove

$$p \vee (q \wedge r) \ \equiv \ (p \vee q) \wedge (p \vee r) \ .$$

(Hint: start from the most complicated side.)   □

Now we prove that conjunction distributes through disjunction:

$$(p \wedge q) \vee (p \wedge r)$$

=   {   distributivity of disjunction over conjunction (7.13)   }

$$((p \wedge q) \vee p) \wedge ((p \wedge q) \vee r)$$

=   {   absorption (see above)   }

$$p \wedge ((p \wedge q) \vee r)$$

=   {   distributivity of disjunction over conjunction

                           (symmetric version)   }

$$p \wedge (p \vee r) \wedge (q \vee r)$$

=   {   absorption   }

$$p \wedge (q \vee r) \ .$$

Exercise 7.14. Prove the following laws.

Modus Ponens: $p \wedge (p \equiv q) \ \equiv \ p \wedge q \ .$

De Morgan: $\neg(p \wedge q) \equiv \neg p \vee \neg q$.

De Morgan: $\neg(p \vee q) \equiv \neg p \wedge \neg q$.

Distributivity: $p \wedge (q \equiv r) \equiv p \wedge q \equiv p \wedge r \equiv p$.

Hint: always try to begin with the most complicated term. If you get stuck try to simplify the remaining term(s). Prove the two De Morgan rules in the order given, exploiting the first when proving the second.   □

Exercise 7.15. Prove that the following are all equivalent.

(a) $(p \vee q) \wedge (q \vee r) \wedge (r \vee p)$.

(b) $p \vee q \equiv q \vee r \equiv r \vee p$.

(c) $p \wedge q \equiv q \wedge r \equiv r \wedge p$.

(d) $(p \wedge q) \vee (q \wedge r) \vee (r \wedge p)$.

Hint: work towards the middle. That is, starting from (a) derive (b), and starting from (d) derive (c). (These two calculations are completely dual.) Then show that (b) and (c) are equivalent. (The statement

$$(p \wedge q) \vee (q \wedge r) \vee (r \wedge p)$$

expresses the fact that at least two of p, q or r is true. One of the other three equivalent expressions may be preferred in some calculations. See, for example, Exercises 7.36 and 7.37, where the middle expressions are more handy.)   □

7.3 Implication

Many constructions and proofs involve a logical implication rather than a logical equivalence. Put simply, implications are 'if' statements rather than 'is' statements. An example is: John and Sue are cousins *if* their fathers are brothers. This is an 'if' statement because the condition given for John and Sue to be cousins is not exhaustive. Another condition is, for example, that their mothers are sisters.

Confusingly, in normal conversation the English word 'if' is often used when an equivalence is meant. For instance we might say, Ann and Dave are siblings *if* they have the same father or the same mother. What is meant here, however, is that the definition of *sibling* is having the same father or mother. That is, Ann and Dave are siblings *is* they have the same father or the same mother. In mathematical texts, the distinction between 'if' and 'is' is often made by saying 'if and only if' when an equivalence is intended.

The notation we use for the statement 'p if q' is $p \Leftarrow q$. The notation we use for 'p only if q' is $p \Rightarrow q$. The expression $p \Leftarrow q$ is often verbalized as 'p follows from q' and $p \Rightarrow q$ is verbalized as 'p implies q'.

The statements $p \Leftarrow q$ and $q \Rightarrow p$ mean the same thing. It is useful to use both notations. Sometimes, an argument can be easier to construct in one direction than in the other.

7.3.1 Definitions and Basic Properties

Implications are defined equationally. One definition of $p \Leftarrow q$ is as follows:

$$\textbf{[Definition of If]} \quad p \Leftarrow q \ \equiv \ p \ \equiv \ p \lor q \ . \tag{7.16}$$

Note that the precedence of '$\Leftarrow$' is higher than the precedence of '$\equiv$', as suggested by the spacing. Henceforth, we give '$\Leftarrow$' and '$\Rightarrow$' lower precedence than '$\lor$' and '$\land$'.

Equation (7.16) defines '$\Leftarrow$' in terms of equivalence and disjunction. Alternatively, in terms of equivalence and conjunction,

$$\textbf{[Definition of If]} \quad p \Leftarrow q \ \equiv \ q \ \equiv \ p \land q \ . \tag{7.17}$$

The two definitions are the same because, by the golden rule, $p \equiv p \lor q$ and $q \equiv p \land q$ are the same.

Turning the arrows around, we get two definitions of $p \Rightarrow q$.

$$\textbf{[Definition of Only-If]} \quad p \Rightarrow q \ \equiv \ q \ \equiv \ p \lor q \ . \tag{7.18}$$

$$\textbf{[Definition of Only-If]} \quad p \Rightarrow q \ \equiv \ p \ \equiv \ p \land q \ . \tag{7.19}$$

Immediate consequences of these definitions are obtained by suitable instantiations of the variables p and q. For example, (7.16) gives us

$$\textbf{[Strengthening]} \quad p \lor q \ \Leftarrow \ q \ . \tag{7.20}$$

(Note that the precedence of '$\Leftarrow$' is lower than the precedence of '$\lor$', as suggested by the spacing.) The specific details of the calculation are as follows:

$$
\begin{aligned}
& p \lor q \ \Leftarrow \ q \\
=& \qquad \{ \qquad (7.16), p,q \ := \ p \lor q, q \ \} \\
& p \lor q \ \equiv \ (p \lor q) \lor q \\
=& \qquad \{ \qquad \text{associativity and idempotence of disjunction} \ \} \\
& p \lor q \ \equiv \ p \lor q \\
=& \qquad \{ \qquad \text{reflexivity of} \equiv \ \} \\
& \text{true} \ .
\end{aligned}
$$

The rule is called 'strengthening' because it is used to replace a proof requirement $p \lor q$ by the stronger requirement q. For example, a programming problem may involve us in establishing the inequality $l \leqslant r$. But $l \leqslant r$ is the same as $l < r \lor l = r$. So, rather than establishing $l \leqslant r$ we may choose to establish $l = r$. The requirement $l = r$ is 'stronger' than the requirement $l \leqslant r$.

A second immediate consequence of the definitions is another strengthening rule:

$$\textbf{[Strengthening]} \quad p \ \Leftarrow \ p \land q \ . \tag{7.21}$$

This is obtained by instantiating q to $p \land q$ in (7.16).

Exercise 7.22. Express the strengthening rules for the operator '$\Rightarrow$' rather than '$\Leftarrow$'. Note that turning the arrows around turns a strengthening rule into a *weakening* rule.   □

Other immediate consequences are

$$p \Leftarrow \mathsf{false} \;\; ,$$

$$\mathsf{true} \Leftarrow p \;\; ,$$

and

$$p \Leftarrow p \;\; .$$

Exercise 7.23. The only other entry in the truth table of '$\Leftarrow$' not covered by these three properties is $\mathsf{false} \Leftarrow \mathsf{true}$. Calculate what its value is.   □

Exercise 7.24. Show that $p \Leftarrow q \;\equiv\; p \vee \neg q$.   □

Exercise 7.25. Prove $(p \Leftarrow q) \vee (p \Rightarrow q)$.   □

Exercise 7.26. Prove the following properties.

Contrapositive: $p \Leftarrow q \;\equiv\; \neg p \Rightarrow \neg q$.

Contradiction: $\neg p \;\equiv\; p \Rightarrow \mathsf{false}$.

Distributivity: $(p \equiv q) \Leftarrow r \;\equiv\; p \wedge r \equiv q \wedge r$.

Distributivity: $(p \equiv q) \Leftarrow r \;\equiv\; p \Leftarrow r \equiv q \Leftarrow r$.

Shunting: $p \Leftarrow q \wedge r \;\equiv\; (p \Leftarrow q) \Leftarrow r$.   □

7.3.2 Replacement Rules

The advantage of using equations over other methods for defining the logical connectives is the opportunity to substitute equals for equals. The definition of $p \Leftarrow q$ provides good examples of this.

An important rule of logic is called *modus ponens*. It is the rule that

$$(p \Leftarrow q) \wedge q \;\equiv\; p \wedge q \;\; .$$

(The rule is often stated as the implication $(p \Rightarrow q) \wedge p \;\Rightarrow\; q$, but it is preferable to state it as an equivalence. Whether or not one chooses to state it in terms of '$\Leftarrow$' or '$\Rightarrow$' is a matter of choice.) Here is one way of proving it. The important step is the middle step, the first step paving the way for this step.

$$(p \Leftarrow q) \wedge q$$

$$= \qquad \{ \qquad \text{true is the unit of equivalence} \quad \}$$

$$(p \Leftarrow q) \wedge (q \equiv \mathsf{true})$$

$$= \qquad \{ \qquad \text{substitution of equals for equals:}$$

specifically the value true is substituted for q

in the term $p \Leftarrow q$ }

$(p \Leftarrow \text{true}) \wedge (q \equiv \text{true})$

=   { $p \Leftarrow \text{true} \equiv p$, true is the unit of equivalence   }

$p \wedge q$.

The middle step uses the fact that, if we know that q is true, we can substitute true for q in any expression in which it appears. The rule is called a *meta-rule* because it cannot be expressed in the form of an algebraic law, and we need additional language outwith the language of the propositional calculus to explain how the rule is used. A way of expressing the rule is as follows:

[Substitution] $(e = f) \wedge E[x := e] \equiv (e = f) \wedge E[x := f]$.   (7.27)

The notation $E[x := e]$ is explained as follows. Suppose E is some propositional expression parametrized by the variable x. Then $E[x := e]$ stands for the expression E after replacing all occurrences of x by e. For example, E may be $(p \Leftarrow x) \wedge x$ and e may be $p \vee q$. Then $E[x := e]$ is $(p \Leftarrow p \vee q) \wedge (p \vee q)$. (Recall that parentheses may need to be added during the process of substitution. Refer back to the discussion in Chapter 3 if in doubt.) Similarly, $E[x := f]$ is the expression after replacing all occurrences of x by f. So the rule expresses the idea that, if e and f are equal, e may be replaced by f (and vice versa) in any logical expression E.

Note that the rule does not depend on the type of e and f—they could be numbers, strings, booleans, or whatever. Equivalence of propositions is just equality of boolean values, so the rule applies to equivalences $e \equiv f$ just as well. The types of e, f and x do, however, have to be the same.

The introduction of the variable x in the rule allows the possibility that not every occurrence of e and f is interchanged. For example,

$$(a^2 = b) \wedge (a^2 + 1 = 2a^2 + 3) \equiv (a^2 = b) \wedge (a^2 + 1 = 2b + 3)$$

is an instance of the rule. It is so because

$$(a^2 + 1 = 2x + 3)[x := a^2] \equiv a^2 + 1 = 2a^2 + 3 ,$$

and

$$(a^2 + 1 = 2x + 3)[x := b] \equiv a^2 + 1 = 2b + 3 .$$

Thus, although the subexpression 'a^2' is repeated, the replacement rule allows a substitution of a value equal to a^2 in selected occurrences of the expression.

Substitution 'of equals for equals' is, in fact, an instance of the rule, first formulated by Baron Gottfried Wilhelm von Leibniz, that application of a function to equal values gives equal results: an expression E parametrized by a variable x is a function of x, and $E[x := e]$ and $E[x := f]$ simply denote the result of applying the function to e and to f, respectively. Sometimes, for brevity and to give credit to Leibniz, we use 'Leibniz' as the hint when we mean 'substitution of equals for equals'.

A more direct formulation of Leibniz's rule is the following. Suppose E is an arbitrary expression. Then, assuming e, f and x all have the same type:

$$\textbf{[Leibniz]} \quad (e = f) \equiv (e = f) \wedge (E[x := e] = E[x := f]) \ . \tag{7.28}$$

(Rule (7.28) is a consequence of rule (7.27) because $e = f$ is equivalent to $(e = f) \wedge (E = E)$, to which (7.27) can be applied.)

We use both rules (7.27) and (7.28). Which of the two is being used can be recognized by whether a step does not or does change the number of conjuncts, respectively.

Returning to the properties of logical implication, here is how substitution (of equals for equals) is used to prove that implication is transitive.

$$
\begin{array}{rl}
& (p \Leftarrow q) \wedge (q \Leftarrow r) \\
= & \qquad \{ \qquad \text{definition} \quad \} \\
& (p \ \equiv \ p \vee q) \wedge (q \ \equiv \ q \vee r) \\
= & \qquad \{ \qquad \text{substitution of equals for equals (7.28),} \\
& \qquad\qquad\qquad \text{applied to 2nd term with } E = (p \vee x) \quad \} \\
& (p \ \equiv \ p \vee q) \wedge (q \ \equiv \ q \vee r) \wedge (p \vee q \ \equiv \ p \vee q \vee r) \\
= & \qquad \{ \qquad \text{substitution of equals for equals (7.27):} \\
& \qquad\qquad\qquad \text{the two rightmost occurrences of } p \vee q \\
& \qquad\qquad\qquad \text{are replaced by } p \quad \} \\
& (p \ \equiv \ p \vee q) \wedge (q \ \equiv \ q \vee r) \wedge (p \ \equiv \ p \vee r) \\
= & \qquad \{ \qquad \text{definition} \quad \} \\
& (p \Leftarrow q) \wedge (q \Leftarrow r) \wedge (p \Leftarrow r) \\
\Rightarrow & \qquad \{ \qquad \text{weakening} \quad \} \\
& p \Leftarrow r \ .
\end{array}
$$

Exercise 7.29. Prove the following properties using substitution of equals for equals.

Mutual Implication (Iff): $\quad p \equiv q \ \equiv \ (p \Leftarrow q) \wedge (p \Rightarrow q) \ .$

Distributivity: $\quad p \Leftarrow q \vee r \ \equiv \ (p \Leftarrow q) \wedge (p \Leftarrow r) \ .$

Distributivity: $\quad p \wedge q \Leftarrow r \ \equiv \ (p \Leftarrow r) \wedge (q \Leftarrow r) \ .$ $\qquad\qquad\qquad\square$

7.4   Exercises: Logic Puzzles

The following are exercises in applying the algebraic laws discussed above. For the exercises involving knights and knaves, recall that if person A makes a statement S, then

$$A \equiv S \ ,$$

where A is 'A is a knight'.

Exercise 7.30. The following is a list of statements that might be made by person A on the island of knights and knaves. In each case, the problem is to determine what can be deduced about A and B.

(a) If I am a knight, B is a knight.

(b) If I am a knave, B is a knight.

(c) If I am a knight, B is a knave.

(d) If I am a knave, B is a knave.

(e) If B is a knight, I am a knight.

(f) If B is a knave, I am a knight.

(g) If B is a knight, I am a knave.

(h) If B is a knave, I am a knave.

All statements are implications in which either the premise or the conclusion is a statement about person A. One method is to use (7.19) in the case that the statement about A is the premise, and (7.18) in the case that the statement about A is the conclusion. This allows easy use of the elementary properties of equivalence. We illustrate the method on two cases and leave its application in the other cases to you.

Sample Solutions.   (a) We are required to simplify $A \equiv A {\Rightarrow} B$. In this case, we choose (7.19).

$$A \equiv A {\Rightarrow} B$$

$$= \qquad \{ \qquad (7.19) \quad \}$$

$$A \equiv A \equiv A \wedge B$$

$$= \qquad \{ \qquad \text{reflexivity of equivalence} \quad \}$$

$$A \wedge B \ .$$

So, both A and B are knights.

(e) We are required to simplify $A \equiv B \Rightarrow A$. In this case, we choose (7.18).

$$A \equiv B \Rightarrow A$$

$$= \qquad \{ \qquad (7.18) \quad \}$$

$$A \equiv A \equiv A \vee B$$

$$= \qquad \{ \qquad \text{reflexivity of equivalence} \quad \}$$

$$A \vee B \ .$$

So, at least one of A and B is a knight, but which it is is not clear.

Note that another method is to restate (e), (f), (g) and (h) using the contrapositive rule (see Exercise 7.26). This maps each of the four problems into one of (a), (b), (c) and (d).   □

Exercise 7.31. You encounter two inhabitants. Pose a question that will determine whether or not both are knights. Pose a question that will determine whether or not at least one of them is a knight.   □

Exercise 7.32. Inhabitant A says 'either I am a knave or B is a knight'. What can you deduce about A and B?   □

Exercise 7.33. According to this problem, three of the inhabitants—A, B and C— were standing together in the garden. A stranger passed by and asked A, 'Are you a knight or a knave?'. A answered, but rather indistinctly, so the stranger could not make out what was said. The stranger then asked B, 'What did A say?'. B replied, 'A said that he is a knave'. At this point the third, C, said 'Don't believe B; he's lying!'. The question is, what are B and C?   □

Exercise 7.34. Suppose the stranger asked A, 'How many knights are among you?'. Again, A answers indistinctly. So, the stranger asks B, 'What did A say?' B replies, 'A said there is one knight among us'. Then C says, 'Don't believe B; he's lying!'. Now what are B and C?   □

In Shakespeare's *Merchant of Venice*, Portia had three caskets: gold, silver and lead. Inside one of these is her portrait, and on each an inscription. Portia explained to her suitor that each inscription could be either true or false, but on the basis of the inscriptions, he was to choose the casket containing the portrait. If he succeeded, he could marry her. The first exercise below is a simpler version. We demonstrate how to solve the problem and then leave the remaining exercises to you.

Exercise 7.35. Suppose there are two caskets, gold and silver, into one of which Portia placed her portrait. The inscriptions are as follows.

Gold: the portrait is not in here.
Silver: exactly one of these inscriptions is true.

Which casket contains the portrait?   □

The solution involves introducing several variables. Let G stand for 'the portrait is in the gold casket', let S stand for 'the portrait is in the silver casket', g stand for 'the inscription on the gold casket is true' and s for 'the inscription on the silver casket is true'. Let U stand for 'the portrait is in exactly one of the caskets'. Then we are given

$$(g \equiv \neg G) \;\wedge\; (s \equiv g \equiv \neg s) \;\wedge\; U \;,$$

where

$$U \equiv G \not\equiv S \;.$$

The middle term simplifies to $\neg g$, so we conclude

$$(g \equiv \neg G) \;\wedge\; \neg g \;\wedge\; (G \not\equiv S) \;.$$

That is, $G \wedge \neg g \wedge \neg S$. Formally, the calculation is as follows:

> true
>
> =   {   problem statement   }
>
> $(g \equiv \neg G) \;\wedge\; (s \equiv g \equiv \neg s) \;\wedge\; (G \not\equiv S)$
>
> =   {   contrapositive applied to 1st conjunct,
>
>   simplification of continued equivalences
>
>   applied to 2nd conjunct,
>
>   definition of inequivalence applied to 3rd conjunct   }
>
> $(\neg g \equiv G) \;\wedge\; \neg g \;\wedge\; (\neg G \equiv S)$
>
> =   {   substitution of equals for equals   }
>
> $G \;\wedge\; \neg g \;\wedge\; \neg S \;.$

So the portrait is in the gold casket (and the inscription on the gold casket is false, but nothing can be concluded about the inscription on the silver casket).

In the following exercises, there are three caskets rather than two. Each inscription gives one item of data which is to be added to the information that the portrait is in exactly one of the caskets.

Exercise 7.36. Suppose that Portia put the following inscriptions on the three caskets.

Gold: the portrait is in here.
Silver: the portrait is in here.
Lead: at least two of these caskets bears a false inscription.

Which casket should the suitor choose? Use the abbreviations L for 'the portrait is in the lead casket' and l for 'the inscription on the lead casket is true' in formulating your answer. Hint: use Exercise 7.15 to formulate the inscription on the lead casket.   □

Exercise 7.37. In this version of the problem, Portia puts a dagger into one of the caskets. The suitor must choose a casket that does *not* contain the dagger. The inscriptions on the caskets are as follows.

Gold: the dagger is in this casket.
Silver: the dagger is not in this casket.
Lead: at most one of these caskets bears a true inscription.

   Which casket should the suitor choose?   □

7.5   Summary

This chapter completes the axiomatization of calculational logic. Axioms for disjunction were added to the axioms for equivalence and negation. Briefly, disjunction is associative, symmetric and idempotent, and distributes through equivalence. In addition, it satisfies the law of the excluded middle.

   The axioms for equivalence, negation and disjunction were used as a basis for the study of the remaining logical connectives—conjunction, follows-from and implies—with the golden rule acting as the linchpin. The solution of logic puzzles demonstrated the effectiveness of mathematical calculation based on equational reasoning.

Bibliographic Remarks

This chapter is heavily influenced by Dijkstra and Scholten's development of propositional calculus (Dijkstra and Scholten, 1990), as well as the textbook by Gries and Schneider (1993). Most of the logic puzzles are from Smullyan (1978).

8
Maximum and Minimum

In this chapter, we put logic to work. Rather, we put you, the reader, to work, with calculational logic as the main tool. The chapter is about the algebraic properties of the maximum and minimum operators on real numbers. The definitions we give of these operators are equivalences which relate them to the propositional connectives. (Formally, the definitions are instances of the general concept of a Galois connection mentioned in Chapter 6, but it is not necessary to know that here.) So, maximum and minimum inherit many of their properties directly from the properties of the logical connectives.

8.1 Definition of Maximum

Denoting the maximum function on real numbers by the infix operator $\uparrow$, we have, for all x, y and z,

$$[\text{Maximum}] \quad x \uparrow y \leqslant z \;\equiv\; x \leqslant z \land y \leqslant z \;. \tag{8.1}$$

Note that this is a distributivity property. It is the property that the boolean-valued function $(\leqslant z)$ distributes through maximum, turning it into a conjunction. In this way properties of maximum are translated into properties of conjunction.

What can be deduced from this definition? Three properties can be deduced very easily. First, we use the fact that true is a unit of equivalence and $\leqslant$ is reflexive—specifically, by instantiating z to $x \uparrow y$, the left side of the definition becomes true so that

$$x \leqslant x \uparrow y \land y \leqslant x \uparrow y \;.$$

Second and third, we use the fact that true is a unit of conjunction and, again, $\leqslant$ is reflexive—by instantiating z to x and z to y we get, respectively,

$$x \uparrow y \leqslant x \;\equiv\; y \leqslant x$$

and

$$x \uparrow y \leqslant y \;\equiv\; x \leqslant y \; .$$

A fourth property can be obtained from the fact that $\leqslant$ is a *total* ordering. That is, for all x and y,

$$x \leqslant y \;\vee\; y \leqslant x \; .$$

Using this fact, we calculate:

$$x \uparrow y = x \;\vee\; x \uparrow y = y$$
$$=\qquad\{\qquad \text{antisymmetry of } \leqslant \quad \}$$
$$(x \uparrow y \leqslant x \;\wedge\; x \leqslant x \uparrow y) \;\vee\; (x \uparrow y \leqslant y \;\wedge\; y \leqslant x \uparrow y)$$
$$=\qquad\{\qquad \text{above, substitution of equals for equals} \quad \}$$
$$(y \leqslant x \;\wedge\; \text{true}) \;\vee\; (x \leqslant y \;\wedge\; \text{true})$$
$$=\qquad\{\qquad \text{true is the unit of conjunction} \quad \}$$
$$y \leqslant x \;\vee\; x \leqslant y$$
$$=\qquad\{\qquad \leqslant \text{ is a total ordering} \quad \}$$
$$\text{true} \; .$$

So maximum is a *choice* function: $x \uparrow y$ chooses between x and y.

Here are a couple of very short exercises.

Exercise 8.2. Show that $x \uparrow y \leqslant x \;\equiv\; x \uparrow y = x$. $\qquad\qquad$ □

Exercise 8.3. Simplify the statement $x \uparrow y \leqslant x + y$. $\qquad\qquad$ □

8.2 Using Indirect Equality

To derive additional *equalities*, we recall the *rule of indirect equality*: in order to establish the equality $x = y$, show that, for arbitrary z of the same type as x and y,

$$x \leqslant z \;\equiv\; y \leqslant z \; .$$

Here are two examples. In the first example, we show that maximum is associative because conjunction is associative. We have, for all w,

$$(x \uparrow y) \uparrow z \leqslant w$$
$$=\qquad\{\qquad \text{definition of max} \quad \}$$

$$x \uparrow y \leqslant w \wedge z \leqslant w$$

$=$ {   definition of max   }

$$(x \leqslant w \wedge y \leqslant w) \wedge z \leqslant w$$

$=$ { $\wedge$ is associative   }

$$x \leqslant w \wedge (y \leqslant w \wedge z \leqslant w)$$

$=$ {   definition of max (applied twice)   }

$$x \uparrow (y \uparrow z) \leqslant w \quad .$$

Thus, by indirect equality,

$$(x \uparrow y) \uparrow z = x \uparrow (y \uparrow z) \quad .$$

Note how short and straightforward this proof is. In contrast, if maximum is defined in the conventional way by case analysis, it would be necessary to consider six different cases, six being the number of ways to order three values x, y and z.

In the second example, we derive a distributivity property of maximum. We have, for all w,

$$x + (y \uparrow z) \leqslant w$$

$=$ {   shunt '$x +$' out of the way in order to be

                able to apply the definition of maximum   }

$$y \uparrow z \leqslant w - x$$

$=$ {   definition of max   }

$$y \leqslant w - x \wedge z \leqslant w - x$$

$=$ {   shunt '$x +$' back in order to be

                able to apply the definition of maximum   }

$$x + y \leqslant w \wedge x + z \leqslant w$$

$=$ {   definition of max   }

$$(x + y) \uparrow (x + z) \leqslant w \quad .$$

Thus, by indirect equality,

$$x + (y \uparrow z) = (x + y) \uparrow (x + z) \quad .$$

Try the following for yourself, observing carefully the properties of conjunction that you exploit.

Exercise 8.4. Prove the following.

(a) $x \uparrow x = x$.

(b) $x \uparrow y = y \uparrow x$. $\square$

Another property we can derive from the definition is by using contraposition:

true

$=$ {   definition of maximum   }

$x \uparrow y \leqslant z \;\equiv\; x \leqslant z \wedge y \leqslant z$

$=$ {   contrapositive }

$\neg (x \uparrow y \leqslant z) \;\equiv\; \neg (x \leqslant z \wedge y \leqslant z)$

$=$ {   De Morgan   }

$\neg (x \uparrow y \leqslant z) \;\equiv\; \neg (x \leqslant z) \vee \neg (y \leqslant z)$

$=$ { $\neg (u \leqslant v) \equiv v < u$ }

$z < x \uparrow y \;\equiv\; z < x \vee z < y$.

Thus we have derived

$$z < x \uparrow y \;\equiv\; z < x \vee z < y \text{ .}$$

This too is a distributivity property: the function $(z <)$ distributes over maximum turning it into a disjunction. Now we verify that the function $(z \leqslant)$ also distributes over maximum using the properties of disjunction as opposed to the properties of conjunction.

$z \leqslant x \vee z \leqslant y$.

$=$ {   definition   }

$(z = x \vee z < x) \vee (z = y \vee z < y)$

$=$ {   rearrangement of terms

(allowed because disjunction is symmetric and

associative)   }

$(z = x \vee z = y) \vee (z < x \vee z < y)$

$=$ {   in the second disjunct: $z < x \uparrow y \;\equiv\; z < x \vee z < y$ }

$z = x \vee z = y \vee z < x \uparrow y$

$=$ {   See the calculation below.   }

$z \leqslant x \uparrow y$.

The last step in the above needs justification. On the face of it, it looks like the step is an easy one. After all,

$$z \leqslant x \uparrow y \;\equiv\; z = x \uparrow y \vee z < x \uparrow y \text{ ,}$$

so that it looks like we just need to replace $z = x \vee z = y$ by $z = x \uparrow y$. But it is not the case that $z = x \vee z = y \;\equiv\; z = x \uparrow y$ in general. A bit more thought is necessary.

To complete the proof, we use a *ping-pong* argument. That is, we prove an equivalence by mutual implication. Here is how it goes.

$$z = x \ \lor \ z = y \ \lor \ z < x \uparrow y$$

$\Leftarrow \qquad \{ \qquad x \uparrow y = x \ \lor \ x \uparrow y = y \ \}$

$$z = x \uparrow y \ \lor \ z < x \uparrow y$$

$= \qquad \{ \qquad \text{definition of } \leqslant \ \}$

$$z \leqslant x \uparrow y$$

$\Leftarrow \qquad \{ \qquad x \leqslant x \uparrow y, y \leqslant x \uparrow y \ \}$

$$z = x \ \lor \ z = y \ \lor \ z < x \uparrow y \ .$$

Note that the first two steps of this calculation prove that

$$z = x \ \lor \ z = y \ \lor \ z < x \uparrow y \ \Leftarrow \ z \leqslant x \uparrow y$$

and the final step proves that

$$z \leqslant x \uparrow y \ \Leftarrow \ z = x \ \lor \ z = y \ \lor \ z < x \uparrow y \ .$$

(Formally, the final step involves the use of the rule

$$p \Leftarrow q \lor r \ \equiv \ (p \Leftarrow q) \land (p \Leftarrow r) \ .$$

The two hints establish that $z \leqslant x \uparrow y \Leftarrow z = x$ and $z \leqslant x \uparrow y \Leftarrow z = y$, respectively, and the final conjunct is the straightforward property $z \leqslant x \uparrow y \Leftarrow z < x \uparrow y$. The final step is thus not as simple as it looks.) The required equivalence follows by the rule of mutual implication.

Summarizing, we have proved that

$$z \leqslant x \uparrow y \ \equiv \ z \leqslant x \lor z \leqslant y \ . \tag{8.5}$$

So the function $(z \leqslant)$ also distributes over maximum turning it into a disjunction.

8.3 Exercises

Try the following exercises. The definition of minimum is dual to the definition of maximum. That is, its definition is obtained by 'turning the ordering around': replacing maximum by minimum, and at-most by at-least, in the definition of maximum:

$$\textbf{[Minimum]} \quad z \leqslant x \downarrow y \ \equiv \ z \leqslant x \land z \leqslant y \ . \tag{8.6}$$

Begin by dualizing all the results given above. Observe the similarity in the properties of $\downarrow$ and $\lor$, and $\uparrow$ and $\land$. Property 8.7 (a) is like the distributivity law,

$$p \lor (q \land r) \equiv (p \lor q) \land (p \lor r) \ ,$$

whilst 8.7 (b) is like the absorption law

$$p \vee (q \wedge p) \equiv p \ .$$

Finally, 8.7 (c) is like the identity between the first and last expressions in Exercise 7.15.

Exercise 8.7. Prove the following.

(a) $x{\downarrow}(y{\uparrow}z) = (x{\downarrow}y){\uparrow}(x{\downarrow}z)$.

(b) $x{\downarrow}(y{\uparrow}x) = x$.

(c) $(x{\downarrow}y){\uparrow}(y{\downarrow}z){\uparrow}(z{\downarrow}x) = (x{\uparrow}y){\downarrow}(y{\uparrow}z){\downarrow}(z{\uparrow}x)$.   □

Exercise 8.8. The absolute value $|x|$ of real number x is $x{\uparrow}(-x)$. Identify some immediate consequences of this definition (by instantiating the properties of maximum above). Then prove the triangular inequality

$$|x{+}y| \leqslant |x|{+}|y| \ ,$$

and also

$$||x|{-}|y|| \leqslant |x{-}y| \ .$$

Hint: in each case use the rule of *indirect order*: to prove that $u \leqslant v$, prove that, for an arbitrary w of the same type as u and v,

$$u \leqslant w \Leftarrow v \leqslant w \ .$$

The absolute value of a real number is often defined by a case analysis on whether the number is positive or not. This leads to so-called 'tedious but straightforward' proofs by case analysis of the above properties. Your proofs should not involve any case analysis; they should be straightforward, but not tedious.   □

Exercise 8.9. Prove that $\lfloor x \rfloor {\downarrow} \lfloor y \rfloor = \lfloor x {\downarrow} y \rfloor$.   □

The final example is about maximum and minimum, but not with respect to the usual at-most relation on real numbers. Instead, the ordering relation is divisibility of natural numbers.

Exercise 8.10. Every (strictly) positive integer has a unique prime factorization. That is, every (strictly) positive integer n can be expressed as a product of the form $p_0^{a_0} \times p_1^{a_1} \times p_2^{a_2} \times \ldots$, where $p_0, p_1, p_2, \ldots$ is a list of all prime numbers[1] and each a_i is a natural number.

Suppose p is a prime number. We call a the *p-exponent of* n if p^a is a term in the prime factorization of n. This question is about the algebraic properties of exponents.

First, note that the relation 'divides' is a partial ordering on positive integers since it is reflexive (n divides n for all n), transitive (if k divides m and m divides

---

[1] A prime number is a number greater than 1 that is divisible by only itself and the number 1.

n, then k divides n) and antisymmetric (if m divides n and n divides m then m and n are equal). We shall write $m \backslash n$, meaning m divides n.

The minimum of two numbers in the partially ordered set of positive numbers ordered by divisibility is their greatest common divisor. Their maximum is their least common multiple. That is, for all k, m and n,

$$k \backslash m \,\wedge\, k \backslash n \;\equiv\; k \backslash \gcd(m, n) \;,$$

and

$$m \backslash k \,\wedge\, n \backslash k \;\equiv\; \mathsf{lcm}(m, n) \backslash k \;.$$

Given prime number p, we let $\mathsf{exp}.n$ denote the p-exponent of n. It is defined by the Galois connection: for all natural numbers m and n,

$$m \leqslant \mathsf{exp}.n \;\equiv\; p^m \backslash n \;.$$

(Read '$\mathsf{exp}.n$ is the greatest m such that p^m divides n'.)

With these preliminaries we can now pose the following questions.

(a) Show that $\mathsf{exp}.p = 1$.

(b) Derive an operator $\ominus$ such that

$$\mathsf{exp}.\gcd(m, n) \;=\; \mathsf{exp}.m \ominus \mathsf{exp}.n \;.$$

(c) Derive an operator $\otimes$ such that

$$\mathsf{exp}.(m \times n) \;=\; \mathsf{exp}.m \otimes \mathsf{exp}.n \;.$$

(You will need to use existential quantification—see Section 11.3.2—to complete this final part of the exercise. Specifically, for prime number p,

$$p^k \backslash m \times n \;=\; \langle \exists\, i, j : k = i + j : p^i \backslash m \,\wedge\, p^j \backslash n \rangle \;.)$$

$\square$

8.4 Summary

The maximum and minimum operators can be defined by an equivalence relation connecting the operators to conjunction and disjunction in the propositional calculus. This facilitates proving that maximum and minimum share many properties in common with conjunction and disjunction (such as associativity, idempotence and absorption). In particular, the tedious case analyses, unavoidable when maximum and minimum are defined by a conditional statement, are avoided entirely.

Bibliographic Remarks

Much of this chapter is drawn from Feijen and Bijlsma (1990).

9

The Assignment Statement

This chapter introduces the formal specification and construction of programs. A notation for formally specifying programs is introduced and applied to assignment statements. Simple illustrations of how assignments are constructed to meet their specifications are given.

9.1 Hoare Triples

When writing computer programs, it is very good practice to comment them thoroughly in order to explain what is going on. It helps the programmer to avoid errors by enforcing greater clarity, and it helps others who need to modify the program at a later date (including the one who wrote the program in the first place!). It is a good discipline, for example, to comment every variable declaration with a statement about the variable's function in the program. This has the additional benefit of disciplining the programmer to use distinct variables for distinct functions, rather than overloading a variable with several different functions.

Comments can also be almost useless. The comment

```
increment i by 1
```

immediately preceding the C/Java statement

```
i++
```

is completely useless to the experienced programmer who can be expected to know that 'i++' means 'increment i by one' in C/Java idiom.

Useless comments are ones that simply repeat in natural language (with all its complexities, nuances and ambiguities) what is stated simply and precisely in the program statements. They are *operational* in the sense that they repeat in words the instructions given to the computer in symbols. Good comments, on the other hand, should have added value. They should supplement the program text with explanations of the program's function and why the code that is used achieves that function.

In this text, comments will be indicated by enclosing them in curly brackets—'{' and '}'. The comments we write state formal properties of the program variables at a particular point in the execution of the program. For example, the text of a program may look like

$$\ldots \quad \{i = 0\} \quad \ldots \quad ,$$

where the dots represent some arbitrary program statements. The intended meaning is that, when execution of the program has reached the point in the program text where the comment appears, the value of the variable i is guaranteed to be zero[1]. Such comments are called *assertions*, *conditions* or *properties*. They are boolean-valued functions of the values of the program variables; by adding them to the program, the claim is being made that they are true at that point in the program's execution. Typical examples of such assertions (albeit written in English rather than as mathematical expressions) can be seen by referring back to the search program shown in Figure 4.1.

When a program statement is bracketed by two comments, as for example in

$$\{\, 0 < i \,\}\; i := i-1 \;\{\, 0 \leqslant i \,\} \; ,$$

we reason about the correctness of the program statement (here '$i := i-1$') on the basis that the first comment (here '$0 < i$') acts as an assumption. That is, we understand the comments as claiming that *if* $0 < i$ before the statement $i := i-1$ is executed, *then* $0 \leqslant i$ after the assignment has been executed. (This is, of course, a valid claim in this particular instance provided that i has type integer.)

An expression of the form

$$\{\, P \,\}\, S \,\{\, Q \,\} \; ,$$

where P and Q are properties of the program variables and S is a program statement (some portion of the program text), is called a *Hoare triple*. The property P is called the *precondition*, and the property Q is called the *postcondition* of the statement S. We read such a triple as the claim that, if the program variables satisfy property P before execution of statement S, execution of S is guaranteed to terminate and, afterwards, the program variables will satisfy property Q. A Hoare triple thus denotes a boolean value; if the value is true, we say the triple is *valid*, and, if it is false, we say the triple is *invalid*.

---

[1] **Important warning to C/Java programmers**: the equality symbol '=' really means equality here and not assignment.

The following are examples of *valid* Hoare triples:

$$\{\, i = 0 \,\}\ i := i+1 \ \{\, i = 1 \,\} \ ,$$
$$\{\, i+j = 0 \,\}\ i := i+1 \ ; j := j-1 \ \{\, i+j = 0 \,\} \ ,$$
$$\{\, \mathsf{true} \,\}\ i := 1 \ \{\, i = 1 \,\} \ .$$

Note the use of the precondition true in the final example. A true precondition describes all states of the program variables; the claim is thus that *whatever the initial value of the program variables* (in particular the variable i) after execution of the assignment $i := 1$ the property $i = 1$ will hold.

The following are examples of *invalid* Hoare triples:

$$\{\, i = 1 \,\}\ i := i+1 \ \{\, i = 0 \,\} \ ,$$
$$\{\, i+j \neq 0 \,\}\ i := i+1 \ ; j := j-1 \ \{\, i+j = 0 \,\} \ ,$$
$$\{\, \mathsf{true} \,\}\ i := 1 \ \{\, i = 0 \,\} \ .$$

The first and last are obviously not valid. The middle example is shown to be invalid by supposing, for example, that i and j are initially 0 and 1. Then the precondition $i+j \neq 0$ is indeed satisfied but, after execution of the two assignment statements, i and j have values 1 and 0, respectively, and $i+j$ is 1. So, the postcondition $i+j = 0$ is not satisfied.

Exercise 9.1. Using your current knowledge, say which of the following are valid Hoare triples. Assume that i, j and N are integers. (Shortly we show how to validate Hoare triples formally.)

(a) $\{\, i = 1 \,\}\ j := i \ \{\, i = j = 1 \,\} \ .$

(b) $\{\, i = 1 \,\}\ i := j \ \{\, i = j = 1 \,\} \ .$

(c) $\{\, 0 \leqslant i < N \,\}\ i := i+1 \ \{\, 0 < i \leqslant N \,\} \ .$

(d) $\{\, \mathsf{true} \,\}\ i := j+1 \ \{\, i < j \,\} \ .$

(e) $\{\, i = 1 \,\}\ i := 0 \ \{\, \mathsf{true} \,\} \ .$

(f) $\{\, i = 0 \,\}\ i := 1 \ \{\, \mathsf{false} \,\} \ .$

(g) $\{\, \mathsf{false} \,\}\ i := 1 \ \{\, i = 0 \,\} \ .$ □

9.2   Ghost Variables

Consider the following sequential composition of three statements:

$$t := x \ ; x := y \ ; y := t \ .$$

Its purpose is to interchange the values of x and y, the variable t being used as a scratch variable. We can see this by the following chain of reasoning. After the first assignment, both x and t have the original value of x, and y has its original value. After the second assignment, t has the original value of x, and x and y have the original value of y. Finally, after the third assignment, x has the original value of y, and y has the original value of x.

To document this argument effectively, we need to adopt some notational conventions. Firstly, we need a mechanism for expressing predicates like 't has the original value of x'. Secondly, we need a notation for saying that 'if the program segment is executed, then, afterwards, x will have the original value of y'. The notation we use is the following:

$$\{\, x = \mathsf{X} \,\wedge\, y = \mathsf{Y} \}$$
$$t := x \,;\, x := y \,;\, y := t$$
$$\{\, x = \mathsf{Y} \,\wedge\, y = \mathsf{X} \} \;.$$

The assertions added before and after the assignment statements refer to variables X and Y that appear nowhere in the assignments themselves. These are called *ghost* variables. Their function is to relate the final values of the program variables to their initial values. In general, an expression of the form

$$\{\, P \,\}\, S \,\{\, Q \,\} \;,$$

where P and Q are predicates on a collection of program variables and ghost variables, means that, *for all possible values of the ghost variables*, if the program variables satisfy property P before execution of statement S, execution of S is guaranteed to terminate, and, afterwards, the program variables will satisfy property Q. So, the claim above is that, for all values of X and Y, if $x = \mathsf{X} \,\wedge\, y = \mathsf{Y}$ before executing the sequence of assignments $t := x \,;\, x := y \,;\, y := t$, then, afterwards, $x = \mathsf{Y} \,\wedge\, y = \mathsf{X}$.

Using the same notation, we can expand the claim, giving details of its justification:

$$\{\, x = \mathsf{X} \,\wedge\, y = \mathsf{Y} \}$$
$$t := x \,;$$
$$\{\, t = x = \mathsf{X} \,\wedge\, y = \mathsf{Y} \}$$
$$x := y \,;$$
$$\{\, t = \mathsf{X} \,\wedge\, x = y = \mathsf{Y} \}$$
$$y := t$$
$$\{\, x = \mathsf{Y} \,\wedge\, y = \mathsf{X} \} \;.$$

A sequence of statements, parenthesized in this way by assertions, is called a *tableau*. We can read such a tableau as a collection of three claims, one for each of the individual assignments as shown below.

(1) $\{x = \mathsf{X} \wedge y = \mathsf{Y}\}$ If $x = \mathsf{X}$ and $y = \mathsf{Y}$ when
     $t := x$ $t := x$ is executed
     $\{t = x = \mathsf{X} \wedge y = \mathsf{Y}\}$ then afterwards $t = x = \mathsf{X}$ and $y = \mathsf{Y}$.

(2) $\{t = x = \mathsf{X} \wedge y = \mathsf{Y}\}$ If $t = x = \mathsf{X}$ and $y = \mathsf{Y}$ when
     $x := y$ $x := y$ is executed
     $\{t = \mathsf{X} \wedge x = y = \mathsf{Y}\}$ then afterwards $t = \mathsf{X}$ and $x = y = \mathsf{Y}$.

(3) $\{t = \mathsf{X} \wedge x = y = \mathsf{Y}\}$ If $t = \mathsf{X}$ and $x = y = \mathsf{Y}$ when
     $y := t$ $y := t$ is executed
     $\{x = \mathsf{Y} \wedge y = \mathsf{X}\}$ then afterwards $x = \mathsf{Y}$ and $y = \mathsf{X}$.

Additionally, we can read the tableau as making claims about subsequences of the three assignments. For instance, omitting the last-but-one assertion, the tableau asserts the following about the last two assignments.

(4) $\{t = x = \mathsf{X} \wedge y = \mathsf{Y}\}$ If $t = x = \mathsf{X}$ and $y = \mathsf{Y}$ when
     $x := y \,;\, y := t$ $x := y$ followed by $y := t$ is executed
     $\{x = \mathsf{Y} \wedge y = \mathsf{X}\}$ then afterwards $x = \mathsf{Y}$ and $y = \mathsf{X}$.

We shall see in Chapter 10 that, provided the claims about each of the individual assignments (claims (1), (2) and (3) above) are valid, any claim about a composition of assignments, obtained by omitting the intermediate assertions as we did in (4) above, is also valid.

9.3   Hoare Triples as Program Specifications

The specification of a program, in its simplest form, is a relation between input values and output values. The specification of a sorting program, for example, would require that the input is an array of values and the output is the same array but sorted according to some given function on the elements of the array. The precise and clear specification of computer programs is a demanding task that needs to be done with great care and attention to detail. Here, we only consider very simple specifications.

It is important to note that specifications are, commonly, *non-deterministic*. That is, the output values are typically not completely determined by the input values, thus giving some latitude in what is acceptable output for given input. For example, when sorting the entries in a table by, say, date of last access, the program is free to list entries last accessed on the same day in an arbitrary order. In mathematical terms, specifications are truly *relations* and not *functions*.

The emphasis in this text is on methods for *constructing* programs to meet their specifications (so-called *correct-by-construction* design methods). A program *S* is specified by stating a *precondition P* and a *postcondition Q* (possibly involving ghost variables in order to relate input and output values) and requiring that *S* be constructed to satisfy

$$\{ P \} S \{ Q \} .$$

If so, we say that *S establishes* (postcondition) *Q under the assumption of* precondition *P*.

The notation $\{ P \} S \{ Q \}$ is so important that it is worth repeating its meaning and making it stand out.

$\{ P \} S \{ Q \}$ means that, for all possible values of the variables in *P*, *S* and *Q*, if, initially, the state of the program variables satisfies the predicate *P* and the statement *S* is executed, *S* is guaranteed to terminate and, on termination of *S*, the final state will satisfy the predicate *Q*.

Although we use Hoare triples exclusively in this text to specify programs, they do have a number of inadequacies which we need to overcome. The reason for choosing Hoare triples as specification mechanism is that they fit in well with the simple process of adding comments to the program text.

Four problems with the use of Hoare triples are

(a) we are forced to name the variables to be used in the program (whereas the names are irrelevant to the specification),

(b) there is no way of saying which variables may be altered in the course of execution of the program and which should remain constant (that is, there is no distinction between input and output variables),

(c) there is no way of limiting the mechanisms for updating the values of the output variables,

(d) an artificial mechanism—the 'ghost' variables discussed above—often needs to be employed to relate the input values of variables to their desired output values.

We ignore the first problem. It is a nuisance rather than a serious issue, and one that is impossible to avoid entirely.

The second problem is more serious. It is illustrated by a very simple example. If we require that program *S* satisfies

$$\{ \text{ true } \} S \{ i = j \} ,$$

then this can be achieved by the assignments

$$i := j$$

and

$$j := i ,$$

there being no way to distinguish between the two variables. In reality, however, one of i and j would store the input value and the other the output value, and the requirement would be to assign a value to the output variable so as to meet the specification, leaving the value of the input variable unchanged. A program to determine whether a student is registered for a module would not be acceptable if it altered the register in the process!

It is possible to avoid this problem formally using a so-called *specification statement*. (See the bibliographic notes for references.) The problem is resolved here informally—we state which are the input and which are the output variables in the text accompanying the formal specification.

Problem (c) is also resolved informally. The issue here is that implementations are limited by the implementation language. The limitations are sometimes imposed to improve efficiency. For example, when sorting a very large collection of data, it is undesirable to make copies of large portions. Sometimes, a requirement is that the implementation be limited to functions supplied by a given library. For example, a hardware implementation of a given specification might require that the implementation be composed of circuits from a small base collection.

Problem (d) is exemplified by the specification of sorting programs. Sorting a list of values involves permuting the values in the list. But, if we simply require that the output list is sorted, the requirement can be met by outputting any list that is sorted without regard to the contents of the input list. The remedy for this problem, as already discussed in Section 9.2, is to introduce ghost variables. (Some authors call these *rigid* variables because their values do not change throughout the execution of the program. Some authors call them *auxiliary* variables.)

It is worthwhile giving another illustration of the use of ghost variables. Suppose we want to specify that the sum of two variables i and j should remain constant. For example, i and j may be initially zero. The requirement is then that, on termination, $i+j$ should also be zero. If, however, i and j are initially 1 and 2, we require that $i+j$ is 3 on termination of the program. We specify this by introducing a ghost variable C. This variable should not be used anywhere else in the program. Then the program S is specified by

$$\{\, i+j = \mathsf{C} \,\} \, S \, \{\, i+j = \mathsf{C} \,\} \;.$$

This says that if the sum of i and j has the value C before execution of statement S, execution of statement S is guaranteed to terminate in a state in which the sum of i and j still has the value C.

In summary, we specify a program S by supplying a precondition P and a post-condition Q and requiring that S be constructed to satisfy

$$\{\, P \,\} \, S \, \{\, Q \,\} \;.$$

In addition, we (informally) specify the input variables and the output variables of the program and their types. Ghost variables may be used to link the precondition to the postcondition. Ghost variables are treated just like ordinary program variables but the program code may not refer to them in any way. To distinguish ghost variables from normal program variables we use a sans serif type. Finally, we sometimes impose limitations on the primitives that may be used in the implementation of the specification. These limitations are stated informally.

9.4   Assignment Statements

The very simplest specifications can be met by assignment statements. An *assignment statement* has the form

$$x := e \ ,$$

where x is a program variable and e is an expression. It is executed by evaluating the expression e and then updating the value of the variable x to the value obtained. For example,

$$x := 2 \times y$$

evaluates twice the value of variable y and 'assigns' this value to x.

It is convenient to allow *simultaneous assignments*. In a simultaneous assignment, the left side is a list of variables and the right side is a list of expressions of the same length as the list of variables. A simultaneous assignment to three variables x, y and z is, for example,

$$x,y,z := 2 \times y, x+y, 3 \times z \ .$$

A simultaneous assignment

$$x_0, x_1, \ldots, x_n := e_0, e_1, \ldots, e_n$$

is executed by evaluating all of the expressions $e_0, e_1, \ldots, e_n$ and then, for each i, updating the value of the variable x_i to the value obtained for expression e_i. In the above example, $2 \times y$, $x+y$ and $3 \times z$ are all evaluated before assigning their values to x, y and z, respectively.

Simultaneous assignments are not allowed in many programming languages (C and Java, for example) but they are allowed in some (Perl, for example). It is unfortunate when they are not allowed because it is very simple to program a compiler to handle them, and their use contributes to the avoidance of error. An example is the assignment

$$x,y := y,x \ ,$$

which has the effect of swapping the values stored in variables x and y. Barred from using simultaneous assignments, the programmer is forced to introduce a local variable t, say, and write

$$t := x \ ; \ x := y \ ; \ y := t \ .$$

The number of times that programmers have had to write such a sequence of statements *and made a mistake*, for example in the order, must be countless.

There are, of course, restrictions on the use of simultaneous assignments. Basically, the variables on the left side should be pairwise distinct. For example, the assignment

$$x,x := 0,1$$

does not make sense (because it tries to assign the distinct values 0 and 1 simultaneously to the variable x) and is disallowed. Very occasionally it is useful to relax this requirement. The statement

$$a[i],a[j] := a[j],a[i]$$

swaps the array elements indexed by i and j. The statement makes sense whatever the values of i and j, including when they are equal. (When i and j are equal the statement means 'do nothing'.) Because it is convenient to do so, we also allow such statements. The rule is that, if a variable occurs more than once on the left side of an assignment, the corresponding expressions on the right side must be guaranteed to denote equal values.

9.5 The Assignment Axiom

We have already used the notation of simultaneous assignment in hints accompanying proof steps. There we used the notation to explain how a law is instantiated to a particular case. The coincidence of notations is deliberate. Rather than understanding the way an assignment is executed, we can also understand an assignment in terms of syntactic substitution. The key insight involves working *backwards* from postconditions to preconditions.

Suppose the assignment $x := e$ is required to establish the postcondition Q. The postcondition is any boolean-valued expression in the program variables, one of which is x. We can regard it as a local law governing the program variables immediately after execution of the assignment statement.

After the assignment, x will have the value of expression e before the assignment. So, if Q is to apply to x *after* the assignment, it should apply to e *before* the assignment. That is, the property $Q[x := e]$—the property Q but with all occurrences of 'x' replaced by 'e'—must hold in advance of executing the assignment. This is stated in the *assignment axiom*:

$$\textbf{[Assignment Axiom]} \quad \{\, Q[x := e] \,\}\, x := e \,\{\, Q \,\} \,. \tag{9.2}$$

The assignment axiom is a very straightforward rule, at least after having seen a number of examples! The dynamics of its use, something that is difficult to convey in the static pages of a textbook, is to work *backwards* from the postcondition.

The simplest example is provided by a postcondition of the form $x = c$, where c is some constant independent of the value of x and the assignment is $x := c$. For concreteness, let us consider the assignment $i := 0$ and postcondition $i = 0$. Then the assignment axiom requires us to replace 'i' everywhere it occurs in the postcondition '$i = 0$' by '0'. (This is a syntactic substitution, which is why we have used inverted commas.) This gives the precondition '$0 = 0$'. So, application of the assignment axiom gives

$$\{ 0 = 0 \} \; i := 0 \; \{ i = 0 \} \; .$$

Of course, $0 = 0$ simplifies to true. The conclusion is, thus,

$$\{ \text{true} \} \; i := 0 \; \{ i = 0 \} \; .$$

(Replacing $0 = 0$ by true is a semantic replacement as it depends on the meaning of equality.) In words, beginning in an arbitrary state, execution of the assignment $i := 0$ is guaranteed to terminate in a state satisfying $i = 0$.

As a second example, consider the assignment $i := 2 \times i$ and postcondition $i < 10$. Replacing 'i' by '$2 \times i$' in the postcondition gives '$2 \times i < 10$' so that application of the assignment axiom results in

$$\{ 2 \times i < 10 \} \; i := 2 \times i \; \{ i < 10 \} \; .$$

Again, the precondition can be simplified, this time to $i < 5$. We conclude that

$$\{ i < 5 \} \; i := 2 \times i \; \{ i < 10 \} \; .$$

In words, beginning in a state in which i is less than 5, execution of the assignment $i := 2 \times i$ is guaranteed to terminate in a state satisfying i is less than 10.

The assignment axiom is equally valid when x is a list of variables and e is an equal-length list of expressions. If x is the list $x_0, x_1, \ldots, x_n$ and e is the list $e_0, e_1, \ldots, e_n$, then $Q[x := e]$ denotes the *simultaneous* substitution of e_0 for x_0, e_1 for x_1, and so on.

To illustrate this, consider the postcondition $i + j = \mathsf{C}$ and the simultaneous assignment $i, j := i+1, j-1$. Then, simultaneously substituting '$i+1$' for 'i' and '$j-1$' for 'j', application of the assignment axiom gives

$$\{ (i+1) + (j-1) = \mathsf{C} \} \; i, j := i+1, j-1 \; \{ i+j = \mathsf{C} \} \; .$$

Simplifying the precondition, we get

$$\{ i+j = \mathsf{C} \} \; i, j := i+1, j-1 \; \{ i+j = \mathsf{C} \} \; .$$

Thus, simultaneously incrementing i by 1 and decrementing j by 1 keeps the value of $i + j$ constant.

Note that we introduced parentheses around '$i+1$' and '$j-1$' when performing the above substitutions. This is because one has to take care with precedence conventions when making such substitutions. An example of where things can go wrong is as follows. Suppose the postcondition is $i-j = C$ and the assignment is as above $i,j := i+1, j-1$. Then the assignment axiom gives

$$\{ (i+1) - (j-1) = C \} \, i,j := i+1, j-1 \{ i-j = C \} \; ,$$

which simplifies to

$$\{ (i-j)+2 = C \} \, i,j := i+1, j-1 \{ i-j = C \} \; .$$

Had we omitted to parenthesize '$j-1$' when performing the substitution we would have got

$$\{ i+1-j-1 = C \} \, i,j := i+1, j-1 \{ i-j = C \} \; ,$$

which simplifies to

$$\{ i-j = C \} \, i,j := i+1, j-1 \{ i-j = C \} \; .$$

This is of course wrong: take C to be 0 and i and j to be 1 before the assignment. Then the precondition $i-j = C$ is satisfied. But, after the assignment, i has value 2 and j has value 0. So, $i-j = 2$, which is not equal to the value of C.

Exercise 9.3. Using the assignment axiom (9.2), determine preconditions for the following statements and postconditions. Simplify the preconditions you obtain.

	Statement	Postcondition
(a)	$x := x+1$	$x+y < 10$
(b)	$x := x-1$	$x^2 + 2 \cdot x = 0$
(c)	$x,y := x-y, x+y$	$x \cdot y = 1$
(d)	$x,y,z := z,x,y$	$x = 0 \lor y = 1 \lor z = 2$

□

9.6 Calculating Assignments

Given a specification in terms of a precondition-postcondition pair, it is often possible to *calculate* an assignment statement that does the job. Many examples involve a property that is to be maintained invariant whilst progress is made by incrementing (or decrementing) a counter.

We begin with a simple example. Suppose the requirement is to maintain the value of the sum $j+k$ constant whilst incrementing k by 1. We can formulate this requirement by introducing a ghost variable C; the precondition is then $j+k = C$ and the postcondition is also $j+k = C$. Our task is to calculate an expression X such that

$$\{ j+k = C \} \, j,k := X, k+1 \{ j+k = C \} \; .$$

Applying the assignment axiom, we get

$$\{ X+k+1 = C \} \, j,k := X, k+1 \{ j+k = C \} \; .$$

Comparing the precondition so obtained with the given precondition, the specification is met if

$$j+k = \mathsf{C} \Rightarrow X+k+1 = \mathsf{C} \ .$$

In words, the postcondition $j+k = \mathsf{C}$ is guaranteed to hold after execution of the assignment $j,k := X,k+1$ if before its execution $X+k+1 = \mathsf{C}$. But the latter is true before execution if it is implied by the given precondition $j+k = \mathsf{C}$.

In this way, we have constructed a functional specification of the expression X in terms of j, k and C. Our task is complete if we can find a solution for X not involving the ghost variable C. This we do by manipulating the left side of the implication until something of the same shape as the right side is obtained. Now,

$$
\begin{aligned}
& j+k \\
= \quad & \{ \qquad \text{arithmetic—introducing `}k+1\text{' } \} \\
& j+k+1-1 \\
= \quad & \{ \qquad \text{rearranging } \} \\
& (j-1)+k+1 \ .
\end{aligned}
$$

So, for all C,

$$j+k = \mathsf{C} \equiv (j-1)+k+1 = \mathsf{C} \ .$$

Recalling the above discussion, it thus follows that a suitable value of X is $j-1$. That is,

$$\{ j+k = \mathsf{C} \} \ j,k := j-1,k+1 \ \{ j+k = \mathsf{C} \} \ .$$

A more complicated example is this. Suppose variables s and n satisfy the property

$$s = n^2$$

and we want to increment n by 1 whilst maintaining this relationship between s and n. Of course this is trivially satisfied by the assignment

$$s,n := (n+1)^2,n+1 \ .$$

(Note that this takes no account of the given precondition.) However, we add the further requirement that squaring is not allowed—the computation of s should only involve additions and not multiplications. So, our goal is to calculate an expression X involving only addition such that

$$\{ s = n^2 \} \ s,n := s+X,n+1 \ \{ s = n^2 \} \ .$$

Applying the assignment axiom, we get

$$\{ s+X = (n+1)^2 \} \ s,n := s+X,n+1 \ \{ s = n^2 \} \ .$$

Comparing with the specification we calculate X so that

$$s = n^2 \;\Rightarrow\; s + X = (n+1)^2 \;.$$

Now,

$$(n+1)^2$$

$=$ {   arithmetic—introducing 'n^2' }

$$n^2 + 2n + 1$$

$=$ {   assume $s = n^2$ }

$$s + 2n + 1 \;.$$

That is,

$$s = n^2 \;\Rightarrow\; s + 2n + 1 = (n+1)^2 \;.$$

In this way, we have calculated the required assignment statement:

$$\{\, s = n^2 \,\}\; s,n \;:=\; s + 2n + 1 \,,\, n+1 \;\{\, s = n^2 \,\} \;.$$

Some of these examples and the exercises below may seem quite trivial. It is tempting in some cases to guess the appropriate assignment and then verify it. Calculation is, however, much more reliable. It is in solving 'trivial' problems like these that so-called 'one-off' errors are made, often because it is human nature to guess and then *not bother* to verify. The consequences can be disastrous.

The use of simultaneous assignments increases reliability if the discipline of calculating right sides is applied. If a sequential composition of assignments is used instead, mistakes occur because of confusion over the right order in which to apply the assignments. Sometimes, sequencing the assignments can be more efficient, but the efficiency gains are minor and it is much more reliable to leave such details to an optimizing compiler.

Exercise 9.4. Suppose there are two integer variables m and n. Suppose a given precondition is that m is even. Calculate the assignment to n that maintains invariant the product $m \times n$ under the division of m by two. In other words, calculate X such that for arbitrary C

$$\{\, m \times n = C \,\wedge\, \text{even}.m \,\}\; m,n \;:=\; m \div 2, X \;\{\, m \times n = C \,\} \;.$$

$\square$

Exercise 9.5. Suppose there are three program variables n, s and t. Calculate assignments to s and t that maintain invariant the relationship

$$s = n^2 \,\wedge\, t = n^3 \;.$$

In other words, calculate X and Y such that

$$\{\, s = n^2 \,\wedge\, t = n^3 \,\}\; s,t,n \;:=\; s + X, t + Y, n + 1 \;\{\, s = n^2 \,\wedge\, t = n^3 \,\} \;.$$

The assignments to s and t should involve additions only. Multiplications are not allowed.   □

Exercise 9.6. The factorial function $n!$ satisfies the equations

$$0! = 1$$

and, for all natural numbers n,

$$(n{+}1)! \;=\; (n{+}1) \times n! \;\;.$$

Suppose program variables f and n satisfy the property

$$f \;=\; n!$$

and it is required to maintain this property by a suitable assignment to f whilst simultaneously incrementing n by 1. Calculate the assignment.   □

Exercise 9.7. The Fibonacci function fib satisfies the equations

$$\text{fib}.0 = 0$$
$$\text{fib}.1 = 1$$

and, for all natural numbers n,

$$\text{fib}.(n{+}2) \;=\; \text{fib}.(n{+}1) + \text{fib}.n \;\;.$$

Suppose program variables f, g and n satisfy the property

$$f = \text{fib}.n \;\wedge\; g = \text{fib}.(n{+}1)$$

and it is required to maintain this property by suitable assignments to f and g whilst simultaneously incrementing n by 1. Calculate the assignments.   □

9.7 Complications

The assignment axiom, as we have presented it, is not completely correct because it ignores the problems of undefined expressions. It ignores, for example, the problem of division by zero in an arithmetic expression. It also ignores overflow and underflow errors (calculating numbers that are too large or too small for the computer to handle) and out-of-bound errors in array indexing.

A more complete statement of the assignment axiom is

$$\{\; \text{`}e\text{'} \text{ is well defined} \;\wedge\; Q[x := e] \;\} \; x := e \; \{\, Q \,\} \;\;.$$

Determining whether 'e' is well defined depends on the primitive operators used in 'e' (for example '$m/0$' is not well defined) and, possibly, the size limitations of the computer on which the program is to be executed. (The inverted commas are there because it is the syntactic form of the expression that is relevant. For example, '$(m \times n)/n$' may be simplified to 'm'. The former may cause a divide-by-zero error, whereas the latter will not. Similarly, examples can be given where overflow may occur, whereas an equivalent expression does not cause overflow.)

In addition to taking account of the well-definedness of the right side of an assignment, it is also necessary to take account of whether the left and right sides have the same type and, if not, the effect of automatic type conversions. Some of the issues surrounding the latter have been discussed in Chapter 4. However, a full discussion of all these complications is beyond the scope of this text.

9.8 Summary

In this chapter, we have seen how to specify programs using precondition-postcondition pairs. We have also shown how to calculate assignment statements that meet a given specification. The basis is the assignment axiom, which is applied by working backwards from the postcondition to the precondition. Other topics that have been discussed are the use of ghost variables and complications arising from undefined right sides of assignments.

Bibliographic Remarks

The 'Hoare' triple notation for program specification, and the assignment axiom—crucially, in a form working backwards from the postcondition to the precondition—were introduced by C. A. R. Hoare in 1969 (see Hoare and Jones 1989, Chapter 4). Actually, the notation used by Hoare—$P\{S\}Q$—bracketed the program statement rather than the preconditions and postconditions. More significantly, $P\{S\}Q$ was defined to be *conditional* on the guaranteed termination of S. (Proving termination is something we return to later.)

It is becoming increasingly common for programming languages to include provision for assertions to be added to a program and processed by the compiler. The assertions are evaluated while the program is run in test mode, and their failure indicates where the printout of a diagnostic trace is needed. Sometimes they are evaluated in a running system, to trigger automatic re-initialization of data or a restart of the program (Hoare, 2001).

10

Sequential Composition and Conditional Statements

This chapter continues the discussion of the formal construction of programs. We discuss the decomposition of a programming problem into constructing a number of statements to be executed sequentially. We also discuss the decomposition of a programming problem into a number of distinct cases, solutions to which are then combined in a conditional statement. We observe a lack of symmetry in conventional if-then-else statements and propose, in their place, a so-called 'guarded command' for defining conditional statements. The rules governing the construction of sequential and conditional statements are applied to a number of examples.

10.1 Sequential Composition

It is common to decompose a problem into two (or more) simpler problems which are to be solved in some specific order. Many examples can be given. Finding the k best entries in a database can be solved, for example, by sorting all the entries and then extracting the first k entries. The amount of fuel that a car consumes on a journey of k kilometres is computed by determining the number of litres consumed per kilometre and then multiplying this amount by k. Counting the proportion of times that a particular letter occurs in the words in a text—say the proportion of words in this text that contain the letter 'e'—is computed by counting the total number of words in the text and, of these, the number that contain the given letter, and then finally dividing the latter by the former.

This problem-solving strategy is captured in programming terms by the sequential composition of statements, here denoted by an infix semicolon. Hoare triples are used to provide the mathematical basis for the strategy.

Suppose a programming problem is specified by giving a precondition P and postcondition Q. We are required to construct a program statement S to satisfy

$$\{ P \} \ S \ \{ Q \} \ .$$

We can decompose this problem by inventing a suitable *intermediate assertion R* and then constructing program statements $S1$ and $S2$ such that

$$\{ P \} \ S1 \ \{ R \}$$

and

$$\{ R \} \ S2 \ \{ Q \} \ .$$

Examples of intermediate assertions are 'the deck of cards is sorted' (in the case of finding the best k entries in a deck of cards), 'lpk is the number of litres consumed per kilometre' (in the case of computing fuel consumption over a given number of kilometres), or 'w is the number of words in the text and l is the number of such words containing the given letter' (in the case of counting the proportion of times that a particular letter occurs in a sequence of words).

The *sequential composition $S1$; $S2$* of statements $S1$ and $S2$ is executed by first executing statement $S1$ and then statement $S2$. If $S1$ has been constructed to satisfy

$$\{ P \} \ S1 \ \{ R \} \ , \tag{10.1}$$

it means that, if execution of $S1$ is begun in a state satisfying P, termination is guaranteed in a state satisfying R. Also, if $S2$ has been constructed to satisfy

$$\{ R \} \ S2 \ \{ Q \} \ , \tag{10.2}$$

it means that, if execution of $S2$ is begun in a state satisfying R, termination is guaranteed in a state satisfying Q. Clearly then, if execution of $S1$; $S2$ is begun in a state satisfying P, termination is guaranteed in a state satisfying Q. That is, given (10.1) and (10.2), it is the case that

$$\{ P \} \ S1 ; S2 \ \{ Q \} \ . \tag{10.3}$$

This is the *rule of sequential composition*: for all statements $S1$ and $S2$ and all assertions P, Q and R,

[Sequence] $\{P\}\ S1;S2\ \{Q\}\ \Leftarrow\ \{P\}\ S1\ \{R\}\ \wedge\ \{R\}\ S2\ \{Q\}$.

$$(10.4)$$

We have introduced the rule of sequential composition in terms of inventing a suitable intermediate assertion R. This is just one way the rule may be used. Another way is that we *invent* a program statement $S1$ that we think may be of use in solving the given programming problem. From the specification of $S1$, we *calculate* a postcondition R that is guaranteed to hold after executing $S1$ beginning in a state satisfying P. Finally, we solve the problem of constructing a program statement $S2$ that will guarantee the postcondition Q if execution of it is begun in a state satisfying precondition R.

Symmetrically, we may *invent* a program statement $S2$ that we think may be of use in solving the given programming problem. From the specification of $S2$, we *calculate* a precondition R that will guarantee Q after executing $S2$. Finally, we solve the problem of constructing a program statement $S1$ that will guarantee the postcondition R if execution of it is begun in a state satisfying precondition P.

These three different strategies (first inventing R, first inventing $S1$, or first inventing $S2$) are interrelated but it can be helpful for the more difficult problems to keep them separate in one's mind. It is difficult to give realistic but simple examples at this stage. An example combining the rule of sequential composition with the construction of conditional statements is discussed in Section 10.6.

10.2 The skip Statement

Sequential composition is associative. That is, it does not matter whether we read $S;T;U$ as $(S;T);U$ or as $S;(T;U)$. The statement $(S;T);U$ is executed by first executing $S;T$ and then executing U; the statement $S;(T;U)$ is executed by first executing S and then executing $T;U$. Both boil down to executing S then T then U. This is a rule that we use in many places, but always without explicit mention of the fact.

Sequential composition also has a unit. It is the 'do-nothing' statement. Most often, there is no need to waste ink on doing nothing. Sometimes, we do want to make the operation explicit, in which case we denote it by skip. Doing nothing means leaving the state of the program variables unchanged. So, clearly,

$$\text{skip};S\ =\ S\ =\ S;\text{skip} ,$$

confirming that skip is the (left and right) unit of sequential composition.

Doing nothing does not seem a very useful operation to do, so introducing a notation for it does not seem useful either. Like the introduction of zero in the number system, the consideration of extreme cases often meets with resistance but is, in fact, very important. We will see that the skip statement does have its uses.

Formally, { P } skip { Q } means that, beginning in a state satisfying P, the act of doing nothing is guaranteed to terminate in a state satisfying Q. It is thus equivalent to [$P \Rightarrow Q$], where the square brackets mean that the statement $P \Rightarrow Q$ is true in *all* states. This is the skip rule:

[Skip]   { P } skip { Q } $\equiv$ [$P \Rightarrow Q$] .   (10.5)

We recommend that the square brackets are read as 'in all states'. The skip rule is then read as 'beginning in a state satisfying P, execution of skip (i.e. doing nothing) is guaranteed to terminate in a state satisfying Q if, in all states, P implies Q'.

In most cases, skip is not explicit (think of it as being written with zero amount of ink). The skip rule is thus most often used in the form:

[Weakening]   { P } { Q } $\equiv$ [$P \Rightarrow Q$] .   (10.6)

So, if two assertions appear consecutively in a program, the intended meaning is that the first assertion is always true at that point in the program's execution, but may be weakened to the second assertion without affecting the program's correctness.

We have already made use of (10.6) without making it explicit. Indeed, the assignment axiom gives the *weakest* precondition that will guarantee a given postcondition after execution of an assignment. For example, $0 < k+1$ is the precondition obtained by applying the assignment axiom given postcondition $0 < k$ and assignment $k := k+1$. However, the given precondition might be $0 < k$. (In words, we might be interested in showing that the assignment $k := k+1$ maintains invariant the property that k is strictly positive.) In terms of Hoare triples, we have

$$\{ 0 < k \} \{ 0 < k+1 \} \ k := k+1 \ \{ 0 < k \} .$$

The precondition $0 < k+1$ is the weakest property guaranteeing that $0 < k$ after the assignment $k := k+1$; it is calculated using the assignment rule. The precondition $0 < k$ is stronger than $0 < k+1$. (That is, for all k, $0 < k \Rightarrow 0 < k+1$.) So, using the rule of sequential composition (10.4), with $S1$ the skip statement, combined with the weakening rule (10.6), we infer that

$$\{ 0 < k \} \ k := k+1 \ \{ 0 < k \} .$$

Examples of the use of skip in constructing programs are given in Section 10.6.

10.3 Conditional Statements

Every programming language has some way of expressing the execution of a statement conditional on some property of the program variables. The most common form is the if-then-else statement. A statement of the form

if b **then** S **else** T

is executed by evaluating the boolean expression b; if b evaluates to true, the statement S is executed, otherwise ('else') the statement T is executed. For example, the statement

if $x \leqslant 0$ **then** $y := -x$ **else** $y := x$

assigns to y the absolute value of x.

The use of **'else'** leads to an asymmetry in the branches of a conditional statement. In the evaluation of the absolute value of x, the case $x = 0$ can be handled by either the assignment $y := -x$ or by the assignment $y := x$; it does not matter which is chosen. The asymmetry becomes more pronounced when there are more cases to be considered, as in, for example,

if $a[i] < b[j]$

then $i := i+1$

else if $b[j] < a[i]$

    then $j := j+1$

    else $i,j := i+1, j+1$.

A modest improvement can be obtained if each branch of a conditional statement is 'guarded' by the condition under which it is executed. An example is the statement

if $x \leqslant 0 \longrightarrow y := -x$

$\square\ x \geqslant 0 \longrightarrow y := x$

fi .

This statement consists of two *guarded* statements

$y := -x$

and

$y := x$,

the guards being $x \leqslant 0$ and $x \geqslant 0$, respectively.

The conditional statement is executed by evaluating the guards and then executing any one of the statements whose guard evaluates to true. (If one such guard is found, the subsequent execution of its associated statement need not wait for all the guards to be evaluated.)

Note that this makes evaluation of a conditional statement *non-deterministic* in that it may be the case that both guards evaluate to true. This is illustrated by the example: in the case that $x = 0$ it is permitted to execute either the assignment

$y := -x$ or the assignment $y := x$. But, it does not matter which is executed since both will assign the value 0 to y. It is precisely this non-determinism that is the advantage of the guarded command style of writing conditionals. It saves the programmer from making arbitrary and possibly confusing distinctions. Also, efficiency improvements can be automated in an optimizing compiler. (Freeing the programmer from the task of making detailed efficiency improvements improves reliability and eases program reuse.)

The number of guarded commands in a conditional statement is finite but otherwise unbounded. An example with three guards is

$$\text{if } a[i] < b[j] \longrightarrow i := i+1$$
$$\square \;\; a[i] = b[j] \longrightarrow i,j := i+1,j+1$$
$$\square \;\; a[i] > b[j] \longrightarrow j := j+1$$
$$\text{fi } .$$

Compare this statement with the equivalent if-then-else statement above to see which you think is clearer.

An if-then statement (i.e. a conditional statement without an else clause) is expressed using the skip statement. The statement **if** b **then** S is expressed as

$$\text{if } b \longrightarrow S$$
$$\square \;\; \neg b \longrightarrow \text{skip}$$
$$\text{fi } .$$

Conditional statements with just *one* guard are used in concurrent programming. (Concurrent programs consist of a collection of programs that are run at the same time. They include synchronization mechanisms which allow communication between the component programs at certain times.) In a concurrent program, the statement

$$\text{if } b \longrightarrow S$$
$$\text{fi}$$

waits until the guard b becomes true. In general, with multiple guards, a concurrent program waits until one of the guards becomes true. We will not be considering concurrent programs in this text; so, if none of the guards evaluates to true, execution of the conditional statement will be forever 'stuck' (because there is no other program running concurrently that can make the guard true) and the program is incorrect.

10.4 Reasoning about Conditional Statements

When we reason about conditional statements, we can take into account the fact that a guarded statement is only executed when its guard is true. So, suppose we consider a conditional statement with precondition P and postcondition Q and, for concreteness, two branches:

$$\{ \; P \; \}$$
$$\text{if } b1 \longrightarrow S1$$
$$\square \; b2 \longrightarrow S2$$
$$\text{fi}$$
$$\{ \; Q \; \} \;.$$

The assumption is that the statement will begin execution in a state satisfying P; it will, therefore, begin execution of statement $S1$ in a state satisfying $P \wedge b1$ and statement $S2$ in a state satisfying $P \wedge b2$. Also, we require that on termination the state must satisfy Q. So, it must be the case that execution of statement $S1$ guarantees termination in a state satisfying Q assuming an initial state satisfying $P \wedge b1$; moreover, execution of statement $S2$ must guarantee termination in a state satisfying Q assuming an initial state satisfying $P \wedge b2$. We can summarize this by an extended annotation of the program with additional assertions:

$$\{ \; P \; \}$$
$$\text{if } b1 \longrightarrow \{ \; P \wedge b1 \; \} \; S1 \; \{ \; Q \; \}$$
$$\square \; b2 \longrightarrow \{ \; P \wedge b2 \; \} \; S2 \; \{ \; Q \; \}$$
$$\text{fi}$$
$$\{ \; Q \; \} \;.$$

Note that the statement $S1$ is now bracketed by precondition $P \wedge b1$ and postcondition Q, whilst statement $S2$ is bracketed by precondition $P \wedge b2$ and postcondition Q.

For example, consider the correctness of the assignment to y of the absolute value of x. The precondition is true and the postcondition is $y = |x|$. The fully annotated program is, thus,

$$\{ \; \text{true} \; \}$$
$$\text{if } x \leqslant 0 \longrightarrow \{ \; \text{true} \wedge x \leqslant 0 \; \} \; y := -x \; \{ \; y = |x| \; \}$$
$$\square \; x \geqslant 0 \longrightarrow \{ \; \text{true} \wedge x \geqslant 0 \; \} \; y := x \; \{ \; y = |x| \; \}$$
$$\text{fi}$$
$$\{ \; y = |x| \; \} \;.$$

Since it is the case that either $x \leqslant 0$ or $x \geqslant 0$, one of the two assignments will be chosen for execution. The correctness of the conditional statement is thus reduced to the correctness of the two assignment statements. Simplifying true $\land p$ to p, we have to verify

$$\{ x \leqslant 0 \} \ y := -x \ \{ y = |x| \}$$

and

$$\{ x \geqslant 0 \} \ y := x \ \{ y = |x| \} \ .$$

Using the assignment axiom, we have

$$\{ -x = |x| \} \ y := -x \ \{ y = |x| \} \ .$$

That is, the assignment $y := -x$ establishes the postcondition $y = |x|$ if the precondition $-x = |x|$ holds. But, it is indeed a property of absolute values that

$$x \leqslant 0 \ \equiv \ -x = |x| \ .$$

Substituting equals for equals ($x \leqslant 0$ for $-x = |x|$), we have thus verified the correctness of the first assignment. Also, again using the assignment axiom,

$$\{ x = |x| \} \ y := x \ \{ y = |x| \} \ .$$

But

$$x \geqslant 0 \ \equiv \ x = |x| \ .$$

Substituting equals for equals again (this time $x \geqslant 0$ for $x = |x|$), the second assignment is valid. We conclude that the conditional statement correctly assigns the absolute value of x to y.

The Conditional Rule. The above discussion can be summarized by saying that the proposition

$$\{ P \}$$
$$\text{if} \ \ b1 \longrightarrow S1$$
$$\square \ \ b2 \longrightarrow S2$$
$$\text{fi}$$
$$\{ Q \}$$

is equivalent to the conjunction of three propositions:

$$[P \ \Rightarrow \ b1 \lor b2] \ ,$$

$$\{ P \land b1 \} \ S1 \ \{ Q \} \ ,$$

and

$$\{ P \land b2 \} \ S2 \ \{ Q \} \ .$$

The first proposition guarantees that at least one branch of the conditional statement can be chosen (recall that the square brackets around $P \Rightarrow b1 \vee b2$ mean that the property is true in all states); the second and third propositions specify the correctness of the individual branches.

Exercise 10.7. Introduce additional assertions into the following Hoare triples so that every assignment statement is bracketed by a precondition and a postcondition. Use the assignment axiom to verify the correctness of each assignment with respect to its precondition and postcondition.

(a)
$$\{ \ m \times n = p \ \}$$
if even.$m \ \longrightarrow \ m,n \ := \ m \div 2 , 2 \times n$
$\square$ true $\ \longrightarrow \ m,p \ := \ m-1 , p-n$
fi
$$\{ \ m \times n = p \ \} \ .$$

(b)
$$\{ \ 0 \leqslant m \ \wedge \ 0 \leqslant n \ \wedge \ \gcd(m,n) = \mathsf{C} \ \}$$
if $m < n \ \longrightarrow \ n \ := \ n-m$
$\square \ n < m \ \longrightarrow \ m \ := \ m-n$
fi
$$\{ \ 0 \leqslant m \ \wedge \ 0 \leqslant n \ \wedge \ \gcd(m,n) = \mathsf{C} \ \}$$

(gcd stands for greatest common divisor). $\qquad\square$

Exercise 10.8. Rather than assign the absolute value of x to a new variable y as we did above, it may be required to *update x* to its absolute value. To specify such an update operation it is necessary to use a ghost variable. The program segment complete with precondition and postcondition is shown below, variable X being the ghost variable.

$$\{ \ \mathsf{X} = |x| \ \}$$
if $x \leqslant 0 \ \longrightarrow \ x \ := \ -x$
$\square \ x \geqslant 0 \ \longrightarrow$ skip
fi
$$\{ \ \mathsf{X} = x \ \} \ .$$

Use the conditional rule, skip rule and assignment axiom to verify that this program segment is indeed correct. $\qquad\square$

10.5 Constructing Conditional Statements

We use conditional statements in programming when a problem can be split into a (small) number of cases and these cases solved independently. The conditional rule neatly captures this problem-solving strategy.

The conditional rule can be used to construct conditional statements in several different ways. We illustrate two.

Suppose a specification of a program statement S is given in terms of a precondition P and a postcondition Q. So, P and Q are given and we are required to construct S. Then we can meet the specification in three steps.

(a) Split the precondition into two (or possibly more) cases $b1$ and $b2$. Formally, 'splitting the precondition' means identifying $b1$ and $b2$ such that $[P \Rightarrow b1 \vee b2]$.

(b) Construct a program statement $S1$ that guarantees termination in a state satisfying Q given the precondition $P \wedge b1$.

(c) Construct a program statement $S2$ that guarantees termination in a state satisfying Q given the precondition $P \wedge b2$.

(If the problem is split into more than two cases, a program statement has to be constructed for each of the cases.)

This strategy involves the invention of the cases $b1$ and $b2$. This is a creative step that relies on the programmer's problem-solving ability. Having taken this step, the specifications of $S1$ and $S2$ are easy to derive.

Let us show how this strategy is used to construct assignments that will assign the maximum of x and y to z (all assumed to be real values).

The problem is specified formally by the precondition true (so the state before execution of the program is arbitrary) and the postcondition $z = x \uparrow y$ where the maximum $x \uparrow y$ is as defined in Chapter 8.

In Chapter 8, we observed that maximum has the following elementary properties:

$$x \uparrow y = x \;\equiv\; y \leqslant x \;, \tag{10.9}$$

and

$$x \uparrow y = y \;\equiv\; x \leqslant y \;. \tag{10.10}$$

Since

$$x \leqslant y \vee y \leqslant x \;,$$

we are led to consider splitting the problem into two cases: the case that $x \leqslant y$ and the case that $y \leqslant x$. (Formally, step (a) above is satisfied by the fact that

$$\text{true} \Rightarrow x \leqslant y \vee y \leqslant x$$

for all x and y.) So, our goal is to calculate expressions $e1$ and $e2$ such that

$$\{ \text{ true } \}$$
$$\text{if } x \leqslant y \longrightarrow \{ x \leqslant y \} \; z := e1 \; \{ z = x \uparrow y \}$$
$$\square \; y \leqslant x \longrightarrow \{ y \leqslant x \} \; z := e2 \; \{ z = x \uparrow y \}$$
$$\text{fi}$$
$$\{ z = x \uparrow y \} \; .$$

Using the assignment axiom we calculate that

$$\{ e = x \uparrow y \} \; z := e \; \{ z = x \uparrow y \} \; .$$

In particular,

$$\{ x = x \uparrow y \} \; z := x \; \{ z = x \uparrow y \} \; .$$

Thus, by (10.9),

$$\{ y \leqslant x \} \; z := x \; \{ z = x \uparrow y \} \; .$$

Similarly, using the assignment axiom and (10.10),

$$\{ x \leqslant y \} \; z := y \; \{ z = x \uparrow y \} \; .$$

We have thus determined expressions $e1$ and $e2$, and conclude that

$$\{ \text{ true } \}$$
$$\text{if } x \leqslant y \longrightarrow \{ x \leqslant y \} \; z := y \; \{ z = x \uparrow y \}$$
$$\square \; y \leqslant x \longrightarrow \{ y \leqslant x \} \; z := x \; \{ z = x \uparrow y \}$$
$$\text{fi}$$
$$\{ z = x \uparrow y \} \; .$$

Exercise 10.11. Given are two variables x and y. It is required to update the values stored in these variables so that the value of x is at most the value of y. In other words, it is required to sort the values of x and y.

Using ghost variables X and Y to record the initial values of x and y, formulate an appropriate precondition and postcondition and construct a conditional statement that implements the specification. Take care to specify that the initial values of x and y are not lost in the process of sorting. □

Exercise 10.12. A program has two real variables x and y and one integer variable k. Initially, k is strictly positive. It is required to decrease the value of k to a positive value whilst maintaining the value of $x^k \times y$ constant. Using ghost variable C to record the initial value of $x^k \times y$ and ghost variable K to record the initial value of k, the precondition is

$$0 < k = \text{K} \; \wedge \; x^k \times y = \text{C}$$

and the postcondition is

$$0 \leqslant k < K \ \wedge \ x^k \times y \ = \ C \ .$$

(Observe how the combination of the conjunct $k = K$ in the precondition and the conjunct $k < K$ in the postcondition express the requirement that k is decreased.)

It is of course always possible to decrease k by subtracting 1. When k is even, however, it is possible to decrease it at least as much, and generally more, by dividing by 2. So, we are interested in constructing expressions a, b, c and d such that

$$\{ \ 0 < k = K \ \wedge \ x^k \times y \ = \ C \ \}$$

$$\mathsf{if} \ \ \mathsf{true} \ \longrightarrow \ k,x,y \ := \ k-1,a,b$$

$$\square \ \ \mathsf{even}.k \ \longrightarrow \ k,x,y \ := \ k \div 2,c,d$$

$$\mathsf{fi}$$

$$\{ \ 0 \leqslant k < K \ \wedge \ x^k \times y \ = \ C \ \} \ .$$

Calculate appropriate values for a, b, c and d.

(Note: the guard 'true' may of course be replaced by 'odd.k'. We choose the weaker guard because correctness is not compromised. In fact, when $k = 2$ the assignments $k := k-1$ and $k := k \div 2$ are equivalent. The non-determinism in the conditional statement thus allows us to postpone the decision on how to handle such cases until the complete program has been calculated. At this later stage, we may choose to strengthen either of the guards in order to improve the efficiency of the program.) $\qquad \square$

10.6   Combining the Rules

In this section, we show how the rule of sequential composition is combined with the skip rule and the conditional rule in constructing a small program.

Suppose that a programming language does not have a direct implementation of integer division by 2. However, it is required to write a program that will implement the assignment $m := m \div 2$ for a given positive integer m. Formally, using ghost variable M to record the initial value of m, the problem is to construct a statement S such that

$$\{ \ 0 \leqslant m = M \ \} \ S \ \{ \ m = M \div 2 \ \} \ .$$

If the programming language does not provide a division-by-two operation, it must provide some other more primitive operation. Let us suppose that the language does have a division-by-two operation in the case that the supplied argument is positive and even. Let us denote this operation by rot (short for *rotate*). Then, what we may assume is that the function rot satisfies, for all k,

$$0 \leqslant k \ \wedge \ \mathsf{even}.k \ \Rightarrow \ rot.k = k \div 2 \ . \tag{10.13}$$

That is, $rot.k$ correctly computes the integer division $k \div 2$ in the case that k is positive and even. We also assume that the language implements a test **even** that determines whether a given argument k is even or not. Finally, we assume that the language has an operation dec (short for *decrement*) that subtracts one from a given strictly positive integer. That is, dec satisfies, for all k,

$$0 < k \;\Rightarrow\; dec.k = k-1 \;. \tag{10.14}$$

(The problem statement is a bit artificial—this is an inevitable consequence of trying to keep the problem simple. If this concerns you, think in terms of a Java class `FunnyInteger` that provides the methods described, but no others. Alternatively, the following scenario might put your mind at rest. Suppose k is stored as a binary numeral, and suppose the operation $rot.k$ rotates the bits one place so that the rightmost bit becomes the leftmost bit. Then, this implements division by two, provided that the number is even. The operation **even**.k simply converts the rightmost bit to a boolean value. That is, if the rightmost bit of the binary representation of k is 0, **even**.k is true, and if it is 1, **even**.k is false.)

At some stage, the program must compute $rot.k$ for some k. This operation computes $k \div 2$ reliably only when k is even (see (10.13)). The input value M is not necessarily even. So, it is reasonable to seek a program that ensures that m gets an even value and then assigns $rot.m$ to m. That is, we use the rule of sequential composition to replace the original problem by the problem of determining a statement S and an intermediate assertion P satisfying

$$\{\, 0 \leqslant m = \text{M} \,\}\; S \;\{\, 0 \leqslant m \,\wedge\, \text{even}.m \,\wedge\, P \,\} \tag{10.15}$$

and

$$\{\, 0 \leqslant m \,\wedge\, \text{even}.m \,\wedge\, P \,\}\; m := rot.m \;\{\, m = \text{M} \div 2 \,\} \;. \tag{10.16}$$

We begin by calculating P. Applying the assignment axiom, we have

$$\{\, rot.m = \text{M} \div 2 \,\}\; m := rot.m \;\{\, m = \text{M} \div 2 \,\} \;.$$

So, P must satisfy, for all m and M,

$$0 \leqslant m \,\wedge\, \text{even}.m \,\wedge\, P \;\Rightarrow\; rot.m = \text{M} \div 2 \;.$$

Comparing this with the property (10.13) of rot, it is clear that

$$P \;\equiv\; m \div 2 = \text{M} \div 2$$

will do. (In more detail, it is a consequence of (10.13) that

$$0 \leqslant m \,\wedge\, \text{even}.m \,\wedge\, m \div 2 = \text{M} \div 2 \;\Rightarrow\; rot.m = m \div 2 \,\wedge\, m \div 2 = \text{M} \div 2 \;.$$

But then, by the transitivity of equality,

$$rot.m = m \div 2 \,\wedge\, m \div 2 = \text{M} \div 2 \;\Rightarrow\; rot.m = \text{M} \div 2 \;.$$

So, by the transitivity of implication,

$$0 \leqslant m \wedge \text{even}.m \wedge m \div 2 = \mathsf{M} \div 2 \Rightarrow rot.m = \mathsf{M} \div 2 \ .)$$

Substituting the calculated value for P in (10.16) and (10.15) gives us

$$\{\, 0 \leqslant m \wedge \text{even}.m \wedge m \div 2 = \mathsf{M} \div 2 \,\}$$
$$m := rot.m \tag{10.17}$$
$$\{\, m = \mathsf{M} \div 2 \,\}$$

and the specification of S:

$$\{\, 0 \leqslant m = \mathsf{M} \,\}$$
$$S \tag{10.18}$$
$$\{\, 0 \leqslant m \wedge \text{even}.m \wedge m \div 2 = \mathsf{M} \div 2 \,\} \ .$$

In words, S must compute a positive, even number m which has the same integer division by 2 as M.

The specification of S suggests that a conditional statement is appropriate. After all, $m \div 2 = m \div 2$, so that, if m is even, nothing needs to be done. Formally,

$$\{\, 0 \leqslant m = \mathsf{M} \wedge \text{even}.m \,\}$$
$$\text{skip} \tag{10.19}$$
$$\{\, 0 \leqslant m \wedge \text{even}.m \wedge m \div 2 = \mathsf{M} \div 2 \,\} \ .$$

If m is odd, doing nothing is not valid and we must seek a property of division-by-two that will allow us to proceed. The appropriate property is, of course, that for an odd positive integer m, $m \div 2 = (m-1) \div 2$ and $m-1$ is even. Moreover, we are told that the operation dec calculates $m-1$ when m is a strictly positive number (see (10.14)). All odd, positive integers are strictly positive, so it is thus the case that

$$\{\, 0 \leqslant m = \mathsf{M} \wedge \text{odd}.m \,\}$$
$$m := dec.m \tag{10.20}$$
$$\{\, 0 \leqslant m \wedge \text{even}.m \wedge m \div 2 = \mathsf{M} \div 2 \,\} \ .$$

(Use the assignment axiom to check the claim, making sure that no details have been overlooked.)

The final step is to put (10.19) and (10.20) together using the conditional rule given in Section 10.4. Every number is either even or odd. So

$$\{\, 0 \leqslant m = \mathsf{M} \,\}$$
$$\text{if } \text{even}.m \longrightarrow \text{skip}$$
$$\square \ \text{odd}.m \longrightarrow m := dec.m$$
$$\text{fi}$$
$$\{\, 0 \leqslant m \wedge \text{even}.m \wedge m \div 2 = \mathsf{M} \div 2 \,\} \ .$$

The construction of S satisfying (10.15) is thereby solved. To complete the construction, we combine the above with (10.17) using the rule of sequential composition to get

$$\{\ 0 \leqslant m = \mathsf{M}\ \}$$

if even.m $\longrightarrow$ skip

$\square$ odd.m $\longrightarrow$ $m := dec.m$

fi ;

$$\{\ 0 \leqslant m \wedge \text{even}.m \wedge m \div 2 = \mathsf{M} \div 2\ \}$$

$m := rot.m$

$$\{\ m = \mathsf{M} \div 2\ \}\ .$$

Note that the middle assertion could now be omitted. It is included in order to document the program better.

Exercise 10.21. This exercise is a variation on Exercise 10.12. Recall the statement of the problem. A program has two real variables x and y and one integer variable k. Initially, k is strictly positive. It is required to decrease the value of k to a positive value whilst maintaining the value of $x^k \times y$ constant.

In this exercise, the requirement is to develop a program that is the sequential composition of two statements using the fact that decreasing an odd number by one always yields an even number.

Construct statement $S2$ and assertion P such that executing $S2$ beginning in a state satisfying

$$P \ \wedge \ \text{even}.k \ \wedge \ x^k \times y = \mathsf{C} \tag{10.22}$$

is guaranteed to terminate in a state satisfying

$$0 \leqslant k < \mathsf{K} \ \wedge \ x^k \times y = \mathsf{C}\ . \tag{10.23}$$

(Hint: a simple assignment statement is all that is needed—make use of Exercise 10.11. You can then use the assignment axiom to determine what P should be.)

Now construct statement $S1$ with precondition

$$0 < k = \mathsf{K} \ \wedge \ x^k \times y = \mathsf{C} \tag{10.24}$$

and postcondition (10.22).

In this way, you will have constructed statements $S1$ and $S2$ such that the sequential composition $S1 ; S2$ has precondition (10.24) and postcondition (10.23). $\square$

10.7   Summary

This chapter completes the discussion of non-looping programs. Rules for sequential composition, the skip statement and conditional statements have been given and applied to a number of simple programming problems. The use of guarded commands and non-determinism, rather than the conventional if-then(-else) statements, helps to avoid error and offers increased scope for improving the efficiency of programs without compromising reliability.

Bibliographic Remarks

The guarded command language was introduced by Dijkstra (1975).

Exercises 10.11 and 10.21 are based on the so-called 'SX' method for computing powers described by Knuth (1969, pp. 398–422). Exercise 13.15 in Chapter 13 completes the discussion of this method.

A recommended text on concurrent programming that practises a correct-by-construction methodology is *A Method of Multiprogramming* by Feijen and van Gasteren (1996).

11
Quantifiers

Before moving on to add iteration to the control structures in our simple programming language, it is convenient to first extend the specification language to allow so-called *quantifiers*. Quantifiers allow one to denote the operation of applying some binary operator (like addition or multiplication, conjunction or disjunction) to an arbitrary, possibly infinite, bag[1] of values.

In this chapter, we introduce a uniform notation for quantifiers. We compare the notation with existing notations, pointing out its advantages and disadvantages. We also give rules for manipulating quantifiers and illustrate their use with several examples.

Two quantifiers that are particularly important are *universal* quantification and *existential* quantification. Additional rules governing such quantifications are also presented.

11.1 DotDotDot and Sigmas

Most readers will have encountered the *dotdotdot* notation already. It is a notation that is rarely introduced properly; mostly, it is just used without explanation as in, for example, '$1 + 2 + \ldots + 20 = 210$' and 'let $x_0, x_1, \ldots, x_n$ be'.

The dotdotdot notation is used when some operation is to be applied to a bag of values in cases where the bag is too large to be enumerated, or the size of the bag is given by some variable. In the case of '$1 + 2 + \ldots + 20 = 210$', the operation is addition and there are 20 values to be enumerated; in the case of 'let $x_0, x_1, \ldots, x_n$ be', the operation is sequencing (indicated by a comma) and the number of values is given by the variable n.

---

[1]A bag is a set in which elements may occur more than once (and the number of occurrences is significant).

The dotdotdot notation is convenient in the very simplest cases. But it has a number of disadvantages in more complicated cases. It can become cumbersome and it is prone to error. Most importantly, however, it puts a major burden on the reader, requiring them to interpolate from a few example values to the general term in a bag of values.

The so-called 'Sigma' notation is a popular notation for continued summations. An example is the sum of the squares of all numbers from 0 up to and including the number n which, in Sigma notation, is written

$$\sum_{k=0}^{n} k^2 \ .$$

Similarly, the 'Pi' notation is used to denote a continued product. For example, the factorial of number n is defined to be the product of all numbers from 1 up to and including the number n. In dotdotdot notation this would be written

$$n! = 1 \times 2 \times \ldots \times n \ .$$

The equivalent in Pi notation is

$$n! = \prod_{k=1}^{n} k \ .$$

The two-dimensional nature of the Sigma and Pi notations makes them very readable because it is easy to identify the constituent components of the notation. There is a *quantifier*—$\sum$ or $\prod$ in the two examples—which identifies the operation to be carried out (addition in the case of $\sum$ and multiplication in the case of $\prod$). There is also a so-called *bound variable* (k in both examples above) which has a certain *range* (from 0 to n in the first example and from 1 to n in the second example). Finally, there is a *term* defining a function of the bound variable which is to be evaluated at each point in the range (k^2 in the first example and k in the second example). The bound variable is always to the left of the equals sign in the expression below the quantifier, and it ranges over a consecutive sequence of numbers, where the lower bound is given to the right of the equals sign and the upper bound is placed above the quantifier. The function of the bound variable is written immediately to the right of the quantifier. The general form of the Sigma and Pi notations is thus

$$\bigoplus_{bv=lb}^{ub} E \ ,$$

where $\oplus$ is the quantifier, bv is an identifier denoting the bound variable, lb and ub are expressions denoting the lower and upper bounds of the range of the quantification, respectively, and E is an expression denoting the function of the bound variable that is to be evaluated at each point in the range of the bound variable.

Because of their readability, the Sigma and Pi notations are widely used. A major drawback, however, is that they are limited to quantifications over a consecutive sequence of numbers. Problems arise if the notation is to be used for quantifications over non-consecutive numbers.

In some cases it is possible to get around the problems. For example, if we want an expression denoting the sum of all *odd* numbers in, say, the range $1..n$, we can write

$$\sum_{k=0}^{n \div 2} 2k + 1 \ .$$

But this is unsatisfactory, first because the intention is obscured—the reader is burdened with the task of relating the complicated expressions ('$n \div 2$' and '$2k+1$') to the intended sequence of numbers—and, second, because the process is error prone. In the example, that the smallest value of k is 0 and not 1, and that the largest value is $n \div 2$, is far from obviously correct!

In other cases, it is not possible to circumvent the problem of the range being a sequence of consecutive numbers. It is impracticable, for example, to use the notation to express the sum of all prime numbers below a given value as there is no simple arithmetic function denoting the kth prime number.

In order to overcome these drawbacks, some authors use a more flexible form of the Sigma–Pi notation in which the range of the bound variable is indicated by a predicate. The notation takes the form

$$\bigoplus_{p(k)} f(k) \ ,$$

where $p(k)$ and $f(k)$ are expressions typically (but not necessarily) dependent on k (as indicated by '(k)'). For example, the sum of the odd numbers in the range $1..n$ would be denoted by

$$\sum_{1 \leqslant k \leqslant n \ \wedge \ \mathrm{odd}.k} k \ .$$

Once again, this notation can be said to work—in the simple cases. But, its greater flexibility has a major shortcoming—the notation is inherently ambiguous! The problem is that the identity of the bound variable has become obscured. If we write

$$\sum_{m \leqslant k \leqslant n} k \times n \ .$$

then the meaning appears to be clear: k is the bound variable and the entire expression denotes a function of the variables m and n. But, taking m equal to n,

$$\sum_{n \leqslant k \leqslant n} k \times n$$

simplifies to

$$\sum_{n\,=\,k} k \times n \ .$$

Now the meaning is not clear. The variables n and k are used in identical ways and it is not clear which is the bound variable. Does the quantification denote a function of n or is it a function of k? If we write

$$\sum_{k\,=\,n} n \times k \ ,$$

using the symmetry of equality and multiplication to interchange n and k, does this change the meaning?

Another serious problem is that the *scope* of the quantifier is not made clear. Does

$$\sum_{1\,\leqslant\,j\,\leqslant\,3} j + 1$$

mean $(1+1) + (2+1) + (3+1)$ or does it mean $(1+2+3) + 1$? In other words, is the function that is being quantified given by 'j' or by '$j + 1$'. Most of us would assume the latter. But, if '1' is replaced by another quantified expression, the meaning suddenly becomes different:

$$\sum_{1\,\leqslant\,j\,\leqslant\,3} j \ + \ \sum_{k\,=\,1} k$$

is normally understood to mean $(1+2+3) + 1$ and not $(1+1) + (2+1) + (3+1)$! (The spacing around the plus symbol is commonly used to indicate the intended meaning but it is a bad notation that is susceptible to the presence or absence of spaces—as many a C programmer will verify.)

The ambiguity of the more flexible Sigma–Pi notation is its main drawback. Less serious, but still important, is that the use of a two-dimensional notation does not scale up either. Here, the problem is that the predicate p used to delimit the range of the bound variable, being written as a subscript, cannot be allowed to get too complicated. Moreover, it should not itself make use of any two-dimensional notation. Try reading

$$\sum_{1\,\leqslant\,k\,\leqslant\,n\,\wedge\,\mathsf{odd}.\left(\sum_{j=\sum_{i=0}^{k} i^2}^{\sum_{i=0}^{k+1} i^2} j^2\right)} k^3 \ ,$$

and you will understand the problem.

In the next section, we introduce a uniform notation for quantified expressions that avoids all the problems mentioned above.

11.2   Introducing Quantifier Notation

Summation and multiplication are just two examples of the quantifiers we want to consider. In general, it is meaningful to 'quantify' over a non-empty range with respect to any binary operator that is associative and symmetric. Addition, multiplication, equivalence, inequivalence, set union, set intersection, minimum, maximum, conjunction, disjunction, highest common factor and least common multiple are all examples of associative and symmetric operators. In each case, it is meaningful (and useful) to consider the operator applied to a (non-zero) number of values rather than just a pair of values. Moreover, quantifying over an empty range is meaningful provided the operator in question has a *unit*[2]. Most of the operators just listed have units, minimum, maximum and highest common factor being the exceptions. (The unit of addition is zero (that is, $x+0 = x$ for all x), the unit of multiplication is one ($x \times 1 = x$ for all x), the unit of conjunction is true (that is, $x \wedge \text{true} = x$), and so on. Minimum and maximum can be given units by adding so-called 'fictitious' values, respectively ∞ and $-\infty$, to their domains but care has to be taken in defining how these values behave in combination with other arithmetic operators. The unit of highest common factor is the number 0, so long as its domain is not restricted to only strictly positive numbers.)

We use a uniform notation to denote quantifications over a number of values. In this way, we can also present a uniform set of laws for manipulating quantifiers, resulting in a substantial reduction in the number of laws one has to remember.

We begin by explaining the particular case of summation, comparing our notation with the Sigma notation discussed above. Then, we consider quantifications with respect to conjunction and disjunction ('for all' quantifications and 'there exist' quantifications, respectively) before considering the general case.

11.2.1   Summation

Our notation for summation has the form

$$\langle \Sigma\, bv : range : term \rangle \ .$$

There are five components to the notation, which we explain in turn.

The first component is the *quantifier*, in this case Σ. By a long-standing convention among mathematicians, Σ denotes summation of some arbitrary number of values. The second component is the *dummy bv*. The dummy is said to be *bound* to the quantifier; it is also called the *bound variable*. We use identifiers like i, j and k, or x, y and z as dummies. Later, we allow the possibility of a list of dummies rather than just a single one. The third component is the *range* of the dummy. The range is a boolean-valued expression that determines a set of values of the dummy: specifically, the set of all values of the bound variable for

---

[2]Recall that a unit of a symmetric binary operator $\oplus$ is a value $1_\oplus$ satisfying $1_\oplus \oplus x = x$, for all x.

which the range evaluates to true. (Quantifications are not always well defined if the range defines an *infinite* range set; we postpone discussion of this problem until later.) The fourth component is the *term*. In the case of summation, the term is an integer or real-valued expression. The final component of the notation is the angle brackets; these serve to delimit the *scope* of the bound variable.

The value of a summation of the form $\langle \Sigma bv : range : term \rangle$ is determined as follows: evaluate the term for each value of the dummy described by the range, and then sum all these values together. For example, the value of

$$\langle \Sigma k : 1 \leqslant k \leqslant 3 : k^3 \rangle$$

is

$$1^3 + 2^3 + 3^3 \quad .$$

Here, the range $1 \leqslant k \leqslant 3$ determines the set $\{k \mid 1 \leqslant k \leqslant 3\}$ (read 'the set of k such that $1 \leqslant k \leqslant 3$'). That is, the dummy k ranges over the three values 1, 2 and 3. The term k^3 is evaluated at these three values and then the values are summed together.

The range can be any boolean expression, and the term any integer or real-valued expression as in, for example,

$$\langle \Sigma k : even.k \wedge 0 \leqslant k < N : k^3 + k^2 + N + 1 \rangle \quad .$$

Sometimes there may be no value of the dummy in the range, for example, if the dummy is k, the range is $0 \leqslant k < N$, and N happens to be zero. In this case, the summation is defined to be zero. (In words, a sum of no values is zero.)

The dummy has a certain *type*, the knowledge of which is crucial in certain circumstances. A long-standing mathematical convention is that variables i, j and k denote *integer* values, whereas x, y and z denote *real* values. Such conventions help for small-scale problems (like the ones considered in this text) but are inadequate for the large-scale problems commonly encountered in programming. Where necessary, the type of the dummy can be indicated by adding it immediately after the first occurrence of the dummy, as in

$$\langle \Sigma k \in \mathbb{Z} : even.k \wedge 0 \leqslant k < N : k^3 + k^2 + N + 1 \rangle \quad .$$

(The symbol $\mathbb{Z}$ is commonly used in mathematics to denote the set of all integers. The symbols $\mathbb{N}$ and $\mathbb{R}$ are used for the natural numbers and reals, respectively.) Mostly, however, we will indicate the type of the dummies in the accompanying text rather than in the quantification itself.

Rather than have just one dummy, it is convenient to allow a number of variables to be bound to the same quantifier. An example is

$$\langle \Sigma i,j : 0 \leqslant i < j \leqslant N : i + j \rangle \quad .$$

This denotes the sum of all values $i+j$ such that i and j satisfy the property $0 \leqslant i < j \leqslant N$. Taking N to be 2, the possible values of i and j are $i=0$ and $j=1$, $i=0$ and $j=2$, $i=1$ and $j=2$, so that

$$\langle \Sigma i,j : 0 \leqslant i < j \leqslant 2 : i+j \rangle \;\; = \;\; (0+1) + (0+2) + (1+2) \;\; .$$

Note that the variables in a list of dummies must all be distinct. It does not make sense to repeat dummies. For example, $\langle \Sigma i,i : 0 \leqslant i < 2 : 0 \rangle$ is not meaningful.

Exercise 11.1. Evaluate the following summations.

(a) $\langle \Sigma k : 1 \leqslant k \leqslant 3 : k \rangle$.

(b) $\langle \Sigma k : 0 \leqslant k < 5 : 1 \rangle$.

(c) $\langle \Sigma i,j : 0 \leqslant i < j \leqslant 2 \wedge \text{odd}.i : i+j \rangle$.

(d) $\langle \Sigma i,j : 0 \leqslant i < j \leqslant 2 \wedge \text{odd}.i \wedge \text{odd}.j : i+j \rangle$. □

Exercise 11.2. What is the value of $\langle \Sigma k : k^2 = 4 : k^2 \rangle$ in the case that the type of k is

(a) a natural number,

(b) an integer? □

11.2.2 Free and Bound Variables

In the next section, we formulate general properties of summation. Several of these rules have so-called *side conditions* that prevent improper use of the rule. The side conditions are, primarily, *syntactic* and not semantic. This means they are conditions on the way expressions are written (their syntax) rather than conditions on the values of the expressions (their semantics). So, the conditions may apply to one expression but not to an equal expression. For example, the condition 'the symbol '0' occurs in the expression' is a syntactic condition on expressions, which is true of '0' but not true of '$1-1$', even though 0 and $1-1$ are equal.

A consequence of the syntactic nature of the side conditions is that they are cumbersome to state even though they are, in fact, quite straightforward. In order to understand them, we need to have a clear understanding of the notions of 'free' and 'bound' variables in an expression. (These notions provide the semantic justification for the syntactic side conditions.)

Note that although all the examples given in this section are of summations, the discussion applies equally well to all quantifiers.

Recall that a dummy in a summation is said to be *bound*. For example, all occurrences of 'k' in $\langle \Sigma k : 1 \leqslant k \leqslant 3 : k \rangle$ are bound to the Σ quantifier. Variables that have occurrences in an expression that are *not* bound to a quantifier are called *free* variables. For example, n is free in 2^n, and m and n are free in $\langle \Sigma k : 0 \leqslant k < m : k^n \rangle$.

Free and bound variables have different roles. The value of an expression depends on the value of its free variables. For example, the value of 2^n depends on the value of the free variable n, and the value of $\langle \Sigma k : 0 \leqslant k < m : k^n \rangle$ depends on the values of the free variables m and n. However, it is meaningless to say that the value of an expression depends on the value of any bound variables occurring in the expression. Also, the names given to bound variables can be changed, whereas those given to free variables cannot. So, $\langle \Sigma k : 1 \leqslant k \leqslant 3 : k^n \rangle$ and $\langle \Sigma j : 1 \leqslant j \leqslant 3 : j^n \rangle$ both have the same meaning—the change of dummy name from 'k' to 'j' is irrelevant. But 2^m and 2^n are quite different—the free variables m and n cannot be interchanged at will.

Dummies bound to quantifiers act like local variables in a program. The first occurrence is comparable to a declaration of the variable, the scope of the declaration being delimited by the angle brackets. This means that dummy names may be reused, i.e. different quantifications may use the same bound variables, as in, for example,

$$\langle \Sigma k : 0 \leqslant k < n : k \rangle \times \langle \Sigma k : 1 \leqslant k \leqslant n : k^2 \rangle \ .$$

In this expression, there are two distinct dummies, both having the same name 'k'. The first is bound to the leftmost Σ and the second to the rightmost Σ. The angle brackets avoid confusion between the two because they clearly delimit the scope of the bindings (the subexpressions in which the dummies have meaning).

(Mathematicians do not usually make the effort to delimit the scope of their dummies; the errors that occur from not doing so have taught computing scientists that it is always a good idea to make scopes explicit. So always remember to include the brackets, even though others may be more sloppy.)

Reuse of dummy names is quite common. After all, the name of a dummy is irrelevant, so why bother to think of different names. Reuse of dummy names is not a problem, except where the scope of the bindings overlaps. The only time that scopes overlap is when they are 'nested'.

Nesting of quantifications is when one quantification is a subexpression in another quantification—as in, for example,

$$\langle \Sigma j : 0 \leqslant j < n : \langle \Sigma k : 0 \leqslant k < n : j \times k^2 \rangle \rangle \ .$$

A variable that is bound at one level in an expression is free within subexpressions. In the above example, all occurrences of 'j' are bound, but in the expression

$$\langle \Sigma k : 0 \leqslant k < n : j \times k^2 \rangle \ ,$$

'j' is free. (This is just like nested declarations in a block-structured programming language. Variables are local to the block in which they are declared but global in any nested blocks.)

Variables may be both free and bound in the same expression. An example is

$$\langle \Sigma k : 0 \leqslant k < n : k^2 \rangle + k \ .$$

In this expression, the rightmost occurrence of 'k' is free, whereas all other occurrences are bound to the Σ quantifier. The rightmost occurrence of 'k' is distinct from all other occurrences, as is evident from the fact that the other occurrences can be renamed to, say, 'j'. An equivalent (and perhaps more readable) expression is

$$\langle \Sigma j : 0 \leqslant j < n : j^2 \rangle + k \ .$$

The names of dummies may also be reused in nested quantifications. The summation

$$\langle \Sigma i : i = 0 \lor i = 1 : \langle \Sigma i : i = 2 \lor i = 3 : i \rangle - 4 \times i \rangle$$

is perfectly meaningful. It evaluates to $((2+3) - 4 \times 0) + ((2+3) - 4 \times 1)$. Renaming the innermost dummy to j, we get the equivalent expression

$$\langle \Sigma i : i = 0 \lor i = 1 : \langle \Sigma j : j = 2 \lor j = 3 : j \rangle - 4 \times i \rangle \ .$$

The rule is that in nested quantifications, the innermost bindings take precedence. (The analogy with variable declarations in block-structured languages is again useful.)

A variable can be *captured* by a quantifier when dummies are renamed. Earlier, we gave

$$\langle \Sigma k : 1 \leqslant k \leqslant 3 : k^n \rangle \ = \ \langle \Sigma j : 1 \leqslant j \leqslant 3 : j^n \rangle$$

as a valid use of renaming. But it would be wrong to rename 'k' to 'n'. Clearly,

$$\langle \Sigma k : 1 \leqslant k \leqslant 3 : k^n \rangle \ \neq \ \langle \Sigma n : 1 \leqslant n \leqslant 3 : n^n \rangle \ .$$

In the left-hand summation, n is free; in the right-hand summation, all occurrences of 'n' are bound to the quantifier. The left side depends on the value of n, whilst the right side does not (it equals $1^1 + 2^2 + 3^3$). So, a proviso on dummy renaming is that the new name is not free anywhere in the scope of the quantifier.

Care must be taken when manipulating quantifications to ensure that free variables are not 'captured' by a quantifier and, conversely, bound variables are not 'released' from their binding. As a general rule, you should always be aware of which variable occurrences in an expression are free and which are bound. Application of algebraic laws is invalid if free variables become bound or, vice versa, bound variables become free. Care is also needed to ensure that a dummy name does not occur twice in a list of dummies. (This can occur, for example, when unnesting quantifications.) And care is needed in the process of substitution — substituting an expression for a variable should only replace *free* occurrences of the variable. Understanding the distinction between free and bound occurrences of variables will enable you to easily avoid any pitfalls.

Exercise 11.3. Identify all occurrences of free variables in the following expressions.

(a) $4 \times i$.

(b) $\langle \Sigma j : 1 \leqslant j \leqslant 3 : 4 \times i \rangle$.

   (c) $\langle \Sigma j : 1 \leqslant j \leqslant 3 : 4 \times j \rangle$.

   (d) $\langle \Sigma j : 1 \leqslant j \leqslant 3 : m \times j \rangle + \langle \Sigma j : 1 \leqslant j \leqslant 3 : n \times j \rangle$.

   (e) $\langle \Sigma j : 1 \leqslant j \leqslant 3 : m \times j \rangle + \langle \Sigma k : 1 \leqslant k \leqslant 3 : n \times j \rangle$. $\square$

Exercise 11.4. Evaluate the left and right sides of the following equations. Hence, state which are true and which are false.

   (a) $\langle \Sigma j : 1 \leqslant j \leqslant 3 : 4 \times i \rangle = \langle \Sigma k : 1 \leqslant k \leqslant 3 : 4 \times i \rangle$.

   (b) $\langle \Sigma j : 1 \leqslant j \leqslant 3 : 4 \times j \rangle = \langle \Sigma k : 1 \leqslant k \leqslant 3 : 4 \times j \rangle$.

   (c) $\langle \Sigma j : 1 \leqslant j \leqslant 3 : \langle \Sigma k : k = 0 : 4 \times j \rangle \rangle = \langle \Sigma i : 1 \leqslant i \leqslant 3 : \langle \Sigma k : k = 0 : 4 \times i \rangle \rangle$.

   (d) $\langle \Sigma j : 1 \leqslant j \leqslant 3 : \langle \Sigma j : j = 1 : 4 \times j \rangle \rangle = \langle \Sigma k : 1 \leqslant k \leqslant 3 : \langle \Sigma j : j = 1 : 4 \times k \rangle \rangle$. $\square$

11.2.3 Properties of Summation

The main advantage of a formal quantifier notation over the informal dotdotdot notation is that it is easier to formulate and use calculational rules. In this subsection, we formulate rules for summation. Later, we will see that these rules are all instances of more general rules.

    We formulate the rules in terms of each of the components of a quantification. So there are rules governing the use of dummies, rules exploiting the structure of the range, and rules exploiting the structure of the term. Additionally, there are two so-called *trading* rules that allow information to be moved to and from the range of the quantification.

Side Condition. A general side condition on all the rules is that their application should not result in the capture of free variables or release of bound variables, and should not result in a variable occurring more than once in a list of dummies.

Dummy Rules. There are three rules governing the use of dummies. The first rule expresses the fact that a 'dummy' is just a place holder, the particular name chosen for the dummy is not relevant provided it does not clash with the names of other variables in the quantified expression. (The rule has already been discussed in Section 11.2.2 but is repeated here for convenience.) Renaming is often used when performing other algebraic manipulations in order to avoid capture of free variables or release of bound variables.

    Let $R[j := k]$ and $T[j := k]$ denote, respectively, the expressions obtained by replacing every *free* occurrence of 'j' in R and T by 'k'. Then

[Dummy Renaming] $\langle \Sigma j : R : T \rangle = \langle \Sigma k : R[j := k] : T[j := k] \rangle$.   (11.5)

    As discussed earlier, the general side condition on application of rules demands that R and T be expressions not containing any free occurrence of 'k'.

The second rule states, essentially, that the use of more than one dummy is a convenient abbreviation for a collection of quantifications. We use '*js*' in the statement of the rule to denote any list of variables:

[Nesting] $\langle \Sigma\, j, js : R \wedge S : T \rangle \;=\; \langle \Sigma j : R : \langle \Sigma js : S : T \rangle \rangle$.   (11.6)

There are two side conditions on this rule. The first side condition is that expression R may not depend on any variable in the list *js*. The reason for this is that the scope of the variables in the list *js* on the right side of the equality is delimited by the innermost angle brackets and, thus, does not extend to the range R of the bound variable j. Were R to depend on variables in *js*, those variables would be released in the process of replacing the left side by the right side.

This is an example of avoiding the circumstance that a bound variable becomes free—were the rule to be used from left to right when R does depend on some variable in the list *js*, that variable would be bound in the left-hand occurrence of R but free in the right-hand occurrence of R. The right side would, thus, be an expression that depends on the value of this variable, whereas the left side does not.

The second side condition is that the list *js* may not include the variable j. This is because 'j, js' in the left side of the equality would then include two occurrences of 'j', and it would not be possible to distinguish between related and unrelated occurrences of 'j' in the range and term. For example, a naive attempt to apply the nesting rule to

$$\langle \Sigma i : i = 0 \vee i = 1 : \langle \Sigma i : i = 2 \vee i = 3 : i \rangle \;-\; 2 \times i \rangle$$

gives

$$\langle \Sigma\, i, i \;:\; (i = 0 \vee i = 1) \wedge (i = 2 \vee i = 3) \;:\; i \;-\; 2 \times i \rangle \;.$$

This is meaningless because it is impossible to determine which occurrences of i are related, and which not.

It is always possible to avoid such complications by suitably renaming bound variables before using the nesting rule. Using the renaming rule, the above summation equals

$$\langle \Sigma i : i = 0 \vee i = 1 : \langle \Sigma j : j = 2 \vee j = 3 : j \rangle \;-\; 2 \times i \rangle \;,$$

which, by the nesting rule, equals

$$\langle \Sigma\, i, j \;:\; (i = 0 \vee i = 1) \wedge (j = 2 \vee j = 3) \;:\; j \;-\; 2 \times i \rangle \;.$$

It is worth remarking that the rule is used both from left to right—from which the name 'nesting' is derived—and from right to left—in which case quantifications become *un*nested. So the rule is both a *nesting* and an *unnesting* rule. The first side condition relates to the use of the rule in a left-to-right direction, and the second side condition to its use in a right-to-left direction.

The third rule is very powerful because, in combination with the nesting rule, it allows us to rearrange the order in which the values in a summation are added together. Formally, however, the rule is very simple. It simply states that the order in which the dummies are listed in a summation is irrelevant.

[Rearranging] $\langle \Sigma j,k:R:T \rangle = \langle \Sigma k,j:R:T \rangle$.   (11.7)

Here is an example of how the nesting and rearranging rules are combined. The parenthesization corresponds to the nesting of the summations.

$$(1\times1 + 1\times2 + 1\times3) + (2\times2 + 2\times3) + 3\times3$$

=   {   definition of Σ }

$$\langle \Sigma i : 1\leqslant i \leqslant 3 : \langle \Sigma j : i\leqslant j \leqslant 3 : i\times j \rangle \rangle$$

=   {   (un)nesting: $1\leqslant i \leqslant 3 \wedge i\leqslant j \leqslant 3 \equiv 1\leqslant i \leqslant j \leqslant 3$ }

$$\langle \Sigma i,j : 1\leqslant i \leqslant j \leqslant 3 : i\times j \rangle$$

=   {   rearranging   }

$$\langle \Sigma j,i : 1\leqslant i \leqslant j \leqslant 3 : i\times j \rangle$$

=   {   nesting: $1\leqslant i \leqslant j \leqslant 3 \equiv 1\leqslant j \leqslant 3 \wedge 1\leqslant i \leqslant j$ }

$$\langle \Sigma j : 1\leqslant j \leqslant 3 : \langle \Sigma i : 1\leqslant i \leqslant j : i\times j \rangle \rangle$$

=   {   definition of Σ }

$$1\times1 + (1\times2 + 2\times2) + (1\times3 + 2\times3 + 3\times3) .$$

Note that repeated use of nesting and rearranging allows the rearrangement of the order of the values to be summed. The rules depend crucially on the associativity and symmetry of addition.

Range Part. We now come to the laws governing manipulation of the range part. There are four rules. The first two rules govern the case that the range defines the empty set, and the case that the range defines a set with exactly one element.

[Empty Range] $\langle \Sigma k:\mathsf{false}:T \rangle = 0$.   (11.8)

[One-Point] $\langle \Sigma k : k=e : T \rangle = T[k := e]$.   (11.9)

The general side condition on use of rules prohibits the use of the one-point rule when e is an expression containing free occurrences of 'k', the reason being that this would result in their release when using the rule from left to right and in their capture when using the rule from right to left.

The third rule allows a summation to be split into separate summations:

[Splitting] $\langle \Sigma k:P:T \rangle + \langle \Sigma k:Q:T \rangle = \langle \Sigma k : P \vee Q : T \rangle + \langle \Sigma k : P \wedge Q : T \rangle$.

(11.10)

The splitting rule gets its name because it is most often used when P and Q 'split' the range into two disjoint sets, that is, when $P \wedge Q$ is everywhere false. In this case, $\langle \Sigma k : P \wedge Q : T \rangle$ is zero, by the empty-range rule, and may be eliminated from the right side of the rule. Here is the most common example, where we 'split' predicate P into $P \wedge Q$ and $P \wedge \neg Q$.

$$\langle \Sigma k : P \wedge Q : T \rangle + \langle \Sigma k : P \wedge \neg Q : T \rangle$$

$$= \qquad \{ \qquad \text{splitting (11.10) with } P,Q := P \wedge Q , P \wedge \neg Q \quad \}$$

$$\langle \Sigma k : (P \wedge Q) \vee (P \wedge \neg Q) : T \rangle + \langle \Sigma k : P \wedge Q \wedge P \wedge \neg Q : T \rangle$$

$$= \qquad \{ \qquad \text{predicate calculus} \quad \}$$

$$\langle \Sigma k : P : T \rangle + \langle \Sigma k : \mathsf{false} : T \rangle$$

$$= \qquad \{ \qquad \text{empty range (11.8), arithmetic} \quad \}$$

$$\langle \Sigma k : P : T \rangle \ .$$

We have thus derived the rule:

$$\langle \Sigma k : P : T \rangle = \langle \Sigma k : P \wedge Q : T \rangle + \langle \Sigma k : P \wedge \neg Q : T \rangle \ . \tag{11.11}$$

This rule can now be combined with the one-point rule to split off one term in a summation, as in, for example,

$$\langle \Sigma i : 0 \leqslant i \leqslant N : 2^i \rangle$$

$$= \qquad \{ \qquad \text{splitting on } i = 0 \vee i \neq 0$$

$$\qquad\qquad\qquad \text{(i.e. (11.11) with } Q \text{ instantiated to } i = 0) \quad \}$$

$$\langle \Sigma i : 0 \leqslant i \leqslant N \wedge i = 0 : 2^i \rangle + \langle \Sigma i : 0 \leqslant i \leqslant N \wedge i \neq 0 : 2^i \rangle$$

$$= \qquad \{ \qquad \text{simplification of ranges (assuming } 0 \leqslant N) \quad \}$$

$$\langle \Sigma i : i = 0 : 2^i \rangle + \langle \Sigma i : 1 \leqslant i \leqslant N : 2^i \rangle$$

$$= \qquad \{ \qquad \text{one-point rule} \quad \}$$

$$2^0 + \langle \Sigma i : 1 \leqslant i \leqslant N : 2^i \rangle$$

$$= \qquad \{ \qquad \text{arithmetic} \quad \}$$

$$1 + \langle \Sigma i : 1 \leqslant i \leqslant N : 2^i \rangle \ .$$

(It is more common to state the splitting rule in the form (11.11). However, the beautiful symmetry of (11.10) makes it more attractive and easier to remember.)

The final rule is a consequence of the rearrangement rule given earlier. It also allows the terms in a summation to be rearranged.

Suppose function f maps values of type J to values of type K, and suppose g is a function that maps values of type K to values of type J. Suppose, further, that f and g are *inverses*. That is, suppose that, for all $j \in J$ and $k \in K$,

$$f.j = k \equiv j = g.k \ .$$

Then

[Translation] $\langle \Sigma\, k{\in}K : R : T \rangle \;=\; \langle \Sigma\, j{\in}J : R[k := f.j] : T[k := f.j] \rangle$.   (11.12)

If a function has an inverse, it is called a *bijection*. The most common use of the translation rule is when the source, J, and target, K, of the function f are the same. A bijection that maps a set to itself simply permutes the elements of the set. So, in this case, (11.12) says that it is permissible to arbitrarily permute the values being added.

The rule is, in fact, a combination of the one-point rule (11.9), the nesting rule (11.6) and the rearrangement rule (11.17). See exercise 11.19. We call it the *translation* rule because, in general, it translates a summation over elements of one type into a summation of elements of another type. It is useful to list it separately, because it is a quite powerful combination of these earlier rules, which finds frequent use.

When we use the translation rule, the function f is indicated in the accompanying hint by giving the substitution '$k := f.j$'. See Section 11.2.4 for an example.

Trading Rules.   The range part of a summation is very convenient to use but, in a formal sense, it is redundant because the information can always be shifted either to the type of the dummy or to the term part. Shifting the information to the type of the dummy is expressed by the rule:

[Trading] $\langle \Sigma\, k{\in}K : P \wedge Q : T \rangle \;=\; \langle \Sigma\, k \in \{k{\in}K \mid P\} : Q : T \rangle$.   (11.13)

Here the type K of the dummy k is replaced by the subset $\{k{\in}K \mid P\}$. For example, we might consider the natural numbers $\mathbb{N}$ to be a subset of the integers $\mathbb{Z}$, specifically $\{k{\in}\mathbb{Z} \mid 0 \leqslant k\}$.

Rule (11.13) is most often used implicitly; in order to avoid specific mention of the range (for example, if it is not explicitly used in a calculation) the information about the types of the dummies is given in the text and then omitted in the formal quantifications. In this case, the form

$$\langle \Sigma k :: T \rangle$$

of the notation is used. Formally, $\langle \Sigma k :: T \rangle$ is a shorthand for $\langle \Sigma\, k{\in}K : \mathsf{true} : T \rangle$, where K is the declared type of k.

Shifting the information in the range to the term part is achieved by exploiting the fact that zero is the unit of addition. For values k not in the given range, we add zero to the sum:

[Trading] $\langle \Sigma k : P \wedge Q : T \rangle \;=\; \langle \Sigma k : Q : \mathsf{if}\ P \longrightarrow T \ \square\ \neg P \longrightarrow 0\ \mathsf{fi} \rangle$.   (11.14)

(Some texts use a trick peculiar to summation to simplify this rule. The trick is to note that $0{\times}x = 0$ and $1{\times}x = 1$; the boolean value false is mapped to 0 and the boolean value true is mapped to 1. Denoting this mapping by square brackets, the rule reads

$$\langle \Sigma k : P \wedge Q : T \rangle \;=\; \langle \Sigma k : Q : [P]{\times}T \rangle \ .)$$

Term Part. There are two rules governing the term part. The first allows us to combine two summations over the same range (or, conversely, split up an addition within a summation into two summations):

[Rearranging] $\quad \langle \Sigma k : R : T_0 + T_1 \rangle \;\; = \;\; \langle \Sigma k : R : T_0 \rangle \, + \, \langle \Sigma k : R : T_1 \rangle$. $\hfill (11.15)$

Like the translation rule, this rule is also a combination of the nesting (11.6) and rearranging rules (11.7) given earlier (because

$$T_0 + T_1 \;\; = \;\; \langle \Sigma j : j = 0 \vee j = 1 : T_j \rangle \quad).$$

It is worth listing separately because it is used very frequently.

The final rule allows us to 'factor out' multiplication by a constant from a summation. (Conversely, it allows one to 'distribute' multiplication by a constant into a summation.)

[Distributivity] $\quad \langle \Sigma k : R : c \times T \rangle \;\; = \;\; c \times \langle \Sigma k : R : T \rangle$. $\hfill (11.16)$

The general side condition on the application of rules prohibits the use of distributivity when 'k' occurs free in the expression c. (Otherwise, any such occurrences would be released/captured by application of the rule.)

11.2.4 The Gauss Legend

In order to illustrate the summation rules, we recall a well-known legend. According to the legend, when he was just nine years old, the famous mathematician Karl Friedrich Gauss was told to add all the numbers from 1 to 100 by his teacher. The teacher wanted to keep Gauss occupied for some time, but Gauss foiled him by simply writing down

$$1 \;+\;\;\;\; 2 \;+\;\;\; \cdots \;+\;\;\;\; 100 \;,$$

and immediately below it

$$100 \;+\;\;\;\; 99 \;+\;\;\; \cdots \;+\;\;\;\;\; 1 \;.$$

He then proceeded to add the two rows together:

$$101 \;+\;\;\;\; 101 \;+\;\;\; \cdots \;+\;\;\;\; 101 \;,$$

and, from the fact that there are 100 occurrences of 101, he concluded that the sum is $(100 \times 101)/2$, i.e. 5050.

To do the same sum formally, for the more general case of summing $a + bk$ for $k = 0, 1, \ldots, N$, we calculate as follows. The crucial step in Gauss's calculation, the reversal of the sequence of numbers, is the use of the translation rule in the second step.

$$\langle \Sigma k : 0 \leqslant k \leqslant N : a + bk \rangle$$

=   {   arithmetic (in order to introduce two summations)   }

$$(\langle \Sigma k : 0 \leqslant k \leqslant N : a + bk \rangle + \langle \Sigma k : 0 \leqslant k \leqslant N : a + bk \rangle) / 2$$

=   {   rearranging (11.12) the second summation,

using permutation $k := N{-}k$ }

$$(\langle \Sigma k : 0 \leqslant k \leqslant N : a + bk \rangle + \langle \Sigma k : 0 \leqslant N{-}k \leqslant N : a + b(N{-}k) \rangle) / 2$$

=   { $0 \leqslant N{-}k \equiv k \leqslant N$

$N{-}k \leqslant N \equiv 0 \leqslant k$ }

$$(\langle \Sigma k : 0 \leqslant k \leqslant N : a + bk \rangle + \langle \Sigma k : 0 \leqslant k \leqslant N : a + b(N{-}k) \rangle) / 2$$

=   {   addition is associative and symmetric: (11.15)   }

$$\langle \Sigma k : 0 \leqslant k \leqslant N : (a + bk) + (a + b(N{-}k)) \rangle / 2$$

=   {   arithmetic   }

$$\langle \Sigma k : 0 \leqslant k \leqslant N : 2a + bN \rangle / 2$$

=   {   multiplication distributes through summation   }

$$\frac{2a + bN}{2} \times \langle \Sigma k : 0 \leqslant k \leqslant N : 1 \rangle$$

=   {   1 summed $N{+}1$ times is clearly $N{+}1$ }

$$\frac{2a + bN}{2} \times (N{+}1) \quad .$$

11.2.5   Warning

We conclude this discussion of summation with a warning. The warning is that care must be taken when quantifying over an infinite range. In this case, the value of the expression is defined as a *limit* of a sequence of finite quantifications, and, in some cases, the limit may not exist. For example, $\langle \Sigma i : 0 \leqslant i : (-1)^i \rangle$ is not defined because the sequence of finite quantifications $\langle \Sigma i : 0 \leqslant i < N : (-1)^i \rangle$, for N increasing from 0 onwards, alternates between 0 and 1. So, it has no limit. The rules we have given are not always valid when the range of the summation is infinite. The so-called *convergence* of infinite summations is a well-studied part of mathematics but is beyond the scope of this text.

Exercise 11.17. Derive the trading rule (11.14) from the splitting rule (11.10). You may assume that $\langle \Sigma k : R : 0 \rangle = 0$ for all ranges R.   □

Exercise 11.18. Prove the generalized distributivity law

$$\langle \Sigma j : P : S \rangle \times \langle \Sigma k : Q : T \rangle = \langle \Sigma j, k : P \wedge Q : S \times T \rangle \quad .$$

What are the side conditions on using this rule?   □

Exercise 11.19. Derive (11.12) from the one-point rule (11.9), the nesting rule (11.6) and the rearrangement rule (11.7). Hint: your derivation should head for using the fact that f is a bijection, i.e. that there is a function g such that for all $j \in J$ and $k \in K$

$$f.j = k \equiv j = g.k \ .$$

Use the one-point rule to introduce a second dummy so that you can exploit this property. □

11.3 Universal and Existential Quantification

Summation is just one example of the quantifiers we want to consider. Readers already familiar with the $\prod$ notation for continued multiplications will probably have no difficulty rewriting each of the properties of summation into a form that is applicable to multiplication. In general, it is meaningful to 'quantify' with respect to any binary operator that is associative and symmetric. As mentioned earlier, addition, multiplication, equivalence, inequivalence, minimum, maximum, conjunction, disjunction, highest common factor, and least common multiple are all examples of associative and symmetric operators and, in each case, it is meaningful (and useful) to consider the operator applied to a number of values rather than just a pair of values.

Two quantifications that are particularly important in program specification are so-called *universal quantification* and *existential quantification*. Universal quantification extends conjunction to a set of booleans of arbitrary size. Just as for summation, there is a widely accepted symbol denoting universal quantification, namely the '$\forall$' ('for all') symbol.

The notation $\langle \forall k : R : T \rangle$ means the logical 'and' ('$\wedge$') of all values of the boolean expression T determined by assigning to dummy k all values in the range R. In words, it reads

for all	k	in the range	R	it is the case that	T
$\langle \forall$	k	:	R	:	$T \rangle$.

For example,

$$\langle \forall k : 0 \leqslant k < N : a[k] = 0 \rangle$$

states that all elements in the array a indexed from 0 up to (but not including) N are zero. In dotdotdot notation this is

$$a[0] = 0 \ \wedge \ a[1] = 0 \ \wedge \ \ldots \ \wedge \ a[N-1] = 0 \ .$$

When disjunction is extended to an arbitrary set of boolean values, the long-standing mathematical convention is to use the '$\exists$' ('there exists') symbol. The notation $\langle \exists k : R : T \rangle$ means the logical 'or' ('$\vee$') of all values of the boolean expression T determined by assigning to dummy k all values in the range R. In words, it reads

$$\begin{array}{cccccc}
\text{there exists} & k & \text{in the range} & R & \text{such that} & T \\
\langle \exists & k & : & R & : & T \rangle \ .
\end{array}$$

For example,

$$\langle \exists k : 0 \leqslant k < N : a[k] = 0 \rangle$$

states that there is some element in the array a indexed from 0 up to (but not including) N that is zero. In dotdotdot notation this is

$$a[0] = 0 \ \vee \ a[1] = 0 \ \vee \ \ldots \ \vee \ a[N-1] = 0 \ .$$

11.3.1 Universal Quantification

Just as for summation, we can enumerate a list of rules that govern the algebraic properties of universal and existential quantification. The rules have much the same shape. In this section, we list the rules for universal quantification. Only the splitting rule differs in a non-trivial way from the rules for summation.

The side conditions on application of the rules will not be repeated for individual rules. As a reminder, here, once more, is the statement of the condition.

Side Condition. The application of a rule is invalid if it results in the capture of free variables or release of bound variables, or it results in a variable occurring more than once in a list of dummies.

The rules governing the dummies are identical to the rules for summation except for the change of quantifier. The side conditions concerning capture of free variables and/or release of bound variables remain as before.

[Dummy Renaming] $\langle \forall j : R : T \rangle = \langle \forall k : R[j := k] : T[j := k] \rangle$.   (11.20)

[Nesting] $\langle \forall j, js : R \wedge S : T \rangle = \langle \forall j : R : \langle \forall js : S : T \rangle \rangle$.   (11.21)

[Rearranging] $\langle \forall j, k : R : T \rangle = \langle \forall k, j : R : T \rangle$.   (11.22)

The rules governing the range are obtained by replacing the quantifier 'Σ' by '$\forall$', replacing '$+$' by '$\wedge$' and replacing 0 (the unit of addition) by true (the unit of conjunction). The proviso on the one-point rule (e contains no occurrences of 'k') still applies.

[Empty Range] $\langle \forall k : \mathsf{false} : T \rangle = \mathsf{true}$.   (11.23)

[One-Point] $\langle \forall k : k = e : T \rangle = T[k := e]$.   (11.24)

[Splitting] $\langle \forall k : P : T \rangle \wedge \langle \forall k : Q : T \rangle = \langle \forall k : P \vee Q : T \rangle$.   (11.25)

The splitting rule for universal quantification is simpler than that for summation. The difference is that conjunction is idempotent whereas addition is not. When splitting the range in a universal quantification it *does not* matter whether some elements of the range are repeated in the two conjuncts. When splitting the range in a summation it *does* matter whether elements of the range are repeated.

This additional flexibility allows the range in the splitting rule to be generalized from a disjunction $P \vee Q$ of two predicates on the dummy to an arbitrary disjunction of predicates on the dummy. That is, we replace an 'or' by an existential quantification:

[Splitting] $\quad \langle \forall j : R : \langle \forall k : S : T \rangle \rangle \;=\; \langle \forall k : \langle \exists j : R : S \rangle : T \rangle$. $\hfill (11.26)$

(The side condition on this rule, when used from right to left, demands that 'k' is not free in R.)

Trading terms in the range is the same as summation, with the appropriate replacements for the operators and constants. In particular, 0 (the unit of summation) is replaced by true (the unit of conjunction). But, since

$$\text{if } P \longrightarrow T \;\square\; \neg P \longrightarrow \text{true fi}$$

is the same as $P \Rightarrow T$, trading with the term part can be simplified.

[Trading] $\quad \langle \forall\, k \in K : P \wedge Q : T \rangle \;=\; \langle \forall\, k \in \{k \in K \mid P\} : Q : T \rangle$. $\hfill (11.27)$

[Trading] $\quad \langle \forall k : P \wedge Q : T \rangle \;=\; \langle \forall k : Q : P \Rightarrow T \rangle$. $\hfill (11.28)$

The final rules govern the term part. The distributivity law is just one example of a distributivity property governing universal quantification. We see shortly that there are several more distributivity laws.

[Rearranging] $\quad \langle \forall k : R : T_0 \wedge T_1 \rangle \;=\; \langle \forall k : R : T_0 \rangle \wedge \langle \forall k : R : T_1 \rangle$. $\hfill (11.29)$

[Distributivity] $\quad \langle \forall k : R : p \vee T \rangle \;=\; p \vee \langle \forall k : R : T \rangle$. $\hfill (11.30)$

11.3.2 Existential Quantification

These are the rules for existential quantification. Not surprisingly, they are entirely dual to the rules for universal quantification. (In the rule (11.39), if $P \longrightarrow T \;\square\; \neg P \longrightarrow \text{false fi}$ has been simplified to $P \wedge T$.) Once again, the side condition that free variables may not be captured, and bound variables may not be released, applies to all rules.

[Dummy Renaming] $\quad \langle \exists j : R : T \rangle \;=\; \langle \exists k : R[j := k] : T[j := k] \rangle$. $\hfill (11.31)$

[Nesting] $\quad \langle \exists j, js : R \wedge S : T \rangle \;=\; \langle \exists j : R : \langle \exists js : S : T \rangle \rangle$. $\hfill (11.32)$

[Rearranging] $\quad \langle \exists j, k : R : T \rangle \;=\; \langle \exists k, j : R : T \rangle$. $\hfill (11.33)$

[Empty Range] $\quad \langle \exists k : \text{false} : T \rangle \;=\; \text{false}$. $\hfill (11.34)$

[One-Point] $\quad \langle \exists k : k = e : T \rangle \;=\; T[k := e]$. $\hfill (11.35)$

[Splitting]	$\langle \exists k : P : T \rangle \vee \langle \exists k : Q : T \rangle \;=\; \langle \exists k : P \vee Q : T \rangle$.	(11.36)
[Splitting]	$\langle \exists j : R : \langle \exists k : S : T \rangle \rangle \;=\; \langle \exists k : \langle \exists j : R : S \rangle : T \rangle$.	(11.37)
[Trading]	$\langle \exists k \in K : P \wedge Q : T \rangle \;=\; \langle \exists k \in \{ k \in K \mid P \} : Q : T \rangle$.	(11.38)
[Trading]	$\langle \exists k : P \wedge Q : T \rangle \;=\; \langle \exists k : Q : P \wedge T \rangle$.	(11.39)
[Rearranging]	$\langle \exists k : R : T_0 \vee T_1 \rangle \;=\; \langle \exists k : R : T_0 \rangle \vee \langle \exists k : R : T_1 \rangle$.	(11.40)
[Distributivity]	$\langle \exists k : R : p \wedge T \rangle \;=\; p \wedge \langle \exists k : R : T \rangle$.	(11.41)

11.3.3 De Morgan's Rules

In addition, De Morgan's rules (Section 7.2) apply not just to binary conjunctions and disjunctions:

[De Morgan]	$\neg \langle \exists k : R : T \rangle \;=\; \langle \forall k : R : \neg T \rangle$,	(11.42)
[De Morgan]	$\neg \langle \forall k : R : T \rangle \;=\; \langle \exists k : R : \neg T \rangle$.	(11.43)

The warning about existence of summations over an infinite range does not apply to universal or existential quantifications. Any universal or existential quantification you care to write down has meaning and the rules above apply.

11.4 Quantifier Rules

We have now seen four different quantifiers: summation, product, universal quantification and existential quantification. We have also seen that the rules governing the manipulation of these quantifiers have much in common. In this section, we generalize the rules to an arbitrary quantifier. The technical name for the process is *abstraction*; we 'abstract' *from* particular operators *to* an arbitrary associative and symmetric operator, which we denote by $\oplus$.

The rules are grouped, as before, into rules for manipulating the dummy, rules for the range part and the term part, and trading rules. The process of abstraction has the added benefit of enabling us to relate different quantifiers, based on distributivity properties of the operators involved. A separate section discussing distributivity has, therefore, also been added.

Warning! In general, the rules given in this section apply only when the range of the quantification is finite. They can all be proved by induction on the size of the range (see Chapter 12). Fortunately, in the case of universal and existential quantification, this restriction can be safely ignored. In all other cases, it is not safe to ignore the restriction. We have previously mentioned the dangers of infinite summations. An example of a meaningless quantification involving a logical operator is the (associative) equivalence of an infinite sequence of **false** values (denoted by

$\langle\equiv i:0\leqslant i:\mathsf{false}\rangle)$. It is undefined because the sequence of finite quantifications $\langle\equiv i:0\leqslant i<N:\mathsf{false}\rangle$ alternates between true and false and has no limit.

How to handle infinite quantifications (other than universal and existential quantifications) is beyond the scope of this text.

11.4.1 The Notation

The quantifier notation extends a binary operator, $\oplus$ say, to an arbitrary bag of values, the bag being defined by a function (the *term*) acting on a set (the *range*). The form of a quantified expression is

$$\langle\oplus\,bv\in type:range:term\rangle\ ,$$

where $\oplus$ is the quantifier, bv is the dummy or bound variable and $type$ is its type, $range$ defines a subset of the type of the dummy over which the dummy ranges, and $term$ defines a function on the range. The value of the quantification is the result of applying the operator $\oplus$ to all the values generated by evaluating the term at all instances of the dummy in the range.

Strictly, the type of the dummy should always be explicitly stated because the information can be important (as in, for example, the stronger relation between the less-than and at-most orderings on integers compared with their properties on reals). It is, however, information that is often cumbersome to repeat. For this reason, the information is often omitted and a convention on the naming of dummies (such as i, j and k denote integer values) is adopted. This means that the most common use of the notation is in the form

$$\langle\oplus bv:range:term\rangle\ .$$

In addition, the $range$ is sometimes omitted (again to avoid unnecessary repetition in calculations). In this case the form of the quantification is

$$\langle\oplus bv :: term\rangle\ .$$

Formally, omitting the range is equivalent to a true range:

$$\langle\oplus bv :: term\rangle\ =\ \langle\oplus bv:\mathsf{true}:term\rangle\ .$$

As we have defined it, a quantification only has meaning if the operator $\oplus$ is associative and symmetric[3]. The operator $\oplus$ should also have a unit in order to make quantification over an empty range meaningful. We denote the unit of $\oplus$ by $1_\oplus$.

There is often an existing, long-standing, mathematical convention for the choice of the symbol $\oplus$ corresponding to the operator $\oplus$. If so, we follow that

---

[3]This assumption can be avoided if an order is specified for enumerating the elements of the range—this is what is done in so-called 'list comprehensions' in functional programming languages. The rules on nesting and rearrangement would then no longer apply.

convention. If not we use the same operator symbol, made larger if the printer will allow it. Examples of quantifications are as follows.

summation	$\langle \Sigma \, bv : range : term \rangle$
product	$\langle \Pi \, bv : range : term \rangle$
universal (and)	$\langle \forall \, bv : range : term \rangle$
existential (or)	$\langle \exists \, bv : range : term \rangle$
minimum	$\langle \Downarrow bv : range : term \rangle$
maximum	$\langle \Uparrow bv : range : term \rangle$
equivalence	$\langle \equiv bv : range : term \rangle$
inequivalence	$\langle \not\equiv bv : range : term \rangle$

11.4.2   Free and Bound Variables

The notions of 'free' and 'bound' occurrences of variables were discussed in Section 11.2.2 in the context of summation. The definitions apply to all quantifications, as do the side conditions on the use of rules. (Briefly, capture or release is forbidden, as is repetition of a variable in a list of dummies.) We do not repeat the side conditions below but trust in the reader's understanding of the concepts.

11.4.3   Dummies

The dummies (or bound variables) in a quantification serve to relate the range and term. There are three rules governing their use.

[Dummy Renaming] $\langle \bigoplus j : R : T \rangle \; = \; \langle \bigoplus k : R[j := k] : T[j := k] \rangle$.   (11.44)

[Nesting] $\langle \bigoplus j,js : R \wedge S : T \rangle \; = \; \langle \bigoplus j : R : \langle \bigoplus js : S : T \rangle \rangle$.   (11.45)

[Rearranging] $\langle \bigoplus j,k : R : T \rangle \; = \; \langle \bigoplus k,j : R : T \rangle$.   (11.46)

11.4.4   Range Part

The range part is a boolean-valued expression that determines the set of values over which the dummy ranges. There are four rules, two simplification rules and two splitting rules.

[Empty Range] $\langle \bigoplus k : \mathsf{false} : T \rangle \; = \; 1_{\oplus}$.   (11.47)

[One-Point] $\langle \bigoplus k : k = e : T \rangle \; = \; T[k := e]$.   (11.48)

[Splitting] $\langle \bigoplus k : P : T \rangle \oplus \langle \bigoplus k : Q : T \rangle \; = \; \langle \bigoplus k : P \vee Q : T \rangle \oplus \langle \bigoplus k : P \wedge Q : T \rangle$.   (11.49)

In the case that $\oplus$ is idempotent, the splitting rule can be simplified to

$$\langle \bigoplus k : P : T \rangle \oplus \langle \bigoplus k : Q : T \rangle \; = \; \langle \bigoplus k : P \vee Q : T \rangle \; . \qquad (11.50)$$

Furthermore, the right side can be generalized from a disjunction of two propositions P and Q to a disjunction of an arbitrary number (i.e. existential quantification) of propositions. We obtain the following.

If $\oplus$ is idempotent,

[Splitting] $\quad \langle \oplus j : R : \langle \oplus k : S : T \rangle \rangle \;=\; \langle \oplus k : \langle \exists j : R : S \rangle : T \rangle$. $\hspace{2cm}$ (11.51)

11.4.5 Trading

Two trading rules allow information to be traded between the type of the dummy and the range, and between the range and the term part.

[Trading] $\quad \langle \oplus k \in K : P \wedge Q : T \rangle \;=\; \langle \oplus k \in \{k \in K \mid P\} : Q : T \rangle$. $\hspace{1cm}$ (11.52)

[Trading] $\quad \langle \oplus k : P \wedge Q : T \rangle \;=\; \langle \oplus k : Q : \text{if } P \longrightarrow T \;\square\; \neg P \longrightarrow 1_{\oplus} \text{ fi} \rangle$. $\hspace{0.3cm}$ (11.53)

11.4.6 Term Part

We give just one rule pertaining to the term part. See the discussion of distributivity below as well.

[Rearranging] $\quad \langle \oplus k : R : T_0 \oplus T_1 \rangle \;=\; \langle \oplus k : R : T_0 \rangle \oplus \langle \oplus k : R : T_1 \rangle$. $\hspace{1cm}$ (11.54)

11.4.7 Distributivity Properties

Distributivity properties are very important in mathematical calculations; they are also very important in computations because they are used to reduce the number of calculations that are performed.

A typical distributivity property is the property that negation distributes through addition:

$$-(x+y) \;=\; (-x) + (-y) \ .$$

The property is used to 'factor out' negation, in order to replace subtractions by additions. Similarly, the fact that multiplication distributes through addition

$$x \times (y+z) \;=\; x \times y + x \times z$$

is used to reduce the number of multiplications.

Another example is the distributivity of addition through minimum:

$$x + (y \downarrow z) \;=\; (x+y) \downarrow (x+z) \;.$$

We use this rule all the time when giving directions. Suppose you are standing on a street corner and a stranger asks you the way to, say, the nearest supermarket. Suppose also that you know the route well but realize that it is complicated, too complicated for the stranger to remember. So, you point in a particular direction and say 'go down this street and, at the next junction, ask the way again'. You can be confident that your directions will not send the stranger out of their way because of the distributivity of addition through minimum! To see this, just think of x as the distance to the next junction, and y and z the distances from the next junction to the supermarket by alternative routes. The distance to the supermarket from where you are standing is $(x+y) \downarrow (x+z)$—this is the choice you make in your head—but it is also $x + (y \downarrow z)$, this corresponding to walking a distance x to the next junction and then choosing the route again. Since the two are equal, it makes no difference whether the choice of route from the junction is decided immediately or postponed until the junction has been reached.

Sometimes distributivity properties involve a change in the operator. Multiplication of real numbers is translated into addition, and vice versa, by the rules of logarithms and exponentiation:

$$\ln(x \times y) \;=\; \ln x + \ln y \;,$$
$$e^{x+y} \;=\; e^x \times e^y \;.$$

In words, the logarithm function distributes through multiplication turning it into addition, and exponentiation distributes through addition turning it into multiplication.

It is clear that a distributivity property can be extended from two operands to a finite, non-zero number of operands. We have, for example,

$$a \times (x + y + z) \;=\; a \times x + a \times y + a \times z \;.$$

Extending a distributivity property to *zero* operands amounts to requiring that units be preserved. And, by good fortune, that is indeed the case in all the examples given above. Specifically, we have

$$-0 = 0 \quad \text{(minus preserves the unit of addition),}$$
$$x \times 0 = 0 \quad \text{(multiplying by } x \text{ preserves the unit of addition),}$$
$$\ln 1 = 0 \quad \text{(the unit of multiplication becomes the unit of addition),}$$
$$e^0 = 1 \quad \text{(the unit of addition becomes the unit of multiplication).}$$

In addition, we can postulate that minimum has a unit ∞ and that

$$x + \infty = \infty \quad \text{(addition of } x \text{ preserves the unit of minimum).}$$

So, in each case, the distributivity property with respect to a binary operator extends to a distributivity property with respect to any finite number of operands, including zero. (The case when there is only one operand is trivial.)

Formally, the general distributivity for quantifications is as follows. Suppose both $\oplus$ and $\otimes$ are associative and symmetric operators, with units $1_\oplus$ and $1_\otimes$, respectively. Suppose f is a function with the properties that

$$f.1_\oplus = 1_\otimes$$

and, for all x and y,

$$f.(x \oplus y) = f.x \otimes f.y \ .$$

Then

[Distributivity] $\quad f.\langle \oplus k : R : T \rangle = \langle \otimes k : R : f.T \rangle \ .$ $\hfill (11.55)$

Exercise 11.56. Derive the rule

$$\langle \oplus k : P : T \rangle = \langle \oplus k : P \wedge Q : T \rangle \oplus \langle \oplus k : P \wedge \neg Q : T \rangle \ .$$

Use this rule to derive (11.50) from (11.49) in the case that $\oplus$ is idempotent. $\hfill \square$

Exercise 11.57 (Translation, idempotent operators). The translation rule for summations (11.12) requires function f to be a bijection. The rule is applicable to all quantifications, and not just summations. (Exercise 11.19, which asked you to derive the rule for summations, can be repeated with Σ replaced by an arbitrary quantifier.)

In the case that the quantifier is idempotent, the rule can be simplified. The translation rule for idempotent quantifiers is as follows. Suppose f is a function from the type of dummy j to the type of dummy k such that

$$\langle \forall k :: \langle \exists j :: k = f.j \rangle \rangle \ .$$

Then

$$\langle \oplus k : R : T \rangle = \langle \oplus j : R[k := f.j] : T[k := f.j] \rangle \ .$$

Prove this rule. $\hfill \square$

Exercise 11.58. The following table shows a number of associative and symmetric binary operators together with their units. For each, give an instance of the distributivity rule (11.55) not already mentioned in the text.

Operator	Unit	Quantifier
$\wedge$	true	$\forall$
$\vee$	false	$\exists$
$+$	0	Σ
$\times$	1	Π
$\downarrow$	∞	$\Downarrow$
$\uparrow$	$-\infty$	$\Uparrow$
$\equiv$	true	$\equiv$
$\not\equiv$	false	$\not\equiv$
$\cup$	ϕ	$\bigcup$
$\cap$	$\mathcal{U}$	$\bigcap$

$\square$

Exercise 11.59 (Pigeon-Hole Principle). Show that, for $n > 0$,

$$\frac{\langle \Sigma k : 0 \leqslant k < n : x_k \rangle}{n} \;\leqslant\; \langle \Uparrow k : 0 \leqslant k < n : x_k \rangle \ .$$

In words, the average of a finite, non-empty set of (real) numbers is at most the maximum value in the set. Deduce that, for integers m_k $(0 \leqslant k < n)$,

$$\left\langle \exists k : 0 \leqslant k < n : \left\lceil \frac{\langle \Sigma k : 0 \leqslant k < n : m_k \rangle}{n} \right\rceil \;\leqslant\; m_k \right\rangle \ .$$

(In words, at least one of the integers is at least the ceiling of the average value of the integers.)

What is the dual property (involving the floor function)?

Suppose p items are put into n pigeon holes. Let m_k denote the number of items placed in pigeon hole k. What does this formula predict in the case that $p = n+1$? What does it predict in the case that $p > j \times n$? $\square$

Exercise 11.60. Recall the proof given in Section 3.4 of the fact that $\sqrt{2}$ is irrational. Suppose the goal is to determine exact conditions when $\sqrt{k}$ is irrational, for arbitrary k. Can you see how to generalize the proof in Section 3.4 to solve this problem? As a hint, note that the first step in the proof of Section 3.4 is a weakening step. In general, the statement that $\exp(m) = \exp(n)$ is weaker than the statement $m = n$. This is why the step is an only-if step. However, the fundamental theorem of arithmetic says that, for all strictly positive natural numbers m and n, $m = n$ is the same as, for all primes p, the number of times that p divides m is equal to the number of times that p divides n. Formally, for all strictly positive natural numbers m and n,

$$m = n \;\equiv\; \langle \forall p :: \exp_p(m) = \exp_p(n) \rangle \ .$$

The problem is to find an expression equivalent to

$$\left\langle \exists m, n :: \sqrt{k} = \frac{m}{n} \right\rangle$$

that does not involve an existential quantification. Your solution should exhibit appropriate values for m and n.   □

11.5 Summary

The general concept of a quantification has been introduced and furnished with a uniform notation. Summation, universal quantification and existential quantification have been discussed in detail. Rules for manipulating quantifications have been presented.

Bibliographic Remarks

Properties of summation are discussed extensively in the book *Concrete Mathematics, A Foundation for Computer Science* by Graham, Knuth and Patashnik (1989). This excellent text is about 'the controlled manipulation of mathematical formulas, using a collection of techniques for problem solving'. Thus, although the subject matter is different, we share the same goal. Knuth (1969) points out the ambiguities of the Sigma notation.

The formulation of the splitting rule for non-idempotent quantifiers and Exercise 11.19 (in the more general form where summation is replaced by an arbitrary quantifier) are due to Gries and Schneider (1993). Gries and Schneider use ordinary parentheses to delimit the scope of the dummies in a quantification. Which parentheses you choose to use is not significant, but we hope you will adopt the advice of always delimiting the scope in this way!

The calculational formulation of the pigeon-hole principle (Exercise 11.59) is due to Edsger W. Dijkstra. ('The undeserved status of the pigeon-hole principle', EWD 1094, 21 March 1991. The principle is called the 'Dirichlet box principle' in Graham, Knuth and Patashnik (1989).) Dijkstra points out how counterproductive the metaphor of pigeons in holes is, and how much easier it is to apply a simple mathematical formula. Dijkstra's (handwritten) documents are available from http://www.cs.utexas.edu/~ewd and are well worth reading. Several examples of the use of the formula can be found in Gries and Schneider (1993).

Although it is beyond the scope of this text to discuss in detail, it is worth mentioning that quantifications are used extensively in database query languages. Below is a typical database query.

```
select author: Y
from biblio._ X,
     X.author Y,
     X.title Z
where "Quantification in database queries" in Z
```

It selects the authors of articles with 'Quantification in database queries' in the title. We recognize 'select' as the quantifier (essentially set union, or bag union if duplicates are allowed) 'X', 'Y' and 'Z' as bound variables, 'author: Y' as the term and 'biblio._ X', 'X.author Y' and 'X.title Z' as conjuncts determining the range of the quantification (with a comma indicating conjunction). In complicated queries, database query languages can exhibit the ambiguities discussed above, since the scope of the bound variables is not precisely defined.

12

Inductive Proofs and Constructions

The logician, the mathematician, the physicist, and the engineer.
'Look at this mathematician', said the logician. 'He observes that the first ninety-nine numbers are less than a hundred and infers hence, by what he calls induction, that all numbers are less than a hundred.'

'A physicist believes', said the mathematician, 'that 60 is divisible by all numbers. He observes that 60 is divisible by 1, 2, 3, 4, 5 and 6. He examines a few more cases, as 10, 20, 30, taken at random as he says. Since 60 is divisible also by these, he considers the experimental evidence sufficient.'

'Yes, but look at the engineer', said the physicist. 'An engineer suspected that all odd numbers are prime numbers. At any rate, 1 can be considered a prime number, he argued. Then there come 3, 5 and 7, all indubitably primes. Then there comes 9; an awkward case, it does not seem to be a prime number. Yet 11 and 13 are certainly primes. 'Coming back to 9', he said, 'I conclude that 9 must be an experimental error.'

George Polya

This chapter explores the process of inductive reasoning, linking it to the identification of invariants. Inductive reasoning lies at the heart of problem solving; it

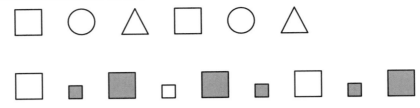

Figure 12.1 Sequences.

is the process whereby one makes informed conjectures from a limited number of experimental observations and then subjects these conjectures to the rigours of proof.

12.1 Patterns and Invariants

An *invariant* is a constant, something that is not changing. Paradoxically, in a world which seems to be changing faster than ever, invariants can be said to dominate our lives. Some of the first that a child learns are the formation of plurals,

dog*s*, cat*s*, hand*s*, arm*s*, leg*s*,

and the past tense,

kick*ed*, jump*ed*, walk*ed*.

The fact that there are exceptions to these rules can be perplexing to the child and frustrating to the parents: it can take many years to dissuade a child from saying 'foots' or 'buyed' instead of 'feet' or 'bought'.

The human brain seems to have a particular aptitude for recognizing invariants—or 'patterns' as they are more commonly called—and many intelligence tests involve just that. Consider, for example, the tests shown in Figure 12.1 which ask you to find the next two shapes in a sequence.

The questions appear to ask for the next *change* but, in fact, are solved by recognizing what *does not* change. In the first, it is easy to see that the sequence square, circle, triangle is repeated and, hence, the next two are a square and a circle. The second is more difficult (but only just), because it exploits *two* invariants, the first being that there is always a large square followed by a small square and the second that there is one white square followed by two shaded squares. We conclude that the next two are a small white square and a large shaded square.

Recognition of invariants often provides a simple solution to a seemingly difficult problem. Exercises 2.2 and 2.3, in Chapter 2, provided a couple of examples. Here is another one.

Suppose it is required to move a square armchair sideways by a distance equal to its own width (see Figure 12.2). However, the chair is so heavy that it can only be moved by rotating it through 90°, around one of its four corners. Is it possible to move the chair as desired? If so, how? If not, why not?

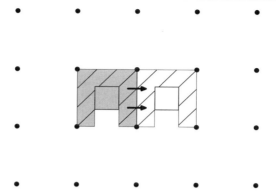

Figure 12.2 Moving a heavy armchair.

The answer is that it is impossible. Suppose the armchair is initially positioned along a north–south axis. Suppose, also, that the floor is painted alternately with black and white squares, like a chess board, with each of the squares being the same size as the armchair. Suppose the armchair is initially on a black square. The requirement is to move the armchair from a north–south position on a black square to a north–south position on a white square.

This cannot be achieved because an invariant property of rotating the armchair around a corner point is

the chair is on a black square $\equiv$ the chair is facing north–south ,

which is false when the chair is on a white square and facing north–south (see Figure 12.3).

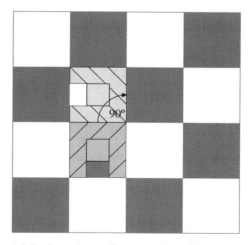

Figure 12.3 Invariant when moving a heavy armchair.

The word 'invariant' is synonymous with 'pattern', 'rule' or 'law'. Recognition of an invariant is synonymous with understanding. When scientists formulate a law, for example the law of motion, they believe they have significantly increased their understanding. But, the understanding associated with the recognition of invariants is much more fundamental than this. Whenever we use a word—'arm', 'cup', 'home'—we are naming an invariant, the property that is common to all the objects which go by that name. Sometimes it is very difficult, if not impossible, for us to define what is unchanging—what, for instance, is meant by 'living' and 'non-living'—nonetheless, we are naming something that is unchanging. The fact that the 'something' is imprecise signifies that our understanding is incomplete.

And so it is with computer programs. We shall find, in Chapter 13, that the way to understand loops, statements that continually *change* the program variables, is to examine what is left *unchanged* by the loop—the so-called *loop invariant*.

Here are some more exercises aimed at getting you to think in terms of invariant properties. They all describe some sort of game (sometimes one-person, sometimes two-person) in which every move has to obey the given rules of the game. They are all solved by identifying an invariant property of the game, i.e. a property of the position reached in the game that is true no matter how many moves have been made. All the invariant properties are very simple—even 'obvious' once pointed out. Finding them can be difficult, however, because thinking in terms of invariants is a skill that is rarely taught properly, if at all. Try not to consult the solutions too soon, and have fun!

Exercise 12.1. Several tumblers are placed in a line on a table. Some tumblers are upside down, some are the right way up. It is required to turn all the tumblers the right way up. However, the tumblers may not be turned individually; an allowed move is to turn any *two* tumblers simultaneously. Describe the initial states of the tumblers from which it is possible to turn all the tumblers the right way up, and describe the strategy for doing so. □

Exercise 12.2.

(a) In this game there are two players. A pile of matches is placed on a table; a move is to remove one, two or three matches from the pile. The winner is the one who removes the last match.

Suppose an odd number of matches is placed on the table. Who should win and what is the winning strategy?

(b) Suppose that the players are allowed to remove any number of matches from 1 up to $2m + 1$, where m is a natural number (fixed by mutual agreement between the players in advance of the game). The initial pile of matches contains an odd number of matches. Who should win and what is the winning strategy?

(c) Suppose that the players are allowed to remove any number of matches from 1 up to m, where m is a natural number (fixed by mutual agreement between the players in advance of the game). What property should the initial position satisfy for one of the players to always have a winning strategy?   □

Exercise 12.3 (The Grid Game). In this game, players A and B are provided with a grid of any size (see Figure 12.4). On each turn, player A draws a solid horizontal line or a solid vertical line between two adjacent points in the grid. Player B draws a dashed horizontal line or a dashed vertical line between two adjacent points. One player cannot play in a place that the other has already played. Player A wins by completing a closed curve of solid lines; player B wins by preventing A from completing a closed curve. Who should win and what is the winning strategy?   □

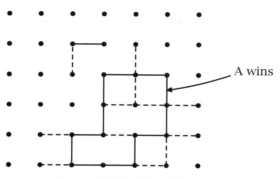

Figure 12.4   The grid game.

Exercise 12.4. Consider an urn filled with a number of balls each of which is either black or white. There are also enough balls outside the urn to play the following game. We want to reduce the number of balls in the urn to one by repeating the following process as often as necessary.

Take any two balls out of the urn. If both have the same colour, throw them away, but put another black ball into the urn; if they have different colours, then return the white one to the urn and throw the black one away.

Each execution of the above process reduces the number of balls in the urn by one; when only one ball is left the game is over. What, if anything, can be said about the colour of the final ball in the urn in relation to the original number of black balls and white balls?

Hint: denote the original number of black balls and white balls by b_0 and w_0, respectively. Let b and w be the number of black balls and white balls after an arbitrary number of executions. Then, on the next execution the values of b and w are changed according to the following rules:

$$b := b-2 \; ; \; b := b+1 \qquad \text{if the balls are both black,}$$
$$w := w-2 \; ; \; b := b+1 \qquad \text{if the balls are both white,}$$
$$b := b-1 \qquad\qquad\qquad\quad \text{if the balls are different colours.}$$

Can you see what is invariant about b and/or w? .   □

Exercise 12.5.

(a) Suppose a daisy has 16 petals arranged symmetrically around its centre. There are two players. A move involves removing one petal or two adjacent petals. The winner is the one who removes the last petal. Who should win and what is the winning strategy?

(b) Generalize your solution to part (a) to the case that there are initially n petals and a move consists of removing between 1 and m adjacent petals (where m is fixed in advance of the game).

(c) Two players are seated at a rectangular table which is initially bare. They each have an unlimited supply of circular coins of varying diameter. The players take it in turns to place a coin on the table, such that it does not overlap any coin already on the table. The winner is the one who puts the last coin on the table. Who should win and what is the winning strategy? (*Harder.*) What, if anything, do you assume about the coins in order to justify your answer? □

Figure 12.5   A 16-petal daisy.

12.2 Mathematical Induction

The process by which one infers an invariant property from a set of observations is called *inductive reasoning*. *In*duction, as opposed to *de*duction, is about abstracting general laws from specific instances. It is a process that is vital to the progress of science.

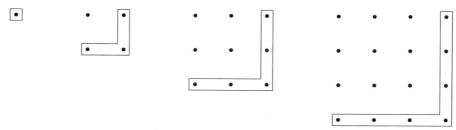

Figure 12.6   An inductive proof.

Induction proceeds from observation to conjectures to proof. Conjectures that are proved become laws. For example, we may observe that $1 = 1^2$, $1 + 3 = 2^2$, $1 + 3 + 5 = 3^2$ and $1 + 3 + 5 + 7 = 4^2$. We recognize a pattern and so make the conjecture that

$$1 + 3 + \ldots + (2m + 1) \;=\; (m + 1)^2 \; .$$

We test the conjecture—for the case $m = 3$ and possibly others—and then we prove the conjecture. Figure 12.6 shows a diagrammatic proof. Note that, at each stage, the square of size m is increased in size by adding $2m + 1$ dots, as indicated by the boxes[1].

Typically, inductive reasoning is not so straightforward. More often than not, the conjectures we make are unfounded. They do not stand up to proof and have to be discarded or, at best, modified in some way. In order to improve the effectiveness of inductive reasoning, it is important to limit the amount of guesswork, reducing induction as far as possible to deduction. Of course, it is never possible to eliminate guesswork altogether—otherwise the creative element of inductive reasoning would be eliminated, and that is too much to expect.

The Principle of Mathematical Induction

The principle of mathematical induction provides a method of proving that a property P predicated on natural numbers is true for all natural numbers[2]. An example is the predicate S defined by

$$\text{S}.n \;\equiv\; \langle \Sigma k : 1 \leqslant k \leqslant n : k \rangle = \tfrac{1}{2}n(n+1) \; . \tag{12.6}$$

(Using the dotdotdot notation: $\text{S}.n \;\equiv\; 1 + 2 + \ldots + n = \tfrac{1}{2}n(n+1)$. We prefer to use the quantifier notation in order to be precise and unambiguous. In particular, the quantifier notation makes it clear that S.0 is well defined, whereas the dotdotdot notation appears to exclude the case that n equals 0.)

---

[1]The leftmost square in the diagram has zero dots, but you cannot see them! The inability to handle important special cases—here, the case $m = 0$—is a major drawback of diagrams.

[2]Recall that a natural number is a non-negative integer. So the natural numbers are the numbers 0, 1, 2, etc.

The essence of the principle of mathematical induction is that an arbitrary property P of the natural numbers is provably true for all natural numbers, n, if it is possible to prove

(i) $P.0$ is true, and

(ii) for all n, $P.(n+1)$ follows from the assumption that $P.n$ is true.

Example 12.7. To illustrate the principle let us apply it to the predicate S defined in (12.6). We begin by proving S.0. This first step is called the *basis* of the proof. We have

> S.0
>
> $=$ {   definition   }
>
> $\langle \Sigma k : 1 \leqslant k \leqslant 0 : k \rangle = \frac{1}{2}0(0+1)$
>
> $=$ {   empty-range rule to simplify the summation,
>
>   arithmetic for the right side of the equality   }
>
> $0 = 0$
>
> $=$ {   reflexivity of equality   }
>
> true .

The next step, called the *induction step*, is to show that S.$(n+1)$ follows from the assumption S.n. We have

> S.$(n+1)$
>
> $=$ {   definition   }
>
> $\langle \Sigma k : 1 \leqslant k \leqslant n+1 : k \rangle = \frac{1}{2}(n+1)((n+1)+1)$
>
> $=$ {   range splitting applied to the summation   }
>
> $\langle \Sigma k : 1 \leqslant k \leqslant n : k \rangle + (n+1) = \frac{1}{2}(n+1)((n+1)+1)$
>
> $=$ {   •   assume S.n . That is, assume that
>
> $\langle \Sigma k : 1 \leqslant k \leqslant n : k \rangle = \frac{1}{2}n(n+1)$ }
>
> $\frac{1}{2}n(n+1) + (n+1) = \frac{1}{2}(n+1)((n+1)+1)$
>
> $=$ {   arithmetic   }
>
> true .

The crucial step in this calculation is the bulleted step in which the assumption is made that S.n is true. This assumption is called the *induction hypothesis*.

The final step is to cite the principle of mathematical induction to combine the basis and the induction step in the conclusion that property S.n is true for all natural numbers n.   □

Formally, the principle of (simple) mathematical induction is the following.

Principle of Simple Mathematical Induction.

Let P be a predicate on the natural numbers. Then, with dummy n ranging over the natural numbers,

$$\langle \forall n :: P.n \rangle \ \equiv \ P.0 \land \langle \forall n :: P.(n+1) \Leftarrow P.n \rangle \ .$$

The principle is most often used in the form

$$\langle \forall n :: P.n \rangle \ \Leftarrow \ P.0 \land \langle \forall n :: P.(n+1) \Leftarrow P.n \rangle$$

but we will see, shortly, why it is advantageous to express it as an equivalence.

The informal justification for the principle is this. The basis is the proof of $P.0$, and the induction step is the proof that, for arbitrary n, $P.(n+1) \Leftarrow P.n$. Having proved the basis and the induction step we know

$$P.0$$

and we also know (by instantiating n to 0 in the induction step)

$$P.1 \ \Leftarrow \ P.0 \ .$$

By *modus ponens*, we infer

$$P.0 \land P.1 \ .$$

But, from the induction step (by instantiating n to 1) we also have

$$P.2 \ \Leftarrow \ P.1 \ .$$

So, applying *modus ponens* again, we infer

$$P.0 \land P.1 \land P.2 \ .$$

In this way, one can see (informally) that $P.(n+1)$ can be inferred by n applications of *modus ponens*. This, together with the basis $P.0$, gives a proof of $\langle \forall n :: P.n \rangle$, where n ranges over all natural numbers.

Example 12.8. In this example we prove that, for all natural numbers n,

$$\langle \Sigma k : 0 \leqslant k < n : 2^k \rangle \ = \ 2^n - 1 \ .$$

(In the dotdotdot notation, $2^0 + 2^1 + \ldots + 2^{n-1} = 2^n - 1$.)

There are two steps in the proof, the basis and the induction step. To make the process clear, let us give the predicate a name, say E. That is, by definition,

$$\mathsf{E}.n \ \equiv \ \langle \Sigma k : 0 \leqslant k < n : 2^k \rangle \ = \ 2^n - 1 \ .$$

Then the proof proceeds as follows.

Basis.

$\quad\quad$ E.0

$=\quad\quad\quad$ {$\quad$ definition $\quad$}

$\langle \Sigma k : 0 \leqslant k < 0 : 2^k \rangle \ = \ 2^0 - 1$

$=\quad\quad\quad$ {$\quad$ empty-range rule to simplify the summation,

$\quad\quad\quad\quad\quad\quad\quad\quad$ arithmetic for the right side of the equality $\quad$}

$0 = 1 - 1$

$=\quad\quad\quad$ {$\quad$ arithmetic and reflexivity of equality $\quad$}

true .

Induction step.

$\quad\quad$ E.$(n{+}1)$

$=\quad\quad\quad$ {$\quad$ definition $\quad$}

$\langle \Sigma k : 0 \leqslant k < n{+}1 : 2^k \rangle \ = \ 2^{n+1} - 1$

$=\quad\quad\quad$ {$\quad$ range splitting applied to the summation $\quad$}

$\langle \Sigma k : 0 \leqslant k < n : 2^k \rangle + 2^n = 2^{n+1} - 1$

$=\quad\quad\quad$ {$\quad$ • $\quad$ assume E.n . That is, assume that

$\quad\quad\quad\quad\quad\quad\quad \langle \Sigma k : 0 \leqslant k < n : 2^k \rangle \ = \ 2^n - 1 \quad$}

$(2^n - 1) + 2^n = 2^{n+1} - 1$

$=\quad\quad\quad$ {$\quad$ property of exponentiation and simple arithmetic $\quad$}

true .

We conclude, by the principle of mathematical induction, that E.n is true, for all natural numbers n. $\quad\quad\quad\quad\quad\quad\quad\quad\quad\quad\quad\quad\quad\quad\quad\quad\quad\quad$ □

Doing Nothing Right. In this text, the natural numbers are defined to be the integers from 0 onwards. Curiously, texts on mathematics often define the natural numbers to be the integers from 1 onwards, and take $n = 1$ as the base case for an inductive proof on n, thus omitting the case $n = 0$! The case $n = 0$ is very important, and should never be forgotten. (Recall, for example, the discussion of the skip statement in Chapter 10.) It is particularly important in programming, because the body of a loop—see Chapter 13—may be executed zero times. A slogan to help you remember this is: *make sure to do 'nothing' right!*

Exercise 12.9. Suppose that instead of (12.6), it is required to prove the property

$$\langle \Sigma k : 0 \leqslant k \leqslant n : k \rangle = \tfrac{1}{2} n(n+1) \ ,$$

for all natural numbers n. (Note the change in the lower bound on the range of k, from 1 to 0.) How does this affect the proof?   □

Exercise 12.10. Prove the following. (The type of dummy k is the set of natural numbers.)

(a) $\langle \Sigma k : 1 \leqslant k \leqslant n : k^2 \rangle = \tfrac{1}{6} n(n+1)(2n+1)$, for all natural numbers n.

(b) $\langle \Sigma k : 1 \leqslant k \leqslant n : k^3 \rangle = \tfrac{1}{4} n^2 (n+1)^2$, for all natural numbers n.

(c) $\langle \Sigma k : 0 \leqslant k \leqslant n : x^k \rangle = \dfrac{x^{n+1} - 1}{x - 1}$, for all (real) x, $x \neq 1$, and all natural numbers n.

(d) $(1+x)^n \geqslant 1 + n \times x$, for all x, $x > -1$, and all natural numbers n.

(e) $\left\langle \Sigma k : 1 \leqslant k \leqslant n : \dfrac{1}{k \times (k+1)} \right\rangle = \dfrac{n}{n+1}$, for all natural numbers n.

(f) $\left\langle \Sigma k : 1 \leqslant k \leqslant n : \dfrac{k}{2^k} \right\rangle = 2 - \dfrac{n+2}{2^n}$, for all natural numbers n.   □

12.3 Strong Induction

A variation on the principle of mathematical induction is the so-called *strong induction* principle[3]. Formally, in a proof by strong induction, there is no separate basis step and the induction step uses the assumption $\langle \forall k : 0 \leqslant k < n : P.k \rangle$ in order to prove $P.n$. The precise formulation is as follows.

Principle of Strong Mathematical Induction.

Let P be a predicate on the natural numbers. Then, with dummy n ranging over the natural numbers,

$$\langle \forall n :: P.n \rangle \ \equiv \ \langle \forall n :: P.n \Leftarrow \langle \forall k : 0 \leqslant k < n : P.k \rangle \rangle \ .$$

The word 'strong' is used because the induction hypothesis when proving $P.(n+1)$ is $P.0 \wedge P.1 \wedge \ldots \wedge P.n$, which is stronger than the hypothesis $P.n$ used in simple mathematical induction. The absence of a base case is sometimes illusory; occasionally, a special case needs to be made for $n = 0$ in the induction step as the induction hypothesis is $\langle \forall k : 0 \leqslant k < 0 : P.k \rangle$, i.e. true, which is just the same as in simple induction.

---

[3]The principle is sometimes called *course-of-values induction*.

Example 12.11. Very often in the analysis of algorithms we are faced with a *recurrence relation* whose solution expresses, for example, the worst-case running time of the algorithm. An example is the following:

$$T.0 = 1 ,$$
$$T.(n+1) = 1 + \langle \Sigma k : 0 \leqslant k \leqslant n : T.k \rangle .$$

The problem is to find a closed formula for $T.n$. In this case, by writing down a few values,

$$T.0 = 1 \quad , \quad T.1 = 2 \quad , \quad T.2 = 4 \quad , \quad T.3 = 8 \quad , \quad T.4 = 16 ,$$

it is plausible to guess that $T.n = 2^n$. This we prove using the principle of strong induction. The induction hypothesis $P.n$ is thus $T.n = 2^n$.

Although the principle of strong induction does not specifically mention a base case, we have to treat the case $n = 0$ separately because the definition of $T.0$ is a special case.

For $n = 0$, $T.n = 1$ by definition. But $1 = 2^0$. So, for $n = 0$, $T.n = 2^n$ as required. Also, for $n > 0$,

$$T.n$$
$$= \quad \{ \quad \text{definition} \quad \}$$
$$1 + \langle \Sigma k : 0 \leqslant k < n : T.k \rangle$$
$$= \quad \{ \quad \bullet \quad \text{assume that } \langle \forall k : 0 \leqslant k < n : T.k = 2^k \rangle . \quad \}$$
$$1 + \langle \Sigma k : 0 \leqslant k < n : 2^k \rangle$$
$$= \quad \{ \quad \text{by example 12.8, } \langle \Sigma k : 0 \leqslant k < n : 2^k \rangle = 2^n - 1 \quad \}$$
$$1 + (2^n - 1)$$
$$= \quad \{ \quad \text{arithmetic} \quad \}$$
$$2^n .$$

The property thus follows by the principle of strong mathematical induction. □

Example 12.12. The recurrence relation

$$F.0 = 0 ,$$
$$F.1 = 1 ,$$
$$F.(n+2) = F.(n+1) + F.n ,$$

where n is a natural number, defines the *Fibonacci numbers*. The first few elements in the sequence are

$$0 , 1 , 1 , 2 , 3 , 5 , 8 .$$

The Fibonacci sequence has a number of remarkable properties which are discussed in depth in many textbooks. Many involve its relationship to the *golden ratio*, G, where

$$G = \tfrac{1}{2}(1 + \sqrt{5}) \ .$$

G is one of the roots of the equation in x

$$x^2 - x - 1 = 0 \ .$$

(In other words, $G^2 - G - 1 = 0$.) The other root is

$$G' = \tfrac{1}{2}(1 - \sqrt{5}) \ .$$

Here we use strong induction to prove that, for all n such that $n \geqslant 1$,

$$G^{n-2} \leqslant F.n \leqslant G^{n-1} \ .$$

The exercises ask you to prove further properties of $F.n$.

Basis. It is important to be very careful in the proof of any theorem about the Fibonacci numbers because there are three separate cases in the definition; it is very easy to make the mistake of applying the rule $F.(n+2) = F.(n+1) + F.n$ when n is not defined. (See Exercise 12.14 for an example). In addition, in this case, the property we have to prove is claimed to be true only for n such that $n \geqslant 1$. (It is false when n equals 0.) A mistake that is easily made in the induction step is to assume that the property is true when n equals 0. This means that we are obliged to prove the property for the cases $n = 1$ and $n = 2$ before proceeding to the induction step. For $n = 1$, we have

$$G^{1-2} \leqslant F.1 \leqslant G^{1-1}$$

$\quad = \qquad \{ \qquad$ arithmetic, definition of $F.1 \quad \}$

$$G^{-1} \leqslant 1 \leqslant 1$$

$\quad = \qquad \{ \qquad G = \tfrac{1}{2}(1 + \sqrt{5}) > 1. \text{ So } G^{-1} \leqslant 1. \quad \}$

$\quad$ true .

For $n = 2$, we have

$$G^{2-2} \leqslant F.2 \leqslant G^{2-1}$$

$\quad = \qquad \{ \qquad$ arithmetic, definition of $F.2 \quad \}$

$$1 \leqslant 1 \leqslant G$$

$\quad = \qquad \{ \qquad G = \tfrac{1}{2}(1 + \sqrt{5}) > 1. \quad \}$

$\quad$ true .

Induction step. In the induction step we assume that $n \geqslant 2$. This means that

$$F.(n+1) = F.n + F.(n-1)$$

and the use of strong induction is valid.

$$G^{(n+1)-2} \leqslant F.(n+1) \leqslant G^{(n+1)-1}$$

$=$ {   arithmetic, definition of F (see remarks above) }

$$G^{n-1} \leqslant F.n + F.(n-1) \leqslant G^n$$

$=$ {   heading for the induction hypothesis, we note that

                 $G^2 - G - 1 = 0$. So, $G^{n-1} = G^{n-3} \times G^2 = G^{n-2} + G^{n-3}$.

                 Similarly, $G^n = G^{n-1} + G^{n-2}$. }

$$G^{n-2} + G^{n-3} \leqslant F.n + F.(n-1) \leqslant G^{n-1} + G^{n-2}$$

$\Leftarrow$ {   addition is monotonic }

$$G^{n-2} \leqslant F.n \leqslant G^{n-1} \ \wedge \ G^{n-3} \leqslant F.(n-1) \leqslant G^{n-2}$$

$=$ {   by the principle of strong induction,

                 and the fact that $n \geqslant 2$, we may assume that

                 $G^{n-2} \leqslant F.n \leqslant G^{n-1}$ and $G^{n-3} \leqslant F.(n-1) \leqslant G^{n-2}$ }

true .

Look again at this proof to ensure that you have understood the use of strong induction. Its use, rather than simple induction, was necessary in the very last step above.

It is also worth looking again at the warnings we made before establishing the basis of the proof. The real significance of these warnings only becomes apparent in the last step. Satisfy yourself that the step is valid and why it would be invalid if the basis had excluded the case $n = 2$.   □

Exercise 12.13. Prove that $F.(n+1) \times F.(n-1) - (F.n)^2 = (-1)^n$ for all n, $n \geqslant 1$. Does your proof use strong induction or simple induction?   □

Exercise 12.14. Here is a proof that $F.n = 0$ for all n. What is wrong with it?

Basis. $F.0 = 0$ by definition.

Induction step. We have, for all n, $n \geqslant 0$,

$$F.(n+1)$$

$=$ {   definition }

$$F.(n-1) + F.n$$

$=$ {   by the principle of strong induction

$$\text{we may assume that } F.(n-1) = 0 \text{ and } F.n = 0 \quad \}$$

$$0 + 0$$

$$= \qquad \{ \qquad \text{arithmetic} \quad \}$$

$$0 \ .$$

$\square$

12.4   From Verification to Construction

So far, we have used induction to *verify* known mathematical formulae. Verification is important but has a major drawback—it seems that a substantial amount of clairvoyance is needed to come up with the formula that is to be verified. And, if one's conjecture is wrong, verification gives little help in determining the correct formula.

Induction is *not* important in computing science as a verification principle but because it is a fundamental principle in the *construction* of computer programs. This section introduces the use of induction in the construction of mathematical formulae.

The problem we consider is how to determine a closed formula for the sum of the kth powers of the first n natural numbers.

Three instances of this problem were given in Section 12.2. You will recall that the section began by showing how to verify that

$$\langle \Sigma k : 1 \leqslant k \leqslant n : k \rangle = \tfrac{1}{2}n(n+1) \ .$$

Also, Exercises 12.10 (a) and 12.10 (b) were about verifying that

$$\langle \Sigma k : 1 \leqslant k \leqslant n : k^2 \rangle = \tfrac{1}{6}n(n+1)(2n+1)$$

and

$$\langle \Sigma k : 1 \leqslant k \leqslant n : k^3 \rangle = \tfrac{1}{4}n^2(n+1)^2 \ .$$

As well as being good examples of the strength of the principle of mathematical induction, the examples also illustrate the weakness of verification: the technique works if the answer is known, but what happens if the answer is not already known! Suppose, for example, that you were now asked to determine a closed formula for the sum of the 4th powers of the first n numbers:

$$\langle \Sigma k : 1 \leqslant k \leqslant n : k^4 \rangle = ? \ .$$

How would you proceed? Verification, using the principle of mathematical induction, does not seem to be applicable unless we already know the right side of the equation. Can you guess what the right side would be in this case? Can you guess

what the right side would be in the case that the term being summed is, say, k^{27}?
Almost certainly not!

Constructing solutions to non-trivial problems involves a creative process. This
means that a certain amount of guesswork is necessary, and trial and error cannot
be completely eliminated. Reducing the guesswork to a minimum, replacing it by
mathematical calculation is, however, the key to success.

Induction can be used to construct closed formulae for such summations. The
general idea is to seek a pattern, formulate the pattern in precise mathematical
terms and then verify the pattern. The key to success is simplicity. Do not be
over ambitious. Leave the work to mathematical calculation.

A simple pattern in the formulae displayed above is that, for m equal to 1, 2
and 3, the sum of the mth powers of the first n numbers is a polynomial in n of
degree $m+1$. (The sum of the first n numbers is a quadratic function of n, the sum
of the first n squares is a cubic function of n, and the sum of the first n cubes is
a quartic function of n.) This pattern is also confirmed in the (oft-forgotten) case
that m is 0:

$$\langle \Sigma k : 1 \leqslant k \leqslant n : k^0 \rangle \ = \ n \ .$$

A strategy for determining a closed formula for, say, $\langle \Sigma k : 1 \leqslant k \leqslant n : k^4 \rangle$ is thus
to guess that it is a fifth-degree polynomial in n and then *use induction to calculate
the coefficients*. The calculation in this case is quite long so let us illustrate the
process by showing how to construct a closed formula for $\langle \Sigma k : 1 \leqslant k \leqslant n : k \rangle$.

We conjecture that the required formula is a second-degree polynomial in n,
say $a + bn + cn^2$, and then calculate the coefficients a, b and c. Here is how the
calculation goes.

For brevity, let us use $P.n$ to denote the proposition

$$\langle \Sigma k : 1 \leqslant k \leqslant n : k \rangle \ = \ a + bn + cn^2 \ .$$

Then

$$\langle \forall n :: \langle \Sigma k : 1 \leqslant k \leqslant n : k \rangle \ = \ a + bn + cn^2 \rangle$$

$=$ {   principle of mathematical induction,

                     definition of $P.n$ }

$$\langle \Sigma k : 1 \leqslant k \leqslant 0 : k \rangle \ = \ a + b0 + c0^2$$

$$\wedge \langle \forall n :: P.(n+1) \Leftarrow P.n \rangle$$

$=$ {   empty range and arithmetic   }

$$0 = a \ \wedge \ \langle \forall n :: P.(n+1) \Leftarrow P.n \rangle \ .$$

So the basis of the induction has allowed us to deduce that a, the coefficient of
n^0, is 0. Now we calculate b and c. To do so, we make the induction hypothesis

that $0 \leqslant n$ and $P.n$ is true. Then

$\qquad P.(n+1)$

$= \qquad \{ \qquad \text{definition of } P, a = 0 \quad \}$

$\langle \Sigma k : 1 \leqslant k \leqslant n+1 : k \rangle \; = \; b(n+1) + c(n+1)^2$

$= \qquad \{ \qquad \text{range splitting} \quad \}$

$\langle \Sigma k : 1 \leqslant k \leqslant n : k \rangle + n + 1 \; = \; b(n+1) + c(n+1)^2$

$= \qquad \{ \qquad \text{assumption: } P.n, a = 0.$

$\qquad\qquad \text{That is, } \langle \Sigma k : 1 \leqslant k \leqslant n : k \rangle \; = \; bn + cn^2 \quad \}$

$bn + cn^2 + n + 1 \; = \; b(n+1) + c(n+1)^2$

$= \qquad \{ \qquad \text{arithmetic} \quad \}$

$cn^2 + (b+1)n + 1 \; = \; cn^2 + (b+2c)n + b + c$

$\Leftarrow \qquad \{ \qquad \text{comparing coefficients} \quad \}$

$1 = 2c \;\wedge\; 1 = b + c$

$= \qquad \{ \qquad \text{arithmetic} \quad \}$

$\frac{1}{2} = c \;\wedge\; \frac{1}{2} = b \;\; .$

From the conjecture that the sum of the first n numbers is a quadratic in n, we have thus calculated that

$$\langle \Sigma k : 1 \leqslant k \leqslant n : k \rangle \; = \; \tfrac{1}{2}n + \tfrac{1}{2}n^2 \;\; .$$

Extrapolating from this calculation, one can see that it embodies an algorithm to express $\langle \Sigma k : 1 \leqslant k \leqslant n : k^m \rangle$ as a polynomial function for any given natural number m. The steps in the algorithm are as follows.

(i) Postulate that the summation is a polynomial in n with degree $m+1$.

(ii) Use the principle of mathematical induction together with the empty-range and range-splitting rules to determine a system of simultaneous equations in the coefficients.

(iii) Finally, solve the system of equations.

Exercise 12.15. Use the technique just demonstrated to construct closed formulae for

$$\langle \Sigma k : 1 \leqslant k \leqslant n : k^0 \rangle \quad \text{and} \quad \langle \Sigma k : 1 \leqslant k \leqslant n : k^2 \rangle \;\; .$$

$\square$

12.5   Summary

This chapter has introduced the principle of mathematical induction. Induction is about identifying patterns or 'invariants', a process that is vital to the construction of computer programs. The emphasis has been on the use of mathematical induction in *verifying* known mathematical formula and only briefly have we illustrated its use in *constructing* novel properties. The next chapter continues the discussion of the latter, much more important, aspect of inductive reasoning.

Bibliographic Remarks

The exercises and examples used in this chapter are mostly standard, and appear in lots of places. Exercises 12.3 and 12.4 are from Gries (1981).

Although not directly related to programming, George Polya's books (1954, 1981) are warmly recommended. Polya's concern is with the process of problem solving, including the formulation of conjectures and their subsequent verification or refutation. He illustrates his ideas with a tremendous collection of examples, taken from many branches of mathematics. The tale of the logician, the mathematician and the physicist at the head of this chapter is from Polya (1954).

13

Iteration

This chapter is about designing programs that involve iterating the execution of a statement whilst some condition on the program state holds. The key elements are *invariant properties* and *bound functions*, both of which were introduced in Chapter 1.

13.1 The do-od Statement

All but the most trivial programs involve some sort of iterative process whereby the values of the program variables are continually updated until the desired final state is reached.

Iteration in conventional programming languages is usually signalled by the keyword **while**. A while statement has two parts, a *condition* and a *body*. The condition is a boolean-valued function of the program variables and the body is a statement. The body is repeatedly executed so long as ('while') the condition is true.

In this text, iteration is indicated by parenthesizing a collection of guarded commands by 'do' and 'od'. The statement denoted by `while (b) S` in Java, or **while** b **do** S in Pascal, is denoted here by

$$\text{do } b \longrightarrow S \text{ od} \ .$$

Here, b is the *condition* and S is the *body* of the loop. The use of a parenthesis pair improves readability and minimizes the use of additional brackets which are otherwise needed to delimit the extent of the loop body.

As for conditional statements, it is convenient to allow a (finite) set of guarded commands rather than just one. The notation

$$\text{do } b_1 \longrightarrow S_1$$
$$\square \quad b_2 \longrightarrow S_2$$
$$\square \quad \dots$$
$$\square \quad b_n \longrightarrow S_n$$
$$\text{od },$$

where, for each i, b_i is a boolean-valued expression and S_i is a statement, denotes a program that is executed by iterating the process of choosing an i such that the guard b_i evaluates to true, and then executing the statement S_i. If none of the guards evaluates to true, execution terminates. (Note that non-determinism is allowed; it may be that more than one guard evaluates to true, in which case an arbitrary choice is made as to which statement to execute.) We call a statement of this form a *loop*.

An example of a loop is the statement

$$\text{do } m < n \; \longrightarrow \; d,m \; := \; d+1, m+1$$
$$\square \quad m > n \; \longrightarrow \; d,n \; := \; d+1, n+1$$
$$\text{od },$$

which adds to the initial value of d the absolute difference between (integer) variables m and n, resetting m and n in the process to the maximum of their initial values.

Allowing multiple guards does not increase the power of the language since

$$\text{do } b_1 \longrightarrow S_1 \square \dots \square b_n \longrightarrow S_n \text{ od}$$

is equivalent to

$$\text{do } b_1 \vee \dots \vee b_n \longrightarrow \quad \text{if } b_1 \longrightarrow S_1 \square \dots \square b_n \longrightarrow S_n$$
$$\text{fi}$$
$$\text{od }.$$

So loops with multiple guards are easily rewritten as while statements. But, as in the case of conditional statements, multiple guards improve readability as well as helping to avoid error.

13.2 Constructing Loops

Invariants and Bound Functions. When constructing loops, the notions of an *invariant* property and a *bound function*[1] are crucial. Loops are designed so that

---

[1]Not to be confused with bound *variable*. The word 'bound' is used in two different ways. In 'bound variable', it signifies 'binding', i.e. tying together. In 'bound function', it signifies a restriction or limitation.

each iteration of the loop body *maintains* the invariant whilst *making progress* to the required postcondition by always decreasing the bound function. Let us formulate this design principle in detail.

Suppose a problem is specified by precondition P and postcondition Q. We design a loop to meet this specification by identifying an invariant property inv and a bound function bf.

The bound function is a measure of the size of the problem to be solved. It is required to be an integer-valued function of the program variables that is guaranteed to be greater than zero when the loop is executed. A guarantee that the value of such a bound function is always decreased at each iteration is a guarantee that the number of times the loop body is executed is at most the initial value of the bound function.

The invariant property is designed, in combination with the termination condition, by generalizing the required postcondition. The idea is to split the postcondition, Q, into a termination condition, *done* say, and the invariant property, inv, in such a way that

$$[inv \wedge done \Rightarrow Q] \ . \tag{13.1}$$

(As in the rule for conditional statements, we use square brackets to mean that the property is true in all states.) The termination condition is typically related to the bound function. (Often the termination condition is equivalent to the value of the bound function being zero.) The invariant should also guarantee that, in all states, the value of the bound function is greater than zero, unless the loop has terminated. That is,

$$[inv \Rightarrow bf > 0 \vee done] \ . \tag{13.2}$$

The invariant property is chosen so that it is easy to design an initialization statement, S, that *establishes* the invariant property inv. That is, we construct S such that

$$\{ P \} \ S \ \{ inv \} \ . \tag{13.3}$$

The design is completed by constructing a loop body T that *maintains the invariant* whilst *making progress* towards the termination condition. That is, using the ghost variable C to relate the values of the bound function before and after execution of T, we construct T to satisfy the specification

$$\{ inv \wedge \neg done \wedge bf = \mathsf{C} \} \ T \ \{ inv \wedge (bf < \mathsf{C} \vee done) \} \ . \tag{13.4}$$

(Note that (13.4) allows execution of T to *not* decrease the bound function, provided that *done* becomes true.)

If the termination condition, *done*, the bound function, bf, the invariant, inv, and the loop body, T, have all been constructed so as to satisfy (13.1), (13.2) and (13.4), it is the case that

$$\{ inv \} \ \mathsf{do} \ \neg done \longrightarrow T \ \mathsf{od} \ \{ Q \} \ . \tag{13.5}$$

Moreover, if statement S has been constructed to satisfy (13.3), we can use the rule of sequential composition to infer that

$$\{\ P\ \}\ S\ ;\ \text{do}\ \neg done \longrightarrow T\ \text{od}\ \{\ Q\ \}\ . \tag{13.6}$$

Loops and Induction.   The validity of (13.5) is proved by a case analysis on $bf \leqslant 0$ and $bf > 0$. The first case involves combining (13.2) and (13.1). The case $bf > 0$ is proved by (strong) induction on the value of the ghost variable C in (13.4). Formally, the inductive hypothesis is

$$\langle \forall n :: \{\ inv \wedge bf = n\ \}\ \text{do}\ \neg done \longrightarrow T\ \text{od}\ \{\ Q\ \}\rangle\ , \tag{13.7}$$

where the type of n is the set of all natural numbers. (We assume, of course, that n is not one of the program variables.) Property (13.5) is then a consequence, because of (13.2).

We will not go into the full details of the proof of (13.7). Briefly, (13.1) provides the basis of the inductive proof, whilst (13.4) establishes the induction step. (Equation (13.1) states that Q is guaranteed to hold if the loop body is executed zero times, and (13.4) enables the proof that, if the loop body T is executed at least once, postcondition Q will still hold on termination.) The case that $bf \leqslant 0$ needs to be considered separately.

Design Steps.   The design of a loop is a non-trivial process, because there are several aspects to keep in mind. With practice, however, it becomes second nature. In order to reinforce this introduction, let us summarize the different items and their roles.

We assume that the precondition P and the postcondition Q are given. The task is to construct an initialization S and a loop with termination condition *done* and body T to meet the specification

$$\{\ P\ \}\ S\ ;\ \text{do}\ \neg done \longrightarrow T\ \text{od}\ \{\ Q\ \}\ . \tag{13.8}$$

We do this with the aid of an invariant, inv, and a bound function (measure of progress), bf. The invariant and termination condition, *done*, are chosen so that, in all states, their conjunction implies the postcondition, Q:

$$[inv \wedge done\ \Rightarrow\ Q]\ . \tag{13.9}$$

The invariant should also guarantee that, in all states, the bound function is greater than zero, unless the termination condition is true:

$$[inv\ \Rightarrow\ bf > 0 \vee done]\ . \tag{13.10}$$

The initialization statement, S, is constructed to establish the invariant:

$$\{\ P\ \}\ S\ \{\ inv\ \}\ . \tag{13.11}$$

Finally, the loop body, T, is constructed so as to guarantee progress towards the termination condition whilst maintaining the invariant:

$$\{\ inv \wedge \neg done \wedge bf = \mathsf{C}\ \}\ T\ \{\ inv \wedge (bf < \mathsf{C} \vee done)\ \}\ . \tag{13.12}$$

13.3   Basic Arithmetic Operations

In this section, we present several simple arithmetic problems, the objective being to illustrate the use of invariants in loop construction in the simplest possible context. In the first few examples, the bound function is simply a counter. Later examples involve (slightly) more complex bound functions.

13.3.1   Summing the Elements of an Array

The problem of summing the elements of an array is an elementary example of the use of invariants. Suppose $0 \leqslant N$ and it is required to compute $\langle \Sigma i : 0 \leqslant i < N : a[i] \rangle$. An obvious solution is to introduce a variable s and assign to s successively 0, $a[0]$, $a[0]+a[1]$, $a[0]+a[1]+a[2]$, and so on. Using index variable k to count the number of values that have been added, the invariant property is

$$0 \leqslant k \leqslant N \;\wedge\; s = \langle \Sigma i : 0 \leqslant i < k : a[i] \rangle \;,$$

and the termination condition is $k = N$. The appropriate initialization is the assignment

$$k,s := 0,0$$

and the bound function is $N-k$. Maintaining the invariant property whilst making progress towards the termination condition is achieved by the assignment

$$k,s := k+1, s+a[k] \;.$$

The complete program is, thus,

$$\{\; 0 \leqslant N \;\}$$

$$k,s := 0,0 \;;$$

$\{$ **Invariant:** $0 \leqslant k \leqslant N \;\wedge\; s = \langle \Sigma i : 0 \leqslant i < k : a[i] \rangle$

Bound function: $N-k \;\}$

do $k < N \longrightarrow k,s := k+1, s+a[k]$

od

$\{\; s = \langle \Sigma i : 0 \leqslant i < N : a[i] \rangle \;\} \;.$

Let us check that this meets all the requirements for constructing a loop.

The requirement (13.9) enables us to check that the termination condition has been implemented correctly. In this case, instantiating *done* to $k \geqslant N$ and *inv* to the invariant, we get

$$k \geqslant N \;\wedge\; 0 \leqslant k \leqslant N \;\wedge\; s = \langle \Sigma i : 0 \leqslant i < k : a[i] \rangle$$

$$\Rightarrow \quad s = \langle \Sigma i : 0 \leqslant i < N : a[i] \rangle \;.$$

This is clearly true (since $k \geqslant N$ and $k \leqslant N$ together imply that $k = N$).

The requirement (13.11) checks the initialization. We have to verify that

$$\{ 0 \leqslant N \}\ k,s := 0,0\ \{ 0 \leqslant k \leqslant N\ \wedge\ s = \langle \Sigma i:0 \leqslant i < k : a[i] \rangle \}\ .$$

Using the assignment axiom, this follows from

$$0 \leqslant N\ \equiv\ 0 \leqslant 0 \leqslant N\ \wedge\ 0 = \langle \Sigma i:0 \leqslant i < 0 : a[i] \rangle\ ,$$

which is true by the empty-range rule for summations.

The requirement (13.12) checks the loop body. We have to verify that

$$\{\ 0 \leqslant k \leqslant N\ \wedge\ s = \langle \Sigma i:0 \leqslant i < k : a[i] \rangle\ \wedge\ k < N\ \wedge\ N-k = \mathsf{C}\ \}$$

$$k,s := k+1, s+a[k]$$

$$\{\ 0 \leqslant k \leqslant N\ \wedge\ s = \langle \Sigma i:0 \leqslant i < k : a[i] \rangle\ \wedge\ N-k < \mathsf{C}\ \}\ .$$

Again, use of the assignment axiom is called for. We get

$$0 \leqslant k \leqslant N\ \wedge\ s = \langle \Sigma i:0 \leqslant i < k : a[i] \rangle\ \wedge\ k < N\ \wedge\ N-k = \mathsf{C}$$

$$\Rightarrow\quad 0 \leqslant k+1 \leqslant N\ \wedge\ s+a[k] = \langle \Sigma i:0 \leqslant i < k+1 : a[i] \rangle\ \wedge\ N-(k+1) < \mathsf{C}\ .$$

This is true by virtue of the splitting and one-point rules for summation (and simple arithmetic).

The final condition (13.10) is clearly satisfied:

$$0 \leqslant k \leqslant N\ \wedge\ s = \langle \Sigma i:0 \leqslant i < k : a[i] \rangle\ \Rightarrow\ N-k \geqslant 0\ .$$

13.3.2 Evaluating a Polynomial

Evaluating a polynomial involves a more complicated summation and is the basis of several other algorithms. Suppose we are required to evaluate

$$\langle \Sigma i:0 \leqslant i < N : a[i] \times X^i \rangle$$

for given real number X and array a.

It is possible, of course, to regard this problem as a specific instance of the summation problem just discussed. Doing so means the introduction of variables s and k satisfying the invariant property

$$0 \leqslant k \leqslant N\ \wedge\ s = \langle \Sigma i:0 \leqslant i < k : a[i] \times X^i \rangle\ .$$

The problem is that each iteration of the loop body involves executing the assignment

$$k,s\ :=\ k+1, s+a[k] \times X^k$$

and thus evaluating X^k.

An alternative method, called *Horner's rule*, is preferable because it uses fewer multiplications. Horner's rule involves computing the values

$$a[N-1] \; ,$$
$$a[N-1] \times X \; + \; a[N-2] \; ,$$
$$(a[N-1] \times X + \; a[N-2]) \times X \; + \; a[N-3] \; ,$$

and so on.

Functionally, we can describe Horner's rule as maintaining invariant the property

$$0 \leqslant k \leqslant N \;\; \wedge \;\; s \times X^k = \langle \Sigma i : k \leqslant i < N : a[i] \times X^i \rangle \; .$$

This property is established, initially, by the assignment

$$k,s := N,0 \; ,$$

and the required postcondition is satisfied when

$$k = 0 \; .$$

We, therefore, consider an algorithm of the form

$$\{ \; 0 \leqslant N \; \}$$

$$k,s := N,0 \; ;$$

$\{$ **Invariant:** $\; 0 \leqslant k \leqslant N \;\; \wedge \;\; s \times X^k = \langle \Sigma i : k \leqslant i < N : a[i] \times X^i \rangle$

Bound function: $\; k \; \}$

$$\text{do } k > 0 \; \longrightarrow \; k,s := k-1,S$$

$$\text{od}$$

$$\{ \; s = \langle \Sigma i : 0 \leqslant i < N : a[i] \times X^i \rangle \; \} \; ,$$

where S, the value to be assigned to s in the body of the loop, is the only missing element.

We calculate the appropriate value of S using the assignment axiom. The specification of the assignment in the body of the loop is given by the Hoare triple:

$$\{ \; 0 \leqslant k \leqslant N \;\; \wedge \;\; s \times X^k = \langle \Sigma i : k \leqslant i < N : a[i] \times X^i \rangle \;\; \wedge \;\; k > 0 \; \}$$

$$k,s := k-1,S$$

$$\{ \; 0 \leqslant k \leqslant N \;\; \wedge \;\; s \times X^k = \langle \Sigma i : k \leqslant i < N : a[i] \times X^i \rangle \; \} \; .$$

Applying the assignment axiom, the requirement reduces to

$$0 \leqslant k \leqslant N \;\; \wedge \;\; s \times X^k = \langle \Sigma i : k \leqslant i < N : a[i] \times X^i \rangle \;\; \wedge \;\; k > 0$$

$$\Rightarrow \quad 0 \leqslant k-1 \leqslant N \;\; \wedge \;\; S \times X^{k-1} = \langle \Sigma i : k-1 \leqslant i < N : a[i] \times X^i \rangle \; .$$

Clearly,

$$0 \leqslant k \leqslant N \ \wedge \ k > 0 \ \Rightarrow \ 0 \leqslant k-1 \leqslant N \ .$$

So, it is indeed only the appropriate value of S that needs to be determined.

We now use the summation rules to calculate the appropriate value of the unknown S:

$$S \times X^{k-1} \ = \ \langle \Sigma i : k-1 \leqslant i < N : a[i] \times X^i \rangle$$

$$= \qquad \{ \qquad \text{splitting the range on } i = k-1, \text{ assuming } 0 < k \leqslant N \ \}$$

$$S \times X^{k-1} \ = \ \langle \Sigma i : k \leqslant i < N : a[i] \times X^i \rangle \ + \ a[k-1] \times X^{k-1}$$

$$= \qquad \{ \qquad \text{assume } s \times X^k = \langle \Sigma i : k \leqslant i < N : a[i] \times X^i \rangle \ \}$$

$$S \times X^{k-1} \ = \ s \times X^k + a[k-1] \times X^{k-1}$$

$$\Leftarrow \qquad \{ \qquad \text{factor out } X^{k-1} \ \}$$

$$S \ = \ s \times X + a[k-1] \ .$$

We have thus determined that

$$0 < k \leqslant N \ \wedge \ s \times X^k = \langle \Sigma i : k \leqslant i < N : a[i] \times X^i \rangle \ \wedge \ S = s \times X + a[k-1]$$

$$\Rightarrow \quad 0 \leqslant k-1 \leqslant N \ \wedge \ S \times X^{k-1} = \langle \Sigma i : k-1 \leqslant i < N : a[i] \times X^i \rangle \ .$$

So the loop body is

$$k,s \ := \ k-1 \ , \ s \times X + a[k-1]$$

and the complete algorithm is as follows:

$$\{ \ 0 \leqslant N \ \}$$

$$k,s \ := \ N,0 \ ;$$

$$\{ \ \textbf{Invariant:} \quad 0 \leqslant k \leqslant N \ \wedge \ s \times X^k = \langle \Sigma i : k \leqslant i < N : a[i] \times X^i \rangle$$

$$\textbf{Bound function:} \quad k \ \}$$

$$\textbf{do } k > 0 \ \longrightarrow \ k,s \ := \ k-1 \ , \ s \times X + a[k-1]$$

$$\textbf{od}$$

$$\{ \ s = \langle \Sigma i : 0 \leqslant i < N : a[i] \times X^i \rangle \ \} \ .$$

Note that this derivation of the algorithm constitutes a formal proof of Horner's rule. Note also how the calculation of S (as opposed to guessing what it should be) avoids making a 'one-off' error. With problems like this one, it is very easy for array indices to be 'one-off'. For example, we might have guessed the value $s \times X + a[k]$ for S. The consequences are often noticed immediately, but not always. And, in the digital world, a small error of this nature can be disastrous!

Exercise 13.13. Verify the correctness of the initialization and the termination condition.   □

13.3.3   Evaluation of Powers

The problem of evaluating X^M for $M \geqslant 0$ seems a trivial one but, in fact, has been studied for thousands of years and an algorithm that is optimal for all values of M is not known. This subsection discusses a number of algorithms for this purpose.

Elementary Algorithm.   The simplest solution is to use the invariant

$$0 \leqslant k \leqslant M \ \wedge \ y = X^k$$

in a loop that initializes k to 0 and continually increments it until it equals M:

$$\{ \ 0 \leqslant M \ \}$$

$$k,y := 0,1 \ ;$$

$$\{ \ \textbf{Invariant:} \quad 0 \leqslant k \leqslant M \ \wedge \ y = X^k$$

$$\quad \textbf{Bound function:} \quad M - k \ \}$$

$$\text{do} \ k \neq M \ \longrightarrow \ k,y := k+1, y \times X$$

$$\text{od}$$

$$\{ \ y = X^M \ \} \ .$$

Using Horner's Rule.   Another method, which is commonly used for large values of M, makes use of Horner's rule. Suppose the binary representation of M is stored in array a. Specifically, we assume that

$$M = \langle \Sigma i : 0 \leqslant i < N : a[i] \times 2^i \rangle \ , \tag{13.14}$$

where

$$\langle \forall i : 0 \leqslant i < N : a[i] = 0 \vee a[i] = 1 \rangle \ .$$

Then, Horner's rule suggests the computation, in succession, of

$$X^{a[N-1]}$$
$$X^{a[N-1] \times 2 + a[N-2]}$$
$$X^{(a[N-1] \times 2 + a[N-2]) \times 2 + a[N-3]} \ ,$$

and so on.

Within the algorithm, we use y to record the powers of X, and we use the value of counter k as bound function. For the purpose of explaining the algorithm, we also employ a variable s which records the exponent of X. This variable plays no role in updating y and so can be eliminated from the algorithm. (It is a so-called *auxiliary* variable, meaning that it is used to establish correctness but is irrelevant to the computation.) The precise roles of y, s and k are expressed by the invariant:

$$0 \leqslant k \leqslant N \ \wedge \ y = X^s \ \wedge \ s \times 2^k = \langle \Sigma i : k \leqslant i < N : a[i] \times 2^i \rangle \ .$$

The invariant is established initially by the assignment

$$k,s,y := N,0,1$$

and, when $k = 0$, we have

$$y = X^s \ \wedge \ s = \langle \Sigma i : 0 \leqslant i < N : a[i] \times 2^i \rangle \ .$$

Using (13.14), it is thus the case that, when $k = 0$,

$$y = X^M \ .$$

Now, we know from our discussion of Horner's rule that the property of s is maintained invariant by the assignment

$$k,s := k-1 , 2 \times s + a[k-1] \ .$$

We, therefore, consider an algorithm of the form

$$\{ \ 0 \leqslant M = \langle \Sigma i : 0 \leqslant i < N : a[i] \times 2^i \rangle \ \}$$

$$k,s,y := N,0,1 \ ;$$

$$\{ \ \textbf{Invariant:} \ \ 0 \leqslant k \leqslant N \ \wedge \ y = X^s \ \wedge \ s \times 2^k = \langle \Sigma i : k \leqslant i < N : a[i] \times 2^i \rangle$$

$$\textbf{Bound function:} \ \ k \ \}$$

$$\text{do} \ k > 0 \ \longrightarrow \ k,s,y := k-1 , 2 \times s + a[k-1] , Y$$

$$\text{od}$$

$$\{ \ y = X^M \ \} \ ,$$

where Y, the value to be assigned to y in the body of the loop, is the missing element.

We calculate the appropriate value of Y using the assignment axiom. The specification of the assignment in the body of the loop is given by the Hoare triple:

$$\{ \ 0 \leqslant k \leqslant N \ \wedge \ y = X^s \ \wedge \ s \times 2^k = \langle \Sigma i : k \leqslant i < N : a[i] \times 2^i \rangle \ \wedge \ k > 0 \ \}$$

$$k,s,y := k-1 , 2 \times s + a[k-1] , Y$$

$$\{ \ 0 \leqslant k \leqslant N \ \wedge \ y = X^s \ \wedge \ s \times 2^k = \langle \Sigma i : k \leqslant i < N : a[i] \times 2^i \rangle \ \} \ .$$

Applying the assignment axiom, and ignoring the requirements on k and s in the postcondition (as they have already been verified), the requirement reduces to

$$0 < k \leqslant N \ \wedge \ y = X^s \ \wedge \ s \times 2^k = \langle \Sigma i : k \leqslant i < N : a[i] \times 2^i \rangle$$

$$\Rightarrow \quad Y = X^{2 \times s + a[k-1]} \ .$$

We now use properties of exponentiation to calculate the appropriate value of the unknown Y:

$$Y = X^{2 \times s + a[k-1]}$$

$$= \quad \{ \quad \text{exponentiation} \quad \}$$

$$Y = (X^s)^2 \times X^{a[k-1]}$$

$$= \quad \{ \quad \text{assume } y = X^s \quad \}$$

$$Y = y^2 \times X^{a[k-1]} .$$

So, to maintain invariant the property $y = X^s$, we must simultaneously perform the assignment

$$y := y^2 \times X^{a[k-1]} .$$

In this way, we have constructed the following algorithm:

$$\{ \ 0 \leqslant M = \langle \Sigma i : 0 \leqslant i < N : a[i] \times 2^i \rangle \ \}$$

$$k,s,y := N,0,1 \ ;$$

$\{$ **Invariant:** $0 \leqslant k \leqslant N \ \wedge \ y = X^s \ \wedge \ s \times 2^k = \langle \Sigma i : k \leqslant i < N : a[i] \times 2^i \rangle$

Bound function: $k \ \}$

do $k > 0 \ \longrightarrow \ k,s,y := k-1, 2 \times s + a[k-1], y^2 \times X^{a[k-1]}$

od

$$\{ \ y = X^M \ \} \ .$$

Two small changes are required before our task is complete. The first is to remove the assignment to s, as forewarned. The second is to take account of the binary value of $a[k-1]$. When $a[k-1] = 0$, $y^2 \times X^{a[k-1]}$ simplifies to y^2 and, when $a[k-1] = 1$, $y^2 \times X^{a[k-1]}$ simplifies to $y^2 \times X$. In this way, we obtain the algorithm's final version, shown in Figure 13.1.

(The use of 'where' in the invariant is informal. Formally, the invariant is

$$0 \leqslant k \leqslant N \ \wedge \ \langle \exists s : s \times 2^k = \langle \Sigma i : k \leqslant i < N : a[i] \times 2^i \rangle : y = X^s \rangle \ .$$

We discuss the use of auxiliary variables, and their elimination using existential quantifications, in detail in Section 15.2.)

Exercise 13.15. The previous algorithm made use of the bits in the binary representation of M starting with the most significant bit and ending with the least significant bit. There is an advantage in processing them in the opposite order, because they can be computed as the remainders resulting from successive divisions by 2. (Thus $a[0] = M \bmod 2$, $a[1] = (M \div 2) \bmod 2$, $a[2] = (M \div 4) \bmod 2$, etc.) An algorithm that uses this approach is based on the invariant

$$0 \leqslant k \ \wedge \ y \times z^k = X^M \ .$$

Develop such an algorithm.

$$\{\ 0 \leqslant M = \langle \Sigma i : 0 \leqslant i < N : a[i] \times 2^i \rangle\ \}$$

$$k, y := N, 1\ ;$$

$\{$ **Invariant:**

$\quad 0 \leqslant k \leqslant N\ \wedge\ y = X^s\ \text{ where }\ s \times 2^k = \langle \Sigma i : k \leqslant i < N : a[i] \times 2^i \rangle$

$\quad$ **Bound function:**$\quad k\ \}$

$\textbf{do}\ k > 0\ \longrightarrow\quad k, y := k-1, y^2\ ;$

$\qquad\qquad\qquad\quad \textbf{if}\ a[k] = 0 \longrightarrow \textsf{skip}$

$\qquad\qquad\qquad\quad \square\ a[k] = 1 \longrightarrow y := y \times X$

$\qquad\qquad\qquad\quad \textsf{fi}$

$\textbf{od}$

$\{\ y = X^M\ \}\ .$

Figure 13.1 Evaluation of powers.

You should make use of Exercise 10.21 in order to develop the loop body. (In fact, the reason Exercise 10.21 was included was in order to prepare the way for the current exercise.) You will need to make the substitutions X^M for C and z for x. $\square$

Exercise 13.16 (All Zeros). Given an array of integers, specify formally and develop an algorithm that will determine whether all values stored in the array are zero. Specify formally and develop an algorithm that will determine whether at least one of the values stored in the array is zero. $\square$

Exercise 13.17 (Binary Split). Given an array of booleans, specify formally and develop an algorithm that will determine whether there is an index k such that all array elements with index less than k are true and all elements with index at least k are false. What answer should be returned if

   (a) the length of the array is zero,

   (b) all elements of the array are true, and

   (c) all elements of the array are false? $\square$

Exercise 13.18 (Array Equality). Given are two arrays a and b both of length M. Given also is a binary relation R. (Think of the equality relation, or the less-than relation.) Specify formally and develop a program to determine whether corresponding elements of a and b are all related by relation R. $\square$

13.4   Summary

This chapter has shown how bound functions and invariant properties are used in the design of loops. The clear, mathematical formulation of an invariant is an invaluable aid to avoiding errors when designing loops. For example, formulating the function of the delimiters of array segments helps to avoid the so-called 'one-off' errors that can plague programs (and cause systems to crash!).

This chapter completes our introduction to the principles of program construction. Rules have been formulated for the design of assignment statements, sequential composition of statements, conditional statements and loops. Each of the rules expresses formally the creative element of the use of the particular type of statement. For conditionals, there is a creative element involved in deciding how to split the problem into different cases. In the case of sequential composition, the creative element is in deciding what intermediate condition should be satisfied after the first statement in the sequence is executed. These problem-solving strategies will probably ring a bell of familiarity with the reader. In the case of loops, the creative element is the design of a suitable invariant property. This strategy may be quite new to you. But, its unfamiliarity should not put you off. It is an important skill that is invaluable in program construction. The skill can only be acquired with practice and perseverance. Make the necessary time, and your effort will be well rewarded.

Bibliographic Remarks

Knuth's books (1968, 1969) are a mine of historical information on the development of algorithms. For a history of methods of calculating powers (briefly mentioned in Section 13.3.3) see Knuth (1969, pp. 398–422). It is worth looking at Knuth's discussion of the 'SX' method for computing powers, which was written before the importance of invariants had been clearly identified in the development of algorithms. What is interesting is that his (textual) description of the algorithm is highly operational, making it extremely difficult to understand why the method works (at least in my view), but the algorithm itself does include a comment which is precisely the invariant property!

The chapters that follow provide more extensive examples of program construction. Other texts that practise 'correct-by-construction' methods for developing non-trivial algorithms are Gries (1981), Dijkstra and Feijen (1984), Kaldewaij (1990), Morgan (1990) and van de Snepscheut (1993). Consult these texts for yet more examples.

14

Sorting and Searching Algorithms

Now that the basis for program construction has been laid, we can begin to study more extensive problems. This chapter treats some classic problems involving a combination of searching and sorting.

Section 14.2 is about finding the kth largest element in an array. The problem, and an informal solution, was introduced earlier in Chapter 2. An algorithm solving this problem was one of the very first (non-trivial) algorithms to be published together with a detailed formal proof of correctness. The Dutch National Flag problem, discussed in the next section, is a simple sorting problem that was invented in order to illustrate the principles of program construction.

14.1 The Dutch National Flag

14.1.1 Problem Statement

This section is about a sorting problem, called the Dutch National Flag problem. The problem first arose as a sub-problem in other sorting problems—we will see it being used in this way in Section 14.2—but it was given a (literally!) colourful formulation by Edsger W. Dijkstra, which we repeat here.

The problem, as originally posed by Dijkstra, concerns the control of a robot that has the task of sorting a number of coloured pebbles, contained in a row of buckets. The buckets are arranged in front of the robot, and each contains exactly one pebble, coloured either red, white or blue. The robot is equipped with two arms, on the end of each of which is an eye. Using its eyes, the robot can determine the colour of the pebble in each bucket; it can also swap the pebbles in any pair of buckets. The problem is to issue a sequence of instructions to the robot, causing it to rearrange the pebbles into the order of the colours in the Dutch National Flag, namely red, white and blue.

The motivation for this rather fanciful problem statement is partly to prohibit some obvious solutions and partly to emphasize certain aspects of an efficient solution to the problem. The only way to change the pebbles in the buckets is using a swap function, thus prohibiting a solution that simply counts the number of pebbles of each colour and then replaces the pebbles in the buckets with pebbles of the appropriate colour. Also, it may be assumed that performing a swap is a somewhat inefficient operation so that the number of times it is executed should be kept to a minimum.

In formulating the problem, we minimize the number of assumptions about the data and how it is stored.

We assume a number of values are stored, these values being indexed by numbers i such that $M \leqslant i < N$. The choice of arbitrary numbers M and N as begin and end indices anticipates the later use of a solution to the problem as a subroutine in solving more complex problems. We assume that M is at most N, but do not assume that M is (strictly) smaller than N. In other words, we assume that M is less than or equal to N; if M equals N, the number of stored values is zero.

We assume that boolean-valued functions red, $white$ and $blue$ on the indices determine the colour of the stored values. That is, $red.i$ equivales the value indexed by i is red, and similarly for $white.i$ and $blue.i$. These attributes cover all cases. So, for each index i,

$$red.i \ \lor \ white.i \ \lor \ blue.i \ .$$

We do not assume that there is at least one value of each colour.

Swapping the pebbles in buckets i and j is effected by executing $swap(i,j)$. The effect of $swap(i,j)$ is specified formally by the Hoare triple:

$$\{ \ M \leqslant i = \mathsf{I} < N \ \land \ M \leqslant j = \mathsf{J} < N \ \land \ colour.i = \mathsf{X} \ \land \ colour.j = \mathsf{Y} \ \}$$

$$swap(i,j)$$

$$\{ \ i = \mathsf{I} \ \land \ j = \mathsf{J} \ \land \ colour.i = \mathsf{Y} \ \land \ colour.j = \mathsf{X} \ \} \ ,$$

where the function $colour$ is defined in the obvious way ($colour.i = red \ \equiv \ red.i$, etc.). (Note the use of the ghost variables I, J, X and Y, in particular that it is not i and j that are swapped, but the colours at i and j.) It is convenient to assume that $swap(i,i)$ is valid and has no effect on the state of the stored values (as predicted by the formal specification of $swap$).

We are required to construct a program, making use exclusively of the above operations together with simple arithmetic operations on indices, that will rearrange the stored values in such a way that, on termination, there are indices r and w such that

$$M \leqslant r \leqslant w \leqslant N$$
$$\wedge \quad \langle \forall i : M \leqslant i < r : red.i \rangle$$
$$\wedge \quad \langle \forall i : r \leqslant i < w : white.i \rangle$$
$$\wedge \quad \langle \forall i : w \leqslant i < N : blue.i \rangle \ .$$

Note how the required postcondition has been formulated carefully to allow for the absence of stored values of each colour. Termination with M equal to r indicates that there are no red values, termination with r equal to w indicates no white values, and termination with w equal to N indicates no blue values.

14.1.2   The Solution

It is clear that a solution to the problem will involve an iterative process. Initially, all the colours are mixed and on termination all the colours should be sorted. We therefore seek an invariant property that has both the initial and final states as special cases.

A reasonably straightforward idea is to strive for an invariant that partitions the array of values into four segments, three of the segments containing values all of the same colour (red, white or blue) and the fourth containing a mixture of colours. Four possible ways of arranging the boundaries between the segments are shown in Figure 14.1. In each case, the initial state is that the red, white and blue segments are empty and the 'mixed' segment is the entire array. Also, the final state is that the 'mixed' segment is empty.

Any solutions based on the first and the last of these figures would be entirely symmetrical, as would solutions based on the two inner figures. The real choice is therefore between maintaining the 'mixed' section at one end of the array or in the interior of the array.

The first figure corresponds to a program that uses a simple **for** statement with the control variable initialized to M and incremented at each repetition by one. The last possibility also corresponds to a **for** statement but where the control variable is initialized to N and continually decremented. The idea is that the values are processed one by one in order, and at each stage the set of values already processed is sorted. It is possible to construct a program of this nature, but it is not easy and the resulting program is not efficient! (Try to work out some of the details to see why.) This is the sort of solution that arises from an operational view of program construction, not taking sufficient time and effort to think about and formulate alternative strategies.

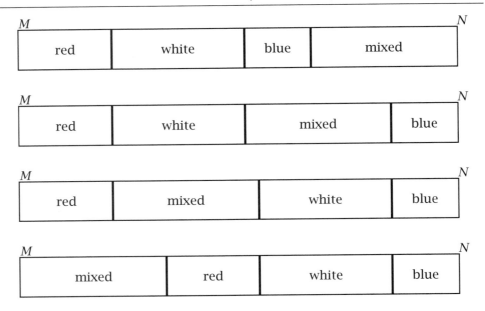

Figure 14.1 Possibilities for the invariant property.

Maintaining the 'mixed' segment in the interior of the array leads to a relatively simple and efficient solution. Adopting the second of the figures as the framework for a solution, we introduce the variables r, w and b with the following specifications.

$$M \leqslant r \leqslant w \leqslant b \leqslant N$$

$$\wedge \quad \langle \forall i : M \leqslant i < r : red.i \rangle$$

$$\wedge \quad \langle \forall i : r \leqslant i < w : white.i \rangle$$

$$\wedge \quad \langle \forall i : b \leqslant i < N : blue.i \rangle \ .$$

Note that the colour of each element is specified for all indices, with the exception of indices i such that $w \leqslant i < b$. This is the 'mixed' segment of the array.

Our goal is to design a simple loop (together with its initialization) that maintains this invariant whilst decreasing the size $b-w$ of the 'mixed' segment.

The chosen invariant property is depicted in Figure 14.2. Drawing a figure helps but *you should never rely on figures*. Figures are often ambiguous and do not properly capture the troublesome extreme cases. Always check your work against the formal specifications and nothing else.

The initialization is easy. The red, white and blue segments are all empty. The assignment

$$r,w,b := M,M,N$$

guarantees that all three universal quantifications are vacuously true.

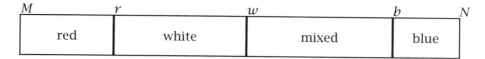

Figure 14.2 Chosen invariant property.

The termination condition for the loop is $w = b$. When this state is reached, the 'mixed' segment is empty and the required postcondition is satisfied.

In order to make progress towards the termination condition, it is reasonable to examine the colour of one of the elements at the boundary of the 'mixed' segment, that is, either the element with index w or the element with index $b-1$ (or both). This way, we may hope to reduce the size of the 'mixed' segment by at least one at each iteration. With foresight, we choose to examine the colour of the element with index w.

An easy case is if the colour of the element with index w is white. If so, the white segment can be extended by incrementing w. That is, execution of

$$white.w \longrightarrow w := w+1$$

is guaranteed to reduce $b-w$ and maintain the invariant.

Another relatively easy case is if the element with index w is blue. If so, the blue segment can be extended if the element with index w is swapped with the element with index $b-1$. That is, execution of

$$blue.w \longrightarrow swap(b-1,w) ; b := b-1$$

is guaranteed to reduce $b-w$ and maintain the invariant.

The most difficult case is if the element with index w is red. If so, the red segment can be extended by swapping the elements with indices w and r. This means that the boundaries of both the red and white segments have been moved up one position. The appropriate code is thus

$$red.w \longrightarrow swap(r,w) ; r,w := r+1,w+1 \ .$$

Note that simultaneously incrementing r and w has no effect on the size $w-r$ of the white segment. If $r < w$, then the white segment is non-empty and a white element is swapped with the newly discovered red element; if $r = w$, the swap statement has no effect.

Each element is known to be either red, white or blue. So the three guarded commands above exhaust all the possibilities and we have completed the design of the program which is shown in Figure 14.3.

14.1.3 Verifying the Solution

In this section, we finish the job off by formally verifying that the claimed invariant property really is invariant. Actually, we consider only the most complicated case, leaving the other two cases as exercises.

$\{\ M \leqslant N\ \}$

$r,w,b := M,M,N$;

$\{$ **Invariant:**

$\qquad M \leqslant r \leqslant w \leqslant b \leqslant N$

$\quad \wedge\ \langle \forall i : M \leqslant i < r : red.i \rangle$

$\quad \wedge\ \langle \forall i : r \leqslant i < w : white.i \rangle$

$\quad \wedge\ \langle \forall i : b \leqslant i < N : blue.i \rangle$

Bound function: $b - w\ \}$

do $w < b \longrightarrow$ if $white.w \longrightarrow w := w + 1$

$\qquad\qquad\qquad\quad \square\ red.w \longrightarrow swap(r,w)\ ;\ r,w := r+1, w+1$

$\qquad\qquad\qquad\quad \square\ blue.w \longrightarrow swap(b-1,w)\ ;\ b := b-1$

$\qquad\qquad\qquad$ fi

od

$\{\qquad M \leqslant r \leqslant w \leqslant N$

$\quad \wedge\ \langle \forall i : M \leqslant i < r : red.i \rangle$

$\quad \wedge\ \langle \forall i : r \leqslant i < w : white.i \rangle$

$\quad \wedge\ \langle \forall i : w \leqslant i < N : blue.i \rangle\ \}$.

Figure 14.3   Dutch National Flag program.

Our task is to check formally the correctness of the guarded command

$$red.w \longrightarrow swap(r,w)\ ;\ r,w := r+1, w+1 \ .$$

In detail, we have to verify the following:

$\{\qquad M \leqslant r \leqslant w \leqslant b \leqslant N$

$\quad \wedge\ \langle \forall i : M \leqslant i < r : red.i \rangle$

$\quad \wedge\ \langle \forall i : r \leqslant i < w : white.i \rangle$

$\quad \wedge\ \langle \forall i : b \leqslant i < N : blue.i \rangle$

$\quad \wedge\ w < b\ \wedge\ red.w\ \}$

$swap(r,w)\ ;\ r,w := r+1, w+1$

$\{\qquad M \leqslant r \leqslant w \leqslant b \leqslant N$

$\wedge \quad \langle \forall i : M \leqslant i < r : red.i \rangle$

$\wedge \quad \langle \forall i : r \leqslant i < w : white.i \rangle$

$\wedge \quad \langle \forall i : b \leqslant i < N : blue.i \rangle \quad \} \quad .$

Using the assignment axiom and simplifying, this is the same as

$\{ \qquad M \leqslant r \leqslant w < b \leqslant N$

$\wedge \quad \langle \forall i : M \leqslant i < r : red.i \rangle$

$\wedge \quad \langle \forall i : r \leqslant i < w : white.i \rangle$

$\wedge \quad \langle \forall i : b \leqslant i < N : blue.i \rangle$

$\wedge \quad red.w \quad \}$

$swap(r,w)$

$\{ \qquad M \leqslant r+1 \leqslant w+1 \leqslant b \leqslant N$

$\wedge \quad \langle \forall i : M \leqslant i \leqslant r : red.i \rangle$

$\wedge \quad \langle \forall i : r+1 \leqslant i \leqslant w : white.i \rangle$

$\wedge \quad \langle \forall i : b \leqslant i < N : blue.i \rangle \quad \} \quad .$

By splitting the postcondition into three separate conjuncts, we can split this proof requirement into three parts. Specifically, the postcondition is the conjunction of, first, the constraints on the indices r, w and b,

$$M \leqslant r+1 \leqslant w+1 \leqslant b \leqslant N \quad ,$$

second, the colour of the parts of the array that should not be affected by the swap,

$\langle \forall i : M \leqslant i < r : red.i \rangle$

$\wedge \quad \langle \forall i : r+1 \leqslant i < w : white.i \rangle$

$\wedge \quad \langle \forall i : b \leqslant i < N : blue.i \rangle \quad ;$

and, finally, the parts that are affected,

$$red.r \wedge \langle \forall i : r+1 \leqslant i = w : white.i \rangle \quad .$$

We verify the correctness of the swap statement with respect to each of these postconditions in turn.

The first postcondition is guaranteed to hold if we can prove that

$\{ \qquad M \leqslant r \leqslant w < b \leqslant N \quad \}$

$swap(r,w)$

$\{ \qquad M \leqslant r+1 \leqslant w+1 \leqslant b \leqslant N \quad \} \quad .$

(Here, we use the fact that it is always permissible to weaken the given precondition.) This is indeed the case because the specification of $swap(r,w)$ states that it does not alter the indices r and w. In other words, $swap(r,w)$ behaves like skip with respect to the indices r, w and b.

The second requirement expresses the fact that the original red and blue segments are unaffected by changes to the elements indexed by r and w. Formally,

$$\{ \quad M \leqslant r \leqslant w < b \leqslant N$$
$$\wedge \ \langle \forall i : M \leqslant i < r : red.i \rangle$$
$$\wedge \ \langle \forall i : r \leqslant i < w : white.i \rangle$$
$$\wedge \ \langle \forall i : b \leqslant i < N : blue.i \rangle \ \}$$

$$swap(r,w)$$

$$\{ \quad \langle \forall i : M \leqslant i < r : red.i \rangle$$
$$\wedge \ \langle \forall i : r+1 \leqslant i < w : white.i \rangle$$
$$\wedge \ \langle \forall i : b \leqslant i < N : blue.i \rangle \ \} \ .$$

This is true because r and w are outside the three ranges in the postcondition ($M \leqslant i < r$, $r+1 \leqslant i < w$ and $b \leqslant i < N$). Executing $swap(r,w)$ behaves like skip with respect to elements within these three ranges.

The final requirement is more subtle. Formally, we have to verify that

$$\{ \quad M \leqslant r \leqslant w < b \leqslant N$$
$$\wedge \ \langle \forall i : M \leqslant i < r : red.i \rangle$$
$$\wedge \ \langle \forall i : r \leqslant i < w : white.i \rangle$$
$$\wedge \ \langle \forall i : b \leqslant i < N : blue.i \rangle$$
$$\wedge \ red.w \ \}$$

$$swap(r,w)$$

$$\{ red.r \ \wedge \ \langle \forall i : r+1 \leqslant i = w : white.i \rangle \ \} \ .$$

Now, the one-point rule can be used to simplify the universal quantification in the postcondition when $r+1 \leqslant w$ (i.e. $r < w$). Also, the empty-range rule can be used to simplify it when $\neg(r+1 \leqslant w)$ (i.e. $r = w$, using the fact that $r \leqslant w$). So the requirement splits into two requirements, the case that $r < w$

$$\{ \quad r < w$$
$$\wedge \ \langle \forall i : M \leqslant i < r : red.i \rangle$$
$$\wedge \ \langle \forall i : r \leqslant i < w : white.i \rangle$$
$$\wedge \ red.w \ \}$$

$$swap(r,w)$$

$$\{\ red.r\ \wedge\ white.w\ \}\ ;$$

and the case that $r = w$

$$\{\quad r = w$$
$$\wedge\quad \langle\forall i: M \leqslant i < r: red.i\rangle$$
$$\wedge\quad \langle\forall i: r \leqslant i < w: white.i\rangle$$
$$\wedge\quad red.w\ \}$$

$$swap(r,w)$$

$$\{\ red.r\ \}\ .$$

The first requirement is met because the quantification $\langle\forall i: r \leqslant i < w: white.i\rangle$ weakens to $white.r$ (using the splitting and one-point rules) when $r < w$. The second holds because $red.w$ and $red.r$ are both equivalent to $red.r \wedge red.w$ when $r = w$.

This completes the verification of the guarded command

$$red.w\ \longrightarrow\ swap(r,w)\ ;\ r,w := r+1, w+1\ .$$

Exercise 14.1. Check formally the correctness of the guarded commands

$$white.w\ \longrightarrow\ w := w+1$$

and

$$blue.w\ \longrightarrow\ b := b-1\ ;\ swap(b,w)\ .$$

$\square$

14.2   Finding the *K* Smallest Values

Exercise 2.1 was about identifying the invariant properties in Hoare's algorithm for finding the 20 best values among 100 values in a deck of cards. In this section, we develop an implementation of the algorithm. If the exercise is no longer fresh in your mind, it may be worthwhile reading through it once more. The implementation developed below differs from Hoare's algorithm, but the essence remains the same.

The algorithm is one of the first truly non-trivial algorithms to be developed with the intention of demonstrating formal program construction techniques; it is called the *Find* algorithm. The algorithm can be used to sort a sequence of values into percentiles without doing a complete sort (for example, finding the best 10% of students in an examination).

Before we can begin the development of the algorithm, we must agree on exactly what is to be computed. Hoare's description of the problem and its solution is informal, a drawback of which is a certain amount of ambiguity. Using a formal, mathematical language to specify the algorithm forces us to be completely precise in our specification of the problem. This is, just by itself, a useful exercise; Section 14.2.1 provides the details. Having agreed on a formal specification, the development of the algorithm is discussed in Section 14.2.2.

14.2.1   The Specification

We suppose we are given an array a of numbers, indexed from 0 onwards, of length N. Informally, we are required to determine those K array elements with the smallest values[1], where $1 \leqslant K \leqslant N$.

This is an 'informal' specification because it is not at all clear what is meant by 'those K array elements with the smallest values'. If all the array values are distinct, there is no problem, but, in general, we can expect that some values in the array are repeated. If so, 'those K array elements with the smallest values' may not be well defined!

To understand the difficulty better, suppose the array contains the following ten values.

$$3 , 5 , 3 , 1 , 1 , 6 , 4 , 1 , 2 , 3 .$$

Now, suppose we are required to find those *two* array elements with the smallest values. Clearly, this is impossible to do as there are *three* array elements with value 1, which is the smallest value of all array elements. The same difficulty occurs if we are required to find those five (or six) array elements with the smallest values.

The problem here is with the use of the word 'those' in 'those K array elements...'. We may try to circumvent the problem by a subtle change in the wording: let us require, instead, that we determine those array elements with the K smallest values. (Note that the position of 'K' has shifted. It now counts values rather than array elements.)

The change of wording makes a great deal of difference in the meaning, but now the specification is ambiguous! Suppose that, as before, we take K to be two. This time we are required to find those array elements with the *two* smallest values. There are two possible answers we can give.

One answer is that 1 and 2 are the two smallest values in the array, and there are four array elements with these values—the fourth, fifth, eighth and ninth.

---

[1] This is, literally, Hoare's statement of the problem generalized to K. Specifically, Hoare states the following: 'It is required to single out those 20 thousand observations with smallest value; perhaps the 20 thousand nearest stars, or the 20 thousand shortest schoolchildren, or the 20 thousand students with lowest marks.' The reason for requiring that both K and N be strictly positive is explained later.

An alternative answer is that 1 and 1 are the two smallest values in the array. The value 1 occurs three times in the array, in the fourth, fifth and eighth positions, so that any two of these can be given as the required array elements.

The difference in these answers is attributable to the difference between a *set* and a *bag*. In a set, multiple occurrences of a value are ignored; in a bag, they all count. The first answer corresponds to taking the two smallest values from the *set* of values defined by the array, the second answer corresponds to taking the two smallest values from the *bag* of values defined by the array. The second answer is also the answer one would obtain by sorting the elements of the array (ordering equal array values arbitrarily) and then choosing the first K elements. Studying Hoare's algorithm (see Exercise 2.1), it is clear that his intention is indeed to determine the K smallest values in the *bag* of values defined by the array elements.

One more difficulty remains. Viewing the array as determining a bag of values means that there may be more than K elements that have the K smallest values. The example array above was designed to illustrate this problem. We have agreed that the two smallest values are 1 and 1, but there are three array elements with these values.

One solution is to agree that the specification is non-deterministic. We require that K array elements are identified but, if there is a choice, as in this case, we do not care how the choice is resolved.

The second solution is to require that *all* array elements with the K smallest values are identified. Because this is a tighter requirement and just as easy to achieve, this is the one we choose to implement. (Exercise 14.3 asks you to design an algorithm that meets the non-deterministic specification.)

In summary, the (still-informal) specification is to determine *all* array elements that have the K smallest values among the *bag* of values defined by the array. Additionally, we will require that it is possible to identify the Kth smallest value in the array.

To achieve this, we develop an algorithm that rearranges the array elements to the extent that, on termination, the required array elements are in the initial segment of the array. These elements are smaller than all other elements and there are at least K of them. However, decreasing their number by omitting the elements with the largest value (among the selected array elements) results in there being fewer than K elements remaining.

Formally, our algorithm rearranges the array elements so that, on termination, there are indices s and l with the properties that

$$0 \leqslant s < K \leqslant l \leqslant N$$
$$\land \quad \langle \forall\, i,j : 0 \leqslant i < s \land s \leqslant j < N : a[i] < a[j] \rangle$$
$$\land \quad \langle \forall\, i,j : 0 \leqslant i < l \land l \leqslant j < N : a[i] < a[j] \rangle$$
$$\land \quad \langle \forall\, i,j : s \leqslant i < l \land s \leqslant j < l : a[i] = a[j] \rangle \ .$$

In words, the first s values in the array are (strictly) smaller than any other array elements—see the first universal quantification—and their number is less than K; the last $N-l$ values in the array are (strictly) larger than any other elements—see the second universal quantification—and their number is at most $N-K$; and the remaining array elements are all equal—see the final universal quantification. The K smallest values in the array are thus delimited by the indices 0 and l; the Kth smallest value is the value common to the array elements in the segment delimited by s and l.

Note that it is impossible to satisfy this postcondition unless we impose the precondition

$$1 \leqslant K \leqslant N \ .$$

Otherwise, it would be impossible to determine s such that $0 \leqslant s < K$. This is unavoidable if we are required to determine the Kth smallest value. Note, also, that the postcondition does not formally require that the final array is a rearrangement of the initial array. This requirement is clumsy to specify compared with the ease with which it is met—by ensuring that the only operation used by the algorithm to change array elements is to swap two of them, as detailed in the discussion of the Dutch National Flag program.

14.2.2   The Algorithm

Now that we have agreed a precise formal specification of the precondition and postcondition, we may proceed to the development of the algorithm.

Hoare's description of the problem involves manipulating a deck of cards. This means that his solution involves operations that are not so easy to implement in a computer program. In particular, Hoare's solution puts the 'borderline card' to one side during the process of adding cards to the bottom-left and bottom-right heaps. We will impose the restriction that all changes to the array are effected by swapping array elements. This means that the program we develop is guaranteed to permute the elements of the array (and will not, for example, introduce spurious array elements) but prohibits us from placing any cards to one side. We are seeking a so-called *in situ* sort of the array elements.

The basic idea is to maintain invariant the property that, for some indices s and l, the first s elements of the array are known to be 'small', the next $l-s$ elements are 'medium', and the remaining $N-l$ elements are 'large'. Making precise what we mean by 'small', etc., a suitable invariant property is:

$$0 \leqslant s < K \leqslant l \leqslant N$$

$$\wedge \ \langle \forall \, i,j : 0 \leqslant i < s \wedge s \leqslant j < N : a[i] < a[j] \rangle$$

$$\wedge \ \langle \forall \, i,j : 0 \leqslant i < l \wedge l \leqslant j < N : a[i] < a[j] \rangle \ .$$

The inequality $0 \leqslant s < K$, together with the first universal quantification, defines the function of the variable s during the course of the computation, whilst the

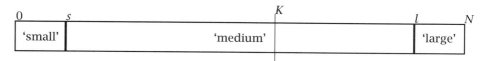

Figure 14.4 Find invariant.

inequality $K \leqslant l \leqslant N$, together with the second universal quantification, does the same for the variable l.

The invariant is depicted in Figure 14.4. (The same warning about reliance on diagrams applies here as it did for the Dutch National Flag problem.)

The computation is complete when it is the case that all values in the 'medium' segment are known to be equal. That is when, in addition to the invariant property, we have

$$\langle \forall\, i,j : s \leqslant i < l \wedge s \leqslant j < l : a[i] = a[j] \rangle \ .$$

We introduce a boolean value *done* whose function is to indicate when this property has been established. Formally, the function of *done* is captured by the invariant property

$$done \Rightarrow \langle \forall\, i,j : s \leqslant i < l \wedge s \leqslant j < l : a[i] = a[j] \rangle \ .$$

Adding this property to the earlier invariant properties of s and l, our loop invariant becomes

$$0 \leqslant s < K \leqslant l \leqslant N$$
$$\wedge \ \langle \forall\, i,j : 0 \leqslant i < s \wedge s \leqslant j < N : a[i] < a[j] \rangle$$
$$\wedge \ \langle \forall\, i,j : 0 \leqslant i < l \wedge l \leqslant j < N : a[i] < a[j] \rangle$$
$$\wedge \ (done \Rightarrow \langle \forall\, i,j : s \leqslant i < l \wedge s \leqslant j < l : a[i] = a[j] \rangle) \ .$$

It is straightforward to establish the invariant. The assignment

$$s, l, done := 0, N, (N \leqslant 1)$$

initializes the 'small' and 'large' segments, each to the empty set. (The initialization of *done* could be to false. Assigning it the value $N \leqslant 1$ enables us to play safe—the specification cannot be satisfied if $N = 0$.)

The bound function is $l-s$. The loop body need not necessarily decrease $l-s$. Instead of decreasing $l-s$, the loop body may truthify *done*. (Since $\neg done$ is the condition for terminating the loop, this can only occur on the final iteration of the loop body.)

In order to make progress to the termination condition whilst maintaining the invariant, Hoare made the observation that it is crucial to choose a borderline value that is known to be in the 'medium' segment. Values in the 'medium' segment are indexed by numbers j such that $s \leqslant j < l$. Because $s < K \leqslant l$ when the loop body is executed, the choice of $a[K-1]$ as borderline value is always appropriate, so this is the one we will choose. (Any value in the 'medium' segment will do, but choosing $a[K-1]$ guarantees termination after exactly one iteration in the fortunate circumstance that the array is already sorted.) Since the loop body may swap the chosen array element with another, it is wise to record this value in some local variable, say X. A crucial property of X, which is immediate from our invariant property, is that all values in the small segment are (strictly) less than X and all values in the large segment are (strictly) greater than X.

In summary, the algorithm we are aiming to develop has the basic structure shown below.

$$\{\ 1 \leqslant K \leqslant N\ \}$$

$$s,l,done := 0,N,(N \leqslant 1)\,;$$

$$\{\ \textbf{Invariant:} \qquad 0 \leqslant s < K \leqslant l \leqslant N$$

$$\wedge\ \langle \forall\, i,j : 0 \leqslant i < s \wedge s \leqslant j < N : a[i] < a[j] \rangle$$

$$\wedge\ \langle \forall\, i,j : 0 \leqslant i < l \wedge l \leqslant j < N : a[i] < a[j] \rangle$$

$$\wedge\ (done \Rightarrow \langle \forall\, i,j : s \leqslant i < l \wedge s \leqslant j < l : a[i] = a[j] \rangle)$$

$$\textbf{Bound function:} \quad l - s\ \}$$

$$\textbf{do}\ \neg done \longrightarrow \quad \{\ \text{choose borderline value in 'medium' segment}\ \}$$

$$X := a[K-1];$$

$$\{\quad \langle \forall\, i : 0 \leqslant i < s : a[i] < X \rangle$$

$$\wedge\ \langle \forall\, j : l \leqslant j < N : X < a[j] \rangle\ \}$$

reduce $l-s$, or truthify $done$,

whilst maintaining invariant

$$\textbf{od}$$

$$\{\quad 0 \leqslant s < K \leqslant l \leqslant N$$

$$\wedge\ \langle \forall\, i,j : 0 \leqslant i < s \wedge s \leqslant j < N : a[i] < a[j] \rangle$$

$$\wedge\ \langle \forall\, i,j : 0 \leqslant i < l \wedge l \leqslant j < N : a[i] < a[j] \rangle$$

$$\wedge\ \langle \forall\, i,j : s \leqslant i < l \wedge s \leqslant j < l : a[i] = a[j] \rangle\ \}\ .$$

It is at this point that the development differs from Hoare's algorithm. The key insight is that it is possible to use the Dutch National Flag program to sort the elements in the 'medium' segment into values less than X (the 'red' values), values equal to X (the 'white' values) and values greater than X (the 'blue' values).

Let us suppose this is done as the first step of maintaining the invariant. Let us also assume that the Dutch National Flag program returns two indices, m and n, delimiting the segment containing values equal to X. This segment is known to

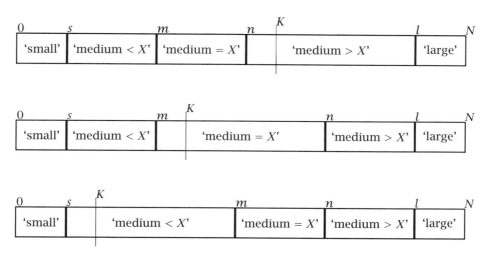

Figure 14.5   Possible outcomes after applying the Dutch National Flag program.

be non-empty, since it includes the array element previously stored at index $K-1$. Figure 14.5 depicts three possible outcomes, depending on the relationship of K to m and n.

In each of the three possible outcomes, the five segments are ordered in the sense that the values stored in the different segments are strictly increasing as one proceeds from left to right. (That is, each value in a segment is at most each value in the segment to its right.)

In the first case depicted in Figure 14.5,

$$n < K \ .$$

This means that all the array elements, up to and including $a[n]$ are among the K smallest values in the array. So, in this case, the assignment

$$s := n$$

may be executed. Moreover, this is bound to increase the value of s (and thus decrease $l-s$) because the segment containing values equal to X is non-empty.

In the second case depicted in Figure 14.5,

$$m < K \leqslant n \ .$$

In this case, the sorting process is complete; the K smallest values in the array have been successfully transferred to the first K positions in the array. So, in this case, the assignment

$$s, l, done := m, n, \text{true}$$

may be executed. Moreover, this is bound to cause the loop to terminate at the next iteration.

In the third case depicted in Figure 14.5,

$$K \leqslant m \ .$$

This means that all the array elements from $a[m]$ onward are among the $N-K$ largest values in the array. So, in this case, the assignment

$$l := m$$

may be executed. Moreover, this is bound to decrease the value of l (and, thus, decrease $l-s$) because the segment containing values equal to X is non-empty.

This completes the development of the algorithm, which is shown in Figure 14.6. Note that the line

$$DNF(s, l, (<X), (=X), (>X), m, n)$$

indicates a call of the Dutch National Flag program applied to the segment of the array a delimited by s and l with predicates red, $white$ and $blue$ set to $(<X)$, $(=X)$ and $(>X)$, respectively. The values of m and n returned by the call delimit the segment of the (partially sorted) array a, all of whose values equal X.

Exercise 14.2. Prove the equivalence of the invariant with the following property:

$$0 \leqslant s < K \leqslant l \leqslant N$$

$$\wedge \ \langle \forall i, j : 0 \leqslant i < s \wedge s \leqslant j < l : a[i] < a[j] \rangle$$

$$\wedge \ \langle \forall i, j : 0 \leqslant i < s \wedge l \leqslant j < N : a[i] < a[j] \rangle$$

$$\wedge \ \langle \forall i, j : s \leqslant i < l \wedge l \leqslant j < N : a[i] < a[j] \rangle \ .$$

State in words what each universal quantification expresses.

The second universal quantification expresses the fact that every element in the 'small' segment is less than every element in the 'large' segment. Is this quantification implied by the other two quantifications? Is it possible to remove this quantification without affecting the meaning? (In other words, is it implied by the remaining terms?) Justify your answer.   □

Exercise 14.3 (Finding the K smallest values). Suppose it suffices to find K smallest values in the array. Formally, the given precondition is $0 \leqslant K \leqslant N$ and the post-condition is

$$\langle \forall i, j : 0 \leqslant i < K \wedge K \leqslant j < N : a[i] \leqslant a[j] \rangle \ .$$

Develop an algorithm to solve this problem.   □

14.3   Summary

Many computer applications involve sorting and searching. This chapter has presented two classic examples of sorting and searching algorithms.

$s, l, done := 0, N, (N \leqslant 1);$

{ **Invariant:** $0 \leqslant s < K \leqslant l \leqslant N$

$\qquad \wedge \; \langle \forall i, j : 0 \leqslant i < s \wedge s \leqslant j < N : a[i] < a[j] \rangle$

$\qquad \wedge \; \langle \forall i, j : 0 \leqslant i < l \wedge l \leqslant j < N : a[i] < a[j] \rangle$

$\qquad \wedge \; (done \Rightarrow \langle \forall i, j : s \leqslant i < l \wedge s \leqslant j < l : a[i] = a[j] \rangle)$

Bound function: $l - s$ }

do $\neg done \longrightarrow$ $X := a[K-1]$ { borderline value in 'medium' region };

$\qquad\qquad$ { apply Dutch National Flag program to the segment

$\qquad\qquad$ delimited by s and l with predicates *red*,

$\qquad\qquad$ *white* and *blue* set to $(< X)$, $(= X)$ and $(> X)$,

$\qquad\qquad$ respectively.

$\qquad\qquad$ Return the boundary values in m and n. }

$\qquad\qquad DNF(s, l, (< X), (= X), (> X), m, n);$

$\qquad\qquad$ { Extend either the 'small' or 'large' segment,

$\qquad\qquad$ or terminate. }

$\qquad\qquad$ if $n < K \longrightarrow s := n$

$\qquad\qquad \square\; m < K \leqslant n \longrightarrow s, l, done := m, n, \text{true}$

$\qquad\qquad \square\; K \leqslant m \longrightarrow l := m$

$\qquad\qquad$ fi

od

{ $\quad 0 \leqslant s < K \leqslant l \leqslant N$

$\quad \wedge \; \langle \forall i, j : 0 \leqslant i < s \wedge s \leqslant j < N : a[i] < a[j] \rangle$

$\quad \wedge \; \langle \forall i, j : 0 \leqslant i < l \wedge l \leqslant j < N : a[i] < a[j] \rangle$

$\quad \wedge \; \langle \forall i, j : s \leqslant i < l \wedge s \leqslant j < l : a[i] = a[j] \rangle$ } .

Figure 14.6 Finding the Kth smallest value.

The problem of the Dutch National Flag illustrates the use of invariant properties in making precise the functions of the variables in a program, making programming decisions straightforward, and avoiding array bound errors that bedevil unsystematic methods. It also illustrates the inappropriateness of 'for' statements, which, being less flexible than do–od loops, can impose an undesir-able straitjacket on program design.

Finding the K smallest values in an array is a challenging programming problem. The first task in solving the problem is to identify its specification, clearly and precisely. Having done so, the use of invariant properties guides the algorithm development. The Dutch National Flag problem emerges as a core subroutine.

Bibliographic Remarks

Dijkstra's original description of the Dutch National Flag problem can be found in his classic text *A Discipline of Programming* (Dijkstra, 1976). There you will also find many other examples of derivations of non-trivial algorithms.

In addition to the informal discussion of the FIND program in his inaugural lecture in 1971 (see Exercise 2.1), Hoare also developed and formally verified an algorithm to solve the problem. His solution, which was one of the very first pub-lished proofs of the formal correctness of a computer program, can be found in Hoare and Jones (1989, pp. 59–74).

15

Remainder Computation

Loosely speaking, the remainder on dividing one number by another is what is left over after the division. For example, if seven pieces of cake are divided among three children, there will be one piece remaining; the remainder after dividing 7 by 3 is 1. Similarly, the remainder after dividing 12 by 4 is 0.

Computing remainders is at the core of two sorts of coding of data: encrypting data so that its content cannot be deciphered by unwanted readers, and adding redundant information to data so that its content can be recovered even when errors are introduced (so-called *error-resilient coding*). In Chapter 16, we consider the latter application in detail. It involves computing remainders after dividing one *polynomial* by another. This chapter is about the more familiar problem of computing remainders after dividing one *integer* by another. We also discuss the calculation of several algebraic properties of remainders.

15.1 Formal Specification

The *remainder*, r, and *quotient*, d, on dividing integer P by strictly positive natural number Q are defined by the properties:

$$0 \leqslant r < Q \quad \wedge \quad P = Q \times d + r \ . \tag{15.1}$$

For example, the remainder after dividing 7 by 3 is 1 because

$$0 \leqslant 1 < 3 \quad \wedge \quad 7 = 3 \times 2 + 1 \ .$$

The quotient is 2, for the same reason. Also, the remainder after dividing -7 by 3 is 2 because

$$0 \leqslant 2 < 3 \quad \wedge \quad -7 = 3 \times (-3) + 2 \ .$$

The quotient is -3.

If we want to specify the computation of remainders only, the quotient is existentially quantified. The formal specification of just the *remainder* on dividing integer P by the strictly positive number Q is thus the number r defined by the properties:

$$0 \leqslant r < Q \quad \wedge \quad \langle \exists d :: P = Q \times d + r \rangle \ . \tag{15.2}$$

The dummy, d, ranges over all integers.

Even when only the remainder is of interest, it helps in the derivation of an algorithm to compute the quotient as well. The quotient plays the role of an *auxiliary variable*—a variable used to relate the computation to the specification—but otherwise plays no role in the computation proper. Auxiliary variables are discarded in the final stages of algorithm design.

We introduce the technique of using auxiliary variables in the next section. Later sections make more extensive use of auxiliary variables.

Our use of 'the' remainder and 'the' quotient presupposes that (15.1) defines r and d uniquely. This is indeed the case, as the following calculation demonstrates. We postulate that both the pair (r, d) and the pair (r', d') satisfy (15.1) and then show that $r = r'$ and $d = d'$.

$$\begin{aligned}
& (0 \leqslant r < Q \quad \wedge \quad P = Q \times d + r) \\
& \wedge \ (0 \leqslant r' < Q \quad \wedge \quad P = Q \times d' + r')
\end{aligned}$$

$=$ {   preparing for next step   }

$$\begin{aligned}
& (0 \leqslant r < Q \quad \wedge \quad P = Q \times d + r) \\
& \wedge \ (Q > r' \geqslant 0 \quad \wedge \quad P = Q \times d' + r')
\end{aligned}$$

$\Rightarrow$ {   introduce $r - r'$ and $d - d'$ by 'subtracting'

                     the bottom line from the top   }

$$-Q < r - r' < Q \quad \wedge \quad 0 = Q \times (d - d') + (r - r')$$

$=$ {   arithmetic and Leibniz   }

$$-Q < -(Q \times (d - d')) < Q \quad \wedge \quad -(Q \times (d - d')) = r - r'$$

$=$ { $0 < Q$, inequalities   }

$$-1 < -(d - d') < 1 \quad \wedge \quad -(Q \times (d - d')) = r - r'$$

$=$ {   (integer) arithmetic and Leibniz   }

$$d = d' \quad \wedge \quad r = r' \ .$$

15.2 Elementary Algorithm

In this section, we develop an elementary algorithm for computing remainders and the corresponding quotients. The algorithm is not efficient, but its existence allows us to identify a number of basic algebraic properties of remainders. The algorithm involves a case analysis on positive and negative numbers P. The case that P is positive is developed in detail below. Exercise 15.5 asks you to develop the algorithm in the case that P is negative.

The elementary algorithm is based on splitting (15.1) into

$$P = Q \times d + r \tag{15.3}$$

and

$$0 \leqslant r < Q \ . \tag{15.4}$$

An easy way to establish (15.3) is by the assignment

$$r,d := P,0 \ .$$

This suggests the construction of a loop with (15.3) as invariant and (15.4) as termination condition.

We note that assigning P to r also establishes $0 \leqslant r$ in the case that $0 \leqslant P$; conversely, it establishes $r < Q$ in the case that $P \leqslant 0$. This suggests a case analysis on $0 \leqslant P$ or $P \leqslant 0$, whereby, in the first case, progress is made to the termination condition by continually decreasing r, and, in the second case, progress is made by continually increasing r.

It is at this point that we make the assumption $0 \leqslant P$ and, as mentioned earlier, leave the other case as an exercise.

Based on the analysis above, we add $0 \leqslant r$ as an invariant property, with the effect that the termination condition can be weakened to $r < Q$. Progress is made by continually decreasing r. The skeleton of an algorithm is thus as shown below, where variables m and n are the unknowns.

$$\{ \ 0 < Q \ \}$$

$$r,d := P,0 \ ;$$

$$\{ \ \textbf{Invariant:} \quad 0 \leqslant r \quad \wedge \quad P = Q \times d + r$$

$$\quad \textbf{Bound function:} \quad r \ \}$$

$$\text{do } r \geqslant Q \quad \longrightarrow \quad r,d := r - m, n$$

$$\text{od}$$

$$\{ \ 0 \leqslant r < Q \quad \wedge \quad P = Q \times d + r \ \}$$

The remaining details are as follows. The loop body is executed when $r \geqslant Q$. So, m and n are required to satisfy

$$0 < m$$

(in order to guarantee progress) and

$$(0 \leqslant r \land P = Q{\times}d + r)\,[r, d := r - m, n]$$
$$\Leftarrow \quad 0 \leqslant r \land P = Q{\times}d + r \land r \geqslant Q$$

(in order to maintain the invariant). Now,

$$(0 \leqslant r \land P = Q{\times}d + r)\,[r, d := r - m, n]$$

$=$ $\qquad\{\qquad$ substitution $\quad\}$

$$0 \leqslant r - m \land P = Q{\times}n + (r - m)$$

$\Leftarrow$ $\qquad\{\qquad$ We may assume $r \geqslant Q$, equivalently $0 \leqslant r - Q$.

$\qquad\qquad\qquad$ This suggests $m = Q$.

$\qquad\qquad\qquad$ (Q is greater than 0 by assumption.) $\quad\}$

$$m = Q \land r \geqslant Q \land P = Q{\times}n + (r - Q)$$

$\Leftarrow$ $\qquad\{\qquad$ Now, heading for the given precondition,

$\qquad\qquad\qquad 0 \leqslant r \land P = Q{\times}d + r$

$\qquad\qquad\qquad$ we choose $n = d + 1$. $\quad\}$

$$n = d + 1 \land m = Q \land r \geqslant Q \land P = Q{\times}(d + 1) + (r - Q)$$

$=$ $\qquad\{\qquad$ arithmetic $\quad\}$

$$n = d + 1 \land m = Q \land r \geqslant Q \land P = Q{\times}d + r\ .$$

We conclude that a loop body consisting of the simple assignment

$$r, d := r - Q, d + 1$$

maintains the invariant and makes progress to the termination condition. The algorithm we have thus obtained is shown in Figure 15.1.

Exercise 15.5 (Elementary remainder algorithm for non-positive *P*). Derive an algorithm to compute the remainder and quotient when $P \leqslant 0$. (Hint: add $r < Q$ to the invariant property (15.3) and weaken the termination condition (15.4) to $0 \leqslant r$.) □

Auxiliary Variables

The algorithm we have developed computes both a remainder and a quotient. Often, however, only the remainder is required, and the quotient is not needed. If this is the case, the algorithm can be simplified, at the expense of making the specification and invariant properties slightly more complicated.

We note that, in Figure 15.1, assignments to d play no role in the computation of r. If only the remainder is required, these assignments can be discarded. The

$$\{ \ 0 \leqslant P \ \wedge \ 0 < Q \ \}$$

$$r, d \ := \ P, 0 \ ;$$

{ **Invariant:** $\ 0 \leqslant r \ \wedge \ P = Q \times d + r$

  Bound function: $\ r \ \}$

do $r \geqslant Q \ \longrightarrow \ r, d \ := \ r - Q, d + 1$

od

$\{ \ 0 \leqslant r < Q \ \wedge \ P = Q \times d + r \ \}$.

Figure 15.1 Elementary remainder and quotient computation (for natural number P).

variable d still has a role in the assertions that establish the algorithm's correctness; it becomes an existentially quantified variable, as shown below.

{ remainder computation—elementary algorithm }

$$\{ \ 0 \leqslant P \ \wedge \ 0 < Q \ \}$$

$$r \ := \ P \ ;$$

{ **Invariant:** $\ 0 \leqslant r \ \wedge \ \langle \exists d :: P = Q \times d + r \rangle$

  Bound function: $\ r \ \}$

do $r \geqslant Q \ \longrightarrow \ r \ := \ r - Q$

od

$\{ \ 0 \leqslant r < Q \ \wedge \ \langle \exists d :: P = Q \times d + r \rangle \ \}$.

Where specifications involve existential quantifications, it is a useful technique to introduce variables into the program in order to compute so-called *witnesses* to the existentially quantified dummies. These are called *auxiliary* variables. With care, the program can often be developed in such a way that the auxiliary variables play no role in the computation proper, and can be discarded once the development of the algorithm is complete. The technique is useful because calculating the implementation from the specification avoids direct manipulation of existential quantifications.

We will use the technique of introducing, and then discarding, auxiliary variables several times throughout this chapter.

15.3 The mod and div Functions

In Section 15.1, we showed that (15.1) defines *at most one* remainder r and quotient d for all integers P and all strictly positive natural numbers Q. The construction of the elementary algorithm in Section 15.2 (for both the cases that $0 \leqslant P$ and $P \leqslant 0$) establishes that there is *at least one* remainder r and quotient d for all integers P and all strictly positive natural numbers Q. Together, we have thus established that there is a *function* that maps given integers P and Q, where $0 < Q$, to the remainder, r, and quotient, d, after dividing P by Q, as specified formally by (15.1).

A specification (a *relation* between input and output values) has a *functional* solution if there is *exactly one* output for each input. Exhibiting an algorithm, no matter how efficient or inefficient, satisfying the specification is the most effective way of demonstrating the existence of *at least one* solution to a specification.

Recognizing that a specification has a functional solution has important consequences for reasoning about the specification. The consequences are realized by naming the function and expressing the functionality by a simple equivalence. (Some logic texts refer to this process as *Skolemization*.)

In the case of the specification (15.1), there are two quantities involved, so we give separate names to each. The standard name in mathematics for the remainder function is 'mod'; the symbol '÷' is used for the quotient.

Given integers P and Q, where $0 < Q$, $P \bmod Q$ denotes the remainder, and $P \div Q$ denotes the quotient, after dividing P by Q. The existence and uniqueness of these functions is expressed by the calculational rule:

$$r = P \bmod Q \; \wedge \; d = P \div Q \;\; \equiv \;\; 0 \leqslant r < Q \; \wedge \; P = Q \times d + r \;\; . \qquad (15.6)$$

Splitting the equivalence into a mutual implication, the '⇒' expresses the *existence* of a solution to (15.1), and the '⇐' expresses the *uniqueness* of a solution to (15.1). We established the existence of a solution by constructing the elementary algorithm of Section 15.2. The uniqueness of the solution was established in Section 15.1.

In Chapter 6, the symbol '÷' was used for integer division, but a different definition was given. We show in Section 15.3.3 that the two definitions are equivalent. For the moment, however, we take care to use only properties of ÷ that are derived from (15.6).

The standard convention in mathematics texts is that mod, like ÷, has higher precedence than addition but lower precedence than multiplication. So, for example, $m + n \bmod Q$ and $m + (n \bmod Q)$ are equal. Also, $m \times n \bmod Q$ and $(m \times n) \bmod Q$ are equal. Giving multiplication precedence over mod is undoubtedly due to the fact that it is common to denote multiplication by juxtaposition, and the eye naturally groups m and n together in $mn \bmod Q$. When multiplication is explicitly denoted, the algebraic properties make it undesirable to give multiplication precedence over mod. Our own preference is therefore for the opposite convention. However, to avoid confusion with other texts, we take the middle road of including parentheses, even though some may be omitted.

15.3.1 Basic Properties

Here is how to use (15.6) in a few simple cases. First, we make the left side of the equivalence trivially true by instantiating r to $P \bmod Q$ and d to $P \div Q$. We get

$$0 \leqslant P \bmod Q < Q \quad \wedge \quad P = Q \times (P \div Q) + P \bmod Q \ . \tag{15.7}$$

Next, we make the second and third conjuncts true by instantiating r to 0 and d to $P \div Q$. We get

$$0 = P \bmod Q \ \equiv \ P = Q \times (P \div Q) \ . \tag{15.8}$$

Now, we instantiate r to $P \bmod Q$ and d to 0. We get

$\qquad$ true

$=\qquad\quad \{ \qquad (15.6) \text{ with } r,d \ := \ P \bmod Q , 0 \ \}$

$\qquad P \bmod Q = P \bmod Q \ \wedge \ 0 = P \div Q$

$\equiv\quad 0 \leqslant P \bmod Q < Q \ \wedge \ P = Q \times 0 + P \bmod Q$

$=\qquad\quad \{ \qquad \text{predicate calculus and arithmetic} \ \}$

$\qquad 0 = P \div Q \ \equiv \ 0 \leqslant P \bmod Q < Q \ \wedge \ P = P \bmod Q$

$=\qquad\quad \{ \qquad (15.7) \ \}$

$\qquad 0 = P \div Q \ \equiv \ P = P \bmod Q \ .$

Summarizing,

$$0 = P \div Q \ \equiv \ P = P \bmod Q \ . \tag{15.9}$$

Now, we consider the case that P satisfies $0 \leqslant P < Q$. We have

$\qquad 0 \leqslant P < Q$

$=\qquad\quad \{ \qquad \text{arithmetic} \ \}$

$\qquad 0 \leqslant P < Q \ \wedge \ P = Q \times 0 + P$

$=\qquad\quad \{ \qquad (15.6) \text{ with } P,r,d \ := \ P,P,0 \ \}$

$\qquad P = P \bmod Q \ \wedge \ 0 = P \div Q$

$=\qquad\quad \{ \qquad (15.9) \ \}$

$\qquad P = P \bmod Q \ .$

Combining with (15.9),

$$(0 \leqslant P < Q) \ = \ (P = P \bmod Q) \ = \ (0 = P \div Q) \ . \tag{15.10}$$

The case that $P = 0$ is important. From (15.10), we get

$$0 = 0 \bmod Q \ . \tag{15.11}$$

Now, we calculate $(Q \times m + n) \bmod Q$ and $(Q \times m + n) \div Q$ for arbitrary m, $0 \leqslant m$:

$$r = (Q \times m + n) \bmod Q \ \wedge \ d = (Q \times m + n) \div Q$$

$$= \qquad \{ \qquad (15.6) \text{ with } P := Q \times m + n \ \}$$

$$0 \leqslant r < Q \ \wedge \ Q \times m + n = Q \times d + r$$

$$= \qquad \{ \qquad \text{arithmetic} \ \}$$

$$0 \leqslant r < Q \ \wedge \ n = Q \times (d - m) + r$$

$$= \qquad \{ \qquad (15.6) \text{ with } P := n \ \}$$

$$r = n \bmod Q \ \wedge \ d - m = n \div Q$$

$$= \qquad \{ \qquad \text{arithmetic} \ \}$$

$$r = n \bmod Q \ \wedge \ d = m + (n \div Q) \ .$$

We conclude that

$$(Q \times m + n) \bmod Q \ = \ n \bmod Q \ \wedge \ (Q \times m + n) \div Q \ = \ m + (n \div Q) \ .$$

$$(15.12)$$

In particular, combining (15.11) and (15.12) by instantiating n to 0,

$$(Q \times m) \bmod Q \ = \ 0 \ \wedge \ (Q \times m) \div Q \ = \ m \ . \qquad\qquad (15.13)$$

Exercise 15.14. Use (15.6) to calculate $P \bmod 1$ and $P \div 1$. $\qquad\qquad\square$

Exercise 15.15. Assume that $-Q \leqslant P < 0$. In this case, can you calculate simpler expressions for $P \bmod Q$ and $P \div Q$ from (15.6)? $\qquad\qquad\square$

Exercise 15.16. Use (15.7) and (15.12) to simplify $(P \bmod (Q \times n)) \bmod Q$, where $0 < n$. $\qquad\qquad\square$

Exercise 15.17. Show that, for all m and n,

$$r \bmod Q \ = \ n$$

is an invariant of the assignment

$$r \ := \ r - Q \times m \ .$$

$$\square$$

Exercise 15.18. Rather than develop separate algorithms for the cases that $0 \leqslant P$ and $P \leqslant 0$, as we did in Section 15.2, an alternative is to express $P \bmod Q$ and $P \div Q$ as functions of $((-(P+1)) \bmod Q)$ and $(-(P+1)) \div Q$, respectively. (Since $P < 0 \ \equiv \ 0 \leqslant -(P+1)$, the existence of such functions means that only the algorithm for positive P is needed.) Calculate these functions using (15.6). $\qquad\qquad\square$

15.3.2 Separating mod from ÷

It is convenient to have a rule for reasoning about the mod function alone, without explicit mention of the ÷ function. This is obtained from (15.6) by existentially quantifying over the variable d. We get that, for all P and all Q, where $0 < Q$,

$$r = P \bmod Q \quad \equiv \quad 0 \leqslant r < Q \land \langle \exists d :: P = Q \times d + r \rangle \ . \tag{15.19}$$

To illustrate the use of (15.19), let us determine when m and n have the same modulus values:

$$m \bmod Q = n \bmod Q$$

$$= \qquad \{ \qquad (15.19) \text{ with } P := m,$$

$$0 \leqslant n \bmod Q < Q \ \}$$

$$\langle \exists d :: m = Q \times d + n \bmod Q \rangle$$

$$= \qquad \{ \qquad (15.7) \text{ with } P := n \ \}$$

$$\langle \exists d :: m = Q \times d + (n - Q \times (n \div Q)) \rangle$$

$$= \qquad \{ \qquad \text{arithmetic} \ \}$$

$$\langle \exists d :: m - n = Q \times (d - n \div Q) \rangle$$

$$= \qquad \{ \qquad \text{range translation: } d := d + n \div Q \ \}$$

$$\langle \exists d :: m - n = Q \times d \rangle$$

$$= \qquad \{ \qquad (15.19) \text{ with } P := m - n \ \}$$

$$(m - n) \bmod Q = 0 \ .$$

We conclude that

$$m \bmod Q = n \bmod Q \quad \equiv \quad (m - n) \bmod Q = 0 \ . \tag{15.20}$$

Note the use of range translation in the calculation. (See Exercise 11.57 for the statement of the rule.) Generally, when using (15.19) instead of (15.6), the use of range translation replaces explicit calculations of the relationship between quotients. This simplifies the calculations, particularly when range translation is used more than once, because it permits the omission of unwanted detail; we know that appropriate witnesses to the existentially quantified variables exist but their exact form is not required.

Exercise 15.21. Express $\langle \exists d :: P = Q \times d + r \rangle$ as an equation involving r and P. (That is, eliminate the existential quantification.)   □

15.3.3 Separating ÷ from mod

A rule for reasoning about the ÷ function, without explicit mention of the mod function, is

$$d = P \div Q \quad \equiv \quad \langle \exists r :: 0 \leqslant r < Q \ \wedge \ P = Q \times d + r \rangle \ . \qquad (15.22)$$

Let us illustrate the use of (15.22) in showing that

$$P \div Q \ = \ \left\lfloor \frac{P}{Q} \right\rfloor \ .$$

(This is the definition of integer division used in Chapter 6.)

$$d = P \div Q$$
$$= \qquad \{ \qquad (15.22) \quad \}$$
$$\langle \exists r :: 0 \leqslant r < Q \ \wedge \ P = Q \times d + r \rangle$$
$$= \qquad \{ \qquad \text{arithmetic and trading (heading towards}$$
$$\text{one-point rule)} \quad \}$$
$$\langle \exists r : r = P - Q \times d : 0 \leqslant r < Q \rangle$$
$$= \qquad \{ \qquad \text{one-point rule} \quad \}$$
$$0 \leqslant P - Q \times d < Q$$
$$= \qquad \{ \qquad \text{arithmetic} \quad \}$$
$$\frac{P}{Q} - 1 < d \leqslant \frac{P}{Q}$$
$$= \qquad \{ \qquad \text{for all real } x \text{ and integer } m,$$
$$\lfloor x \rfloor = m \ \equiv \ x - 1 < m \leqslant x \quad \}$$
$$d = \left\lfloor \frac{P}{Q} \right\rfloor \ .$$

Exercise 15.23. Simplify $(m \times P) \div (m \times Q)$. Hence, simplify $(m \times P) \bmod (m \times Q)$ (when $m > 0$).   □

15.3.4 Modular Arithmetic

A remainder after dividing by Q is called a remainder *modulo Q*. (Indeed, $P \bmod Q$ is sometimes read as P *modulo Q*.) A *modulo-Q number* is any number in the range $0 .. Q - 1$. In this section, we identify addition, multiplication and negation operations on modulo-Q numbers. We do so by seeking distributivity properties of the $\bmod Q$ function over addition, multiplication and negation.

We begin with negation. The problem we consider is whether, for given Q, there is a unary operator $\ominus$ such that, for all P,

$$\ominus(P \bmod Q) \ = \ (-P) \bmod Q \ .$$

An appropriate definition is calculated as follows.

$$(-P) \bmod Q \ = \ r \ \wedge \ (-P) \div Q \ = \ d$$

$$= \qquad \{ \qquad (15.6) \text{ with } P := -P \ \}$$

$$0 \leqslant r < Q \ \wedge \ -P = Q \times d + r$$

$$= \qquad \{ \qquad (15.7), \text{ in order to introduce } P \bmod Q \text{ and } P \div Q \ \}$$

$$0 \leqslant r < Q \ \wedge \ -(Q \times (P \div Q) + P \bmod Q) \ = \ Q \times d + r$$

$$= \qquad \{ \qquad \text{arithmetic—rewriting the second conjunct}$$

$$\text{in the shape of the second conjunct of (15.6)} \ \}$$

$$0 \leqslant r < Q \ \wedge \ -(P \bmod Q) \ = \ Q \times (d + P \div Q) + r$$

$$= \qquad \{ \qquad (15.6) \text{ with } P,d,r \ := \ -(P \bmod Q) , d + P \div Q , r \ \}$$

$$(-(P \bmod Q)) \bmod Q \ = \ r \ \wedge \ (-(P \bmod Q)) \div Q \ = \ d + P \div Q \ .$$

We conclude that

$$(-P) \bmod Q \ = \ (-(P \bmod Q)) \bmod Q \ .$$

Thus, we define the operation $\ominus$ by, for all integers m,

$$\ominus m \ = \ (-m) \bmod Q \ , \tag{15.24}$$

so that

$$(-P) \bmod Q \ = \ \ominus(P \bmod Q) \ . \tag{15.25}$$

Note that $\ominus m$ is a modulo-Q number for all integers m. In particular, $\ominus m$ is a modulo-Q number when m is a modulo-Q number. The operation $\ominus$ is called *negation modulo Q*. We say that the modulo-Q numbers are *closed* under negation modulo Q.

Calling $\ominus$ a 'negation' operator is justified if it has similar algebraic properties to negation in integer (or real) arithmetic. Negation of integers has two properties, namely

$$-0 = 0 \ ,$$

and, for all integers m and n,

$$-m = n \ \equiv \ m = -n \ .$$

(This is equivalent to $-(-m) = m$. It is neater because it is symmetric.) So, let us check that $\ominus$ has similar properties. First,

$$\ominus 0$$
$$=\qquad \{\qquad \text{definition (15.24)}\quad\}$$
$$(-0) \bmod Q$$
$$=\qquad \{\qquad -0 = 0\quad\}$$
$$0 \bmod Q$$
$$=\qquad \{\qquad \text{(15.11)}\quad\}$$
$$0\ .$$

We conclude that

$$\ominus 0 = 0\ .$$

Second, assume that m and n are modulo-Q numbers. Then,

$$\ominus m = n$$
$$=\qquad \{\qquad \text{definition (15.24)}\quad\}$$
$$(-m) \bmod Q = n$$
$$=\qquad \{\qquad \text{(15.19), assumption: } 0 \leqslant n < Q\quad\}$$
$$\langle \exists d :: -m = Q \times d + n \rangle$$
$$=\qquad \{\qquad \text{negation (in integer arithmetic)}\quad\}$$
$$\langle \exists d :: -n = Q \times d + m \rangle$$
$$=\qquad \{\qquad \text{(15.19), assumption: } 0 \leqslant m < Q\quad\}$$
$$(-n) \bmod Q = m$$
$$=\qquad \{\qquad \text{definition (15.24)}\quad\}$$
$$\ominus n = m\ .$$

We conclude that, for all modulo-Q numbers m and n,

$$\ominus m = n \ \equiv\ \ominus n = m\ .$$

We next consider whether remainder computation distributes through addition. That is, we seek an operator $\oplus$ such that

$$(m+n) \bmod Q \ =\ (m \bmod Q) \oplus (n \bmod Q)\ .$$

We have

$$(m+n) \bmod Q$$
$$=\qquad \{\qquad \text{(15.7) in order to introduce } m \bmod Q\quad\}$$

$$(Q \times (m \div Q) + m \bmod Q + n) \bmod Q$$
$$= \qquad \{ \qquad (15.12) \quad \}$$
$$(m \bmod Q + n) \bmod Q \ .$$

That is,

$$(m+n) \bmod Q \ = \ (m \bmod Q + n) \bmod Q \ . \tag{15.26}$$

We can now exploit the symmetry of addition:

$$(m+n) \bmod Q$$
$$= \qquad \{ \qquad (15.26) \quad \}$$
$$(m \bmod Q + n) \bmod Q$$
$$= \qquad \{ \qquad \text{addition is symmetric} \quad \}$$
$$(n + m \bmod Q) \bmod Q$$
$$= \qquad \{ \qquad (15.26) \text{ with } m,n := n, m \bmod Q \quad \}$$
$$(n \bmod Q + m \bmod Q) \bmod Q \ .$$

We have thus calculated that

$$(m+n) \bmod Q \ = \ (m \bmod Q) \oplus (n \bmod Q) \ ,$$

where

$$p \oplus q \ = \ (p + q) \bmod Q \ .$$

Just as for negation, we observe that $m \oplus n$ is a modulo-Q number for all integers m and n, but, in particular, for modulo-Q numbers m and n. The $\oplus$ operator is called *addition modulo Q*.

The operators $\ominus$ and $\oplus$, together with the multiplication operator $\otimes$ you are asked to construct in Exercise 15.27 (see below), form the basis of *modular arithmetic*—arithmetic modulo some number Q. The exercises below ask you to establish that these three operators have some algebraic properties in common with their counterparts in normal arithmetic. Some properties of normal arithmetic do not carry over to modular arithmetic, however. One example is the subject of Exercise 15.29. The bibliographic remarks point you to practical applications of modular arithmetic.

Exercise 15.27. Calculate an operator $\otimes$ such that

$$(m \times n) \bmod Q \ = \ (m \bmod Q) \otimes (n \bmod Q) \ .$$

$\square$

Exercise 15.28. Show that addition modulo Q and multiplication modulo Q are symmetric and associative. To be precise, show that, for all integers m, n and p,

$$m \oplus n = n \oplus m \ ,$$
$$(m \oplus n) \oplus p = m \oplus (n \oplus p) \ ,$$
$$m \otimes n = n \otimes m$$

and

$$(m \otimes n) \otimes p = m \otimes (n \otimes p) \ .$$

Show, also, that negation modulo Q distributes through addition modulo Q. That is, show that, for all integers m and n,

$$\ominus(m \oplus n) = (\ominus m) \oplus (\ominus n) \ .$$

(This is the hardest part of this exercise. Hint: formulate a lemma like (15.26).)

Show that multiplication modulo Q distributes through addition modulo Q. That is, show that, for all integers m and n,

$$m \otimes (n \oplus p) = (m \otimes n) \oplus (m \otimes p) \ .$$

$\square$

Exercise 15.29 (Cancellation Properties). Show that addition of any modulo-Q number is a bijection on modulo-Q numbers. That is, show that for all modulo-Q numbers m, n and p,

$$m \oplus n = m \oplus p \ \equiv \ n = p \ .$$

Show, on the contrary, that multiplication by a non-zero modulo-Q number is not necessarily a bijection on modulo-Q numbers. That is, exhibit modulo-Q numbers m, n and p such that

$$m \neq 0 \ \wedge \ (m \otimes n = m \otimes p \ \not\equiv \ n = p) \ .$$

$\square$

15.4 Long Division

The elementary remainder computation algorithm, developed in Section 15.2, repeatedly subtracts Q from an approximation to the remainder. The efficiency can be substantially improved if, for some positive number m, $Q \times m$ is subtracted, in one go, where m is as large as possible. *Long division*, which has been designed for efficient manual calculation of remainders and quotients, does just that.

Figure 15.2(a) shows the computation by long division of the remainder 6 and quotient 521 on dividing 3653 by 7. (The presentation is in the format used in British schools. Other nations may use a different format.)

$$
\begin{array}{r@{\qquad}l}
 & 1 \qquad m_3 \\
 & 20 \qquad m_2 \\
521 & 500 \qquad m_1 \\
\overline{7)3653} & \overline{7)3653} \qquad r_0 \quad (\doteq P) \\
35 & 3500 \qquad m_1 \times Q \\
\overline{15} & \overline{153} \qquad r_1 \\
14 & 140 \qquad m_2 \times Q \\
\overline{13} & \overline{13} \qquad r_2 \\
7 & 7 \qquad m_3 \times Q \\
\overline{6} & \overline{6} \qquad r_3 \\
(a) & (b)
\end{array}
$$

Figure 15.2 Remainder computation in decimal arithmetic ($P = 3653$, $Q = 7$). (a) Long division; (b) filling in details.

In this section, we develop an implementation of this manual technique of computing remainders and quotients. A method designed for paper-and-pencil calculations need not be the best method for implementation on a digital computer, but we hope that your familiarity with the method will help you to understand the use of invariant properties in the design of such an implementation.

Figure 15.2(b) explains long division in detail. From it, we see that the technique begins with the remainder, r_0, equal to P (3653). At each subsequent step, a multiple $Q \times m$ of Q is subtracted from r, thus forming the sequence of ever-decreasing remainders r_0, r_1, r_2 and r_3. The process is terminated when the remainder is less than Q. In decimal arithmetic, all the multiples take the form $Q \times n \times 10^k$ for some k, where $0 \leqslant n < 10$. (Thus, m_1 is 5×10^2, m_2 is 2×10^1 and m_3 is 1×10^0. Not shown is m_0, which is 0×10^3.)

Figure 15.3 shows the same process in binary arithmetic. The strategy is identical but the multiples of Q subtracted from r take the form $Q \times n \times 2^k$ for some k, where $0 \leqslant n < 2$. Since binary arithmetic is more suited to computer implementation, we develop long division for binary numerals.

15.4.1 Implementing Long Division

Long division subtracts successive multiples of Q from a remainder value. We introduce variable m, to store the multiples of Q, and variables r and d, to store the remainder and quotient, respectively. The specification of m is simple; in binary arithmetic, it satisfies the invariant property

$$
\langle \exists k : 0 \leqslant k : m = Q \times 2^k \rangle \quad .
$$

```
                              1        m₂
           101              100        m₁
     101)11010        101)11010        r₀(= P)
       101              10100          Q×m₁
       ───              ─────
           110              110        r₁
           101              101        Q×m₂
           ───              ───
             1                1        r₂

          (a)              (b)
```

Figure 15.3 Remainder computation in binary arithmetic ($P = 26$, $Q = 5$). (a) Long division; (b) filling in details.

The existential quantification suggests the introduction of variable k into the algorithm. The two variables m and k satisfy the invariant property

$$0 \leqslant k \ \wedge \ m = Q \times 2^k \ .$$

Later (Section 15.4.2), we consider doing without variable k, reintroducing the existential quantification.

What about the successive values of r and d? We have to identify an invariant property and a termination condition such that their conjunction implies the required postcondition (15.1). Noting that $Q = Q \times 2^0$, a possibility is to replace Q in (15.1) by the variable m. That is, we postulate the invariant property

$$0 \leqslant r < m \ \ \wedge \ \ P = Q \times d + r$$

together with the termination condition

$$m = Q \ .$$

Our algorithm thus has the following shape. (Note that the bound function for the loop has yet to be determined.)

$$\{ \ 0 \leqslant P \ \wedge \ 0 < Q \ \}$$

initialize m, k, r and d to establish invariant ;

{ **Invariant:**

$$0 \leqslant r < m \ \wedge \ P = Q \times d + r \ \wedge \ 0 \leqslant k \ \wedge \ m = Q \times 2^k \ \}$$

do $m \neq Q \ \longrightarrow$ make progress to termination condition

whilst maintaining invariant

od

$$\{ \ 0 \leqslant r < Q \ \wedge \ P = Q \times d + r \ \} \ .$$

The initialization is slightly more complicated than in earlier examples. Let us split the invariant into four separate clauses and consider each in turn. The clauses are

$$0 \leqslant r \ , \tag{15.30}$$

$$r < m \ , \tag{15.31}$$

$$P = Q \times d + r \ , \tag{15.32}$$

$$0 \leqslant k \ \wedge \ m = Q \times 2^k \ . \tag{15.33}$$

Now, (15.32) can be established by the assignment $r,d := P,0$. This also establishes (15.30) because we are given the precondition $0 \leqslant P$. That is,

$$\{ \ 0 \leqslant P \ \}$$

$$r,d := P,0$$

$$\{ \ 0 \leqslant r \ \wedge \ P = Q \times d + r \ \} \ .$$

Clauses (15.31) and (15.33) are left. The code to establish these clauses is to be executed after the initialization of r and d, so should not modify their values.

To establish (15.31) and (15.33), a loop is needed. The loop has (15.33) as invariant and (15.31) as termination condition. Property (15.33) is established by the assignment $m,k := Q,0$, and progress is made towards (15.31) by continually multiplying m by 2. (Multiplying by 2 increases m because $0 < Q$.) This, then, is the initialization of m. It assumes that r has already been assigned the value of P.

$$\{ \ 0 < Q \ \wedge \ 0 \leqslant r \ \}$$

$$m,k := Q,0 \ ;$$

$$\{ \ \textbf{Invariant:} \quad 0 \leqslant k \ \wedge \ m = Q \times 2^k$$

$$\textbf{Bound function:} \quad r - m \ \}$$

$$\text{do } r \geqslant m \ \longrightarrow \ m,k := 2 \times m, k+1$$

$$\text{od}$$

$$\{ \ r < m \ \wedge \ 0 \leqslant k \ \wedge \ m = Q \times 2^k \ \} \ .$$

Because the initialization of m does not alter the value of r or d, the assignment $r,d := P,0$, followed by the above code, fulfils the requirement of initializing m, k, r and d. Let us now turn to the loop body.

The requirement on the loop body is that it should maintain properties (15.30), (15.31), (15.32) and (15.33) whilst making progress to the condition $m = Q$.

We note that the loop body is executed when $m \neq Q$. Since we have also stipulated that it should maintain invariant the property (15.33), $0 \leqslant k \ \wedge \ m = Q \times 2^k$, we conclude that the loop body is executed when $1 \leqslant k$. The assignment

$$m,k := m \div 2, k-1$$

will, therefore, decrease m whilst maintaining (15.33), thus making progress to the termination condition $m = Q$.

Decreasing m may, however, falsify the requirement $r < m$. If this is the case, the value of r must also be decreased, but in a way that maintains all conjuncts of the invariant, in particular property (15.32). We investigate conditions on number n that guarantee that subtracting n from r maintains (15.32). We have

$$(P = Q{\times}d + r)\,[r,d := r - n, d']$$

$=$ $\qquad$ { $\qquad$ substitution $\quad$ }

$$P = Q{\times}d' + r - n$$

$=$ $\qquad$ { $\qquad$ assume $P = Q{\times}d + r$ $\quad$ }

$$Q{\times}d + r = Q{\times}d' + r - n$$

$=$ $\qquad$ { $\qquad$ arithmetic $\quad$ }

$$n = Q{\times}(d'-d)$$

$=$ $\qquad$ { $\qquad$ one-point rule, arithmetic $\quad$ }

$$\langle \exists l : d' = l + d : n = Q{\times}l \rangle \ .$$

So, subtracting any multiple $Q{\times}l$ of Q from r, simultaneously adding l to d, maintains (15.32). Formally, for all l,

$$(P = Q{\times}d + r)\,[r,d := r - Q{\times}l, d+l] \ \Leftarrow \ P = Q{\times}d + r \ .$$

By design, however, m is a multiple of Q; it is $Q{\times}2^k$. Thus, subtracting m from r, at the same time adding 2^k to d, maintains property (15.32).

In summary, the loop body takes the following form:

$$\{\ 0 \leqslant r < m \ \wedge \ P = Q{\times}d + r \ \wedge \ 1 \leqslant k \ \wedge \ m = Q{\times}2^k\ \}$$

$$m, k := m \div 2, k-1 \ ;$$

$\quad$ { **Invariant:** $\quad 0 \leqslant r \ \wedge \ P = Q{\times}d + r \ \wedge \ 0 \leqslant k \ \wedge \ m = Q{\times}2^k$

$\quad$ **Bound function:** $\quad r$ }

$$\textbf{do} \ r \geqslant m \ \longrightarrow \ r, d := r - m, d + 2^k$$

$\textbf{od}$

$$\{\ 0 \leqslant r < m \ \wedge \ P = Q{\times}d + r \ \wedge \ 0 \leqslant k \ \wedge \ m = Q{\times}2^k\ \} \ .$$

So far, we have not made any use of the fact that the algorithm we are developing is based on binary (as opposed to, say, decimal) arithmetic. All our calculations are equally valid if '2' is replaced everywhere by 'B', where $B \geqslant 2$.

Recall the discussion of long division. In decimal arithmetic, each step subtracts a multiple of Q of the form $Q{\times}n{\times}10^k$, for some k and n, where $0 \leqslant n < 10$, from the current remainder r. In binary arithmetic, each step subtracts a multiple of

Q of the form $Q \times n \times 2^k$, for some k and n, where $0 \leqslant n < 2$, from the current remainder r. So, each step subtracts $Q \times 2^k$ at most once.

We can formally justify this within the development of our algorithm. Currently, the loop body we have developed subtracts m repeatedly from r until $r < m$. The following calculation investigates how many times this needs to take place. Specifically, noting that the value subtracted from r is $m \div 2$, where m satisfies $0 \leqslant r < m$, we investigate when $r - m \div 2 \leqslant m \div 2$.

$$r - m \div 2 \; \leqslant \; m \div 2$$

$$= \qquad \{ \qquad \text{arithmetic} \quad \}$$

$$r \; \leqslant \; 2 \times (m \div 2)$$

$$\Leftarrow \qquad \{ \qquad m - 1 \leqslant 2 \times (m \div 2), \text{ transitivity of } \leqslant \quad \}$$

$$r \; \leqslant \; m - 1$$

$$= \qquad \{ \qquad \text{integer arithmetic} \quad \}$$

$$r < m \;\; .$$

So, as expected, the subtraction only needs to take place at most once; the inner loop, which repeatedly checks to see whether m should be subtracted from r, can therefore be replaced by a conditional statement, which checks only once.

Our algorithm is now complete; it is shown in Figure 15.4.

Exercise 15.34. Check your understanding by giving the algorithm for the case that '2' is replaced everywhere by 'B', where $B \geqslant 2$. Why is the lower bound 2 on B needed? $\qquad\qquad\square$

15.4.2 Discarding Auxiliary Variables

As was the case for the elementary remainder computation algorithm, the implementation of long division can be simplified if only the remainder, and not the quotient, is required.

The basis for the simplification is that the computation of remainder r depends only on the variable m; no boolean test uses the value of k or d, and no assignment to r depends on the value of k or d. So, if only r is required, all assignments to k and d can be removed from the program.

The variables do not disappear entirely. They are needed for the specification of r, and for the invariants, in the form of existentially quantified variables. The invariant property of m reverts to

$$\langle \exists k : 0 \leqslant k : m = Q \times 2^k \rangle \;\; ,$$

which is what it was before we decided to introduce k. Also, the quotient d becomes existentially quantified, so that the postcondition satisfied by r is

$$0 \leqslant r < Q \; \wedge \; \langle \exists d :: P = Q \times d + r \rangle \;\; .$$

$\{\ 0 \leqslant P\ \wedge\ 0 < Q\ \}$

$r, m, k, d\ :=\ P, Q, 0, 0\ ;$

$\{\ \textbf{Invariant:}\quad 0 \leqslant k\ \wedge\ m = Q \times 2^k$

$\quad\textbf{Bound function:}\quad r - m\ \}$

$\textsf{do}\ r \geqslant m\ \longrightarrow\ m, k := 2 \times m, k+1$

$\textsf{od}\ ;$

$\{\ \textbf{Invariant:}$

$\quad 0 \leqslant r < m\ \wedge\ P = Q \times d + r\ \wedge\ 0 \leqslant k\ \wedge\ m = Q \times 2^k$

$\quad\textbf{Bound function:}\quad m\ \}$

$\textsf{do}\ m \neq Q\ \longrightarrow\quad m, k := m \div 2, k-1\ ;$

$\qquad\qquad\qquad\qquad\{\quad 0 \leqslant r < 2 \times m\ \wedge\ P = Q \times d + r$

$\qquad\qquad\qquad\qquad\quad \wedge\ 0 \leqslant k\ \wedge\ m = Q \times 2^k\ \}$

$\qquad\qquad\qquad\qquad\textsf{if}\ r < m\ \longrightarrow\ \textsf{skip}$

$\qquad\qquad\qquad\qquad\square\ r \geqslant m\ \longrightarrow\ r, d := r - m, d + 2^k$

$\qquad\qquad\qquad\qquad\textsf{fi}$

$\textsf{od}$

$\{\ 0 \leqslant r < Q\ \wedge\ P = Q \times d + r\ \}$

Figure 15.4 Long division in binary arithmetic.

Removing d and k from the computation proper, introducing them as existentially quantified variables in the assertions, we get the program in Figure 15.5.

Exercise 15.35. Use the equivalence

$$\langle \exists d :: P = Q \times d + r \rangle\ \equiv\ P \bmod Q = r \bmod Q$$

to develop the program in Figure 15.5 afresh, exploiting modular arithmetic (see Section 15.3.4) rather than using the basic specification (15.2) of remainders. Make clear which particular properties you use in your derivation. □

15.5 On-Line Remainder Computation

We now consider an implementation of remainder computation motivated by a desire for an efficient implementation in hardware.

$$\{\ 0 \leqslant P\ \wedge\ 0 < Q\ \}$$

$$r, m\ :=\ P, Q\ ;$$

{ **Invariant:** $\langle \exists k : 0 \leqslant k : m = Q \times 2^k \rangle$

   Bound function: $r - m$ }

do $r \geqslant m\ \longrightarrow\ m := 2 \times m$

od ;

{ **Invariant:**

   $0 \leqslant r < m\ \wedge\ \langle \exists d :: P = Q \times d + r \rangle\ \wedge\ \langle \exists k : 0 \leqslant k : m = Q \times 2^k \rangle$

   Bound function: m }

do $m \neq Q\ \longrightarrow\ \ m := m \div 2\ ;$

            { $0 \leqslant r < 2 \times m\ \wedge\ \langle \exists d :: P = Q \times d + r \rangle$

                $\wedge\ \langle \exists k : 0 \leqslant k : m = Q \times 2^k \rangle\ \}$

            if $r < m\ \longrightarrow$ skip

            □ $r \geqslant m\ \longrightarrow\ r := r - m$

            fi

od

$\{\ 0 \leqslant r < Q\ \wedge\ \langle \exists d :: P = Q \times d + r \rangle\ \}$

Figure 15.5   Remainder computation in binary arithmetic.

Suppose that the number P is stored in binary form as a sequence of bits. We envisage a situation where the requirement is to construct a 'black box' into which the bits are input one by one, most significant bit first. Within a constant delay of inputting each bit, it is expected that the remainder after dividing the number input thus far by Q should be output from the black box. For example, if Q is 11 (the number 3 in binary form) and the bits 1, 0, 1 and 1 are input, in that order, the output should be 1, 10, 10 and 10, these being the remainder after dividing 1, 10, 101 and 1011 by 11, in binary arithmetic. (In decimal, the sequence of numbers is 1, 2, 5 and 11. The sequence of remainders is 1, 2, 2, 2.)

A computation of this form occurs frequently in practice. The requirement of constant delay (that is, a delay that is independent of the history of inputs and outputs) makes the computation a so-called *on-line* algorithm. An on-line algorithm maps a sequence of inputs to a sequence of outputs, each output occurring within at most a constant delay after the associated input.

We can model the input of bits and the computation of the 'number input thus far' as a non-terminating loop that gets a bit b and 'adds' it to the value P input thus far, which is initially zero:

$$P := 0 ;$$

{ **Invariant:** $0 \leqslant P$ }

do true $\longrightarrow$ (*get.b* { $0 \leqslant b \leqslant 1$ } ; $P := 2 \times P + b$)

od .

(We continue to use an upper-case 'P', in spite of the fact that P is not constant, as a warning that no additional assignments to P are allowed. The parentheses around the body of the loop are unnecessary, since guarded commands are always bracketed by if-fi or do-od, but they are included to improve readability.)

The requirement is to add code that establishes and maintains the invariant

$$r = P \bmod Q , \tag{15.36}$$

where Q is a given positive number.

There is no progress requirement on the outer loop, because we choose to ignore the detail of testing for the end of the input. There will, however, be a progress requirement on any inner loop introduced during the development.

Since P is also initialized to 0, and $0 \bmod Q = 0$, the assignment $r := 0$ establishes the invariant. So, our task is to determine m such that the following is valid:

$$P,r := 0,0 ;$$

{ **Invariant:** $0 \leqslant P \wedge r = P \bmod Q$ }

do true $\longrightarrow$ (*get.b* { $0 \leqslant b \leqslant 1$ } ; $P,r := 2 \times P + b, m$; *put.r*)

od .

We calculate m, the right side of the assignment to r, as follows. The formal requirement on m is

$$(r = P \bmod Q) [P,r := 2 \times P + b, m] \Leftarrow r = P \bmod Q ,$$

which is equivalent to

$$m = (2 \times P + b) \bmod Q \Leftarrow r = P \bmod Q .$$

Now,

$$(2 \times P + b) \bmod Q$$

$=$ {   modular addition: (15.26)   }

$$((2 \times P) \bmod Q + b) \bmod Q$$

$=$ {   modular multiplication: Exercise 15.27   }

$$(2 \times (P \bmod Q) + b) \bmod Q$$

$$= \qquad \{ \qquad \text{assume} \quad r = P \bmod Q \quad \}$$

$$(2 \times r + b) \bmod Q \ .$$

That is, $r = P \bmod Q$ is maintained invariant by taking m to be $(2 \times r + b) \bmod Q$.

This still involves a 'mod Q' operation, which we must eliminate. The strategy is to split the assignment to r into the composition of two assignments, the first assigning $2 \times r + b$ to r, and the second assigning $r \bmod Q$ to r, as shown below.

$$\{ \ 0 \leqslant P \ \wedge \ r \ = \ P \bmod Q \ \}$$

$$P, r \ := \ 2 \times P + b, 2 \times r + b \ ;$$

$$\{ \ 0 \leqslant P \ \wedge \ r \bmod Q \ = \ P \bmod Q \ \}$$

$$r \ := \ r \bmod Q$$

$$\{ \ 0 \leqslant P \ \wedge \ r \ = \ P \bmod Q \ \} \ .$$

This simplifies the task to replacing the second assignment by something not involving the 'mod Q' operation.

The assignment $r \ := \ r \bmod Q$ may be replaced by skip if the precondition $r = r \bmod Q$ holds. Now, $r = r \bmod Q$ is equivalent to

$$0 \leqslant r < Q \ . \tag{15.37}$$

Also, by an easy calculation,

$$\{ 0 \leqslant r \wedge 0 \leqslant b \} r \ := \ 2 \times r + b \{ 0 \leqslant r \} \ .$$

So, if the assignment $r \ := \ 2 \times r + b$ falsifies (15.37), it does so by falsifying

$$r < Q \ .$$

However,

$$\{ r < Q \wedge b \leqslant 1 \} r \ := \ 2 \times r + b \{ r < 2 \times Q \} \ .$$

The increase in r, caused by the assignment $r \ := \ 2 \times r + b$, thus makes r at most Q more than the desired greatest value. Moreover, by (15.12) (see Exercise 15.17),

$$\{ r \bmod Q = P \bmod Q \} r \ := \ r - Q \{ r \bmod Q = P \bmod Q \} \ .$$

Re-establishing $r = P \bmod Q$ thus amounts to a conditional statement that subtracts Q from r in the case that $r \geqslant Q$.

We have thus obtained the on-line remainder computation algorithm shown in Figure 15.6.

Exercise 15.38. Suppose the input value b is not constrained to be a binary digit but satisfies $0 \leqslant b < B$. (So the base is B.) Modify the algorithm accordingly. $\qquad \square$

$$P,r := 0,0 ;$$

{ **Invariant:** $0 \leqslant P \wedge r = P \bmod Q$ }

do true $\longrightarrow$ $get.b \{ 0 \leqslant b \leqslant 1 \}$;

               $P,r := 2 \times P + b, 2 \times r + b$;

               { $0 \leqslant P \wedge 0 \leqslant r < 2 \times Q \wedge r \bmod Q = P \bmod Q$ }

               if $r < Q \longrightarrow$ skip

               $\square \ r \geqslant Q \longrightarrow r := r - Q$

               fi ;

               $put.r$

od

Figure 15.6   On-line remainder computation in binary arithmetic.

15.6   Casting Out Nines

In Section 15.3, we showed how to derive properties of the mod function directly from its specification. Some properties are more easily derived by analysing an algorithm to compute the function. This is particularly true of properties that require inductive proof, because these properties can be identified as invariants of the algorithm. This section considers one example.

Decimal numbers can easily be checked to see whether or not they are divisible by 3 and 9. Add the digits of the number, and check whether the sum is divisible by 3 and 9. For example, 23571 is divisible by 3 and 9, because $2+3+5+7+1 = 18$, which is divisible by both; 23475 is divisible by 3 but not by 9, because $2+3+4+7+5 = 21$ which is divisible by 3 but not by 9; 13475 is divisible by neither, because $1+3+4+7+5 = 20$ which is divisible by neither 3 nor 9. This process is called *casting out nines*.

To prove the correctness of casting out nines, it suffices to add the computation of the sum, s, of the input digits to the computation of the remainder, r, after dividing by 9. Then we establish that $s \bmod 9$, the remainder after dividing s by 9, equals r. This we do by showing that it is an invariant of the algorithm for computing remainders. The details are shown below. (Note the additions to the invariant properties and the assignments to s.)

        $P,r,s := 0,0,0$;

        { **Invariant:** $0 \leqslant P \wedge r = P \bmod 9 = s \bmod 9$ }

        do true $\longrightarrow$ $get.b \{ 0 \leqslant b \}$;

$$P, r, s := 10{\times}P + b, 10{\times}r + b, s + b \;\;;$$

{ **Invariant:**

$$0 \leqslant P \;\wedge\; r \bmod 9 \;=\; P \bmod 9 \;=\; s \bmod 9$$

Bound function: r }

do $r \geqslant 9 \;\longrightarrow\; r := r - 9$

od ;

$put.r$

od .

To check the correctness of the added assertions, we have to check their validity with respect to the three assignments involving r and s. That is, we check the truth of

$$(r = s \bmod 9)\,[P, r, s := 0, 0, 0] \;,$$
$$(r \bmod 9 = s \bmod 9)\,[r, s := 10{\times}r + b, s + b] \;\Leftarrow\; r = s \bmod 9 \;,$$

and

$$(r \bmod 9 = s \bmod 9)\,[r := r - 9] \;\Leftarrow\; r \bmod 9 = s \bmod 9 \;.$$

These follow from properties (15.11) and (15.12).

Exercise 15.39. We seem to have forgotten about divisibility by 3! Show that this is not the case by showing how testing for divisibility by 3 follows from a test for divisibility by 9. □

15.7 Summary

This chapter has been about specifying and implementing remainder computation in normal arithmetic. We have seen how to calculate algebraic properties of remainders and how to calculate different implementations (both directly from the specification and exploiting the derived properties). Specifications that involve existential quantifications give rise to the use of auxiliary variables. This important technique is illustrated by the computation of quotients, as well as remainders, these computations being discarded at a later stage of the development.

Bibliographic Remarks

Remainder computation is fundamental to public-key cryptography (Schneier, 1995; Stallings, 1999). The encryption and decryption algorithms involve a combination of remainder computation, as discussed in this chapter, and evaluating powers, as discussed in Section 13.3.3. A different sort of remainder computation is used in error-resilient coding, which is the subject of Chapter 16.

16

Cyclic Codes

The transmission of raw data from one site to another, for example over the Internet or from a CD to a loudspeaker, is rarely error free. Data sent via a satellite may be lost, corrupted or duplicated as a result of atmospheric disturbances; the same may happen to data retrieved from a CD as a result of scratches or dirt.

In order to counteract the errors that occur in data transmission, it is usual to *encode* the data in such a way that errors can be detected and, where possible, repaired. This is achieved by adding redundant information to the data.

Cyclic codes offer an efficient way of protecting data from transmission errors, and their use is recommended in several industry standards. Special-purpose hardware has been developed to implement the associated encoding and decoding algorithms, in order to make the process of transmitting data as efficient as possible. This chapter is about deriving these hardware implementations.

The computation of cyclic codes is effectively a remainder computation, but in an algebra different to ordinary arithmetic—in fact, an algebra that is, in one sense, simpler than ordinary arithmetic. Section 16.2 introduces this algebra, and Section 16.3 explains how remainder computation in this algebra is used to add redundancy to transmitted data. Section 16.4 shows how a long-division algorithm is developed, taking account of the novel algebraic properties, whilst Section 16.5 is about the implementation in hardware of on-line encoding and decoding algorithms.

16.1   Codes and Codewords

One of the simplest possible encoding methods is to add a single *parity bit* to the end of a sequence of bits to ensure that the number of unit bits is always even (Figure 16.1(a)). This method allows a single error in the transmitted data

```
000 | 0                    0 | 00
001 | 1                    1 | 11
010 | 1
011 | 0
100 | 1
101 | 0
110 | 0
111 | 1
    (a)                       (b)
```

Figure 16.1 Two examples of codes. The information bits are to the left of the dotted line. (a) Parity check; (b) threefold repetition code.

to be *detected*. If there are two or more errors, the transmitted data will be indistinguishable from a message containing at most one error; also, error repair is impossible because it is not possible to determine which bit has been incorrectly transmitted.

Another method is to repeat each bit of data some constant number of times. This is called a *repetition* code. The threefold repetition code illustrated in Figure 16.1(b) permits the *repair* of a single error in the data. (We use the word 'repair' rather than 'correction' because it is never possible to guarantee that at most one error has occurred during transmission; 'repair' is less likely to mislead than 'correct'.)

Redundancy in the transmitted data results from the fact that only a fraction of all bit sequences are ever transmitted. Thus, of all sixteen 4-bit sequences, eight may be transmitted when using a single parity bit (Figure 16.1(a)), and, in a threefold repetition code, only two out of eight 3-bit sequences are ever transmitted.

A *code of length n* is a subset of the set of all n-bit sequences[1]. A *codeword* is an element of the code. If there are k information bits in a code of length n, the *rate* of the code is expressed by the pair (k, n).

A mathematical theory has been developed with the aim of predicting codes that maximize both the ratio k/n and the error detection and repair capability. Among such codes the class of *cyclic codes* has assumed a prominent role, and their use is recommended in several industry standards. In this chapter, we develop encoding and decoding algorithms appropriate to the use of cyclic codes for error detection. Algorithms for error repair are beyond the scope of this text.

---

[1] For simplicity, we assume that data to be transmitted are a finite sequence of 0s and 1s—bits. *Block* codes group bits together into larger units, but a full treatment of cyclic codes goes far beyond the scope of this text.

16.2   Boolean Polynomials

The idea behind cyclic codes is that a finite sequence of bits can be represented as a *polynomial*. Polynomial arithmetic has algebraic properties in common with normal arithmetic that allow remainder polynomials to be defined. Data is encoded as the data itself, combined with a remainder, obtained by dividing the data polynomial by a so-called *generator* polynomial.

The sequence of $n+1$ bits $P_0, P_1, \ldots, P_n$ is regarded as a *polynomial* in x:

$$P_n x^n + P_{n-1} x^{n-1} + \ldots + P_1 x + P_0 \; .$$

The bits $P_0, P_1, \ldots, P_n$ are called the *coefficients* of the polynomial, and x is a so-called *indeterminate* value. That is, x is treated like a variable, but no information is given that will allow its value to be determined.

The definition of a polynomial presupposes the definition of 'addition' and 'multiplication' operators on the coefficients. For cyclic codes, *addition* of bits is defined to be addition modulo 2. That is,

$$0+0 = 0 \; ,$$
$$0+1 = 1 \; ,$$
$$1+0 = 1 \; ,$$
$$1+1 = 0 \; .$$

Likewise, *multiplication* of bits is defined to be multiplication modulo 2. This, as it happens, is the same as normal multiplication:

$$0 \times 0 = 0 \; ,$$
$$0 \times 1 = 0 \; ,$$
$$1 \times 0 = 0 \; ,$$
$$1 \times 1 = 1 \; .$$

(Another way of looking at these operations is as operations on the boolean values true and false, where true corresponds to 1 and false to 0. Addition is then boolean inequality, and multiplication is conjunction of boolean values. Alternatively, with true corresponding to 0 and false to 1, addition is boolean equality and multiplication is disjunction. The algebraic properties should thus be familiar to you from Chapter 5.)

A polynomial is said to have *degree n* if n is the index of the largest non-zero coefficient. By convention, '0', the polynomial whose coefficients are all zero, has degree $-\infty$.

Two polynomials are *equal* if they have the same degree and corresponding coefficients are equal.

In defining operations on polynomials, it is useful to regard a polynomial as an infinite sequence of bits that is eventually all zero. This means that we assume that polynomial P satisfies

$$P = \langle \Sigma k : 0 \leqslant k : P_k x^k \rangle \ ,$$

where no upper bound is given on the dummy k. The assumption that $P_k = 0$ for all k greater than the degree of P ensures that problems with infinite summations do not arise. In this way, the rule for equality of polynomials P and Q becomes

$$\langle \Sigma k : 0 \leqslant k : P_k x^k \rangle \ = \ \langle \Sigma k : 0 \leqslant k : Q_k x^k \rangle$$
$$\equiv \quad \langle \forall k : 0 \leqslant k : P_k = Q_k \rangle \ .$$

Also, a precise definition of the degree of polynomial P, denoted *degree.P*, is

$$\langle \forall n :: \ degree.P < n \ \equiv \ \langle \forall k : n \leqslant k : P_k = 0 \rangle \rangle \ .$$

This definition also applies to the zero polynomial. The assumption we make about $-\infty$ is $-\infty < 0$.

We are now in a position to define addition and multiplication of polynomials. Both are defined by *extending* addition and multiplication operations on the coefficients of the polynomials.

Suppose that the addition $p + q$ of coefficients p and q is well defined. Then *addition* of polynomials—also denoted by '+'— is defined as the addition of corresponding coefficients. That is,

$$\langle \Sigma k : 0 \leqslant k : P_k x^k \rangle + \langle \Sigma k : 0 \leqslant k : Q_k x^k \rangle$$
$$= \quad \langle \Sigma k : 0 \leqslant k : (P_k + Q_k) x^k \rangle \ .$$

Note that the '+' in the upper line is the operator we are defining. The '+' in the lower line is assumed to be known. This overloading of the '+' symbol is justified by the fact that addition of polynomials inherits the principle algebraic properties of an 'addition' operator. That is, if addition of coefficients is symmetric and associative, then so is addition of polynomials. Also, if 0 is the unit of addition of coefficients (that is, for all coefficients p, $0 + p = p$) then 0, the polynomial of degree $-\infty$, is the unit of addition of polynomials. (It will also turn out to be the zero of multiplication.)

An immediate consequence of the definition of addition of polynomials is that the degree of $P + Q$ is at most the maximum of the degrees of P and Q. For cyclic codes, there is an additional, important consequence. Recall that, for cyclic codes, the coefficients are bits, and addition is addition modulo 2. In particular, $1 + 1 = 0$. This means that adding two non-zero polynomials of the same degree will result in a polynomial of smaller degree. Formally, since $b + b = 0$, for all bits b,

$$\langle \forall k : k \geqslant n : P_k = Q_k \rangle \ \equiv \ \langle \forall k : k \geqslant n : P_k + Q_k = 0 \rangle \ .$$

Polynomial *multiplication* is defined by the rule

$$P \times Q = R \ ,$$

where, for all k,

$$R_k = \langle \Sigma\, i,j : i+j = k : P_i \times Q_j \rangle \ .$$

This makes polynomial multiplication behave like normal multiplication. For example,

$$(P_1 x + P_0) \times (Q_2 x^2 + Q_1 x + Q_0)$$
$$= (P_1 \times Q_2)x^3 + (P_0 \times Q_2 + P_1 \times Q_1)x^2 + (P_0 \times Q_1 + P_1 \times Q_0)x + P_0 \times Q_0 \ ,$$

which is what one would obtain if x is assumed to be a normal variable, and multiplication and addition obey the rules of real arithmetic.

An immediate consequence of the definition is that, for non-zero polynomials P and Q,

$$degree.(P \times Q) = degree.P + degree.Q \ .$$

For this to be true when P or Q is zero, we require that $-\infty + n = -\infty$, for all n (including $-\infty$).

Exact division of polynomials cannot be defined, just as it is impossible to define exact division of integers. Remainder computation can be defined, however, and it is this which is exploited in cyclic codes.

The precise specification of the remainder r after dividing the polynomial P by the non-zero polynomial Q is

$$degree.r < degree.Q \ \wedge \ \langle \exists d :: P = Q \times d + r \rangle \ .$$

In this specification, d ranges over polynomials.

For example, with arithmetic on the coefficients defined to be modulo 2, the remainder on dividing $x^2 + 1$ by $x+1$ is 0 because

$$x^2 + 1 = (x+1) \times (x+1) + 0$$

and

$$degree.0 = -\infty \ < \ 1 = degree.(x+1) \ .$$

(Remember that addition is modulo 2, so that $1+1 = 0$ and, hence, $x+x = 0$.) The remainder on dividing $x^2 + x + 1$ by $x+1$ is 1 because

$$x^2 + x + 1 = (x+1) \times x + 1$$

and

$$degree.1 = 0 \ < \ 1 = degree.(x+1) \ .$$

16.3   Data and Generator Polynomials

To form a sequence of check bits from a *data polynomial P*, a so-called *generator polynomial Q* is used. Generator polynomials are chosen according to their error detection/repair capabilities, and are published in internationally recognized standards. The most important point, of course, is that both the transmitter and the receiver of the data agree on which generator polynomial to use.

The check bits are defined to be the coefficients of the remainder polynomial after division of the *input polynomial $P \times x^{degree.Q}$* by Q. The coefficients of the data polynomial are then transmitted followed by the coefficients of the remainder polynomial. In effect, this is equivalent to transmitting $P \times x^{degree.Q} + r$, where r is the remainder. But, since addition modulo 2 coincides with subtraction modulo 2, this polynomial equals $P \times x^{degree.Q} - r$, which is divisible by Q. Thus, the receiver may check for errors during transmission by determining whether or not the remainder, after dividing the received data polynomial by Q, is 0.

Example 16.1. Suppose the generator polynomial is $x^5 + x^4 + x^2 + 1$. Then, the message 1000100101, corresponding to the data polynomial $x^9 + x^5 + x^2 + 1$, would be encoded as 100010010100011. This corresponds to the polynomial

$$(x^9 + x^5 + x^2 + 1) \times x^5 + (x+1) \ .$$

The remainder $0 \times x^4 + 0 \times x^3 + 0 \times x^2 + 1 \times x^1 + 1 \times x^0$ is found by determining that

$$(x^9 + x^5 + x^2 + 1) \times x^5$$
$$= (x^5 + x^4 + x^2 + 1) \times (x^9 + x^8 + x^7 + x^3 + x^2 + x + 1) + (x+1) \ .$$

If the transmission occurs without error, the receiver computes the remainder after dividing

$$(x^9 + x^5 + x^2 + 1) \times x^5 + (x+1)$$

by the generator polynomial. This is 0 because

$$(x^9 + x^5 + x^2 + 1) \times x^5 + (x+1)$$
$$= (x^5 + x^4 + x^2 + 1) \times (x^9 + x^8 + x^7 + x^3 + x^2 + x + 1) \ .$$

$\square$

The simple parity check illustrated in Figure 16.1 is the cyclic code resulting from computing the remainder after division of the data polynomial by $x+1$. We can see this from the specification of the remainder. Substituting $x+1$ for Q, the remainder satisfies

$$degree.r < 1 \land \langle \exists d :: P = (x+1) \times d + r \rangle \ .$$

So,

true

$=$ {   above   }

$degree.r < 1 \;\wedge\; \langle \exists d :: P = (x+1){\times}d + r\rangle$

$\Rightarrow$ {   equality of polynomials   }

$degree.r = 0 \;\wedge\; \langle \exists d :: P\,[x := 1] = ((x+1){\times}d + r)\,[x := 1]\rangle$

$=$ {   substitution (P and r are independent of d),

                   $1+1 = 0$ }

$degree.r = 0 \;\wedge\; P\,[x := 1] = r\,[x := 1]$

$=$ { $degree.r = 0 \;\Rightarrow\; r = r\,[x := 1]$

                   assume $P = \langle \Sigma k : 0 \leqslant k : P_k x^k \rangle$; $1^k = 1$, for all k }

$degree.r = 0 \;\wedge\; \langle \Sigma k : 0 \leqslant k : P_k \rangle = r$.

So the remainder, r, is the sum (modulo 2) of the bits of the data polynomial. That is, r is 0 if P has an even number of 1 bits, and r is 1 if P has an odd number of 1 bits.

16.4   Long Division

The process of long division can be used to compute polynomial remainders so long as we remember the appropriate rules of arithmetic. Figure 16.2 shows one such computation presented in two ways. In the first, the powers of x are made explicit, and, in the second, a more concise form is used.

To develop long division formally, we introduce a variable k into the specification of the remainder r:

$$k \leqslant degree.Q \;\wedge\; degree.r < k \;\wedge\; \langle \exists d :: P = Q{\times}d + r\rangle \;.$$

The first conjunct forms the termination condition for a loop with the second and third conjuncts as invariants.

The invariant is established by the assignment

$$\text{if } P = 0 \longrightarrow k := 0 \;\square\; P \neq 0 \longrightarrow k := degree.P + 1 \text{ fi } ; \; r := P \;.$$

(Recall that the degree of the zero polynomial is $-\infty$.)

Since the polynomial Q is assumed to be non-zero, its degree is a natural number. We can therefore make progress to the termination condition, $k \leqslant degree.Q$, by repeatedly decreasing k and then re-establishing the invariant. The structure

$$
\begin{array}{r}
1x^3 + 1x^2 + 0x^1 + 1x^0 \\
1x^2 + 0x + 1\overline{\smash{)}1x^5 + 1x^4 + 1x^3 + 0x^2 + 1x^1 + 0x^0} \\
\underline{1x^5 + 0x^4 + 1x^3} \\
1x^4 + 0x^3 + 0x^2 + 1x^1 + 0x^0 \\
\underline{1x^4 + 0x^3 + 1x^2} \\
1x^2 + 1x^1 + 0x^0 \\
\underline{1x^2 + 0x^1 + 1x^0} \\
1x^1 + 1x^0
\end{array}
$$

Remainder =

$$
\begin{array}{r}
1101 \\
101\overline{\smash{)}111010} \\
\underline{101} \\
100 \\
\underline{101} \\
110 \\
\underline{101} \\
11
\end{array}
$$

Remainder =   11

Figure 16.2   Long division of polynomials.

of the program is thus as follows.

$\{\ 0 \leqslant degree.Q\ \}$

if $P = 0 \longrightarrow k := 0 \ \square\ P \neq 0 \longrightarrow k := degree.P + 1\ \text{fi}\ ;\ r := P\ ;$

$\{\ \textbf{Invariant:}\quad degree.r < k \wedge \langle \exists d :: P = Q \times d + r \rangle$

$\textbf{Bound function:}\quad k\ \}$

do $k > degree.Q \longrightarrow k := k - 1\ ;$

re-establish invariant

od

$\{\ degree.r < degree.Q\ \wedge\ \langle \exists d :: P = Q \times d + r \rangle\ \}$.

Re-establishing the invariant requires no action if the decrementation of k does not falsify $degree.r < k$. If the property is falsified, the degree of r must be reduced by adding a multiple of Q. Now, the precondition

$degree.r \geqslant k - 1$

$\{\ 0 \leqslant degree.Q\ \}$

if $P = 0 \longrightarrow k := 0 \ \square\ P \neq 0 \longrightarrow k := degree.P + 1$ fi ; $r := P$;

$\{\ \textbf{Invariant:}\quad degree.r < k \wedge \langle \exists d :: P = Q \times d + r \rangle$

$\quad \textbf{Bound function:}\quad k\ \}$

do $k > degree.Q \quad \longrightarrow \quad k := k-1$;

$\qquad\qquad\qquad\qquad$ if $degree.r < k \longrightarrow$ skip

$\qquad\qquad\qquad\qquad \square\ degree.r \geqslant k \longrightarrow \{\ degree.r = k\ \}$

$\qquad\qquad\qquad\qquad\qquad r := r + Q \times x^{k - degree.Q}$

$\qquad\qquad\qquad\qquad$ fi

od

$\{\ degree.r < degree.Q \quad \wedge \quad \langle \exists d :: P = Q \times d + r \rangle\ \}$.

Figure 16.3 Long-division algorithm for polynomials.

guarantees the postcondition $\neg(degree.r < k)$ after executing $k := k-1$, but the precondition under which the assignment is executed is $degree.r < k$. We conclude that, if the property $degree.r < k$ is falsified, then $degree.r = k$ is truthified. This determines how to decrease the degree of r. We exploit the property that the degree of the sum of two polynomials both of degree k has degree less than k. We need therefore to add to r a multiple of Q that has degree k. Such a multiple is $Q \times x^{k - degree.Q}$. The complete algorithm is shown in Figure 16.3. You should compare this algorithm with the long-division algorithm for integers.

16.5 Hardware Implementations

The polynomial arithmetic used to compute cyclic codes is simpler than integer arithmetic (because of the absence of 'carrying' when subtracting one number from another) although it is undoubtedly less familiar. Several operations on polynomials are also easily implemented directly in computer hardware. We now investigate the computation of cyclic codes using hardware functions as building blocks.

The requirement on the implementation is to design logic circuitry that inputs the coefficients of the polynomial P one by one. Simultaneously, the coefficients are transmitted to the receiver (see Figure 16.4). When the last coefficient (P_0) has been input, a switch is thrown, so that the coefficients of the remainder polynomial can be transmitted to the receiver.

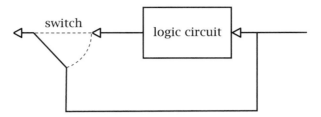

Figure 16.4   Requirement on the implementation.

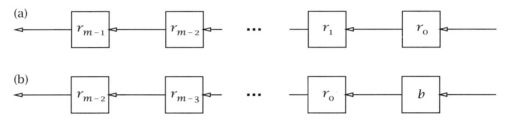

Figure 16.5   Shift register implementation of polynomial operations. (a) Before shift; (b) after shift.

The implementation we seek is, thus, an *on-line* algorithm, similar to the on-line computation of remainders in integer arithmetic (Section 15.5). The circuitry is required to input an arbitrary sequence of bits, computing, at each successive input bit, the remainder after dividing the polynomial input thus far by the given generator polynomial. When a signal is received that all of the data bits have been input, the remainder stored in the register can be output, bit by bit.

A shift register (Figure 16.5) is a fundamental component of computer hardware. It consists of an array of cells, each of which is capable of storing one bit. On receipt of a signal, its basic operation is to simultaneously 'shift' the contents of each cell into the next cell. Suppose the register stores m bits and we regard its contents $r_{m-1}, r_{m-2}, \ldots, r_1, r_0$ as a polynomial r, where

$$r = r_{m-1}x^{m-1} + r_{m-2}x^{m-2} + \ldots + r_1x + r_0 .$$

The shift operation then corresponds to the assignment

$$r := (r \times x + b) \bmod x^m ,$$

where b is the bit that is input to the cell with index 0. In this assignment, '$r \times x$' represents shifting, the addition of 'b' represents the input of a new bit, and 'mod x^m' represents the loss of the bit with index $m-1$.

Using a shift register with m cells, it is easy to implement the combined operation of multiplying a polynomial by x (i.e. shifting) and adding a multiple of a polynomial Q of degree m, all modulo x^m. Figure 16.6 shows the layout of such a circuit. In this figure, the circles marked '+' represent addition modulo 2 (better

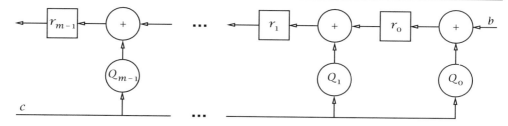

Figure 16.6 Shifting and adding a multiple of Q.

known to hardware designers as exclusive or (xor), and to readers of this text as inequivalence), and those marked Q_i, for some i, represent the 'multiplication' of the input bit by the coefficient Q_i of polynomial Q. Since $1 \times c = c$ and $0 \times c = 0$, the 'multiplication' operation is, in fact, realized by the existence of a connecting wire if $Q_i = 1$ and the absence of a connecting wire if $Q_i = 0$. Thus, the operation of the circuit in Figure 16.6 corresponds to the assignment

$$r \;\; := \;\; (r \times x + b + Q \times c) \bmod x^m \;\; . \tag{16.2}$$

Moreover, if it can be guaranteed that the polynomial $r \times x + b + Q \times c$ has degree less than m, the operation is equivalent to the assignment

$$r \;\; := \;\; r \times x + b + Q \times c \;\; .$$

We can now begin the development of the algorithm. As in Section 15.5, we model an on-line computation by an endless loop that inputs the coefficients of the polynomial bit by bit, as shown below. (Note that 'x' is an indeterminate; it is not a program variable.)

$$P \;\; := \;\; 0 \; ;$$
$$\textbf{do true} \;\; \longrightarrow \;\; (get.b \, \{ \, 0 \leqslant b \leqslant 1 \, \} \; ; \; P \;\; := \;\; P \times x + b)$$
$$\textbf{od} \;\; .$$

The task is to add code to maintain a remainder polynomial r satisfying the invariant property

$$degree.r \; < \; degree.Q \; \wedge \; \langle \exists d :: P = Q \times d + r \rangle \; ,$$

where Q is the given (non-zero) generator polynomial. For convenience, we assume that the degree of Q is m. Clearly, r should be initialized to 0. Within the body of the loop, the property

$$\langle \exists d :: P = Q \times d + r \rangle$$

can be maintained by mimicking the assignment to P:

$$r \;\; := \;\; r \times x + b \;\; .$$

$P,r := 0,0$;

{ **Invariant:** $degree.r < degree.Q \;\wedge\; \langle \exists d :: P = Q{\times}d + r \rangle$ }

do true $\longrightarrow$ $get.b \; \{\, 0 \leqslant b \leqslant 1 \,\}$;

$P := P{\times}x + b$;

$r := r{\times}x + b + Q{\times}r_{m-1}$;

$put.r$

od

Figure 16.7 On-line computation of cyclic codes.

This increases the degree of r by one. Consequently, it may falsify

$$degree.r < degree.Q \;.$$

If it does, the degree of r after the assignment must be equal to the degree of Q. The invariant can thus be re-established by adding Q to r. If it does not, no further action needs to be taken. So the assignments to r that we have to implement are

$r := r{\times}x + b$;

if $degree.r < degree.Q \longrightarrow$ skip

□ $degree.r \geqslant degree.Q \longrightarrow r := r + Q$

fi .

A direct hardware implementation of the conditional statement would be inefficient. However, by observing that the assignment $r := r{\times}x + b$ falsifies $degree.r < degree.Q$ exactly when $r_{m-1} = 1$, we see that it may be replaced by the unconditional assignment

$r := r + Q{\times}r_{m-1}$.

The two assignments can now be combined resulting in the program in Figure 16.7.

The assignment to r does, indeed, have the form of the assignment in (16.2). (The 'mod x^m' can be dropped because the resulting value of r is guaranteed to have degree less than m.) The coefficient, c, in (16.2) takes the value r_{m-1}, the bit of the remainder that is 'shifted out' of the shift register by the operation $r := r{\times}x + b$. So, the assignment to r can be implemented by a simple feedback loop. Figure 16.8 illustrates the circuit for the particular generator polynomial $Q = x^5 + x^4 + x^2 + 1$.

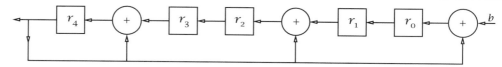

Figure 16.8   Remainder computation with generator $Q = x^5 + x^4 + x^2 + 1$.

Exercise 16.3. Earlier on, we said that what is transmitted is the remainder after dividing $x^m \times P$ by Q, where P is the *data* polynomial. This means that the *input* polynomial is terminated by m zeros. A direct implementation in hardware of the program in Figure 16.7 would therefore involve a delay of m steps—inputting the trailing zeros—before the remainder could be output.

Develop a program that eliminates this undesirable delay by taking as invariant the property

$$degree.r < degree.Q \;\wedge\; \langle \exists d :: x^m \times P = Q \times d + r \rangle \;.$$

$\square$

16.6 Summary

Cyclic codes are used to add redundancy to transmitted data in order to detect and/or repair transmission errors. Computation of cyclic codes involves remainder computation in an algebra of polynomials. Two algorithms have been discussed for computing cyclic codes. One is similar to long division in integer arithmetic, and the second is an on-line algorithm suitable for direct implementation in hardware.

Bibliographic Remarks

More information on cyclic codes can be found in (for example) Blahut (1983).

Appendix

This appendix contains a summary of the mathematical laws discussed in the main text.

Propositional Calculus

Minimal Basis. A minimal basis for the propositional calculus comprises three operators ('logical connectives'), listed below in ascending order of precedence,

- equivalence ($\equiv$) ,

- disjunction ($\vee$) ,

- negation ($\neg$) ,

and the following laws.

Associativity of $\equiv$: $((p \equiv q) \equiv r) \equiv (p \equiv (q \equiv r))$.

Symmetry of $\equiv$: $p \equiv q \equiv q \equiv p$.

Unit of $\equiv$: $\text{true} \equiv p \equiv p$.

Negation: $\neg p \equiv p \equiv \text{false}$.

Distributivity of $\neg$: $\neg(p \equiv q) \equiv \neg p \equiv q$.

Symmetry of $\vee$: $p \vee q \equiv q \vee p$.

Associativity of $\vee$: $(p \vee q) \vee r \equiv p \vee (q \vee r)$.

Idempotence of $\vee$: $p \vee p \equiv p$.

Distributivity of $\vee$: $p \vee (q \equiv r) \equiv p \vee q \equiv p \vee r$.

Excluded middle: $p \vee \neg p$.

Note that, in all but the first law, the associativity of equivalence is assumed.

Additional Operators.   The remaining logical connectives are

- conjunction ($\wedge$) ,

- if ($\Leftarrow$) ,

- only if ($\Rightarrow$) ,

- inequivalence ($\not\equiv$) .

These are defined in terms of equivalence, disjunction and negation in the following laws. The precedence convention is that conjunction has the same precedence as disjunction, and inequivalence has the same precedence as equivalence. 'If' and 'only if' have the same precedence, which is less than conjunction and disjunction, and more than equivalence and inequivalence.

false: $\text{false} \equiv \neg\text{true}$.

Golden rule: $p \wedge q \equiv p \equiv q \equiv p \vee q$.

Inequivalence: $(p \not\equiv q) \equiv \neg(p \equiv q)$.

If: $p \Leftarrow q \equiv p \vee q \equiv p$.

Only-if: $p \Rightarrow q \equiv p \vee q \equiv q$.

Rules of Substitution.

Substitution: $(e = f) \wedge E[x := e] \ \equiv \ (e = f) \wedge E[x := f]$.

Leibniz: $(e = f) \ \equiv \ (e = f) \wedge (E[x := e] = E[x := f])$.

The following subsections enumerate a number of theorems. That is, all the properties can be derived from the above axioms. The names given to the theorems are taken (with a few exceptions) from Gries and Schneider (1993) to which reference should be made for a very full and clear discussion of the principles with many more examples.

Negation

Negation of false: $\text{true} \equiv \neg\text{false}$.

Contrapositive: $p \equiv q \equiv \neg p \equiv \neg q$.

Double negation: $\neg\neg p \equiv p$.

Equivalence and Inequivalence

Symmetry: $(p \not\equiv q) \equiv (q \not\equiv p)$.

Associativity: $((p \not\equiv q) \not\equiv r) \equiv (p \not\equiv (q \not\equiv r))$.

Mutual associativity: $((p \not\equiv q) \equiv r) \equiv (p \not\equiv (q \equiv r))$.

Mutual interchangeability: $((p \not\equiv q) \equiv r) \equiv (p \equiv (q \not\equiv r))$.

Note that, in view of mutual associativity, we can write $p \not\equiv q \equiv r$ without ambiguity. This means, in turn, that the mutual interchangeability rule can be written:

$$p \not\equiv q \equiv r \equiv p \equiv q \not\equiv r .$$

Disjunction

Zero: $p \vee \text{true} \equiv \text{true}$.

Unit: $p \vee \text{false} \equiv p$.

Conjunction

Symmetry: $p \wedge q \equiv q \wedge p$.

Associativity: $(p \wedge q) \wedge r \equiv p \wedge (q \wedge r)$.

Idempotence: $p \wedge p \equiv p$.

Contradiction: $p \wedge \neg p \equiv \text{false}$.

Zero: $p \wedge \text{false} \equiv \text{false}$.

Unit: $p \wedge \text{true} \equiv p$.

Disjunction and Conjunction

Absorption: $p \wedge (p \vee q) \equiv p$.

Absorption: $p \vee (p \wedge q) \equiv p$.

Distributivity: $p \vee (q \wedge r) \equiv (p \vee q) \wedge (p \vee r)$.

Distributivity: $p \wedge (q \vee r) \equiv (p \wedge q) \vee (p \wedge r)$.

De Morgan: $\neg(p \wedge q) \equiv \neg p \vee \neg q$.

De Morgan: $\neg(p \vee q) \equiv \neg p \wedge \neg q$.

Equivalence, Disjunction and Conjunction

Distributivity: $p \wedge (q \equiv r) \equiv p \wedge q \equiv p \wedge r \equiv p$.

Modus ponens: $p \wedge (q \equiv p) \equiv p \wedge q$.

Disjunctive normal form: $p \equiv q \equiv (p \wedge q) \vee (\neg p \wedge \neg q)$.

Disjunctive normal form: $p \not\equiv q \equiv (\neg p \wedge q) \vee (p \wedge \neg q)$.

Implication

Strengthening/weakening: $p \Leftarrow p \wedge q$.

Strengthening/weakening: $p \vee q \Leftarrow q$.

Contrapositive: $p \Leftarrow q \equiv \neg p \Rightarrow \neg q$.

Contradiction: $\neg p \equiv p \Rightarrow \mathsf{false}$.

Mutual implication (iff): $p \equiv q \equiv (p \Leftarrow q) \wedge (p \Rightarrow q)$.

Distributivity: $(p \equiv q) \Leftarrow r \equiv p \wedge r \equiv q \wedge r$.

Distributivity: $(p \equiv q) \Leftarrow r \equiv p \Leftarrow r \equiv q \Leftarrow r$.

Shunting: $p \Leftarrow q \wedge r \equiv (p \Leftarrow q) \Leftarrow r$.

Modus ponens: $(p \Leftarrow q) \wedge q \equiv p \wedge q$.

Right unit: $p \Leftarrow \mathsf{true} \equiv p$.

Left zero: $\mathsf{true} \Leftarrow p \equiv \mathsf{true}$.

Absurdity: $p \Leftarrow \mathsf{false} \equiv \mathsf{true}$.

Reflexivity: $p \Leftarrow p \equiv \mathsf{true}$.

Disjunctive normal form: $p \Leftarrow q \equiv p \vee \neg q$.

(The name given to the strengthening/weakenening rules depends on whether they are used from left to right ('strengthening') or from right to left ('weakening').)

Properties of Numbers

In the rule of indirect equality, z ranges over the type of x and y. (That is, if x and y are reals, z must range over all reals. If x and y are, say, even integers, then z must range over all even integers.)

Indirect equality: $x = y \equiv \langle \forall z :: x \leqslant z \equiv y \leqslant z \rangle$.

Floor: $n \leqslant \lfloor x \rfloor \equiv n \leqslant x$.

Floor: $n = \lfloor x \rfloor \equiv n \leqslant x < n+1$.

Ceiling: $n \geqslant \lceil x \rceil \equiv n \geqslant x$.

Ceiling: $n = \lceil x \rceil \equiv n < x \leqslant n+1$.

Minimum: $m \leqslant n \downarrow p \equiv m \leqslant n \wedge m \leqslant p$.

Maximum: $m \geqslant n \uparrow p \equiv m \geqslant n \wedge m \geqslant p$.

Quantifier Laws

This section summarizes the rules for manipulating quantifiers. We assume that $\oplus$ is associative and symmetric. Some rules assume that $\oplus$ has a unit, which is denoted by $1_\oplus$. If $\oplus$ does not have a unit, quantification over a false range is not defined.

Two cautionary remarks need to be made. First, the rules are not applicable in general to infinite quantifications. (They are, however, all applicable in the case of universal and existential quantification.) Second, 'side' conditions on dummies are not repeated here. Generally, rules are only applicable when (a) application of the rule does not *capture* free variables and, conversely, (b) application of the rule does not *release* bound variables. This must be the case for all subexpressions, and not just the quantified expression itself. Also, application of a rule should not result in a variable occurring more than once in a list of dummies. Dummy renaming can sometimes be used before applying a rule in order to make its application valid (but, of course, the side condition on dummy renaming must also be observed).

Dummies.

Dummy Renaming: $\langle \oplus j : R : T \rangle = \langle \oplus k : R[j := k] : T[j := k] \rangle$.

Nesting: $\langle \oplus j, js : R \wedge S : T \rangle = \langle \oplus j : R : \langle \oplus js : S : T \rangle \rangle$.

Rearranging: $\langle \oplus j, k : R : T \rangle = \langle \oplus k, j : R : T \rangle$.

Translation: if f is a bijection from the type of dummy j to the type of dummy k,

$$\langle \oplus k : R : T \rangle = \langle \oplus j : R[k := f.j] : T[k := f.j] \rangle .$$

Translation (idempotent $\oplus$): if f is a function from the type of dummy j to the type of dummy k such that $\langle \forall k :: \langle \exists j :: k = f.j \rangle \rangle$,

$$\langle \oplus k : R : T \rangle = \langle \oplus j : R[k := f.j] : T[k := f.j] \rangle .$$

Range Part.

Empty Range: $\langle \oplus k : \mathsf{false} : T \rangle = 1_\oplus$.

One-Point: $\langle \oplus k : k = e : T \rangle = T[k := e]$.

Splitting: $\langle \oplus k : P : T \rangle \oplus \langle \oplus k : Q : T \rangle = \langle \oplus k : P \vee Q : T \rangle \oplus \langle \oplus k : P \wedge Q : T \rangle$.

Splitting (idempotent $\oplus$): $\langle \oplus k : \langle \exists j : R : S \rangle : T \rangle = \langle \oplus j : R : \langle \oplus k : S : T \rangle \rangle$.

Trading.

Type and Range: $\langle \bigoplus k{\in}K : P \wedge Q : T \rangle \;=\; \langle \bigoplus k \in \{k{\in}K \mid P\} : Q : T \rangle$.

Range and Term: $\langle \bigoplus k : P \wedge Q : T \rangle \;=\; \langle \bigoplus k : Q : \text{if } P {\longrightarrow} T \;\square\; \neg P \longrightarrow 1_\oplus \text{ fi} \rangle$.

Term Part and Distributivity.

Rearranging: $\langle \bigoplus k : R : T_0 \oplus T_1 \rangle \;=\; \langle \bigoplus k : R : T_0 \rangle \oplus \langle \bigoplus k : R : T_1 \rangle$.

Distributivity: suppose f is a function with the properties that

$$f.1_\oplus \;=\; 1_\otimes$$

and, for all x and y,

$$f.(x \oplus y) \;=\; f.x \otimes f.y \;.$$

Then

$$f.\langle \bigoplus k : R : T \rangle \;=\; \langle \bigotimes k : R : f.T \rangle \;.$$

(If $\oplus$ does not have a unit, the rule is still valid, provided that the range R is not false.)

Laws of Programming

The Hoare triple $\{ P \} \, S \, \{ Q \}$ is either true or false. Its meaning is, if execution of the statement S begins in a state satisfying precondition P, termination is guaranteed in a state satisfying Q. (If P and Q involve ghost variables, then these are universally quantified.)

Square brackets in the statement of the rules mean that the property is true for all instances of the program and ghost variables.

Assignment Axiom.

Simplified form:

$$\{ Q[x := e] \} \, x := e \, \{ Q \} \;.$$

Complete form:

$$\{ \text{'}e\text{' is well defined} \wedge Q[x := e] \} \, x := e \, \{ Q \} \;.$$

Sequential Composition.

$$\{ P \} \, S1; S2 \, \{ Q \} \;\Leftarrow\; \{ P \} \, S1 \, \{ R \} \wedge \{ R \} \, S2 \, \{ Q \} \;.$$

Skip Rule.

$$\{ P \} \, \text{skip} \, \{ Q \} \;\equiv\; [P \Rightarrow Q] \;.$$
$$\{ P \} \, \{ Q \} \;\equiv\; [P \Rightarrow Q] \;.$$

Conditional Statements.

$$\{ \; P \; \}$$

$$\text{if} \; b1 \longrightarrow S1$$

$$\square \; b2 \longrightarrow S2$$

$$\text{fi}$$

$$\{ \; Q \; \}$$

is equivalent to the conjunction of three propositions:

$$[P \Rightarrow b1 \lor b2] \; ,$$

$$\{ \, P \land b1 \, \} \; S1 \; \{ \, Q \, \}$$

and

$$\{ \, P \land b2 \, \} \; S2 \; \{ \, Q \, \} \; .$$

Loops.

$$\{ \, P \, \} \; S \, ; \, \text{do} \; \neg done \longrightarrow T \; \text{od} \; \{ \, Q \, \}$$

is guaranteed by the following construction.

(1) Choose bound function, bf, invariant, inv, and termination condition, $done$, so that

$$[inv \land done \; \Rightarrow \; Q]$$

and

$$[inv \; \Rightarrow \; bf > 0 \lor done] \; .$$

(2) Construct initialization statement, S, to establish the invariant:

$$\{ \, P \, \} \; S \; \{ \, inv \, \} \; .$$

(3) Construct the loop body, T, so as to guarantee progress towards the termination condition whilst maintaining the invariant:

$$\{ \, inv \, \land \, \neg done \, \land \, bf = \mathsf{C} \, \} \; T \; \{ \, inv \, \land \, (bf < \mathsf{C} \lor done) \, \} \; .$$

Solutions to Exercises

Solution 1.1. For $n = 5$, the number of portions is 16. This suggests that the number of portions for arbitrary n is 2^{n-1}. However, for $n = 0$, it does not make sense to say that there are 2^{n-1} portions (even though cutting the cake as stated does make sense). The conclusion might then be that the conjecture only holds for n at least 1. However, for $n = 6$, the number of portions is 31 (see Figure B.1)! Note that $n = 6$ is the first case in which the points are not allowed to be placed at equal distances around the perimeter.) □

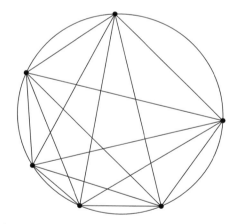

Figure B.1 Cutting the cake. The case $n = 6$.

Solution 2.1.

(a) Hoare assumes that the pack contains 100 cards. The weakest assumption is that the pack contains at least 20 cards.

(b) The number of cards in the top-left heap is always at most 20. The number of cards in the top-right heap is always at most 80.

(c) Each value in the top-left heap is at most all values in the bottom-left heap. Each value in the bottom-left heap is at most all values in the bottom-right heap. And, each value in the bottom-right heap is at most all values in the top-right heap.

Note: the relationship is 'at most'. It is incorrect to claim, for example, that all values in the top-left heap are lower than (or less than) all values in the bottom-left heap.

(d) If all cards in the pack have the same value, each iteration of step (2) adds just the borderline card to the top-left heap. The repetition in step (2) will therefore take place 20 times.

If the pack is sorted and the borderline card is chosen to be the 20th card in the pack, one repetition of step (2) adds 20 cards to the bottom left deck whenever there are exactly 19 cards strictly lower than the 20th card. If there are n cards strictly lower than the 20th, $19 - n$ repetitions are needed.

(e) The borderline card is always either added to the top-left heap (in step (2.3)) or to the top-right heap (in step (2.4)). This means that between every repetition of (2) the size of the middle heap decreases by at least one.

If an arbitrary value is chosen for the borderline, termination is not guaranteed. For example, if the borderline is chosen to be zero and all values in the pack are greater than zero, the algorithm will continually loop between a state in which all cards are in the bottom-right heap and one in which all cards are in the middle heap.

(f) The assumption is that $M \leqslant N$ and (possibly) $N \neq 0$. The algorithm is obtained by replacing 100 by N, 20 by M, 21 by $M+1$, 80 by $N-M$ and 81 by $N-M+1$. When M is zero, the amalgamation in step (2.4) takes place. Also the borderline card is moved to the top-right deck. Thus, the algorithm terminates correctly after one repetition of step (2). When N equals M, the amalgamation in step (2.3) takes place and the borderline card is moved to the top-left deck. Thus, also in this case, the algorithm terminates correctly after one repetition of step (2). The requirement that $N \neq 0$ is unfortunate and depends on how one understands step (2). If one understands it as executing steps (2.1)–(2.5) and *then* testing whether the middle heap is empty, the requirement is necessary because, otherwise, it is not possible to choose a borderline card in step (2.1). This is the way repeat-until statements are normally understood by computer programmers. If, however, the statement means that the test of whether the middle heap is not empty is executed *first* and only when it succeeds are steps (2.1)–(2.5) executed, it is not necessary for N to be non-zero; it may be zero so long as M is also zero. (This is an example, albeit minor, of the ambiguities of natural language.)

□

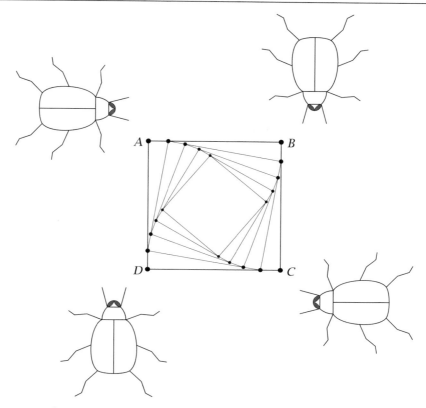

Figure B.2 Invariant: beetles are at the corners of a square.

Solution 2.2. It is not possible to cover the chessboard. Removing the top-left and bottom-right squares removes two squares of the same colour. So more squares of one colour remain than of the other. But, each time a domino is placed on the board it covers one black square and one white square. So, no matter how many dominoes are placed on the board, an equal number of white and black squares will have been covered. □

Solution 2.3. At all times the four beetles occupy the corners of a square (see Figure B.2). Thus at no time does any beetle have any component of velocity away from its pursuer. The distance travelled by any one beetle is therefore identical to the distance it would travel were the pursued beetle to remain stationary. Thus, each beetle travels a distance equal to the length of a side of the square. □

Solution 3.1. The proof assumes the formulae for the area of a triangle and a square, and basic algebraic properties of addition and multiplication. However, the most important omission in the proof is that nowhere is the fact that $\widehat{BAC}$ is a right angle explicitly used. The property is, in fact, implicitly used in the sentence beginning 'Construct a square $IJKL$'. The fact that $IJKL$ is a square relies on the fact that the angles $\hat{I}$, $\hat{J}$, $\hat{K}$ and $\hat{L}$ are all right angles. Less obviously, it also relies on the fact that (for example) the line IBJ is a straight line, i.e. $\widehat{IBJ}$ is 180°, and that (again, for example) $\widehat{BDE}$ is a right angle. These properties are consequences of the fact that the angles of a triangle add up to 180°.   □

Solution 3.4. The rule is that multiplication by a strictly positive number is invertible with respect to the relation X. That is, for X is '<', '=' or '>', all strictly positive numbers a and all numbers b and c,

$$(a{\times}b \ X \ a{\times}c) \ = \ (b \, X \, c) \ .$$

                                                                                                    □

Solution 3.5. We have, for X is '<', '=' or '>',

$$\sqrt{3} + \sqrt{13} \ \ X \ \ \sqrt{5} + \sqrt{11}$$

$=$ {   squaring is invertible with respect to X: (3.3)   }

$$(\sqrt{3} + \sqrt{13})^2 \ \ X \ \ (\sqrt{5} + \sqrt{11})^2$$

$=$ {   arithmetic   }

$$16 + 2\sqrt{39} \ \ X \ \ 16 + 2\sqrt{55}$$

$=$ {   addition is invertible with respect to X: (3.2)   }

$$2\sqrt{39} \ \ X \ \ 2\sqrt{55}$$

$=$ {   squaring is invertible with respect to X: (3.3)   }

$$156 \ X \ 220 \ .$$

We conclude that $\sqrt{3} + \sqrt{13} \, < \, \sqrt{5} + \sqrt{11}$.   □

Solution 3.6. The flaw in the algorithm is the implicit assumption that both sides remain non-negative. The property that squaring preserves each of the orderings is not true for negative numbers. For example, $-1 < 0$ but $(-1)^2 > 0^2$. So, for example, if the algorithm is applied with $a,b,c,d := 0,2,0,1$, v is assigned the value 0 at step (2) and z and y are assigned the values -1 and 0, respectively. This results in the incorrect inference that $\sqrt{0} + \sqrt{2} < \sqrt{0} + \sqrt{1}$.

Each step of the algorithm replaces the left and right sides by new left and right sides, each side being a sum of terms. The invariant that should be maintained by the algorithm is that the ordering relation between the two sides remains the same. In order to maintain this invariant, we add the extra requirement that the terms on each side are non-negative. Thus, when a subtraction is performed, we must ensure that the result is non-negative. Step (2) should therefore subtract the minimum of u and x from both sides. This has repercussions for both steps (3) and (4), with step (4) being modified similarly to step (2).   □

Solution 3.7.

(a) $x+2$.

(b) $y \cdot (x+y)$.

(c) $x+y+y$.

(d) $x+1$.

(e) 0 .

(f) $x - y + (x+y) \cdot (x-y)$.

(g) $x \cdot y + x \cdot y$.

(h) $x + 2 + (x+2) \cdot (x \cdot y)^2$.

□

Solution 3.8. Replacing 2 everywhere by k, exp.l is defined to be the number of times that k divides l. It is required to satisfy

$$\text{exp.}k = 1 ,$$

and, for all m and n,

$$\text{exp.}(m \times n) = \text{exp.}m + \text{exp.}n .$$

The former property is satisfied whatever the value of k. The latter property is satisfied exactly when k is a prime number different from one. So a generalization of the theorem and its proof is that $\sqrt{k}$ is irrational if k is a prime number different from one. (See Exercise 11.60 for a better generalization.) □

Solution 4.1. Immediately before the `return` statement, add the assignment

```
if (1 < N) found= (card[1] == X) ; else found= false ; .
```

□

Solution 4.2.

$$(l+r-1) \div 2 < r$$

$$= \qquad \{ \qquad (l+r-1) \div 2 \text{ and } r \text{ are integers} \quad \}$$

$$(l+r-1) \div 2 \leqslant r-1$$

$$= \qquad \{ \qquad r-1 = (2 \times (r-1)) \div 2 \quad \}$$

$$(l+r-1) \div 2 \leqslant (2 \times (r-1)) \div 2$$

$$\Leftarrow \qquad \{ \qquad \text{division by 2 is monotonic} \quad \}$$

$$l+r-1 \leqslant 2 \times (r-1)$$

$$= \qquad \{ \qquad \text{arithmetic} \quad \}$$

$$l \leqslant r-1$$

$$= \qquad \{ \qquad l \text{ and } r \text{ are integers. } \}$$

$$l < r \ .$$

The proof using $m \div 2 \leqslant m/2 \Leftarrow 0 \leqslant m$ is as follows:

$$(l+r-1) \div 2 < r$$

$$\Leftarrow \qquad \{ \qquad \text{division by 2 rounds towards 0 for non-negative integers.}$$

$$\text{That is, } (l+r-1) \div 2 \leqslant (l+r-1)/2 \Leftarrow 0 \leqslant l+r-1.$$

$$0 \leqslant l+r-1 \Leftarrow 0 \leqslant l < r \ \}$$

$$(l+r-1)/2 < r$$

$$= \qquad \{ \qquad \text{(real) division by 2 is monotonic}$$

$$\text{with respect to the } < \text{ relation } \}$$

$$l-1 < r$$

$$\Leftarrow \qquad \{ \qquad \text{arithmetic } \}$$

$$l < r \ .$$

From this we conclude the (slightly weaker)

$$(l+r-1) \div 2 < r \Leftarrow 0 \leqslant l < r \ .$$

$\square$

Solution 4.3.

(a) This is not the case. For example, $0 < 1$, but $0 \div 2 = 0 = 1 \div 2$.

(b) This is not the case either; $1 \div 2 \leqslant 0 \div 2$ but it is not the case that $1 \leqslant 0$.

(c) The difference is that addition is invertible. (That is, adding m can be undone by subtracting m.) Integer division is not invertible.

(d) Multiplication by a negative number is anti-monotonic. (That is, if $n < 0$,

$$i \times n \leqslant j \times n \ \Leftarrow \ i \geqslant j \ .$$

(Note the reversal of the ordering.) Division inverts multiplication. So any implementation of integer division should also be anti-monotonic. That is, if $n < 0$,

$$i \div n \leqslant j \div n \ \Leftarrow \ j \leqslant i \ .$$

$\square$

Solution 4.4. The assignment $k := l$ is clearly correct, and the assignment $k := r$ clearly incorrect—it will generate an array bound error the very first time the loop body is executed whatever the size of the array.

The assignment $k := (l+r) \div 2$ is correct. The property $l \leqslant k$ is satisfied because $l \leqslant (l+r-1) \div 2$, as proved above, $l+r-1 \leqslant l+r$, and integer division by 2 is monotonic. The proof that $(l+r) \div 2 < r$ is the only time that we need to use the fact that integer division rounds towards zero.

$$(l+r) \div 2 < r$$

$\Leftarrow \qquad \{ \qquad (l+r) \div 2 \leqslant (l+r)/2 \quad \}$

$$(l+r)/2 < r$$

$= \qquad \{ \qquad \text{arithmetic} \quad \}$

$$l < r \ .$$

If integer division is defined to round away from zero, the assignment $k := (l+r-1) \div 2$ is correct, the assignment $k := (l+r) \div 2$ is not. To show that the latter is incorrect consider an array of size 1. Then l and r are initialized to 0 and 1, respectively. So $(l+r)/2$ rounds up to 1. If this value is assigned to k, an array bound error will occur.

A general conclusion is that the assignment $k := (l+r-1) \div 2$ is safer than the assignment $k := (l+r) \div 2$ because its correctness is independent of whether integer division is implemented by rounding down or up. □

Solution 4.5. First, if $card[r-1] = card[l]$, a division-by-zero error will occur. Assuming this not to be the case, the right side of the assignment to k gives a value in the range l up to $r-1$ if

$$card[l] \leqslant X \leqslant card[r-1] \ .$$

But this is not an invariant property of the algorithm. □

Solution 4.6. (a) In the scenario given, hi and lo are initialized to 2 and 0, respectively. The first iteration of the loop sets centre to 1—the fact that there are 'Only two items left' is not observed—and resets lo to 1. In the second iteration, centre is again assigned the value 1. This time, the method erroneously concludes 'Only two items left'. The test v[centre].equals(o) fails and then an array bound error occurs when the test v[centre+1].equals(o) is executed.

Reading the comment 'Only two items left', it would appear that the program implicitly assumes that v.length is at least 2. Indeed, the program will always give an array bound error if its length is zero, and it will also do so if its length is one and the entry being sought is greater than the entry in the array. The clumsy code preceded by the comment 'Only two items left' was possibly inserted to fix a bug that had been found. But, as we have just seen, the fix is not just clumsy, it does not work! (It is very common for additional tests to be added to fix bugs; an abundance of case analyses is indicative of bad programming.) The problem lies in the fact that the assignments to hi and lo are unsystematic: initially, the region to be searched is given by the indices from lo to hi−1 inclusive. If lo is reassigned, however, the region to be searched begins at index lo+1. (This observation makes it possible to identify the error.) The assignments to hi are more systematic, but probably by good fortune rather than good programming! There is no mention of an invariant property in the comments, and no mention of how progress is guaranteed.   □

Solution 5.2. $(p = q) = r$ and $p = (q = r)$ are both true exactly when an odd number of p, q and r is true. (Thus when all are true or just one is true.)   □

Solution 5.3. Parenthesizing the statement as

$$x \times y \text{ is positive } \equiv (x \text{ is positive } \equiv y \text{ is positive}) ,$$

it states that the number $x \times y$ is positive exactly when the signs of x and y are both the same. Parenthesizing it as

$$(x \times y \text{ is positive } \equiv x \text{ is positive}) \equiv y \text{ is positive} ,$$

it states that the operation of multiplying a number x by a number y does not change the sign of x exactly when y is positive. As for the parity of a number, we get four different cases:

$$((x \times y \text{ is positive}) \text{ and } (x \text{ is positive}) \text{ and } (y \text{ is positive}))$$
or $\quad((x \times y \text{ is negative}) \text{ and } (x \text{ is negative}) \text{ and } (y \text{ is positive}))$
or $\quad((x \times y \text{ is negative}) \text{ and } (x \text{ is positive}) \text{ and } (y \text{ is negative}))$
or $\quad((x \times y \text{ is positive}) \text{ and } (x \text{ is negative}) \text{ and } (y \text{ is negative})).$

□

Solution 5.5.

(a) p .

(b) q .

(c) $q \equiv p$.

(d) false .

(e) true .

(f) false .

(g) p .

□

Solution 5.8. Yes. If you ask A if B is a knight you get the answer $A \equiv B$. If you ask B if A is a knight you get the answer $B \equiv A$. But equivalence is symmetric, so they are the same answer.   □

Solution 5.9. We have $A \equiv B \equiv C$, which is true when an odd number of A, B and C is true. Thus either just one is a knight or all three are knights. $\square$

Solution 5.10. We have $C \equiv A \equiv B$. So the question we have to pose to A is $A \equiv A \equiv B$, i.e. B. In words, ask A whether B is a knight. $\square$

Solution 5.11. Let Q be the question. Asking the question Q will produce the response $A \equiv Q$, which we require to be A. So we require that $A \equiv A \equiv Q$, i.e. Q. In words, ask A to confirm or deny any true statement (for example $0 = 0$). $\square$

Solution 5.12. Let Q be the question. Asking the question Q will produce the response $A \equiv Q$, which we require to be B. So we require that $B \equiv A \equiv Q$. In words, ask A whether they are both the same type. $\square$

Solution 5.13. Let Q be the question. Asking the question Q will produce the response $A \equiv Q$ which we require to be $B \equiv A$. So we require that $B \equiv A \equiv A \equiv Q$, i.e. $B \equiv Q$. In words, ask A whether B is a knight. $\square$

Solution 5.14. Let Q be the question. Choose arbitrarily to pose the question to A. Asking the question Q will then produce the response $A \equiv Q$. The proposition whose truth we want to determine is $A \equiv B \equiv C$. So we require that $(A \equiv Q) \equiv (A \equiv B \equiv C)$. Rearranging and simplifying we get $Q \equiv B \equiv C$. That is, the question is: 'are your two companions the same type?'. $\square$

Solution 5.17.

  (a) false .

  (b) false .

  (c) false .

  (d) p .

  (e) false .

  (f) $q \not\equiv r$.

  (g) p .

  (h) true .

$\square$

Solution 5.18.

  (a) $p = q$.

  (b) $p \neq q$.

  (c) $p \equiv q \equiv r \equiv s$.

  (d) $p \not\equiv q \not\equiv r \not\equiv s$.

$\square$

Solution 5.19.

$$\neg\text{true}$$
$$=\quad\{\qquad\text{law }\neg p \equiv p \equiv \text{false with } p := \text{true}\quad\}$$
$$\text{true} \equiv \text{false}$$
$$=\quad\{\qquad\text{law true} \equiv p \equiv p \text{ with } p := \text{false}\quad\}$$
$$\text{false}\;.$$

□

Solution 5.20.

$$\neg\neg p$$
$$=\quad\{\qquad\text{law }\neg p \equiv p \equiv \text{false with } p := \neg p\quad\}$$
$$\neg p \equiv \text{false}$$
$$=\quad\{\qquad\text{law }\neg p \equiv p \equiv \text{false with } p := p$$
$$\text{and symmetry of equivalence}\quad\}$$
$$p\;.$$

□

Solution 5.21. The three most important examples are
$$(p \not\equiv (q \not\equiv r)) \equiv (p \equiv q \equiv r)\;,$$
$$((p \not\equiv q) \not\equiv r) \equiv (p \equiv q \equiv r)\;,$$
$$(p \not\equiv q) \equiv (q \not\equiv r) \equiv p \equiv r\;.$$

The first two establish that inequivalence is associative.   □

Solution 5.22. The process of decryption after encryption computes $a \not\equiv (a \not\equiv b)$. But,

$$a \not\equiv (a \not\equiv b)$$
$$=\quad\{\qquad \not\equiv \text{ is associative}\quad\}$$
$$(a \not\equiv a) \not\equiv b$$
$$=\quad\{\qquad (a \not\equiv a \equiv \text{false})\quad\}$$
$$\text{false} \not\equiv b$$
$$=\quad\{\qquad \text{definition of } \not\equiv\quad\}$$
$$\text{false} \equiv \neg b$$
$$=\quad\{\qquad \text{definition of negation: (5.15)}\quad\}$$
$$b\;.$$

□

Solution 5.23. A's statement is $B \equiv \neg A$. So, what we are given is

$$A \equiv B \equiv \neg A \ .$$

This simplifies to $\neg B$ as follows.

$\quad\quad A \equiv B \equiv \neg A$

$=\quad\quad\quad\{\quad\quad$ rearranging terms $\quad\}$

$\quad\quad \neg A \equiv A \equiv B$

$=\quad\quad\quad\{\quad\quad$ law $\neg p \equiv p \equiv$ false with $p := A \quad\}$

$\quad\quad$ false $\equiv B$

$=\quad\quad\quad\{\quad\quad$ law $\neg p \equiv p \equiv$ false with $p := B$ and rearranging $\quad\}$

$\quad\quad \neg B \ .$

So, B is a knave, but A could be a knight or a knave. $\quad\quad\square$

Solution 5.24. Let Q be the question. Then, $Q \equiv A \equiv A \not\equiv B$, i.e. $Q \equiv \neg B$. In words, ask A whether B is a knave. $\quad\quad\square$

Solution 6.5. Suppose that l and m are given numbers such that for all numbers n,

$$n \leqslant l \equiv n \leqslant m \ .$$

Instantiating n to l (which is allowed because n and l are assumed to have the same type), we get

$$l \leqslant l \equiv l \leqslant m \ .$$

But,

$\quad\quad l \leqslant l \equiv l \leqslant m$

$=\quad\quad\quad\{\quad\quad \leqslant$ is reflexive $\quad\}$

$\quad\quad$ true $\equiv l \leqslant m$

$=\quad\quad\quad\{\quad\quad$ true is the unit of equivalence $\quad\}$

$\quad\quad l \leqslant m \ .$

Thus, we conclude that $l \leqslant m$.

Symmetrically, instantiating n to m (which is allowed because n and m are assumed to have the same type), we get

$$m \leqslant l \equiv m \leqslant m$$

and, hence, $m \leqslant l$.

The conjunction of $l \leqslant m$ and $m \leqslant l$, together with the fact that the at-most relation is antisymmetric establishes that $l = m$, as required. $\quad\quad\square$

Solution 6.6.

(a) We have, for all n,

$$n \leqslant \lfloor x+m \rfloor$$
$$= \qquad \{ \qquad \text{definition of floor} \quad \}$$
$$n \leqslant x+m$$
$$= \qquad \{ \qquad \text{arithmetic} \quad \}$$
$$n-m \leqslant x$$
$$= \qquad \{ \qquad \text{definition of floor} \quad \}$$
$$n-m \leqslant \lfloor x \rfloor$$
$$= \qquad \{ \qquad \text{arithmetic} \quad \}$$
$$n \leqslant \lfloor x \rfloor +m \ .$$

The result follows by indirect equality.

(b) We have, for all n,

$$n \leqslant \lfloor x/m \rfloor$$
$$= \qquad \{ \qquad \text{definition of floor} \quad \}$$
$$n \leqslant x/m$$
$$= \qquad \{ \qquad \text{arithmetic, } m \text{ is positive} \quad \}$$
$$n \times m \leqslant x$$
$$= \qquad \{ \qquad \text{definition of floor} \quad \}$$
$$n \times m \leqslant \lfloor x \rfloor$$
$$= \qquad \{ \qquad \text{arithmetic, } m \text{ is positive} \quad \}$$
$$n \leqslant \lfloor x \rfloor /m$$
$$= \qquad \{ \qquad \text{definition of floor} \quad \}$$
$$n \leqslant \lfloor \lfloor x \rfloor /m \rfloor \ .$$

The result follows by indirect equality.   □

Solution 6.7. The second 'definition of floor' step is invalid since m/n is not an integer. Taking m, n and x to be 1, 2 and $\frac{2}{3}$, we have

$$\tfrac{1}{2} \leqslant \tfrac{2}{3}$$
$$\neq \qquad \{ \qquad \lfloor \tfrac{2}{3} \rfloor = 0 \quad \}$$
$$\tfrac{1}{2} \leqslant \lfloor \tfrac{2}{3} \rfloor \ .$$

This suggests that $2 \times \lfloor \frac{2}{3} \rfloor \neq \lfloor 2 \times \frac{2}{3} \rfloor$, which indeed is the case as $0 \neq 1$.   □

Solution 6.11.

$$\left\lfloor \frac{(-1)+(-1)-1}{-1} \right\rfloor,$$

which equals 3 and is clearly different from $\lceil \frac{1}{1} \rceil$, which is 1. □

Solution 6.12. The second step (with the hint 'inequalities') is invalid. The rule $m < k+1 \equiv m \leqslant k$ is only valid for integers m and k, and not for real numbers.

The mistake made here is an easy one to make because of the overloading of the symbols $<$ and $\leqslant$ for ordering both real and integer numbers. In this case, the mistake is easily spotted, but in other circumstances it may not be so easy to spot. The moral is: beware of overloaded operators! □

Solution 6.13. We have, for all n,

$$n \geqslant -\lfloor x \rfloor$$
$$= \qquad \{ \qquad \text{negation} \quad \}$$
$$-n \leqslant \lfloor x \rfloor$$
$$= \qquad \{ \qquad \text{definition of floor} \quad \}$$
$$-n \leqslant x$$
$$= \qquad \{ \qquad \text{negation} \quad \}$$
$$n \geqslant -x$$
$$= \qquad \{ \qquad \text{definition of ceiling} \quad \}$$
$$n \geqslant \lceil -x \rceil \ .$$

Thus, by indirect equality, the function f is the ceiling function. □

Solution 6.14. The defining equation is

$$k \leqslant m \div n \ \equiv \ k \times n \leqslant m \ .$$

Indirect equality is used to show that

$$m \div n = \left\lfloor \frac{m}{n} \right\rfloor \ .$$

We have, for all integers k,

$$k \leqslant m \div n$$
$$= \qquad \{ \qquad \text{above definition} \quad \}$$
$$k \times n \leqslant m$$
$$= \qquad \{ \qquad \text{arithmetic} \quad \}$$
$$k \leqslant \frac{m}{n}$$

$$= \qquad \{ \qquad \text{definition of the floor function} \quad \}$$
$$k \leqslant \left\lfloor \frac{m}{n} \right\rfloor \; .$$

In the case that $m \div n$ is the smallest integer k such that $k \times n \geqslant m$, the definition becomes

$$k \geqslant m \div n \; \equiv \; k \times n \geqslant m \; .$$

$\square$

Solution 7.4. For continued equivalences, pairs of repeated terms cancel each other out. So for continued equivalences, an even number of occurrences of the same term reduces to none, and an odd number of repeated terms reduces to one. $\square$

Solution 7.7.

$$p \vee \text{true}$$
$$= \qquad \{ \qquad \text{reflexivity of equivalence (5.4)} \quad \}$$
$$p \vee (p \equiv p)$$
$$= \qquad \{ \qquad \text{disjunction distributes over equivalence (7.5)} \quad \}$$
$$p \vee p \equiv p \vee p$$
$$= \qquad \{ \qquad \text{reflexivity of equivalence (5.4)} \quad \}$$
$$\text{true} \; .$$

$\square$

Solution 7.10.

$$p \wedge p$$
$$= \qquad \{ \qquad \text{golden rule, } p,q := p,p \quad \}$$
$$p \equiv p \equiv p \vee p$$
$$= \qquad \{ \qquad \text{disjunction is idempotent} \quad \}$$
$$p \equiv p \equiv p$$
$$= \qquad \{ \qquad \text{reflexivity of equivalence (5.4)} \quad \}$$
$$p \; .$$

$\square$

Solution 7.12.

$$p \wedge (p \vee q)$$
$$= \qquad \{ \qquad \text{golden rule: } p,q := p, p \vee q \quad \}$$
$$p \equiv p \vee q \equiv p \vee (p \vee q)$$

$=$ {   associativity and idempotence of disjunction }

$p \equiv p \vee q \equiv p \vee q$

$=$ {   reflexivity of equivalence (5.4) }

p .

□

Solution 7.13.

$(p \vee q) \wedge (p \vee r)$

$=$ {   golden rule: $p,q := p \vee q, p \vee r$ }

$p \vee q \equiv p \vee r \equiv (p \vee q) \vee (p \vee r)$

$=$ {   associativity, symmetry, idempotence of disjunction }

$p \vee q \equiv p \vee r \equiv p \vee q \vee r$

$=$ {   disjunction distributes over equivalence }

$p \vee (q \equiv r \equiv q \vee r)$

$=$ {   golden rule }

$p \vee (q \wedge r)$.

□

Solution 7.14.

Modus ponens:

$p \wedge (p \equiv q)$

$=$ {   golden rule, $p,q := p, p \equiv q$ }

$p \equiv p \equiv q \equiv p \vee (p \equiv q)$

$=$ {   disjunction distributes over equivalence }

$p \equiv p \equiv q \equiv p \vee p \equiv p \vee q$

$=$ {   simplification of continued equivalence,

                 disjunction is idempotent }

$p \equiv q \equiv p \vee q$

$=$ {   golden rule }

$p \wedge q$.

De Morgan. The more complicated side is the right side (because it contains two negations rather than one).

$$\neg p \vee \neg q$$

$=$ {   definition of negation   }

$$(p \equiv \text{false}) \vee (q \equiv \text{false})$$

$=$ {   disjunction distributes over equivalence

                             (applied twice)   }

$$p \vee q \equiv \text{false} \vee q \equiv p \vee \text{false} \equiv \text{false} \vee \text{false}$$

$=$ {   false is unit of disjunction   }

$$p \vee q \equiv q \equiv p \equiv \text{false}$$

$=$ {   rearranging terms (using symmetry

                             and associativity of equivalence)   }

$$p \equiv q \equiv p \vee q \equiv \text{false}$$

$=$ {   golden rule   }

$$p \wedge q \equiv \text{false}$$

$=$ {   definition of negation   }

$$\neg(p \wedge q) \ .$$

De Morgan. Again we begin with the right side.

$$\neg p \wedge \neg q$$

$=$ {   golden rule   }

$$\neg p \equiv \neg q \equiv \neg p \vee \neg q$$

$=$ {   contrapositive applied to $\neg p \equiv \neg q$

                             rule just proved: $\neg p \vee \neg q \equiv \neg(p \wedge q)$

                             applied to third term   }

$$p \equiv q \equiv \neg(p \wedge q)$$

$=$ {   definition of negation   }

$$p \equiv q \equiv p \wedge q \equiv \text{false}$$

$=$ {   golden rule   }

$$p \vee q \equiv \text{false}$$

$=$ {   definition of negation   }

$$\neg(p \vee q) \ .$$

Distributivity of conjunction over equivalence.

$$p \wedge (q \equiv r)$$

$=$ { golden rule, $p,q := p, q \equiv r$ }

$$p \equiv q \equiv r \equiv p \vee (q \equiv r)$$

$=$ { distributivity of disjunction over equivalence }

$$p \equiv q \equiv r \equiv p \vee q \equiv p \vee r$$

$=$ { rearrange terms (using symmetry and associativity of

equivalence) and add p twice

in order to head for the golden rule. }

$$p \equiv q \equiv p \vee q \equiv p \equiv p \equiv r \equiv p \vee r$$

$=$ { golden rule (twice—once with $p,q := p,q$,

once with $p,q := p,r$) }

$$p \wedge q \equiv p \equiv p \wedge r .$$

We thus conclude that

$$p \wedge (q \equiv r) \equiv p \wedge q \equiv p \equiv p \wedge r .$$

Rearranging terms we get the required result. $\qquad\qquad\square$

Solution 7.15. In this solution, simplification of continued equivalences and disjunctions using the basic laws (symmetry, associativity, idempotence and constants) is not spelt out.

We begin by deriving the equality between (a) and (b).

$$(p \vee q) \wedge (q \vee r) \wedge (r \vee p)$$

$=$ { golden rule, $p,q := p \vee q , (q \vee r) \wedge (r \vee p)$ }

$$p \vee q \equiv (q \vee r) \wedge (r \vee p) \equiv p \vee q \vee ((q \vee r) \wedge (r \vee p))$$

$=$ { distributivity of disjunction over conjunction

and simplification }

$$p \vee q \equiv (q \vee r) \wedge (r \vee p) \equiv p \vee q \vee r$$

$=$ { golden rule, $p,q := q \vee r , r \vee p,$

simplification of continued disjunction }

$$p \vee q \equiv q \vee r \equiv r \vee p \equiv p \vee q \vee r \equiv p \vee q \vee r$$

$=$ { simplification of continued equivalences }

$$p \vee q \equiv q \vee r \equiv r \vee p .$$

Now the equality between (d) and (c) is obtained by replacing conjunction everywhere by disjunction and vice versa.

$$(p \wedge q) \vee (q \wedge r) \vee (r \wedge p)$$

=   {   golden rule, $p,q := p \wedge q , (q \wedge r) \vee (r \wedge p)$ }

$$p \wedge q \equiv (q \wedge r) \vee (r \wedge p) \equiv p \wedge q \wedge ((q \wedge r) \vee (r \wedge p))$$

=   {   distributivity of conjunction over disjunction

        and simplification   }

$$p \wedge q \equiv (q \wedge r) \vee (r \wedge p) \equiv p \wedge q \wedge r$$

=   {   golden rule, $p,q := q \wedge r , r \wedge p$,

        simplification of continued conjunction   }

$$p \wedge q \equiv q \wedge r \equiv r \wedge p \equiv p \wedge q \wedge r \equiv p \wedge q \wedge r$$

=   {   simplification of continued equivalences   }

$$p \wedge q \equiv q \wedge r \equiv r \wedge p \ .$$

Now we prove that (b) and (c) are equal.

$$p \wedge q \equiv q \wedge r \equiv r \wedge p$$

=   {   golden rule, applied to each conjunct   }

$$p \equiv q \equiv p \vee q \equiv q \equiv r \equiv q \vee r \equiv r \equiv p \equiv r \vee p$$

=   {   simplification of continued equivalences   }

$$p \vee q \equiv q \vee r \equiv r \vee p \ .$$

                          □

Solution 7.22.

$$p \wedge q \Rightarrow p \ .$$
$$q \Rightarrow p \vee q \ .$$

                          □

Solution 7.23.

$$\text{false} \Leftarrow \text{true}$$

=   {   definition   }

$$\text{false} \equiv \text{false} \vee \text{true}$$

=   {   true is zero of disjunction   }

$$\text{false} \equiv \text{true}$$

$$= \qquad \{ \qquad \text{true is unit of equivalence} \quad \}$$

$$\textsf{false} \; .$$

□

Solution 7.24.

$$p \Leftarrow q$$

$$= \qquad \{ \qquad \text{definition} \quad \}$$

$$p \; \equiv \; p \lor q$$

$$= \qquad \{ \qquad \text{false is unit of disjunction} \quad \}$$

$$p \lor \textsf{false} \; \equiv \; p \lor q$$

$$= \qquad \{ \qquad \text{disjunction distributes through equivalence} \quad \}$$

$$p \lor (\textsf{false} \equiv q)$$

$$= \qquad \{ \qquad \text{definition of negation} \quad \}$$

$$p \lor \neg q \; .$$

□

Solution 7.25.

$$(p \Leftarrow q) \; \lor \; (p \Rightarrow q)$$

$$= \qquad \{ \qquad (7.24) \quad \}$$

$$p \; \lor \; \neg q \; \lor \; \neg p \; \lor \; q$$

$$= \qquad \{ \qquad \text{symmetry and associativity of disjunction} \quad \}$$

$$p \; \lor \; \neg p \; \lor \; q \; \lor \; \neg q$$

$$= \qquad \{ \qquad \text{excluded middle (twice)} \quad \}$$

$$\textsf{true} \; .$$

□

Solution 7.26.
Contrapositive:

$$\neg p \Rightarrow \neg q$$

$$= \qquad \{ \qquad \text{definition} \quad \}$$

$$\neg p \; \equiv \; \neg p \land \neg q$$

$$= \qquad \{ \qquad \text{De Morgan} \quad \}$$

$$\neg p \; \equiv \; \neg (p \lor q)$$

$$= \qquad \{ \qquad \text{contrapositive} \quad \}$$

$$p \equiv p \vee q$$

$$= \qquad \{ \qquad \text{definition} \quad \}$$

$$p \Leftarrow q \ .$$

Contradiction:

$$p \Rightarrow \text{false}$$

$$= \qquad \{ \qquad \text{definition} \quad \}$$

$$p \equiv p \wedge \text{false}$$

$$= \qquad \{ \qquad \text{false is zero of conjunction} \quad \}$$

$$p \equiv \text{false}$$

$$= \qquad \{ \qquad \text{definition} \quad \}$$

$$\neg p \ .$$

Distributivity:

$$(p \equiv q) \Leftarrow r$$

$$= \qquad \{ \qquad \text{definition} \quad \}$$

$$r \equiv (p \equiv q) \wedge r$$

$$= \qquad \{ \qquad \text{distributivity of conjunction over equivalence} \quad \}$$

$$r \equiv p \wedge r \equiv q \wedge r \equiv r$$

$$= \qquad \{ \qquad \text{simplification of continued equivalences} \quad \}$$

$$p \wedge r \equiv q \wedge r \ .$$

Distributivity:

$$(p \equiv q) \Leftarrow r$$

$$= \qquad \{ \qquad \text{definition} \quad \}$$

$$p \equiv q \equiv (p \equiv q) \vee r$$

$$= \qquad \{ \qquad \text{distributivity of disjunction over equivalence} \quad \}$$

$$p \equiv q \equiv p \vee r \equiv q \vee r$$

$$= \qquad \{ \qquad \text{rearranging terms} \quad \}$$

$$p \equiv p \vee r \equiv q \equiv q \vee r$$

$$= \qquad \{ \qquad \text{definition} \quad \}$$

$$p \Leftarrow r \equiv q \Leftarrow r \ .$$

Shunting:

$$(p \Leftarrow q) \Leftarrow r$$

= { definition (applied twice) }

$$p \equiv p \vee q \equiv (p \equiv p \vee q) \vee r$$

= { distributivity of disjunction over equivalence }

$$p \equiv p \vee q \equiv p \vee r \equiv p \vee q \vee r$$

= { distributivity of disjunction over equivalence }

$$p \equiv p \vee (q \equiv r \equiv q \vee r)$$

= { golden rule }

$$p \equiv p \vee (q \wedge r)$$

= { definition }

$$p \Leftarrow q \wedge r \ .$$

□

Solution 7.29.
Mutual implication:

$$(p \Leftarrow q) \wedge (p \Rightarrow q)$$

= { definition }

$$(p \equiv p \vee q) \wedge (q \equiv p \vee q)$$

= { substitution of equals for equals (7.27),
first occurrence of $p \vee q$ replaced by q }

$$(p \equiv q) \wedge (q \equiv p \vee q)$$

= { substitution of equals for equals (7.27),
second occurrence of p replaced by q }

$$(p \equiv q) \wedge (q \equiv q \vee q)$$

= { disjunction is idempotent,
properties of true }

$$p \equiv q \ .$$

Distributivity:

$$p \Leftarrow q \vee r$$

= { definition of $\Leftarrow$ }

$$p \equiv p \vee q \vee r$$

$= \quad \{ \qquad$ substitution of equals for equals (7.28):

$\qquad\qquad$ with $g.x = (x \vee q)$ $\}$

$$(p \equiv p \vee q \vee r) \wedge (p \vee q \equiv p \vee q \vee r)$$

$= \quad \{ \qquad$ substitution of equals for equals (7.27):

$\qquad\qquad$ specifically, $p \vee q$ for first occurrence of $p \vee q \vee r$ $\}$

$$(p \equiv p \vee q) \wedge (p \vee q \equiv p \vee q \vee r)$$

$= \quad \{ \qquad$ substitution of equals for equals (7.27):

$\qquad\qquad$ specifically, p for last two occurrences of $p \vee q$ $\}$

$$(p \equiv p \vee q) \wedge (p \equiv p \vee r)$$

$= \quad \{ \qquad$ definition of $\Leftarrow$ $\}$

$$(p \Leftarrow q) \wedge (p \Leftarrow r) \ .$$

Distributivity:

$$(p \Leftarrow r) \wedge (q \Leftarrow r)$$

$= \quad \{ \qquad$ definition $\}$

$$(r \equiv p \wedge r) \wedge (r \equiv q \wedge r)$$

$= \quad \{ \qquad$ substitution of equals for equals (7.27)

$\qquad\qquad$ specifically, $p \wedge r$ for last two occurrences of r $\}$

$$(r \equiv p \wedge r) \wedge (p \wedge r \equiv p \wedge q \wedge r)$$

$= \quad \{ \qquad$ substitution of equals for equals (7.27),

$\qquad\qquad$ specifically, $p \wedge q \wedge r$ for first occurrence of $p \wedge r$ $\}$

$$(r \equiv p \wedge q \wedge r) \wedge (p \wedge r \equiv p \wedge q \wedge r)$$

$= \quad \{ \qquad$ substitution of equals for equals (7.28),

$\qquad\qquad$ with $g.x = (p \wedge x)$ $\}$

$$r \equiv p \wedge q \wedge r$$

$= \quad \{ \qquad$ definition $\}$

$$p \wedge q \Leftarrow r \ .$$

$\qquad\qquad\qquad\qquad\qquad\qquad\qquad\qquad\qquad\qquad\qquad\qquad\qquad\qquad \square$

Solution 7.30.

(b) Simplifying $A \equiv \neg A \Rightarrow B$ using (7.19), we get $A \equiv \neg A \equiv \neg A \wedge B$, which equals $A \vee \neg B$. So, either A is a knight or B is a knave.

(c) Simplifying $A \equiv A \Rightarrow \neg B$ using (7.19), we get $A \wedge \neg B$. So A is a knight and B is a knave.

(d) Simplifying $A \equiv \neg A \Rightarrow \neg B$ using (7.19), we get $A \equiv \neg A \equiv \neg A \wedge \neg B$, which equals $A \vee B$. So, at least one of A or B is a knight.

(f) Simplifying $A \equiv \neg B \Rightarrow A$ using (7.18), we get $A \equiv A \equiv \neg B \vee A$, which equals $\neg B \vee A$. So, either A is a knight or B is a knave.

(g) Simplifying $A \equiv B \Rightarrow \neg A$ using (7.18), we get $A \equiv \neg A \equiv \neg A \vee B$, which equals $A \wedge \neg B$. So A is a knight and B is a knave.

(h) Simplifying $A \equiv \neg B \Rightarrow \neg A$ using (7.18), we get $A \equiv \neg A \equiv \neg A \vee \neg B$, which equals $A \wedge B$. So, both A and B are knights.

$\square$

Solution 7.31. Let the natives be A and B. Following the analysis given in Section 5.5, to determine whether both are knights, the question to be posed is $A \equiv A \wedge B$. This is the same as $A \Rightarrow B$. So, in words, the question is 'is it the case that, if you are a knight, then your colleague is also a knight?'.

To determine whether at least one is a knight, the question to be posed is $A \equiv A \vee B$. This is the same as $A \Leftarrow B$. So, in words, the question is 'is it the case that you are a knight if your colleague is a knight?'.

$\square$

Solution 7.32. We are required to simplify $A \equiv \neg A \vee B$.

$$A \equiv \neg A \vee B$$

$$= \qquad \{ \qquad \text{definition of negation} \quad \}$$

$$A \equiv (A \equiv \mathsf{false}) \vee B$$

$$= \qquad \{ \qquad \text{disjunction distributes through equivalence} \quad \}$$

$$A \equiv (A \vee B \equiv \mathsf{false} \vee B)$$

$$= \qquad \{ \qquad \text{associativity of equivalence,}$$

$$\text{false is unit of disjunction} \quad \}$$

$$A \equiv A \vee B \equiv B$$

$$= \qquad \{ \qquad \text{definition of conjunction} \quad \}$$

$$A \wedge B \ .$$

So A and B are both knights. $\square$

Solution 7.33. B's statement is $A \equiv \neg A$. C's statement is $\neg B$. So, what we are given is

$$(B \equiv A \equiv \neg A) \wedge (C \equiv \neg B) \ .$$

We simplify this as follows:

$$(B \equiv A \equiv \neg A) \wedge (C \equiv \neg B)$$

$$= \qquad \{ \qquad (A \equiv \neg A) = \mathsf{false} \quad \}$$

$$\neg B \wedge (C \equiv \neg B)$$

$$= \qquad \{ \qquad \text{modus ponens} \quad \}$$

$$\neg B \wedge C \ .$$

So, B is a knave and C is a knight. □

Solution 7.34. Let U denote the proposition 'One of A, B and C is a knight'. B's statement is then $A \equiv U$. C's statement is $\neg B$. So, what we are given is

$$(B \equiv A \equiv U) \wedge (C \equiv \neg B) \ .$$

We begin by assuming $C \equiv \neg B$ and simplifying U:

$$U$$

$$= \qquad \{ \qquad \text{definition} \quad \}$$

$$(A \wedge \neg B \wedge \neg C) \vee (B \wedge \neg C \wedge \neg A) \vee (C \wedge \neg A \wedge \neg B)$$

$$= \qquad \{ \qquad C \equiv \neg B \quad \}$$

$$(A \wedge \neg B \wedge \neg \neg B) \vee (B \wedge \neg \neg B \wedge \neg A) \vee (\neg B \wedge \neg A \wedge \neg B)$$

$$= \qquad \{ \qquad \neg \neg B \equiv B, \ \neg B \wedge B \equiv \mathsf{false},$$

$$p \wedge p \equiv p \ (\text{Once with } p := B, \text{ once with } p := \neg B),$$

$$\text{constants} \quad \}$$

$$(\neg A \wedge B) \vee (\neg A \wedge \neg B)$$

$$= \qquad \{ \qquad \text{distributivity, excluded middle} \quad \}$$

$$\neg A \ .$$

Hence

$$(B \equiv A \equiv U) \wedge (C \equiv \neg B)$$

$$= \qquad \{ \qquad \text{above, substitution of equals for equals} \quad \}$$

$$(B \equiv A \equiv \neg A) \wedge (C \equiv \neg B)$$

$$= \qquad \{ \qquad A \equiv \neg A \equiv \mathsf{false} \quad \}$$

$$(B \equiv \mathsf{false}) \wedge (C \equiv \neg B)$$

$$= \qquad \{ \qquad \text{substitution of equals for equals}, \ \neg\mathsf{false} \equiv \mathsf{true} \quad \}$$

$$(B \equiv \mathsf{false}) \wedge (C \equiv \mathsf{true})$$

$$= \quad \{ \quad \text{constants} \quad \}$$

$$\neg B \wedge C \ .$$

We conclude that C is a knight and B is a knave. Nothing can be deduced about A.

□

Solution 7.36. We are given a number of properties. The uniqueness of the placement of the portrait is the conjunction of four statements:

   (a) $G \vee S \vee L$,

   (b) $\neg G \vee \neg S$,

   (c) $\neg S \vee \neg L$,

   (d) $\neg L \vee \neg G$.

The inscriptions on the gold and silver caskets amount to

   (e) $G \equiv g$ and

   (f) $S \equiv s$.

Finally, the inscription on the lead casket is

   (g) $l \ \equiv \ (\neg g \wedge \neg s) \vee (\neg s \wedge \neg l) \vee (\neg l \wedge \neg g)$.

Formally, therefore, we want to simplify

$$\text{(a)} \wedge \text{(b)} \wedge \text{(c)} \wedge \text{(d)} \wedge \text{(e)} \wedge \text{(f)} \wedge \text{(g)} \ .$$

We focus on (g) since this is clearly the most crucial property.

Using the hint of applying Exercise 7.15 as first step, the calculation goes as follows:

$$l \ \equiv \ (\neg g \wedge \neg s) \vee (\neg s \wedge \neg l) \vee (\neg l \wedge \neg g)$$

$$= \quad \{ \quad \text{Exercise 7.15} \quad \}$$

$$l \equiv \neg g \vee \neg s \ \equiv \ \neg s \vee \neg l \ \equiv \ \neg l \vee \neg g$$

$$= \quad \{ \quad \text{Here we bring in other information.}$$

                               Since g and G are the same (see (e)) as are s and S (see (f)),

                               property (b) is $\neg g \vee \neg s$. So, substituting equals for equals

                               (true for $\neg g \vee \neg s$) this term can be eliminated. }

$$l \equiv \neg s \vee \neg l \ \equiv \ \neg l \vee \neg g$$

$$= \quad \{ \quad \text{(heading for the elimination of the negation operator}$$

                               applied to l)

                               rearranging, disjunction distributes over equivalence }

$$l \equiv \neg l \lor (\neg g \equiv \neg s)$$

$=$ { $\quad \neg p \lor q \equiv q \equiv p \lor q$, contrapositive }

$$l \equiv g \equiv s \equiv l \lor (g \equiv s)$$

$=$ { $\quad$ golden rule, $p, q := l, g \equiv s$ }

$$l \land (g \equiv s) \ .$$

From this calculation we conclude that the inscription on the lead casket is true and the inscriptions on the gold and silver caskets are as true as each other.

Now we can complete the calculation:

$$(a) \land (b) \land (c) \land (d) \land (e) \land (f) \land (g)$$

$=$ { $\quad$ above calcuation }

$$(a) \land (b) \land (c) \land (d) \land (e) \land (f) \land l \land (g \equiv s)$$

$=$ { $\quad$ (e) $\land$ (f) $\land$ $(g \equiv s)$ $\equiv$ $(g = s = G = S)$

$\quad$ (b) $\land$ $(g = s = G = S)$ $\equiv$ $\neg G \land (g = s = G = S)$,

$\quad$ definitions of (c) and (d) }

$$(G \lor S \lor L) \land \neg G \land g = s = G = S \land l \land (\neg S \lor \neg L)$$

$=$ { $\quad$ substitution of equals for equals and simplification }

$$L \land (g = s = G = S = \mathsf{false}) \land l \ .$$

So the portrait is in the lead casket, the inscription on the lead casket is true, and the inscriptions on the gold and silver caskets are false. □

Solution 7.37. Using G for 'the dagger is in the gold casket', and similarly for S and L, we have the properties (a), (b), (c) and (d), as in Exercise 7.36, together with the three properties

(e) $G \equiv g$,

(f) $S \not\equiv s$,

(g) $l \equiv \neg((g \land s) \lor (s \land l) \lor (l \land g))$.

Again, we focus on simplifying (g). Much is copied from Exercise 7.36.

$$l \equiv \neg((g \land s) \lor (s \land l) \lor (l \land g))$$

$=$ { $\quad$ contrapositive }

$$\neg l \equiv (g \land s) \lor (s \land l) \lor (l \land g)$$

$=$ { $\quad$ Exercise 7.15 and definition of negation }

$$\mathsf{false} \equiv l \equiv g \lor s \equiv s \lor l \equiv l \lor g$$

$=$ { As in Exercise 7.36 we bring in additional information.

This time, we have from (b), (e) and (f),

$G \equiv g$, $s \equiv \neg S$ and $\neg S \equiv G \vee \neg S$. }

false $\equiv l \equiv \neg S \equiv \neg S \vee l \equiv l \vee G$

$=$ { rearranging and negation }

$S \equiv S \vee l \equiv l \vee G$.

But,

$G \vee S \vee (S \equiv S \vee l \equiv l \vee G)$

$=$ { distributivity, idempotence, symmetry of disjunction }

$G \vee S \equiv G \vee S \vee l \equiv G \vee S \vee l$

$=$ { continued equivalences }

$G \vee S$.

That is,

(b) $\wedge$ (e) $\wedge$ (f) $\wedge$ (g) $\Rightarrow$ $G \vee S$.

We conclude that the dagger is in the gold or silver casket and Portia's suitor should choose the lead casket. □

Solution 8.2.

$x \uparrow y = x$

$=$ { antisymmetry }

$x \leqslant x \uparrow y \wedge x \uparrow y \leqslant x$

$=$ { $x \leqslant x \uparrow y$ }

$x \uparrow y \leqslant x$.

□

Solution 8.3.

$x \uparrow y \leqslant x + y$

$=$ { definition of $\uparrow$ }

$x \leqslant x + y \wedge y \leqslant x + y$

$=$ { arithmetic }

$0 \leqslant y \wedge 0 \leqslant x$.

□

Solution 8.4.

(a) We have, for all z,

$$x \uparrow x \leqslant z$$

$= \quad \{ \qquad \text{definition of max} \quad \}$

$$x \leqslant z \wedge x \leqslant z$$

$= \quad \{ \qquad \text{conjunction is idempotent} \quad \}$

$$x \leqslant z .$$

The result follows by indirect equality.

(b) We have, for all z,

$$x \uparrow y \leqslant z$$

$= \quad \{ \qquad \text{definition of max} \quad \}$

$$x \leqslant z \wedge y \leqslant z$$

$= \quad \{ \qquad \wedge \text{ is symmetric} \quad \}$

$$y \leqslant z \wedge x \leqslant z$$

$= \quad \{ \qquad \text{definition of max} \quad \}$

$$y \uparrow x \leqslant z .$$

The result follows by indirect equality.

$\square$

Solution 8.7.

(a) We have, for all u,

$$x \downarrow (y \uparrow z) \leqslant u$$

$= \quad \{ \qquad \text{dual of (8.5), specifically}$

$$x \downarrow y \leqslant z \;\equiv\; x \leqslant z \vee y \leqslant z \quad \}$$

$$x \leqslant u \vee y \uparrow z \leqslant u$$

$= \quad \{ \qquad \text{Galois connection defining maximum} \quad \}$

$$x \leqslant u \vee (y \leqslant u \wedge z \leqslant u)$$

$= \quad \{ \qquad \text{distributivity of } \vee \text{ over } \wedge \quad \}$

$$(x \leqslant u \vee y \leqslant u) \wedge (x \leqslant u \vee z \leqslant u)$$

$= \quad \{ \qquad \text{dual of (8.5): see first step} \quad \}$

$$x{\downarrow}y \leqslant u \ \wedge\ x{\downarrow}z \leqslant u$$

$$=\qquad\{\qquad\text{Galois connection defining maximum}\quad\}$$

$$(x{\downarrow}y){\uparrow}(x{\downarrow}z) \leqslant u\ .$$

The result follows by indirect equality.

(b) We have, for all u,

$$x{\downarrow}(y{\uparrow}x) \leqslant u$$

$$=\qquad\{\qquad\text{dual of (8.5): see first step in (a)}\quad\}$$

$$x \leqslant u \ \vee\ y{\uparrow}x \leqslant u$$

$$=\qquad\{\qquad\text{Galois connection defining maximum}\quad\}$$

$$x \leqslant u \ \vee\ (y \leqslant u \wedge x \leqslant u)$$

$$=\qquad\{\qquad\text{absorptivity of } \vee \text{ and } \wedge\quad\}$$

$$x \leqslant u\ .$$

The result follows by indirect equality.

(c) We have, for all u,

$$(x{\downarrow}y){\uparrow}(y{\downarrow}z){\uparrow}(z{\downarrow}x) \leqslant u$$

$$=\qquad\{\qquad\text{Galois connection defining maximum}\quad\}$$

$$x{\downarrow}y \leqslant u \ \wedge\ y{\downarrow}z \leqslant u \ \wedge\ z{\downarrow}x \leqslant u$$

$$=\qquad\{\qquad\text{(8.5) dual}\quad\}$$

$$(x \leqslant u \vee y \leqslant u) \wedge (y \leqslant u \vee z \leqslant u) \wedge (z \leqslant u \vee x \leqslant u)$$

$$=\qquad\{\qquad\text{Exercise 7.15}\quad\}$$

$$(x \leqslant u \wedge y \leqslant u) \vee (y \leqslant u \wedge z \leqslant u) \vee (z \leqslant u \wedge x \leqslant u)$$

$$=\qquad\{\qquad\text{first two steps reversed using dual properties}\quad\}$$

$$(x{\uparrow}y){\downarrow}(y{\uparrow}z){\downarrow}(z{\uparrow}x) \leqslant u\ .$$

The result follows by indirect equality.

$\square$

Solution 8.8. First part. We have, for all w,

$$|x{+}y| \leqslant w$$

$$=\qquad\{\qquad\text{definition of } |x| \text{ and max}\quad\}$$

$$x{+}y \leqslant w \ \wedge\ -(x{+}y) \leqslant w$$

$\Leftarrow$ {   1st conjunct: $y \leqslant |y|$, and monotonicity;

2nd conjunct: arithmetic }

$$x + |y| \leqslant w \ \wedge \ -x \leqslant w + y$$

$\Leftarrow$ {   1st conjunct: arithmetic;

2nd conjunct: $-y \leqslant |y|$.

So, $-|y| \leqslant y$, and monotonicity }

$$x \leqslant w - |y| \ \wedge \ -x \leqslant w - |y|$$

$=$ {   definition of $|x|$ and max and arithmetic }

$$|x| + |y| \leqslant w \ .$$

Thus by indirect order, $|x + y| \leqslant |x| + |y|$.

    Second part:

$$||x| - |y|| \leqslant w$$

$=$ {   definition of $|x|$ and max }

$$|x| - |y| \leqslant w \ \wedge \ -(|x| - |y|) \leqslant w$$

$=$ {   arithmetic }

$$|x| \leqslant w + |y| \ \wedge \ |y| \leqslant w + |x|$$

$=$ {   definition of $|x|$ and max }

$$x \leqslant w + |y| \ \wedge \ -x \leqslant w + |y| \ \wedge \ y \leqslant w + |x| \ \wedge \ -y \leqslant w + |x|$$

$\Leftarrow$ { $y \leqslant |y|$ and $-y \leqslant |y|$, similarly for x }

$$x \leqslant w + y \ \wedge \ -x \leqslant w - y \ \wedge \ y \leqslant w + x \ \wedge \ -y \leqslant w - x$$

$=$ {   arithmetic and definition of $|x|$ and max }

$$|x - y| \leqslant w \ .$$

Thus, by indirect order, $|x - y| \leqslant ||x| - |y||$. $\square$

Solution 8.9. We have, for all n,

$$n \leqslant \lfloor x \rfloor \downarrow \lfloor y \rfloor$$

$=$ {   definition of $\downarrow$ }

$$n \leqslant \lfloor x \rfloor \ \wedge \ n \leqslant \lfloor y \rfloor$$

$=$ {   definition of floor }

$$n \leqslant x \ \wedge \ n \leqslant y$$

$=$ {   definition of min }

$$n \leqslant x \downarrow y$$

$$= \qquad \{ \qquad \text{definition of floor} \quad \}$$

$$n \leqslant \lfloor x \downarrow y \rfloor \enspace .$$

The result follows by indirect equality. □

Solution 8.10. Indirect equality is used to compute the value of $\mathsf{exp}.p$. We have, for all k,

$$k \leqslant \mathsf{exp}.p$$

$$= \qquad \{ \qquad \text{definition of exponent} \quad \}$$

$$p^k \backslash p$$

$$= \qquad \{ \qquad \text{integer division} \quad \}$$

$$k \leqslant 1 \enspace .$$

Thus, by indirect equality, $\mathsf{exp}.p = 1$.

Indirect equality is also used to derive $\ominus$. We have, for all k,

$$k \leqslant \mathsf{exp.gcd}(m,n)$$

$$= \qquad \{ \qquad \text{definition of exponent} \quad \}$$

$$p^k \backslash \mathsf{gcd}(m,n)$$

$$= \qquad \{ \qquad \text{definition of gcd} \quad \}$$

$$p^k \backslash m \ \wedge \ p^k \backslash n$$

$$= \qquad \{ \qquad \text{definition of exponent} \quad \}$$

$$k \leqslant \mathsf{exp}.m \ \wedge \ k \leqslant \mathsf{exp}.n$$

$$= \qquad \{ \qquad \text{definition of minimum} \quad \}$$

$$k \leqslant \mathsf{exp}.m \downarrow \mathsf{exp}.n \enspace .$$

We have thus derived that $\mathsf{exp.gcd}(m,n) = \mathsf{exp}.m \downarrow \mathsf{exp}.n$.

Indirect equality is used to derive $\otimes$. We have, for all k,

$$k \leqslant \mathsf{exp}.(m \times n)$$

$$= \qquad \{ \qquad \text{definition of exponent} \quad \}$$

$$p^k \backslash m \times n$$

$$= \qquad \{ \qquad \text{prime factorization} \quad \}$$

$$\langle \exists\, i,j \, : \, k = i+j \, : \, p^i \backslash m \ \wedge \ p^j \backslash n \rangle$$

$$= \qquad \{ \qquad \text{definition of exponent} \quad \}$$

$$\langle \exists\, i,j\, :\, k = i+j\, :\, i \leqslant \exp.m \,\wedge\, j \leqslant \exp.n \rangle$$

$$=\qquad\{\qquad \text{arithmetic}\quad\}$$

$$k \leqslant \exp.m + \exp.n\ .$$

We have thus derived that $\exp.(m \times n) = \exp.m + \exp.n$.   □

Solution 9.1.

(a) Valid.

(b) Invalid (the value of i is changed by the assignment).

(c) Valid.

(d) Invalid (a valid postcondition would be $j < i$).

(e) Valid (the triple says nothing about the assignment statement because all states satisfy postcondition true).

(f) Invalid (it is impossible to end up in a state satisfying false).

(g) Valid (the claim is vacuously true because the assumption is that the execution of the assignment is begun in a state satisfying false, which can never be the case).

□

Solution 9.3.

(a) $x + y < 9$.

(b) $x^2 - 1 = 0$.

(c) $x^2 - y^2 = 1$.

(d) $z = 0 \vee x = 1 \vee y = 2$.

□

Solution 9.4. We seek X such that

$$m \times n = C \,\wedge\, \text{even}.m \;\Rightarrow\; (m \div 2) \times X = C\ .$$

Clearly, $X = 2n$ suffices.   □

Solution 9.5. As before, $X = 2n + 1$. To calculate Y, we use that

$$(n+1)^3 \;=\; n^3 + 3n^2 + 3n + 1\ .$$

So,

$$s = n^2 \,\wedge\, t = n^3$$

$$\Rightarrow\; s + 2n + 1 = (n+1)^2 \,\wedge\, t + 3s + 3n + 1 \;=\; (n+1)^3\ .$$

The required assignment is, thus,

$$s, t, n \ := \ s + 2n + 1 \, , \, t + 3s + 3n + 1 \, , \, n + 1 \ .$$

□

Solution 9.6. We seek X such that

$$\{ f \ = \ n! \} \ f, n \ := \ X, n+1 \ \{ f \ = \ n! \} \ .$$

That is, X must satisfy

$$f \ = \ n! \ \Rightarrow \ X \ = \ (n+1)! \ .$$

Now,

$(n+1)!$

$=$ $\qquad$ { $\qquad$ definition of factorials $\quad$ }

$(n+1) \times n!$

$=$ $\qquad$ { $\qquad$ assume $f \ = \ n!$ $\quad$ }

$(n+1) \times f$.

So,

$$f \ = \ n! \ \Rightarrow \ (n+1) \times f \ = \ (n+1)! \ .$$

The required assignment is, thus,

$$f, n \ := \ (n+1) \times f \, , \, n+1 \ .$$

□

Solution 9.7. We seek X and Y such that

$$\{ f = \mathsf{fib}.n \ \wedge \ g = \mathsf{fib}.(n+1) \}$$
$$f, g, n \ := \ X, Y, n+1$$
$$\{ f = \mathsf{fib}.n \ \wedge \ g = \mathsf{fib}.(n+1) \} \ .$$

That is, X and Y must satisfy

$$f = \mathsf{fib}.n \ \wedge \ g = \mathsf{fib}.(n+1) \ \Rightarrow \ X = \mathsf{fib}.(n+1) \ \wedge \ Y = \mathsf{fib}.((n+1)+1) \ .$$

Now,

$\mathsf{fib}.((n+1)+1)$

$=$ $\qquad$ { $\qquad$ arithmetic $\quad$ }

$\mathsf{fib}.(n+2)$

$$= \qquad \{ \qquad \text{definition of fib} \quad \}$$

$$\text{fib.}(n+1) + \text{fib.}n$$

$$= \qquad \{ \qquad \text{assume } f = \text{fib.}n \wedge g = \text{fib.}(n+1) \quad \}$$

$$g+f \ .$$

So,

$$f = \text{fib.}n \wedge g = \text{fib.}(n+1) \ \Rightarrow \ g = \text{fib.}(n+1) \wedge g+f = \text{fib.}((n+1)+1) \ .$$

The required assignment is, thus,

$$f,g,n \ := \ g,g+f,n+1 \ .$$

□

Solution 10.7. (a) Moving the precondition and the postcondition inside the conditional:

$$\{ \ m \times n = p \ \}$$

$$\text{if } \text{even.}m \longrightarrow \{ \ m \times n = p \wedge \text{even.}m \ \} \ m,n := m \div 2, 2 \times n \ \{ \ m \times n = p \ \}$$

$$\square \ \text{true} \longrightarrow \{ \ m \times n = p \wedge \text{true} \ \} \ m,p := m-1, p-n \ \{ \ m \times n = p \ \}$$

$$\text{fi}$$

$$\{ \ m \times n = p \ \} \ .$$

Thus the assignment statements must satisfy

$$\{ \ m \times n = p \wedge \text{even.}m \ \} \ m,n := m \div 2, 2 \times n \ \{ \ m \times n = p \ \} \ ,$$

and

$$\{ \ m \times n = p \wedge \text{true} \ \} \ m,p := m-1, p-n \ \{ \ m \times n = p \ \} \ .$$

Using the assignment axiom, their correctness follows from:

$$m \times n = p \wedge \text{even.}m \ \Rightarrow \ (m \div 2) \times 2 \times n = p$$

and

$$m \times n = p \ \equiv \ (m-1) \times n = p-n \ .$$

(b) For brevity, we use Inv to denote $0 \leqslant m \wedge 0 \leqslant n \wedge \text{gcd}(m,n) = \text{C}$. Moving the precondition and the postcondition inside the conditional:

$$\{ \ Inv \ \}$$

$$\text{if } m < n \longrightarrow \{ \ Inv \wedge m < n \ \} \ n := n-m \ \{ \ Inv \ \}$$

$$\square \ n < m \longrightarrow \{ \ Inv \wedge n < m \ \} \ m := m-n \ \{ \ Inv \ \}$$

$$\text{fi}$$

$$\{ \ Inv \ \} \ .$$

Thus the assignment statements must satisfy

$$\{\ Inv \wedge m < n\ \}\ n := n - m\ \{\ Inv\ \}\ ,$$

and

$$\{\ Inv \wedge n < m\ \}\ m := m - n\ \{\ Inv\ \}\ .$$

Using the assignment axiom, and spelling out the definition of Inv, their correctness follows from

$$0 \leqslant m \wedge 0 \leqslant n \wedge \mathsf{gcd}(m,n) = \mathsf{C} \wedge m < n$$

$$\Rightarrow \quad 0 \leqslant m \wedge 0 \leqslant n - m \wedge \mathsf{gcd}(m, n-m) = \mathsf{C}$$

and

$$0 \leqslant m \wedge 0 \leqslant n \wedge \mathsf{gcd}(m,n) = \mathsf{C} \wedge n < m$$

$$\Rightarrow \quad 0 \leqslant m - n \wedge 0 \leqslant n \wedge \mathsf{gcd}(m-n, n) = \mathsf{C}\ .$$

$\square$

Solution 10.8. The conditional rule requires us to check that $x \leqslant 0 \vee x \geqslant 0$ is true. This is clearly the case. Also, we have to verify each branch of the conditional statement with respect to the appropriate preconditions and postconditions (as given in the conditional rule). That is, we have to verify

$$\{\ \mathsf{X} = |x| \wedge x \leqslant 0\ \}\ x := -x\ \{\ \mathsf{X} = x\ \}$$

and

$$\{\ \mathsf{X} = |x| \wedge x \geqslant 0\ \}\ \mathsf{skip}\ \{\ \mathsf{X} = x\ \}\ .$$

Using the assignment axiom and the skip rule, we get the verification conditions:

$$\mathsf{X} = |x| \wedge x \leqslant 0 \Rightarrow \mathsf{X} = -x$$

and

$$\mathsf{X} = |x| \wedge x \geqslant 0 \Rightarrow \mathsf{X} = x\ .$$

These are both clearly true, thus completing the verification. $\square$

Solution 10.11. The precondition is

$$x = \mathsf{X} \wedge y = \mathsf{Y}\ .$$

The postcondition is

$$x \leqslant y \wedge (x = \mathsf{X} \vee y = \mathsf{X}) \wedge (x = \mathsf{Y} \vee y = \mathsf{Y})\ .$$

We consider two cases: $x \leqslant y$ and $y \leqslant x$. In the first case, there is nothing to do. In the second case, an interchange of x and y establishes the postcondition. Thus the program is

$$\{ \ x = \mathsf{X} \land y = \mathsf{Y} \ \}$$

$$\text{if } x \leqslant y \longrightarrow \text{skip}$$

$$\Box \ y \leqslant x \longrightarrow x, y := y, x$$

$$\text{fi}$$

$$\{ \ x \leqslant y \land (x = \mathsf{X} \lor y = \mathsf{X}) \land (x = \mathsf{Y} \lor y = \mathsf{Y}) \ \} \ .$$

Use of the assignment axiom and the skip rule in order to check the correctness yields the verification conditions:

$$x = \mathsf{X} \land y = \mathsf{Y} \land x \leqslant y \ \Rightarrow \ x \leqslant y \land (x = \mathsf{X} \lor y = \mathsf{X}) \land (x = \mathsf{Y} \lor y = \mathsf{Y})$$

and

$$x = \mathsf{X} \land y = \mathsf{Y} \land y \leqslant x \ \Rightarrow \ y \leqslant x \land (y = \mathsf{X} \lor x = \mathsf{X}) \land (y = \mathsf{Y} \lor x = \mathsf{Y}) \ .$$

Both are clearly true.   □

Solution 10.12. Using the conditional rule, the requirements are

$$\{ \ 0 < k = \mathsf{K} \ \land \ x^k \times y \ = \ \mathsf{C} \ \}$$

$$k, x, y := k{-}1, a, b$$

$$\{ \ 0 \leqslant k < \mathsf{K} \ \land \ x^k \times y \ = \ \mathsf{C} \ \}$$

and

$$\{ \ 0 < k = \mathsf{K} \ \land \ x^k \times y \ = \ \mathsf{C} \ \land \ \text{even.}k \ \}$$

$$k, x, y := k \div 2, c, d$$

$$\{ \ 0 \leqslant k < \mathsf{K} \ \land \ x^k \times y \ = \ \mathsf{C} \ \} \ .$$

Applying the assignment axiom, the requirement on a and b is

$$0 < k = \mathsf{K} \ \land \ x^k \times y \ = \ \mathsf{C} \ \Rightarrow \ 0 \leqslant k{-}1 < \mathsf{K} \ \land \ a^{k-1} \times b \ = \ \mathsf{C} \ .$$

Now,

$$0 < k = \mathsf{K} \ \land \ x^k \times y \ = \ \mathsf{C}$$

$$\Rightarrow \qquad \{ \qquad \text{heading for introducing '}k{-}1\text{' we use the fact that}$$

$$0 < k = \mathsf{K} \ \Rightarrow \ k = (k{-}1){+}1 \ \land \ 0 \leqslant k{-}1 < \mathsf{K} \ \}$$

$$0 \leqslant k{-}1 < \mathsf{K} \ \land \ x^{(k-1)+1} \times y \ = \ \mathsf{C}$$

$$= \qquad \{ \qquad \text{property of powers} \ \}$$

$$0 \leqslant k{-}1 < \mathsf{K} \ \land \ x^{k-1} \times x \times y \ = \ \mathsf{C} \ .$$

So, suitable values for a and b are $a = x$ and $b = x \times y$. (Note the implicit use of the associativity of multiplication!)

Again applying the assignment axiom, the requirement on c and d is

$$0 < k = \mathsf{K} \; \wedge \; x^k \times y = \mathsf{C} \; \wedge \; even.k$$
$$\Rightarrow \quad 0 \leqslant k \div 2 < \mathsf{K} \; \wedge \; c^{k \div 2} \times d = \mathsf{C} \; .$$

Now,

$$0 < k = \mathsf{K} \; \wedge \; x^k \times y = \mathsf{C} \; \wedge \; even.k$$

$\Rightarrow$ $\quad\quad\quad$ { $\quad\quad$ heading for introducing '$k \div 2$' we use the fact that

$$0 < k = \mathsf{K} \; \wedge \; even.k \; \Rightarrow \; k = (k \div 2) \times 2 \; \wedge \; 0 \leqslant k \div 2 < \mathsf{K} \quad \}$$

$$0 \leqslant k \div 2 < \mathsf{K} \; \wedge \; x^{(k \div 2) \times 2} \times y = \mathsf{C}$$

$=$ $\quad\quad\quad$ { $\quad\quad$ property of powers $\quad$ }

$$0 \leqslant k \div 2 < \mathsf{K} \; \wedge \; (x^2)^{k \div 2} \times y = \mathsf{C} \; .$$

So, suitable values for c and d are $c = x^2$ and $d = y$.

In summary, taking account of the fact that x is unchanged when the assignment $k := k-1$ is chosen, and y is unchanged when the assignment $k := k \div 2$ is chosen, the program we have constructed is

$$\{ \; 0 < k = \mathsf{K} \; \wedge \; x^k \times y = \mathsf{C} \; \}$$

$\quad$ if true $\;\longrightarrow\; k, y := k-1, x \times y$

$\quad$ $\square$ $even.k \;\longrightarrow\; k, x := k \div 2, x^2$

$\quad$ fi

$$\{ \; 0 \leqslant k < \mathsf{K} \; \wedge \; x^k \times y = \mathsf{C} \; \} \; .$$

$\hfill \square$

Solution 10.21. Using Exercise 10.12, we have

$$\{ \; 0 \leqslant k \div 2 < \mathsf{K} \; \wedge \; even.k \; \wedge \; x^k \times y = \mathsf{C} \; \}$$

$\quad k, x := k \div 2, x^2$

$$\{ \; 0 \leqslant k < \mathsf{K} \; \wedge \; x^k \times y = \mathsf{C} \; \} \; .$$

So the statement $S2$ is $k, x := k \div 2, x^2$ and the assertion P is $0 \leqslant k \div 2 < \mathsf{K}$.

Now, satisfying the postcondition $even.k$ is achieved by doing nothing in the case that k is already even, and subtracting one in the case that k is odd. So, again making use of Exercise 10.12, we postulate that statement $S1$ is the statement

$\quad$ if $even.k \;\longrightarrow\;$ skip

$\quad$ $\square$ $odd.k \;\longrightarrow\; k, y := k-1, x \times y$

$\quad$ fi .

We have to check that it meets its specification, i.e. we have

$$\{\ 0 < k = \mathsf{K}\ \wedge\ x^k \times y\ =\ \mathsf{C}\ \}$$

if even.$k\ \longrightarrow\ $ skip

$\square$ odd.$k\ \longrightarrow\ k, y\ :=\ k-1, x \times y$

fi

$$\{\ 0 \leqslant k \div 2 < \mathsf{K}\ \wedge\ \text{even}.k\ \wedge\ x^k \times y\ =\ \mathsf{C}\ \}\ .$$

Using the conditional rule and the assignment axiom, this is the case if

$$0 < k = \mathsf{K}\ \wedge\ \text{even}.k\ \wedge\ x^k \times y\ =\ \mathsf{C}$$

$\Rightarrow\quad 0 \leqslant k \div 2 < \mathsf{K}\ \wedge\ \text{even}.k\ \wedge\ x^k \times y\ =\ \mathsf{C}$

and

$$0 < k = \mathsf{K}\ \wedge\ \text{odd}.k\ \wedge\ x^k \times y\ =\ \mathsf{C}$$

$\Rightarrow\quad 0 \leqslant (k-1) \div 2 < \mathsf{K}\ \wedge\ \text{even}.(k-1)\ \wedge\ x^{k-1} \times x \times y\ =\ \mathsf{C}\ .$

Simple properties of arithmetic show that this is indeed the case. The complete program is, thus,

$$\{\ 0 < k = \mathsf{K}\ \wedge\ x^k \times y\ =\ \mathsf{C}\ \}$$

if even.$k\ \longrightarrow\ $ skip

$\square$ odd.$k\ \longrightarrow\ k, y\ :=\ k-1, x \times y$

fi ;

$$\{\ 0 \leqslant k \div 2 < \mathsf{K}\ \wedge\ \text{even}.k\ \wedge\ x^k \times y\ =\ \mathsf{C}\ \}$$

$k, x\ :=\ k \div 2, x^2$

$$\{\ 0 \leqslant k < \mathsf{K}\ \wedge\ x^k \times y\ =\ \mathsf{C}\ \}\ .$$

$\square$

Solution 11.1. (a) 6, (b) 5, (c) 3, (d) 0. (There are no integers i and j such that $0 \leqslant i < j \leqslant 2 \wedge \text{odd}.i \wedge \text{odd}.j$.) $\square$

Solution 11.2. (a) 4 (there is only one natural number k such that $k^2 = 4$). (b) 8 (there are two integers k such that $k^2 = 4$). $\square$

Solution 11.3. (a), (b) The one occurrence of 'i' is free, all other occurrences of variables are bound. (c) There are no free occurrences of variables. (d) The occurrences of 'm' and 'n' are free. (e) The occurrences of 'm' and 'n' are free, as is the rightmost occurrence of 'j'. $\square$

Solution 11.4. (a) Valid—both sides equal $12 \times i$. (b) Invalid—left side equals 24, right side equals $12 \times j$. (c) Valid—both sides equal $24 \times j$. (d) Invalid—left side equals 12, right side equals 24. $\qquad\square$

Solution 11.17.

$$\langle \Sigma k : Q : \text{if } P \longrightarrow T \ \square \ \neg P \longrightarrow 0 \ \text{fi} \rangle$$

$\qquad = \qquad \{ \qquad \text{range splitting} \quad \}$

$$\langle \Sigma k : P \wedge Q : \text{if } P \longrightarrow T \ \square \ \neg P \longrightarrow 0 \ \text{fi} \rangle$$
$$+ \ \langle \Sigma k : \neg P \wedge Q : \text{if } P \longrightarrow T \ \square \ \neg P \longrightarrow 0 \ \text{fi} \rangle$$

$\qquad = \qquad \{ \qquad \text{substitution of equals for equals}$

$\qquad\qquad\qquad\qquad \text{(true for } P \text{ in 1st conditional,}$

$\qquad\qquad\qquad\qquad \text{true for } \neg P \text{ in 2nd conditional)} \quad \}$

$$\langle \Sigma k : P \wedge Q : T \rangle + \langle \Sigma k : \neg P \wedge Q : 0 \rangle$$

$\qquad = \qquad \{ \qquad \langle \Sigma k : R : 0 \rangle = 0 \text{ for all ranges } R, \ R := \neg P \wedge Q \quad \}$

$$\langle \Sigma k : P \wedge Q : T \rangle + 0$$

$\qquad = \qquad \{ \qquad \text{arithmetic} \quad \}$

$$\langle \Sigma k : P \wedge Q : T \rangle \ .$$

$\qquad\qquad\qquad\qquad\qquad\qquad\qquad\qquad\qquad\qquad\qquad\qquad\qquad\square$

Solution 11.18.

$$\langle \Sigma j : P : S \rangle \times \langle \Sigma k : Q : T \rangle$$

$\qquad = \qquad \{ \qquad \text{distributivity} \quad \}$

$$\langle \Sigma j : P : S \times \langle \Sigma k : Q : T \rangle \rangle$$

$\qquad = \qquad \{ \qquad \text{distributivity} \quad \}$

$$\langle \Sigma j : P : \langle \Sigma k : Q : S \times T \rangle \rangle$$

$\qquad = \qquad \{ \qquad \text{nesting} \quad \}$

$$\langle \Sigma j, k : P \wedge Q : S \times T \rangle \ .$$

The side conditions are that k should not be free in P or S, and j should not be free in Q or T. Also, j and k should be different. $\qquad\square$

Solution 11.19.

$$\langle \Sigma k : R : T \rangle$$

$\qquad = \qquad \{ \qquad \text{one-point rule (11.9), } g \text{ is the inverse of } f \quad \}$

$$\langle \Sigma k : R : \langle \Sigma j : j = g.k : T \rangle \rangle$$

$$= \qquad \{ \qquad \text{nesting (11.6)} \quad \}$$

$$\langle \Sigma k, j \ : \ R \wedge j = g.k \ : \ T \rangle$$

$$= \qquad \{ \qquad f.j = k \ \equiv \ j = g.k \quad \}$$

$$\langle \Sigma k, j \ : \ R \wedge f.j = k \ : \ T \rangle$$

$$= \qquad \{ \qquad \text{substitution of equals for equals} \quad \}$$

$$\langle \Sigma k, j \ : \ R[k := f.j] \wedge f.j = k \ : \ T \rangle$$

$$= \qquad \{ \qquad \text{rearranging (11.7),}$$

$$\text{(preparing to nest)} \quad \}$$

$$\langle \Sigma j, k \ : \ R[k := f.j] \wedge f.j = k \ : \ T \rangle$$

$$= \qquad \{ \qquad \text{nesting (11.6), '}k\text{' is not free in } R[k := f.j] \quad \}$$

$$\langle \Sigma j \ : \ R[k := f.j] \ : \ \langle \Sigma k \ : \ f.j = k \ : \ T \rangle \rangle$$

$$= \qquad \{ \qquad \text{one-point rule (11.9)} \quad \}$$

$$\langle \Sigma j \ : \ R[k := f.j] \ : \ T[k := f.j] \rangle \ .$$

$\qquad\qquad\qquad\qquad\qquad\qquad\qquad\qquad\qquad\qquad\qquad\qquad\qquad\qquad$ □

Solution 11.56. For the first part, simply replace '+' by '⊕' and 'Σ' by '⊕' in the derivation of (11.11). Now, for the second part,

$$\langle \oplus k : P \vee Q : T \rangle$$

$$= \qquad \{ \qquad \text{above with } Q := P \wedge Q \quad \}$$

$$\langle \oplus k : (P \vee Q) \wedge P \wedge Q : T \rangle \oplus \langle \oplus k : (P \vee Q) \wedge \neg (P \wedge Q) : T \rangle$$

$$= \qquad \{ \qquad \text{predicate calculus} \quad \}$$

$$\langle \oplus k : P \wedge Q : T \rangle \oplus \langle \oplus k : (P \vee Q) \wedge \neg (P \wedge Q) : T \rangle$$

$$= \qquad \{ \qquad \oplus \text{ is idempotent} \quad \}$$

$$\langle \oplus k : P \wedge Q : T \rangle \oplus \langle \oplus k : P \wedge Q : T \rangle \oplus \langle \oplus k : (P \vee Q) \wedge \neg (P \wedge Q) : T \rangle$$

$$= \qquad \{ \qquad \text{first two steps reversed} \quad \}$$

$$\langle \oplus k : P \wedge Q : T \rangle \oplus \langle \oplus k : P \vee Q : T \rangle$$

$$= \qquad \{ \qquad \text{(11.49)} \quad \}$$

$$\langle \oplus k : P : T \rangle \oplus \langle \oplus k : Q : T \rangle \ .$$

$\qquad\qquad\qquad\qquad\qquad\qquad\qquad\qquad\qquad\qquad\qquad\qquad\qquad\qquad$ □

Solution 11.57.

$$\langle \oplus k : R : T \rangle$$

$$= \qquad \{ \qquad \text{assumption:} \quad \langle \forall k :: \langle \exists j :: k = f.j \rangle \rangle \quad \}$$

$$\langle \oplus k : R \wedge \langle \exists j :: k = f.j \rangle : T \rangle$$

$=$ {   distributivity (11.41),

         preparing for splitting   }

$$\langle \oplus k : \langle \exists j :: R \wedge k = f.j \rangle : T \rangle$$

$=$ {   splitting (11.51)   }

$$\langle \oplus j :: \langle \oplus k : R \wedge k = f.j : T \rangle \rangle$$

$=$ {   nesting (11.45)   }

$$\langle \oplus j,k : R \wedge k = f.j : T \rangle$$

$=$ {   substitution of equals for equals   }

$$\langle \oplus j,k : R[k := f.j] \wedge k = f.j : T \rangle$$

$=$ {   nesting (11.45), $R[k := f.j]$ is independent of k }

$$\langle \oplus j : R[k := f.j] : \langle \oplus k : k = f.j : T \rangle \rangle$$

$=$ {   one-point rule (11.48)   }

$$\langle \oplus j : R[k := f.j] : T[k := f.j] \rangle \ .$$

$\square$

Solution 11.58. (Other solutions to this question are possible.) In all cases the variable p is assumed not to occur free in R or T. (In the fifth example, $p \backslash q$ is to be read as 'p divides q', and p is assumed to be a prime number.)

$$p \Rightarrow \langle \forall j : R : T \rangle = \langle \forall j : R : p \Rightarrow T \rangle \ .$$
$$p \Leftarrow \langle \exists j : R : T \rangle = \langle \forall j : R : p \Leftarrow T \rangle \ .$$
$$- \langle \Sigma i : R : T \rangle = \langle \Sigma i : R : -T \rangle \ .$$
$$p \backslash \langle \Pi i : R : T \rangle = \langle \exists j : R : p \backslash T \rangle \ .$$
$$p + \langle \Downarrow j : R : T \rangle = \langle \Downarrow j : R : p + T \rangle \ .$$
$$\neg \langle \equiv j : R : T \rangle = \langle \not\equiv j : R : \neg T \rangle \ .$$
$$p \wedge \langle \not\equiv j : R : T \rangle = \langle \not\equiv j : R : p \wedge T \rangle \ .$$
$$p \cup \langle \bigcap j : R : T \rangle = \langle \bigcap j : R : p \cup T \rangle \ .$$
$$p \cap \langle \bigcup j : R : T \rangle = \langle \bigcup j : R : p \cap T \rangle \ .$$

$\square$

Solution 11.59.

$$\frac{\langle \Sigma k : 0 \leqslant k < n : x_k \rangle}{n} \ \leqslant \ \langle \Uparrow k : 0 \leqslant k < n : x_k \rangle$$

$=$ {   arithmetic, $n > 0$ }

$$\langle \Sigma k : 0 \leqslant k < n : x_k \rangle \ \leqslant \ n \times \langle \Uparrow k : 0 \leqslant k < n : x_k \rangle$$

$=$ { $n = \langle \Sigma\, k : 0 \leqslant k < n : 1\rangle$,

distributivity of multiplication over addition   }

$\langle \Sigma\, k : 0 \leqslant k < n : x_k\rangle \;\leqslant\; \langle \Sigma\, k : 0 \leqslant k < n : \langle \Uparrow k : 0 \leqslant k < n : x_k\rangle\rangle$

$\Leftarrow$ {   addition is monotonic   }

$\langle \forall\, k \,:\, 0 \leqslant k < n \,:\, x_k \;\leqslant\; \langle \Uparrow k : 0 \leqslant k < n : x_k\rangle\rangle$

$=$ {   maximum   }

true .

When x_k is an integer, for each k, $\langle \Uparrow k : 0 \leqslant k < n : x_k\rangle$ is also an integer. So,

true

$=$ {   above   }

$\dfrac{\langle \Sigma\, k : 0 \leqslant k < n : m_k\rangle}{n} \;\leqslant\; \langle \Uparrow k : 0 \leqslant k < n : m_k\rangle$

$=$ { $\langle \Sigma\, k : 0 \leqslant k < n : m_k\rangle = p$ }

$\dfrac{p}{n} \;\leqslant\; \langle \Uparrow k : 0 \leqslant k < n : m_k\rangle$

$=$ {   definition of ceiling   }

$\left\lceil \dfrac{p}{n} \right\rceil \;\leqslant\; \langle \Uparrow k : 0 \leqslant k < n : m_k\rangle$

$=$ {   for all q, $q \leqslant x \uparrow y \;\equiv\; q \leqslant x \lor q \leqslant y$,

distributivity (valid because $n > 0$)   }

$\langle \exists\, k \,:\, 0 \leqslant k < n \,:\, \left\lceil \dfrac{p}{n} \right\rceil \leqslant m_k\rangle$.

The dual properties are

$\dfrac{\langle \Sigma\, k : 0 \leqslant k < n : x_k\rangle}{n} \;\geqslant\; \langle \Downarrow k : 0 \leqslant k < n : x_k\rangle$

and

$\langle \exists\, k \,:\, 0 \leqslant k < n \,:\, \left\lfloor \dfrac{\langle \Sigma\, k : 0 \leqslant k < n : m_k\rangle}{n} \right\rfloor \geqslant m_k\rangle$.

In the case that $p = n+1$, it follows that there is a pigeon-hole with at least two items in it. In the case that $p > j \times n$, it follows that there is a pigeon-hole with at least j items in it.   □

Solution 11.60.

$\langle \exists\, m,n \,::\, \sqrt{k} = \dfrac{m}{n}\rangle$

$=$ {   Use arithmetic to eliminate the square root operator.   }

$\langle \exists\, m,n \,::\, k \times n^2 = m^2\rangle$

$=$ { Let $\exp_p(l)$ denote the number of times that p divides l.

Fundamental theorem of arithmetic. (Dummy p ranges

over prime numbers.) }

$\langle \exists\, m,n :: \langle \forall p :: \exp_p(k \times n^2) = \exp_p(m^2) \rangle \rangle$

$=$ { For all m and n, and all primes p,

$\exp_p(m \times n) = \exp_p(m) + \exp_p(n)$. }

$\langle \exists\, m,n :: \langle \forall p :: \exp_p(k) + 2 \times \exp_p(n) = 2 \times \exp_p(m) \rangle \rangle$

$=$ { ($\Rightarrow$) Both $2 \times \exp_p(n)$ and $2 \times \exp_p(m)$ are even.

The difference between two even numbers is even.

($\Leftarrow$) $\quad m,n \;:=\; \langle \Pi\, p,j : j = \exp_p(k)/2 : p^j \rangle\,,\, 1$ }

$\langle \forall p :: \exp_p(k) \text{ is even} \rangle$.

So, $\sqrt{k}$ is rational exactly when, for every prime number p, the number of times that p divides k is even. $\qquad\square$

Solution 12.1. If the two tumblers that are chosen on a particular move are both upside down, the move increases the number that are the right way up by two. If the two tumblers that are chosen on a particular move are both the right way up, the move decreases the number that are the right way up by two. If one of the tumblers is the right way up and the other is upside down, the move does not change the number that are the right way up. Thus, in any move the number that are the right way up changes by a multiple of two. The invariant is whether or not the number that are the right way up is even. Starting from an initial position in which an odd number of tumblers is upside down, it is impossible to turn them all the right way up. Starting from an initial position in which an even number of tumblers is upside down, it is possible—choose two tumblers that are upside down at each step. $\qquad\square$

Solution 12.2.

(a) The first player always wins. The strategy is to ensure that the number of matches left is a multiple of 4 equivales it is the second player's turn to move. This invariant property is true initially (because there is an odd number of matches and it is the first player's move). To maintain the invariant, the first player removes $n \bmod 4$ matches on the first move, where n is the number of matches in the pile. ($n \bmod 4$ is the remainder after dividing n by 4. In general, $n \bmod m$ is the number remaining after dividing n by m.) Subsequently, if the second player removes k matches, the first player then removes $4-k$ matches.

(b) The first player always wins. The strategy is to ensure that the number of matches left is a multiple of $2m + 2$ equivales it is the second player's turn to move. (Since 0 is a multiple of $2m + 2$ it follows that the first player makes the last move.) The first player should therefore always remove $n \bmod (2m + 2)$ matches, where n is the number of matches remaining in the pile. The initial position satisfies the invariant property (because an odd number is not divisible by an even number) and every move made by the first or second player guarantees the invariant.

(c) The first player has a winning strategy if the initial number of matches is not divisible by $m+1$. Otherwise the first player is guaranteed to lose if the second player follows the winning strategy.

□

Solution 12.3. The key property is that any closed curve must include the four corners of a rectangle. In particular, a closed curve must have a lower-right corner. That is, in order to complete a closed curve, A must always draw two lines in the shape below.

In order to guarantee winning, one strategy for B is to prevent A from drawing such a shape. So, whenever A draws a horizontal line, B responds by adding a vertical line forming the shape below.

If A draws a vertical line, B responds by adding a horizontal line forming the shape below.

If A's move already forms either of these shapes, then B may make an arbitrary move.

□

Solution 12.4. The value of w remains constant or decreases by 2. So, the invariant is the parity of w (whether or not it is even). Thus the last ball in the bag is white if initially there is an odd number of white balls in the bag, otherwise the last ball in the bag is black. □

Solution 12.5.

(a) The second player always wins. The strategy is to maintain the symmetry of the daisy by always copying the first player's moves, choosing petals diagonally opposite those chosen by the first player. If we number the petals from 0 to 15, then the second player removes petal $8+n$ whenever the first player has removed petal n, the numbers being counted modulo 16. The invariant property that holds after each of the second player's moves is that, for all n in the range $0 \leqslant n \leqslant 15$, there is a petal at position n equivales there is a petal at position $(8+n)$ mod 16. More generally, the invariant property of the game is that it is the first player's turn to move equivales for all n in the range $0 \leqslant n \leqslant 15$, there is a petal at position n equivales there is a petal at position $(8+n)$ mod 16.

Figure B.3 Solution to the daisy problem.

(b) If $n \leqslant m$, then the first player wins (by removing all petals on the first move). Otherwise, the second player has a winning strategy. After the first move, the petals are divided into groups of adjacent petals. (Immediately after the first player's first move there is one such group of petals; later in the game there may be more.) The sizes of these groups varies but the winning strategy is to ensure that, for each k, there is an even number of groups of petals of size k. The second player's first move is to establish this property—by removing enough petals to create two groups of adjacent petals of equal size.

Subsequently, the first player is always obliged to invalidate this property—if his move is to remove l petals from a group of size k, then the number of groups of size k will become odd. The second player can restore the property by copying the first player's move—removing the same l petals from one of the remaining groups of size k.

(c) The first player wins. The first player places a coin over the centre of the table. Thereafter, every move the first player makes is a copy of the second player's move at a position diagonally opposite. Thus, if the second player places a coin at position (x, y), the first player copies the move by placing a coin of the same diameter at the position $(-x, -y)$. The invariant property holding immediately after the first player's move is: there is a coin of diameter d at position (x, y) equivales there is a coin of diameter d at position $(-x, -y)$. The first player can always copy the second player's move provided that all coins are solid and circular. (If there are, say, coins with holes in the centre and the first player places one such coin on the table in his first move, the second player could put another coin in the centre of that coin, thus foiling the first player's winning strategy!)   □

Solution 12.9. The main change is the base case. Instead of the empty-range rule, the one-point rule is used:

$$S.0$$

$$=\qquad\{\qquad\text{definition}\quad\}$$

$$\langle\Sigma k:0\leqslant k\leqslant 0:k\rangle = \tfrac{1}{2}0(0+1)$$

$$=\qquad\{\qquad 0\leqslant k\leqslant 0 \equiv k=0,\ \text{one-point rule to simplify}$$

$$\text{the summation,}$$

$$\text{arithmetic for the right side of the equality}\quad\}$$

$$0=0$$

$$=\qquad\{\qquad\text{reflexivity of equality}\quad\}$$

$$\text{true}\ .$$

The proof of the induction step is essentially the same.   □

Solution 12.10.

(a) **Basis:**

$$\langle\Sigma k:1\leqslant k\leqslant 0:k^2\rangle = \tfrac{1}{6}0\times(0+1)\times(2\times 0+1)$$

$$=\qquad\{\qquad\text{empty-range rule to simplify the summation,}$$

$$\text{arithmetic on the right side.}\quad\}$$

$$0 = 0$$

$=$ {   reflexivity of equality   }

true .

Induction Step:

$$\langle \Sigma k : 1 \leqslant k \leqslant n+1 : k^2 \rangle \;=\; \tfrac{1}{6}(n+1)((n+1)+1)(2(n+1)+1)$$

$=$ {   range splitting, arithmetic   }

$$\langle \Sigma k : 1 \leqslant k \leqslant n : k^2 \rangle + (n+1)^2 \;=\; \tfrac{1}{6}(n+1)(n+2)(2n+3)$$

$=$ {   •   assume that

$$\langle \Sigma k : 1 \leqslant k \leqslant n : k^2 \rangle \;=\; \tfrac{1}{6}n(n+1)(2n+1) . \quad \}$$

$$\tfrac{1}{6}n(n+1)(2n+1) + (n+1)^2 \;=\; \tfrac{1}{6}(n+1)(n+2)(2n+3)$$

$=$ {   arithmetic and reflexivity of equality   }

true .

(b) Basis:

$$\langle \Sigma k : 1 \leqslant k \leqslant 0 : k^3 \rangle \;=\; \tfrac{1}{4}0^2(0+1)^2$$

$=$ {   one-point rule to simplify the summation,

                    arithmetic   }

$$0 = 0$$

$=$ {   arithmetic and reflexivity of equality   }

true .

Induction Step:

$$\langle \Sigma k : 1 \leqslant k \leqslant n+1 : k^3 \rangle \;=\; \tfrac{1}{4}(n+1)^2((n+1)+1)^2$$

$=$ {   range splitting, arithmetic   }

$$\langle \Sigma k : 1 \leqslant k \leqslant n : k^3 \rangle + (n+1)^3 \;=\; \tfrac{1}{4}(n+1)^2(n+2)^2$$

$=$ {   •   assume that

$$\langle \Sigma k : 1 \leqslant k \leqslant n : k^3 \rangle \;=\; \tfrac{1}{4}n^2(n+1)^2 . \quad \}$$

$$\tfrac{1}{4}n^2(n+1)^2 + (n+1)^3 \;=\; \tfrac{1}{4}(n+1)^2(n+2)^2$$

$=$ {   arithmetic and reflexivity of equality   }

true .

(c) **Basis:**

$$\langle \Sigma k : 0 \leqslant k \leqslant 0 : x^k \rangle \;=\; \frac{x^{0+1} - 1}{x - 1}$$

$=$ { one-point rule to simplify the summation,

arithmetic }

$$x^0 \;=\; \frac{x - 1}{x - 1}$$

$=$ { $x \neq 1$, arithmetic and reflexivity of equality }

true .

Induction Step:

$$\langle \Sigma k : 0 \leqslant k \leqslant n+1 : x^k \rangle \;=\; \frac{x^{(n+1)+1} - 1}{x - 1}$$

$=$ { range splitting, arithmetic }

$$\langle \Sigma k : 0 \leqslant k \leqslant n : x^k \rangle + x^{n+1} \;=\; \frac{x^{n+2} - 1}{x - 1}$$

$=$ { • assume that

$$\langle \Sigma k : 0 \leqslant k \leqslant n : x^k \rangle \;=\; \frac{x^{n+1} - 1}{x - 1} \;. \quad \}$$

$$\frac{x^{n+1} - 1}{x - 1} + x^{n+1} \;=\; \frac{x^{n+2} - 1}{x - 1}$$

$=$ { arithmetic and reflexivity of equality }

true .

(d) **Basis:**

$$(1+x)^0 \;\geqslant\; 1 + 0 \times x$$

$=$ { arithmetic }

true .

Induction Step:

$$(1+x)^{n+1} \;\geqslant\; 1 + (n+1) \times x$$

$\Leftarrow$ { transitivity of $\geqslant$

(heading towards using the induction hypothesis,

we introduce the middle term

$(1+x) \times (1 + n \times x)$) }

$$(1+x)^{n+1} \;\geqslant\; (1+x) \times (1 + n \times x) \;\geqslant\; 1 + (n+1) \times x$$

$=$ { • assume that $(1+x)^n \geqslant 1 + n \times x$.

$x > -1$, so $1 + x > 0$. Multiplication by a positive

number is monotonic. That is,

$$(1+x)^{n+1} \geqslant (1+x) \times (1 + n \times x) \quad \}$$

$$(1+x) \times (1 + n \times x) \geqslant 1 + (n+1) \times x$$

$=$ {   arithmetic   }

$$1 + x + n \times x + n \times x^2 \geqslant 1 + x + n \times x$$

$=$ { $n \times x^2 \geqslant 0$. Addition is monotonic.   }

true .

(e) **Basis:**

$$\left\langle \Sigma k : 1 \leqslant k \leqslant 0 : \frac{1}{k \times (k+1)} \right\rangle \;=\; \frac{0}{0+1}$$

$=$ {   empty-range rule to simplify the summation,

           arithmetic on the right side   }

true .

Induction Step:

$$\left\langle \Sigma k : 1 \leqslant k \leqslant n+1 : \frac{1}{k \times (k+1)} \right\rangle \;=\; \frac{n+1}{(n+1)+1}$$

$=$ {   range splitting   }

$$\left\langle \Sigma k : 1 \leqslant k \leqslant n : \frac{1}{k \times (k+1)} \right\rangle + \frac{1}{(n+1) \times ((n+1)+1)} \;=\; \frac{n+1}{n+2}$$

$=$ {   •   assume that

$$\left\langle \Sigma k : 1 \leqslant k \leqslant n : \frac{1}{k \times (k+1)} \right\rangle \;=\; \frac{n}{n+1} \,. \quad \}$$

$$\frac{n}{n+1} + \frac{1}{(n+1) \times (n+2)} \;=\; \frac{n+1}{n+2}$$

$=$ {   arithmetic and reflexivity of equality   }

true .

(f) **Basis:**

$$\left\langle \Sigma k : 1 \leqslant k \leqslant 0 : \frac{k}{2^k} \right\rangle \;=\; 2 - \frac{0+2}{2^0}$$

$=$ {   empty-range rule to simplify the summation,

           arithmetic   }

$$0 = 0$$

$=$ {   reflexivity of equality   }

true .

Induction Step:

$$\left\langle \Sigma k : 1 \leqslant k \leqslant n+1 : \frac{k}{2^k} \right\rangle = 2 - \frac{(n+1)+2}{2^{n+1}}$$

$= \qquad \{ \qquad$ range splitting $\}$

$$\left\langle \Sigma k : 1 \leqslant k \leqslant n : \frac{k}{2^k} \right\rangle + \frac{n+1}{2^{n+1}} = 2 - \frac{n+3}{2^{n+1}}$$

$= \qquad \{ \qquad \bullet \quad$ assume that

$$\left\langle \Sigma k : 1 \leqslant k \leqslant n : \frac{k}{2^k} \right\rangle = 2 - \frac{n+2}{2^n} . \quad \}$$

$$2 - \frac{n+2}{2^n} + \frac{n+1}{2^{n+1}} = 2 - \frac{n+3}{2^{n+1}}$$

$= \qquad \{ \qquad$ arithmetic and reflexivity of equality $\}$

true .

$\square$

Solution 12.13. Basis: the basis is the case $n = 1$. This is because there are individual definitions of $F.0$ and $F.1$. We have

$$F.(1+1) \times F.(1-1) - (F.1)^2$$

$= \qquad \{ \qquad$ definition $\}$

$$1 \times 0 - 1^2$$

$= \qquad \{ \qquad$ arithmetic $\}$

$$-1$$

$= \qquad \{ \qquad$ arithmetic $\}$

$$(-1)^1 .$$

Induction Step: care must be taken in the induction step when expanding the definition of F. Assuming that $n \geqslant 1$, the definitions of $F.(n+2)$ and $F.(n+1)$ are given by the rule $F.(k+2) = F.(k+1) + F.k$, for all k, $k \geqslant 0$. (This is not the case for the definition of $F.n$.)

$$F.((n+1)+1) \times F.((n+1)-1) - (F.(n+1))^2$$

$= \qquad \{ \qquad$ arithmetic $\}$

$$F.(n+2) \times F.n - (F.(n+1))^2$$

$= \qquad \{ \qquad$ definition: $F.(k+2) = F.(k+1) + F.k$

$\qquad\qquad\qquad\qquad$ applied to the cases $k = n$ and $k = n-1$. $\}$

$$(F.(n+1) + F.n) \times F.n - (F.n + F.(n-1)) \times F.(n+1)$$

$= \qquad \{ \qquad$ arithmetic $\}$

$$(F.n)^2 - F.(n-1) \times F.(n+1)$$

$=$ $\{$ •   assume that

$$F.(n+1) \times F.(n-1) - (F.n)^2 = (-1)^n . \quad \}$$

$$-(-1)^n$$

$=$ $\{$ arithmetic and reflexivity of equality $\}$

$$(-1)^{n+1} .$$

The proof uses simple induction only.   □

Solution 12.14. The first step is invalid in the case that $n = 0$.   □

Solution 13.13. To verify the correctness of the initialization, we must verify the Hoare triple

$$\{ \ 0 \leqslant N \ \}$$
$$k,s := N,0$$
$$\{ \ 0 \leqslant k \leqslant N \ \wedge \ s \times X^k = \langle \Sigma i : k \leqslant i < N : a[i] \times X^i \rangle \ \} \ .$$

By the assignment axiom, this reduces to

$$0 \leqslant N \ \Rightarrow \ 0 \leqslant N \leqslant N \ \wedge \ 0 \times X^N = \langle \Sigma i : N \leqslant i < N : a[i] \times X^i \rangle \ .$$

This is **true** by virtue of the empty-range rule (since $N \leqslant i < N$ is **false**) and simple properties of arithmetic.

The termination condition is valid if

$$0 \leqslant k \leqslant N \ \wedge \ s \times X^k = \langle \Sigma i : k \leqslant i < N : a[i] \times X^i \rangle \ \wedge \ \neg (k > 0)$$
$$\Rightarrow \ s = \langle \Sigma i : 0 \leqslant i < N : a[i] \times X^i \rangle \ .$$

This is clearly **true** as $0 \leqslant k \leqslant N \wedge \neg (k > 0)$ reduces to $0 = k \leqslant N$.   □

Solution 13.15. The invariant is established by the assignment

$$k,y,z := M,1,X$$

and, when $k = 0$, we have

$$y = X^M$$

independently of the value of z. As the reader will have seen in solving Exercise 10.21, we also have

$$\{ \ 0 < k = K \ \wedge \ y \times z^k = X^M \ \}$$

$$\textbf{if } \ \text{even}.k \ \longrightarrow \ \textbf{skip}$$

$$\square \ \ \text{odd}.k \ \longrightarrow \ k,y := k-1, y \times z$$

fi ;

$\{\ 0 \leqslant k \div 2 < K \ \wedge \ \text{even}.k \ \wedge \ y \times z^k = X^M \ \}$

$k,z := k \div 2, z^2$

$\{\ 0 \leqslant k < K \ \wedge \ y \times z^k = X^M \ \}$.

(Make the substitutions X^M for C and z for x.) Thus we obtain the following algorithm.

$\{\ 0 \leqslant M \ \}$

$k,y,z := M,1,X$;

$\{\ \textbf{Invariant:} \quad 0 \leqslant k \ \wedge \ y \times z^k = X^M$

$\textbf{Bound function:} \quad k \ \}$

do $k > 0 \longrightarrow$ if even.$k \longrightarrow$ skip

$\square$ odd.$k \longrightarrow k,y := k-1, y \times z$

fi ;

$k,z := k \div 2, z^2$

od

$\{\ y = X^M \ \}$.

$\square$

Solution 14.1. For the first command, using the assignment axiom we have to verify

$M \leqslant r \leqslant w \leqslant b \leqslant N$

$\wedge \ \langle \forall i : M \leqslant i < r : red.i \rangle$

$\wedge \ \langle \forall i : r \leqslant i < w : white.i \rangle$

$\wedge \ \langle \forall i : b \leqslant i < N : blue.i \rangle$

$\wedge \ w < b \ \wedge \ white.w$

$\Rightarrow \quad M \leqslant r \leqslant w+1 \leqslant b \leqslant N$

$\wedge \ \langle \forall i : M \leqslant i < r : red.i \rangle$

$\wedge \ \langle \forall i : r \leqslant i < w+1 : white.i \rangle$

$\wedge \ \langle \forall i : b \leqslant i < N : blue.i \rangle$.

This is clearly true.

For the second command, using the assignment axiom we have to verify

$$
\begin{aligned}
\{ \quad & M \leqslant r \leqslant w \leqslant b \leqslant N \\
\wedge \quad & \langle \forall i : M \leqslant i < r : red.i \rangle \\
\wedge \quad & \langle \forall i : r \leqslant i < w : white.i \rangle \\
\wedge \quad & \langle \forall i : b \leqslant i < N : blue.i \rangle \\
\wedge \quad & w < b \ \wedge \ blue.w \ \}
\end{aligned}
$$

$$ swap(b-1, w) $$

$$
\begin{aligned}
\{ \quad & M \leqslant r \leqslant w \leqslant b-1 \leqslant N \\
\wedge \quad & \langle \forall i : M \leqslant i < r : red.i \rangle \\
\wedge \quad & \langle \forall i : r \leqslant i < w : white.i \rangle \\
\wedge \quad & \langle \forall i : b-1 \leqslant i < N : blue.i \rangle \ \} \ .
\end{aligned}
$$

Here again, we split the postcondition into three separate conjuncts. These are, first, the constraints on the boundary indices,

$$ M \leqslant r \leqslant w \leqslant b-1 \leqslant N \ ; $$

second, the parts of the array that should not be affected,

$$
\begin{aligned}
& \langle \forall i : M \leqslant i < r : red.i \rangle \\
\wedge \ & \langle \forall i : r \leqslant i < w : white.i \rangle \\
\wedge \ & \langle \forall i : b \leqslant i < N : blue.i \rangle \ ;
\end{aligned}
$$

and, finally the one element that is affected,

$$ blue.(b-1) \ . $$

These three conjuncts are verified by checking the following properties of swap. First,

$$ \{ \ M \leqslant r \leqslant w \leqslant b \leqslant N \ \wedge \ w < b \ \} $$
$$ swap(b-1, w) $$
$$ \{ \ M \leqslant r \leqslant w \leqslant b-1 \leqslant N \ \} \ . $$

Second,

$$
\begin{aligned}
\{ \quad & w < b \\
\wedge \quad & \langle \forall i : M \leqslant i < r : red.i \rangle \\
\wedge \quad & \langle \forall i : r \leqslant i < w : white.i \rangle \\
\wedge \quad & \langle \forall i : b \leqslant i < N : blue.i \rangle \ \}
\end{aligned}
$$

$$swap(b-1,w)$$
$$\{ \quad \langle \forall i : M \leqslant i < r : red.i \rangle$$
$$\wedge \ \langle \forall i : r \leqslant i < w : white.i \rangle$$
$$\wedge \ \langle \forall i : b \leqslant i < N : blue.i \rangle \ \} \ .$$

Finally,

$$\{ \ w < b \ \wedge \ blue.w \ \}$$
$$swap(b-1,w)$$
$$\{ \ blue.(b-1) \ \} \ .$$

$\square$

Solution 14.2. We have

$$0 \leqslant s < K \leqslant l \leqslant N$$
$$\wedge \ \langle \forall i,j : 0 \leqslant i < s \wedge s \leqslant j < N : a[i] < a[j] \rangle$$
$$\wedge \ \langle \forall i,j : 0 \leqslant i < l \wedge l \leqslant j < N : a[i] < a[j] \rangle$$

= $\quad\quad$ { $\quad$ range splitting

The first quantification is split on

whether or not $s \leqslant j < l$,

the second quantification is split on

whether or not $s \leqslant i < l$. }

$$0 \leqslant s < K \leqslant l \leqslant N$$
$$\wedge \ \langle \forall i,j : 0 \leqslant i < s \wedge s \leqslant j < l : a[i] < a[j] \rangle$$
$$\wedge \ \langle \forall i,j : 0 \leqslant i < s \wedge l \leqslant j < N : a[i] < a[j] \rangle$$
$$\wedge \ \langle \forall i,j : 0 \leqslant i < s \wedge l \leqslant j < N : a[i] < a[j] \rangle$$
$$\wedge \ \langle \forall i,j : s \leqslant i < l \wedge l \leqslant j < N : a[i] < a[j] \rangle$$

= $\quad\quad$ { $\quad$ idempotence of $\wedge$ $\quad$ }

$$0 \leqslant s < K \leqslant l \leqslant N$$
$$\wedge \ \langle \forall i,j : 0 \leqslant i < s \wedge s \leqslant j < l : a[i] < a[j] \rangle$$
$$\wedge \ \langle \forall i,j : 0 \leqslant i < s \wedge l \leqslant j < N : a[i] < a[j] \rangle$$
$$\wedge \ \langle \forall i,j : s \leqslant i < l \wedge l \leqslant j < N : a[i] < a[j] \rangle \ .$$

The first universal quantification states that every element in the 'small' segment is less than every element in the 'medium' segment, the second universal quantification that every element in the 'small' segment is less than every element in the 'large' segment, and the third universal quantification that every element in the 'medium' segment is less than every element in the 'large' segment.

The second universal quantification is not implied by the other two in the case that the medium segment is empty. Take, for example, N to be 2 and all of s, K and l to be 1. Let the array have elements $a[0] = 20$ and $a[1] = 10$. Then

$$\langle \forall\, i,j : 0 \leqslant i < s \,\wedge\, s \leqslant j < l : a[i] < a[j]\rangle$$

$$\wedge\ \langle \forall\, i,j : 0 \leqslant i < s \,\wedge\, l \leqslant j < N : a[i] < a[j]\rangle$$

$$\wedge\ \langle \forall\, i,j : s \leqslant i < l \,\wedge\, l \leqslant j < N : a[i] < a[j]\rangle$$

is false (because $a[0] \leqslant a[1]$ is false), whereas

$$\langle \forall\, i,j : 0 \leqslant i < s \,\wedge\, s \leqslant j < l : a[i] < a[j]\rangle$$

$$\wedge\ \langle \forall\, i,j : s \leqslant i < l \,\wedge\, l \leqslant j < N : a[i] < a[j]\rangle$$

is (vacuously) true. The first term $(0 \leqslant s < K \leqslant l \leqslant N)$ implies, however, that the medium segment is indeed non-empty. So we have

$$\langle \forall\, i,j : 0 \leqslant i < s \,\wedge\, s \leqslant j < l : a[i] < a[j]\rangle$$

$$\wedge\ \langle \forall\, i,j : s \leqslant i < l \,\wedge\, l \leqslant j < N : a[i] < a[j]\rangle$$

$\Rightarrow$ $\quad\{\quad 0 \leqslant s < K \leqslant l \leqslant N$. In particular, $s < l$.

So, use the one point rule with $j = s$ in the first conjunct

and $i = s$ in the second conjunct. $\}$

$$\langle \forall i : 0 \leqslant i < s : a[i] < a[s]\rangle$$

$$\wedge\ \langle \forall j : l \leqslant j < N : a[s] < a[j]\rangle$$

$\Rightarrow$ $\quad\{\quad$ transitivity of $<\quad\}$

$$\langle \forall\, i,j : 0 \leqslant i < s \,\wedge\, l \leqslant j < N : a[i] < a[j]\rangle\ .$$

$\square$

Solution 14.3. An appropriate invariant property is

$$0 \leqslant s \leqslant K \leqslant l \leqslant N$$

$$\wedge\ \langle \forall\, i,j : 0 \leqslant i < s \,\wedge\, s \leqslant j < N : a[i] \leqslant a[j]\rangle$$

$$\wedge\ \langle \forall\, i,j : 0 \leqslant i < l \,\wedge\, l \leqslant j < N : a[i] \leqslant a[j]\rangle\ .$$

The assignment

$$s, l := 0, N$$

initializes the 'small' and 'large' segments to the empty set and, so, the invariant is vacuously true.

The bound function we use is $l-s$, the size of the 'medium' segment. The termination condition is $s=K$ so that the loop body is executed when $s<K$. In order to make progress to the termination condition whilst maintaining the invariant, we again choose $a[K-1]$ as borderline value, recording it in some local variable, X. (The justification for this choice is unchanged from the earlier algorithm.) The algorithm we are aiming to develop thus has the basic structure shown below:

$$\{\ 0 \leqslant K \leqslant N\ \}$$

$$s,l := 0,N\ ;$$

$\{$ **Invariant:**

$$0 \leqslant s \leqslant K \leqslant l \leqslant N$$

$$\wedge\ \langle \forall i,j : 0 \leqslant i < s \wedge s \leqslant j < N : a[i] \leqslant a[j] \rangle$$

$$\wedge\ \langle \forall i,j : 0 \leqslant i < l \wedge l \leqslant j < N : a[i] \leqslant a[j] \rangle\ \}$$

do $s<K \longrightarrow$ $\{$ choose boundary value in unsorted region $\}$

$$X := a[K-1];$$

reduce $l-s$ whilst maintaining invariant

od

$$\{\ \langle \forall i,j : 0 \leqslant i < K \wedge K \leqslant j < N : a[i] \leqslant a[j] \rangle\ \}\ .$$

Reducing $l-s$ whilst maintaining the invariant is again achieved by applying the Dutch National Flag program to split the medium segment into segments delimited by the indices s, m, n and l, containing values less than X, values equal to X, and values greater than X. After this operation, there are three cases to consider. In the first case, $n \leqslant K$. This means that all the array elements, up to and including $a[n-1]$, are among the K smallest values in the array. So, in this case, the assignment $s := n$ is executed. Moreover, this is bound to increase the value of s (and thus decrease $l-s$) because the segment containing values equal to X is non-empty.

In the second case, $m \leqslant K < n$. In this case the sorting process is complete—the K smallest values in the array have been successfully transferred to the first K positions in the array. So, in this case, the assignment $s,l := K,K$ is executed. Moreover, this is bound to decrease $l-s$ to zero.

In the third case, $K < m$. This means that all the array elements, from $a[m]$ onward, are among the $N-K$ largest values in the array. So, in this case, the assignment $l := m$ is executed. Moreover, this is bound to decrease the value of l (and thus decreases $l-s$) because the segment containing values equal to X is non-empty.

{ $0 \leqslant K \leqslant N$ }

$s,l := 0,N$ { s delimits the 'small' segment, l the 'large' segment };

{ **Invariant:** $\quad 0 \leqslant s \leqslant K \leqslant l \leqslant N$

$\quad\quad\quad \land \ \langle \forall\, i,j : 0 \leqslant i < s \land s \leqslant j < N : a[i] \leqslant a[j] \rangle$

$\quad\quad\quad \land \ \langle \forall\, i,j : 0 \leqslant i < l \land l \leqslant j < N : a[i] \leqslant a[j] \rangle$

Bound function: $\quad l-s$ }

do $s < K \longrightarrow \quad X := a[K-1]$ { borderline value in 'medium' region };

$\quad\quad\quad$ { apply Dutch National Flag program to the segment

$\quad\quad\quad\quad$ delimited by s and l with predicates *red*, *white* and

$\quad\quad\quad\quad$ *blue* set to $(< X)$, $(= X)$ and $(> X)$, respectively.

$\quad\quad\quad\quad$ Return the boundary values in m and n. }

$\quad\quad\quad DNF(s, l, (< X), (= X), (> X), m, n)$

$\quad\quad\quad$ { $\quad s \leqslant m < n \leqslant l$

$\quad\quad\quad\quad \land \ \langle \forall i : s \leqslant i < m : a[i] < X \rangle$

$\quad\quad\quad\quad \land \ \langle \forall i : m \leqslant i < n : a[i] = X \rangle$

$\quad\quad\quad\quad \land \ \langle \forall i : n \leqslant i < l : a[i] > X \rangle$

$\quad\quad\quad$ (Note: $m < n$ by choice of X.) };

$\quad\quad\quad$ { Extend either the 'small' or 'large' segment (or both),

$\quad\quad\quad\quad$ ensuring that the chosen boundary element is added

$\quad\quad\quad\quad$ to one of the heaps. }

$\quad\quad\quad$ if $n \leqslant K \longrightarrow s := n$

$\quad\quad\quad$ ▢ $m \leqslant K < n \longrightarrow s,l := K,K$

$\quad\quad\quad$ ▢ $K < m \longrightarrow l := m$

$\quad\quad\quad$ fi

od

{ $\langle \forall\, i,j : 0 \leqslant i < K \land K \leqslant j < N : a[i] \leqslant a[j] \rangle$ }

Figure B.4 Solution to simplified find problem.

This completes the development of the program. The complete details are shown in Figure B.4.   □

Solution 15.5. Assuming $P \leqslant 0$, the statement $r,d := P,0$ establishes

$$r < Q \;\wedge\; P = Q \times d + r \;.$$

So, we take this as invariant and the condition $0 \leqslant r$ as the termination condition. The development of the loop body proceeds in a similar way, leading to

> { remainder and quotient computation
>
>   —elementary algorithm, assumes that $-P$ is a natural number }
>
> { $P \leqslant 0 \;\wedge\; 0 < Q$ }
>
> $r,d := P,0$;
>
> { **Invariant:** $r < Q \;\wedge\; P = Q \times d + r$
>
>   **Bound function:** r }
>
> do $0 > r \longrightarrow r,d := r+Q,d-1$
>
> od
>
> { $0 \leqslant r < Q \;\wedge\; P = Q \times d + r$ } .

                                                                                          □

Solution 15.14.

$$r = P \bmod 1 \;\wedge\; d = P \div 1$$

$=$ {   (15.6) with $Q := 1$ }

$$0 \leqslant r < 1 \;\wedge\; P = 1 \times d + r$$

$=$ {   integer arithmetic   }

$$r = 0 \;\wedge\; P = d + r$$

$=$ {   substitution and arithmetic   }

$$r = 0 \;\wedge\; P = d \;.$$

That is, $0 = P \bmod 1$ and $P = P \div 1$.   □

Solution 15.15.

$$-Q \leqslant P < 0$$

$=$ {   addition is monotonic with respect to $\leqslant$ and $<$ }

$$0 \leqslant P + Q < Q$$

$=$ {   arithmetic   }

$$0 \leqslant P+Q < Q \ \wedge \ P+Q = Q \times 0 + P + Q$$

$=$ {   arithmetic   }

$$0 \leqslant P+Q < Q \ \wedge \ P = Q \times (-1) + P + Q$$

$=$ {   (15.6)   }

$$P+Q = P \bmod Q \ \wedge \ -1 = P \div Q \ .$$

So,

$$-Q \leqslant P < 0 \ \equiv \ P+Q = P \bmod Q \ \wedge \ -1 = P \div Q \ .$$

$\square$

Solution 15.16.

$\quad$ true

$=$ {   (15.7)   }

$$P \ = \ Q \times n \times (P \bmod (Q \times n)) + P \div (Q \times n)$$

$\Rightarrow$ {   Leibniz   }

$$P \bmod Q \ = \ (Q \times n \times (P \bmod (Q \times n)) + P \div (Q \times n)) \bmod Q$$

$=$ {   (15.12) with $m, n := n \times (P \bmod (Q \times n)), (P \div (Q \times n))$ }

$$P \bmod Q \ = \ (P \bmod (Q \times n)) \bmod Q \ .$$

$\square$

Solution 15.17.

$$(r \bmod Q \ = \ n) [r := r - Q \times m]$$

$=$ {   substitution   }

$$(r - Q \times m) \bmod Q \ = \ n$$

$=$ {   (15.12)   }

$$r \bmod Q \ = \ n \ .$$

$\square$

Solution 15.18. We combine the assumption $P < 0$ with the specification (15.1) and try to work towards the right side of (15.6).

$$0 \leqslant r < Q \ \wedge \ P = Q \times d + r$$

$=$ { $P < 0 \ \equiv \ 0 \leqslant -(P+1)$ suggests replacing

                     'P' in second conjunct by '$-(P+1)$'   }

$$0 \leqslant r < Q \;\land\; -(P{+}1) = -(Q{\times}d + r + 1)$$

= $\quad\quad$ { $\quad$ arithmetic $\quad$ }

$$0 \leqslant r < Q \;\land\; -(P{+}1) = Q{\times}(-d) + (-(r{+}1))$$

= $\quad\quad$ { $\quad$ investigating replacing r by $-(r{+}1)$ in $0 \leqslant r < Q$:

$\quad\quad\quad$ $0 \leqslant r < Q$

$\quad\quad\quad\quad$ = $\quad$ { $\quad$ negation $\quad$ }

$\quad\quad\quad$ $-Q < -r \leqslant 0$

$\quad\quad\quad\quad$ = $\quad$ { $\quad$ addition is monotonic

$\quad\quad\quad\quad\quad\quad\quad\quad$ with respect to $<$ and $\leqslant$ $\quad$ }

$\quad\quad\quad$ $Q{-}Q < Q{-}r \leqslant Q$

$\quad\quad\quad\quad$ = $\quad$ { $\quad$ integer arithmetic,

$\quad\quad\quad\quad\quad\quad\quad\quad$ introducing '$-(r{+}1)$' $\quad$ }

$\quad\quad\quad$ $0 \leqslant Q - (r{+}1) < Q$ $\quad$ }

$$0 \leqslant Q - (r{+}1) < Q \;\land\; -(P{+}1) = Q{\times}(-(d{+}1)) + (Q - (r{+}1))$$

= $\quad\quad$ { $\quad$ (15.6) with $P, r, d := -(P{+}1), Q - (r{+}1), -(d{+}1)$

$\quad\quad\quad$ —assumes $0 \leqslant -(P{+}1)$; but this equivales $P < 0$,

$\quad\quad\quad$ which is the given assumption on P $\quad$ }

$$Q - (r{+}1) = (-(P{+}1)) \bmod Q \;\land\; -(d{+}1) = (-(P{+}1)) \div Q$$

= $\quad\quad$ { $\quad$ arithmetic $\quad$ }

$$r = (Q{-}1) - ((-(P{+}1)) \bmod Q) \;\land\; d = -((-(P{+}1)) \div Q + 1) \;.$$

We have thus calculated that

$$0 \leqslant r < Q \;\land\; P = Q{\times}d + r$$
$$\equiv\; r = (Q{-}1) - ((-(P{+}1)) \bmod Q) \;\land\; d = -((-(P{+}1)) \div Q + 1) \;.$$

Comparing with (15.6), we see that $P \bmod Q$ equals $(Q{-}1) - ((-(P{+}1)) \bmod Q)$ and $P \div Q$ equals $-((-(P{+}1)) \div Q + 1)$. These equalities are valid for all P, but would normally only be used in the case that $P < 0$. $\quad\quad\quad\quad\quad$ $\square$

Solution 15.21.

$$\langle \exists d :: P = Q{\times}d + r \rangle$$

= $\quad\quad$ { $\quad$ arithmetic $\quad$ }

$$\langle \exists d :: P{-}r = Q{\times}d \rangle$$

$$= \qquad \{ \qquad (15.19) \text{ with } P, r := P, r \bmod Q \quad \}$$
$$(P - r) \bmod Q = 0$$
$$= \qquad \{ \qquad (15.20) \quad \}$$
$$P \bmod Q = r \bmod Q \quad .$$

$\square$

Solution 15.23. Using the property just obtained, and arithmetic, we have

$$(m {\times} P) \div (m {\times} Q) \;=\; \left\lfloor \frac{m {\times} P}{m {\times} Q} \right\rfloor \;=\; \left\lfloor \frac{P}{Q} \right\rfloor \;=\; P \div Q \quad .$$

Consequently,

$$(m {\times} P) \bmod (m {\times} Q)$$
$$= \qquad \{ \qquad (15.7) \quad \}$$
$$m {\times} P \;-\; m \times Q \times ((m {\times} P) \div (m {\times} Q))$$
$$= \qquad \{ \qquad \text{above} \quad \}$$
$$m {\times} P \;-\; m \times Q \times (P \div Q)$$
$$= \qquad \{ \qquad \text{arithmetic} \quad \}$$
$$m {\times} (P \;-\; Q \times (P \div Q))$$
$$= \qquad \{ \qquad (15.7) \quad \}$$
$$m \times (P \bmod Q) \quad .$$

We conclude that $(m {\times} P) \bmod (m {\times} Q) \;=\; m \times (P \bmod Q)$. $\square$

Solution 15.27.

$$(m {\times} n) \bmod Q$$
$$= \qquad \{ \qquad \text{introduce } m \bmod Q \text{ using } (15.7) \quad \}$$
$$((Q \times (m \div Q) + m \bmod Q) \times n) \bmod Q$$
$$= \qquad \{ \qquad \text{distributivity of } \times \text{ over } + \quad \}$$
$$(Q \times (m \div Q) \times n \;+\; m \bmod Q \times n) \bmod Q$$
$$= \qquad \{ \qquad (15.12) \quad \}$$
$$(m \bmod Q \times n) \bmod Q \quad .$$

Thus,

$$(m {\times} n) \bmod Q \;=\; (m \bmod Q \times n) \bmod Q \quad . \tag{B.1}$$

Now, we can exploit the symmetry of multiplication:

$$(m \times n) \bmod Q$$
$$= \qquad \{ \qquad (15.26) \quad \}$$
$$(m \bmod Q \times n) \bmod Q$$
$$= \qquad \{ \qquad \text{multiplication is symmetric,}$$
$$\text{(B.1) with } m,n := n,m \quad \}$$
$$(m \bmod Q \times n \bmod Q) \bmod Q \ .$$

We have thus calculated that

$$(m \times n) \bmod Q \ = \ (m \bmod Q) \otimes (n \bmod Q) \ ,$$

where

$$p \otimes q \ = \ (p \times q) \bmod Q \ .$$

$\square$

Solution 15.28. Symmetry and associativity are easy to prove. For example,

$$(m \oplus n) \oplus p$$
$$= \qquad \{ \qquad \text{definition of } \oplus \text{ (twice)} \quad \}$$
$$((m + n) \bmod Q + p) \bmod Q$$
$$= \qquad \{ \qquad (15.26) \quad \}$$
$$((m + n) + p) \bmod Q$$
$$= \qquad \{ \qquad + \text{ is associative} \quad \}$$
$$(m + (n + p)) \bmod Q$$
$$= \qquad \{ \qquad (15.26) \text{ (and symmetry of } +) \quad \}$$
$$(m + (n + p) \bmod Q) \bmod Q$$
$$= \qquad \{ \qquad \text{definition of } \oplus \text{ (twice)} \quad \}$$
$$m \oplus (n \oplus p) \ .$$

Distributivity of $\ominus$ over $\oplus$ is proved in a similar way. The lemma we need emerges during the course of the calculation.

$$(\ominus m) \oplus (\ominus n)$$
$$= \qquad \{ \qquad \text{definition of } \oplus \quad \}$$
$$((-m) \bmod Q + (-n) \bmod Q) \bmod Q$$
$$= \qquad \{ \qquad (15.26) \text{ (applied twice)} \quad \}$$

$$((-m) + (-n)) \bmod Q$$

$=$ { $-$ distributes through $+$ }

$$(-(m+n)) \bmod Q$$

$=$ { Using (15.24) now would give $\ominus(m+n)$;

but we want $\ominus(m \oplus n)$.

Since $m \oplus n = (m+n) \bmod Q$, we need the lemma

$(-P) \bmod Q = (-(P \bmod Q)) \bmod Q$, for all P.

This is proved below. }

$$(-((m+n) \bmod Q)) \bmod Q$$

$=$ { definition of $\oplus$ }

$$(-(m \oplus n)) \bmod Q$$

$=$ { (15.24) }

$$\ominus(m \oplus n) \ .$$

The lemma we need to complete the proof is proved as follows. Assume that $0 \leqslant r < Q$. Then

$$r = (-P) \bmod Q$$

$=$ { (15.19) with $P := -P$,

assumption: $0 \leqslant r < Q$ }

$$\langle \exists d :: -P = Q \times d + r \rangle$$

$=$ { introduce $P \bmod Q$ using (15.7) }

$$\langle \exists d :: -(Q \times (P \div Q) + P \bmod Q) = Q \times d + r \rangle$$

$=$ { arithmetic }

$$\langle \exists d :: -(P \bmod Q) = Q \times (d + Q \times (P \div Q)) + r \rangle$$

$=$ { range translation: $d := d - Q \times (P \div Q)$ }

$$\langle \exists d :: -(P \bmod Q) = Q \times d + r \rangle$$

$=$ { (15.19) with $P := -(P \bmod Q)$,

assumption: $0 \leqslant r < Q$ }

$$r = (-(P \bmod Q)) \bmod Q \ .$$

It follows that, as required,

$$(-(P \bmod Q)) \bmod Q = (-P) \bmod Q \ .$$

$\square$

Solution 15.29. For the case of modulo-Q addition, we have

$$m \oplus n = m \oplus p$$

$=$ {   definition   }

$$(m + n) \bmod Q = (m + p) \bmod Q$$

$=$ {   (15.20)   }

$$((m + n) - (m + p)) \bmod Q = 0$$

$=$ {   arithmetic   }

$$(n - p) \bmod Q = 0$$

$=$ {   (15.20)   }

$$n \bmod Q = p \bmod Q$$

$=$ {   assumption: n and p are modulo-Q numbers

                 i.e. $n \bmod Q = n \ \wedge \ p \bmod Q = p$ }

$$n = p \ .$$

For the case of modulo-Q multiplication, we have

$$m \otimes n = m \otimes p$$

$=$ {   similar to above   }

$$(m \times (n - p)) \bmod Q = 0$$

$=$ {   (15.19), $0 \leqslant 0 < Q$ }

$$\langle \exists d :: m \times (n - p) = Q \times d \rangle \ .$$

So we see that, if Q is not a prime number, we can choose $n - p$ to be a divisor of Q (so that $n \neq p$) and still satisfy $m \otimes n = m \otimes p$. A concrete example is when Q is 4. Take m, n and p to be 2, 3 and 1.   □

Solution 15.34. When the base B is greater than 2, the process of decrementing r by m may be executed several times, and not just at most once. The replacement of the loop by a conditional statement is therefore invalid.

Otherwise, all steps in the development remain valid and we obtain the algorithm below.

$$\{ \ 0 \leqslant P \ \wedge \ 0 < Q \ \}$$

$$r, m, k, d \ := \ P, Q, 0, 0 \ ;$$

$$\{ \ \textbf{Invariant:} \quad 0 \leqslant k \ \wedge \ m = Q \times B^k$$

$$\textbf{Bound function:} \quad r - m \ \}$$

$$\text{do } r \geqslant m \ \longrightarrow \ m, k \ := \ B \times m, k + 1$$

od ;

{ **Invariant:**

$0 \leqslant r < m \ \wedge \ P = Q \times d + r \ \wedge \ 0 \leqslant k \ \wedge \ m = Q \times B^k$

Bound function: m }

do $m \neq Q \ \longrightarrow \quad m, k := m \div B, k-1$;

{ **Invariant:**

$0 \leqslant r \ \wedge \ P = Q \times d + r$

$\wedge \ 0 \leqslant k \ \wedge \ m = Q \times B^k$

Bound function: r }

do $r, d := r - m, d + B^k$

od

od

{ $0 \leqslant r < Q \ \wedge \ P = Q \times d + r$ } .

The lower bound, 2, on B is needed in order to guarantee progress of the two outer loops. □

Solution 15.35. The changes are minor. The invariant of the second loop becomes

$$0 \leqslant r < m \ \wedge \ P \bmod Q = r \bmod Q \ \wedge \ \langle \exists k : 0 \leqslant k : m = Q \times 2^k \rangle \ .$$

That the property

$$P \bmod Q = r \bmod Q$$

is maintained invariant by the assignment

$$r := r - m$$

is a consequence of (15.12). □

Solution 15.38. If b is an arbitrary positive number, an inner loop is needed. The invariant of the loop is

$$0 \leqslant r \ \wedge \ r \bmod Q = P \bmod Q$$

and the termination condition is

$$r \geqslant Q \ .$$

Progress is made to the termination condition by decrementing r by Q.

$P, r := 0, 0$;

{ **Invariant:** $0 \leqslant P \ \wedge \ r = P \bmod Q$ }

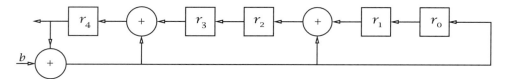

Figure B.5   Remainder of $x^5 \times P$ for generator polynomial $Q = x^5 + x^4 + x^2 + 1$.

$$\textbf{do}\ true\ \longrightarrow\quad get.b\ \{\ 0 \leqslant b < B\ \}\ ;$$

$$P, r\ :=\ B \times P + b, B \times r + b\ ;$$

$$\{\ \textbf{Invariant:}\ \ 0 \leqslant r\ \wedge\ r \bmod Q\ =\ P \bmod Q$$

$$\textbf{Bound function:}\quad r\ \}$$

$$\textbf{do}\ r \geqslant Q\ \longrightarrow\ r\ :=\ r - Q$$

$$\textbf{od}$$

$$\textbf{od}\ .$$

$\square$

Solution 15.39. The property is that, for all m, $m \bmod 3 = (m \bmod 9) \bmod 3$. So $r \bmod 3 = s \bmod 3$ is also invariant. $\square$

Solution 16.3. The initialization remains unchanged. In the body of the loop, the property

$$\langle \exists d :: x^m \times P = Q \times d + r \rangle$$

is maintained by the assignment

$$r\ :=\ x \times r + x^m \times b\ .$$

This will falsify $degree.r < degree.Q$ exactly when $r_{m-1} + b$ is 1. So $Q \times (r_{m-1} + b)$ must also be added to r. The program thus becomes

$$P, r\ :=\ 0, 0\ ;$$

$$\{\ \textbf{Invariant:}\ \ degree.r < degree.Q\ \wedge\ \langle \exists d :: x^m \times P = Q \times d + r \rangle\ \}$$

$$\textbf{do}\ true\ \longrightarrow\quad get.b\ \{\ 0 \leqslant b \leqslant 1\ \}\ ;$$

$$P\ :=\ x \times P + b\ ;$$

$$\{\ degree.r \leqslant degree.Q\ \wedge\ \langle \exists d :: x^m \times P = Q \times d + r \rangle\ \}$$

$$r\ :=\ x \times r + x^m \times b + Q \times (r_{m-1} + b)\ ;$$

$$put.r$$

$$\textbf{od}\ .$$

Now,

$$x \times r + x^m \times b + Q \times (r_{m-1} + b)$$

$$= \qquad \{ \qquad x \times r = (x \times r) \bmod x^m + x^m \times r_{m-1} \quad \}$$

$$(x^m + Q) \times (r_{m-1} + b) + (x \times r) \bmod x^m \ .$$

The subexpression $(x \times r) \bmod x^m$ is implemented by shifting the contents of the register. Also, the polynomial $x^m + Q$ is a fixed polynomial of degree $m - 1$. So it can be hardwired into a circuit in which both the input bit, b, and the feedback bit, r_{m-1}, are combined with the shift operation. The circuit for the generator polynomial $Q = x^5 + x^4 + x^2 + 1$ is shown in Figure B.5. $\qquad \square$

References

Blahut, R. E. 1983 *Theory and Practice of Error Control Coding.* Addison-Wesley.

Buxton, J. N. and Randell, B. 1970 *Software Engineering Techniques.* Report on a Conference Sponsored by the NATO Science Committee, Rome, October 1969. NATO Science Committee.

Dijkstra, E. W. 1975 Guarded commands, nondeterminacy and formal derivation of programs. *Communications of the ACM,* **18,** 453–457.

Dijkstra, E. W. 1976 *A Discipline of Programming.* Prentice Hall.

Dijkstra, E. W. (ed.) 1990 *Formal Development of Programs and Proofs,* pp. 209–228. The UT Year of Programming Series. Addison-Wesley.

Dijkstra, E. W. and Feijen, W. H. J. 1984 *Een Methode van Programmeren.* Academic Service. (Also available as *A Method of Programming.* Addison-Wesley (1988).)

Dijkstra, E. W. and Scholten, C. S. 1990 *Predicate Calculus and Program Semantics.* Texts and Monographs in Computer Science. Springer.

Feijen, W. H. J. and Bijlsma, L. 1990 Exercises in formula manipulation. In *Formal Development of Programs and Proofs* (ed. E. W. Dijkstra). University of Texas at Austin Year of Programming Series. Addison-Wesley.

Feijen, W. H. J. and van Gasteren, A. J. M. 1999 *On a Method of Multiprogramming.* Springer.

Gardner, M. 1959 *Mathematical Puzzles and Diversions.* Penguin Books.

Graham, R. L., Knuth, D. E. and Patashnik, O. 1989 *Concrete Mathematics.* Addison-Wesley.

Gries, D. 1981 *The Science of Programming.* Springer.

Gries, D. and Schneider, F. B. 1993 *A Logical Approach to Discrete Math.* Springer.

Hoare, C. A. R. and Jones, C. B. (eds) 1989 *Essays in Computing Science.* Prentice Hall.

Hoare, T. 2001 Legacy. *Information Processing Letters,* **77,** 123–129.

Hoogerwoord, R. R. 2001 Formality works. *Information Processing Letters,* **77,** 137–142.

Kaldewaij, A. 1990 *Programming. The Derivation of Algorithms.* Prentice Hall International.

Knuth, D. E. 1968 *The Art of Computer Programming,* vol. I. *Fundamental Algorithms.* Addison-Wesley.

Knuth, D. E. 1969 *The Art of Computer Programming,* vol. II. *Seminumerical Algorithms.* Addison-Wesley.

Knuth, D. E. 1973 *The Art of Computer Programming,* vol. III. *Sorting and Searching.* Addison-Wesley.

Morgan, C. 1990 *Programming from Specifications.* Prentice Hall International Series in Computer Science.

Mössner, A. 1951 Eine Bemerkung über die Potenzen der natürlichen Zahlen. *Sitzungsberichte der Bayerischen Akademie der Wissenschaften. Math.–naturwissenschaftliche Klasse,* p. 29.

Nader, R. 1965 *Unsafe At Any Speed: The Designed-in Dangers Of The American Automobile.* Grossman.

Naur, P. and Randell, B. (eds) 1969 *Software Engineering*. Report of a Conference Sponsored by the NATO Science Committee, Garmisch, Germany, 7–11 October 1968. Scientific Affairs Division, NATO, Brussels.

Perron, O. 1951 Beweis der Mössnerschen Satzes. *Sitzungsberichte der Bayerischen Akademie der Wissenschaften. Math.-naturwissenschaftliche Klasse*, pp. 31–34.

Polya, G. 1954 *Mathematics and Plausible Reasoning*, vol. I. *Induction and Analogy in Mathematics*. Princeton University Press.

Polya, G. 1981 *Mathematical Discovery. On Understanding, Learning and Teaching Problem-Solving*. John Wiley & Sons, Ltd/Inc.

Schneier, B. 1995 *Applied Cryptography: Protocols, Algorithms, and Source Code in C*, 2nd edn. John Wiley & Sons, Ltd/Inc.

Smullyan, R. 1978 *What Is The Name Of This Book?* Prentice Hall.

Snepscheut, van de, J. L. A. 1993 *What Computing Is All About*. Springer.

Stallings, W. 1999 *Cryptography and Network Security, Principles and Practice*, 2nd edn. Prentice Hall.

Tarski, A. 1956 *Logic, Semantics, Metamathematics, Papers from 1923 to 1938* (transl. J. H. Woodger). Oxford University Press.

Wiltink, J. G. 1987 A deficiency of natural deduction. *Information Processing Letters*, **25**, 233–234.

Winder, R. and Roberts, G. 1998 *Developing Java Software*. John Wiley & Sons, Ltd/Inc.

Glossary of Symbols

:=	assignment operator, 46		lcm	least common multiple, 103
>	greater than, 27		mod	modulus (remainder), 220
⩾	at least, 34		even	divisible by two, 129
<	less than, 34		odd	not divisible by two, 134
⩽	at most, 34		Σ	summation, 141
false	boolean constant 'false', 65		Π	multiplication, 153
true	boolean constant 'true', 61		∀	'for all' quantifier, 153
∧	conjunction ('and'), 85		∃	'there exists' quantifier, 154
∨	disjunction (inclusive 'or'), 83		≡	equivalence quantifier, 158
=	equals, 35		≢	inequivalence quantifier, 158
≡	equivalence, 35		⇑	maximum quantifier, 158
≢	inequivalence, 67		⇓	minimum quantifier, 158
⇐	if, 36, 88		⊕	(arbitrary) quantifier, 157
⇒	only if, 36, 88		..	range of integers, 43
¬	(boolean) negation, 65		/	real division, 46
⌈ ⌉	ceiling function, 78		**Z**	set of integers, 150
⌊ ⌋	floor function, 72		**N**	set of natural numbers, 150
÷	integer division, 46, 220		φ	empty set, 162
↑	(binary) maximum , 97		𝒰	universe of values, 158
↓	(binary) minimum, 101		\	divides, 103
| |	absolute value, 102		{ }	set comprehension, 142
exp	exponent function, 103		[ ]	in all states, 124
gcd	greatest common divisor, 103			

Index